Armed Conflict and Forcible Displacement

AF695558

This book addresses the involuntary and arbitrary displacement of individuals resulting from armed conflict and gross human rights violations. It shows that forcible displacement constitutes a serious violation of international law and of fundamental community interests.

Armed Conflict and Forcible Displacement provides a critical legal analysis of the contemporary international framework, permeating forcible displacement in these circumstances and explores the rights that individuals possess with specific focus on the right not to be displaced and, where this fails, the right to return home and to receive property restitution. In doing so, this volume marries together different fields of international law and builds on the case studies of Cyprus, Colombia, Cambodia and Syria. While the case studies considered here are far from exhaustive, they are either little explored or present significant challenges due to the magnitude of displacement or contested international jurisprudence.

Through this analysis, the volume exposes some of the legal challenges that individuals encounter in being protected from forcible displacement, as well as the legal obstacles that persist in ensuring the return of and the recovery of property by the displaced. It will be of interest to those interested in the fields of international law, human rights law, as well as conflict and war studies.

Dr Elena Katselli Proukaki is Senior Lecturer in Law, Newcastle University and specialises in public international law and human rights.

Routledge Research in International Law

For a full list of titles in this series, visit https://www.routledge.com/Routledge-Research-in-International-Law/book-series/INTNLLAW

Available:

The Right to Democracy in International Law
Between Procedure, Substance and the Philosophy of John Rawls
Khalifa A Alfadhel

Latin America and the International Court of Justice
Contributions to International Law
Edited by Paula Wojcikiewicz Almeida and Jean-Marc Sorel

Fragmentation vs the Constitutionalisation of International Law
A Practical Inquiry
Edited by Andrzej Jakubowski and Karolina Wierczyńska

Legal Accountability and Britain's Wars 2000-2015
Peter Rowe

Means of Transportation and Registration of Nationality
Transportation Registered by International Organizations
Vincent P. Cogliati-Bantz

Regionalism in International Law
Ján Klučka

The International Criminal Court and Nigeria
Implementing the Complementarity Principle Of The Rome Statute
Muyiwa Adigun

Armed Conflict and Forcible Displacement
Individual Rights under International Law
Elena Katselli Proukaki

Armed Conflict and Forcible Displacement

Individual Rights under International Law

Edited by Elena Katselli Proukaki

Routledge
Taylor & Francis Group
LONDON AND NEW YORK

First published 2018
by Routledge

2 Park Square, Milton Park, Abingdon, Oxfordshire OX14 4RN
52 Vanderbilt Avenue, New York, NY 10017

Routledge is an imprint of the Taylor & Francis Group, an informa business

First issued in paperback 2020

Copyright © 2018 Elena Katselli Proukaki

The right of Elena Katselli Proukaki to be identified as author of this work has been asserted by her in accordance with sections 77 and 78 of the Copyright, Designs and Patents Act 1988.

All rights reserved. No part of this book may be reprinted or reproduced or utilised in any form or by any electronic, mechanical, or other means, now known or hereafter invented, including photocopying and recording, or in any information storage or retrieval system, without permission in writing from the publishers.

Notice:
Product or corporate names may be trademarks or registered trademarks, and are used only for identification and explanation without intent to infringe.

British Library Cataloguing in Publication Data
A catalogue record for this book is available from the British Library

Library of Congress Cataloging in Publication Data
Names: Katselli Proukaki, Elena, editor.
Title: Armed conflict and forcible displacement : individual rights under international law / edited by Elena Katselli Proukaki.
Description: Abingdon, Oxon [UK] ; New York : Routledge, 2018. |
Series: Routledge research in international law | Includes index.
Identifiers: LCCN 2017048889| ISBN 9781138643338 (hardback) |
ISBN 9781317243908 (web pdf) | ISBN 9781317243892 (epub) |
ISBN 9781317243885 (mobipocket)
Subjects: LCSH: Forced migration. | Refugees—Civil rights. | Internally displaced persons—Civil rights. | War.
Classification: LCC KZ6530 .A75 2018 | DDC 341.6/7—dc23
LC record available at https://lccn.loc.gov/2017048889

ISBN: 978-1-138-64333-8 (hbk)
ISBN: 978-0-367-59233-2 (pbk)

Typeset in Galliard
by Keystroke, Neville Lodge, Tettenhall, Wolverhampton

To my Daughter, Ioanna

Contents

List of abbreviations

AC	Appeal Chamber
ACHR	American Convention on Human Rights
AHR	*American Historical Review*
AIDH	*Annuaire International Des Droits De L'Homme*
AJIL	*American Journal of International Law*
APSR	*American Political Science Review*
ASILBrookInst	*American Society of International Law and the Brookings Institution*
ASILP	*American Society of International Law Proceedings*
AUILR	*American University International Law Review*
BHRLR	*Buffalo Human Rights Law Review*
BS	*Balkan Studies*
CILJ	*Cornell International Law Journal*
CJIL	*Columbia Journal of European Law*
CYbELS	*Cambridge Yearbook of European Legal Studies*
DJIL&P	*Denver Journal of International Law & Policy*
DLJ	*Duke Law Journal*
ECHR	European Convention on Human Rights
ECtHR	European Court of Human Rights
EHRLR	*European Human Rights Law Review*
EJIL	*European Journal of International Law*
EJPT	*European Journal of Political Theory*
ERS	*Ethnic and Racial Studies*
FJIL	*Florida Journal of International Law*
FordhamInte'lLJ	*Fordham International Law Journal*
HILJ	*Harvard International Law Journal*
HRC	Human Rights Committee
HRLR	*Human Rights Law Review*
HRQ	*Human Rights Quarterly*
ICCPR	International Covenant on Civil and Political Rights
ICESCR	International Covenant on Economic, Social and Cultural Rights
ICJ	International Court of Justice
ICL	International Criminal Law

ICLR	*International Criminal Law Review*
ICRC	International Committee of the Red Cross
ICTFY	International Criminal Tribunal for the former Yugoslavia
IHL	International Humanitarian Law
IHLS	*International Humanitarian Legal Studies*
IHRL	International Human Rights Law
IJHR	*International Journal of Human Rights*
IJRL	*International Journal of Refugee Law*
ILC	International Law Commission
ILR	*Israel Law Review*
IRRC	*International Review of the Red Cross*
IYbHR	*Israel Yearbook on Human Rights*
JCSL	*Journal of Conflict & Security Law*
JICJ	*Journal of International Criminal Justice*
JISB	*Journal of Intervention and State Building*
JMP	*Journal of Medicine and Philosophy*
JWIT	*Journal of World Investment and Trade*
L&Cont.Problems	*Law and Contemporary Problems*
LJIL	*Leiden Journal of International Law*
MJIL	*Michigan Journal of International Law*
MilLR	*Military Law Review*
MPEncPIL	*Max Planck Encyclopedia of Public International Law*
NJIL	*Nordic Journal of International Law*
NQHR	*Netherlands Quarterly of Human Rights*
NYbIL	*Netherlands Yearbook of International Law*
PCA	Permanent Court of Arbitration
PCIJ	Permanent Court of International Justice
PNAS	*Proceedings of the National Academy of Sciences*
QIL	*Questions of International Law*
RLR	*Ritsumeikan Law Review*
RSQ	*Refugee Survey Quarterly*
SSR	*Social Service Review*
TC	Trial Chamber
UNGA	United Nations General Assembly
UNHCR	United Nations High Commissioner for Refugees
UNOHCR	United Nations Office of High Commissioner for Refugees
UNSC	United Nations Security Council
UNSG	United Nations Secretary General
VJIL	*Virginia Journal of International Law*
VLR	*Vanderbilt Law Review*
WWI	World War I
WWII	World War II
YbIHumL	*Yearbook of International Humanitarian Law*
YbILC	*Yearbook of International Law Commission*
YLJ	*Yale Law Journal*

Acknowledgements

I am deeply indebted to a number of individuals and organisations for the support and assistance they provided in the materialisation of this project. Indeed, this project was able to mature through the generous funding of the British Academy, which made feasible research visits as well as the organisation of a one-day workshop in December 2012 entitled *Displaced Persons and Armed Conflict: The right to Property and to Return Home under Contemporary International Law* held at Newcastle University. Importantly however, I would like to thank all the authors who contributed a chapter in this volume for their excellent work and commitment and without whom this volume would not have been made possible. In particular, I am indebted to Dr Vassilis Tzevelekos, Ms Eleni Meleagrou, Dr Costas Paraskeva, Professor Nicolás Carrillo-Santarelli, Professor Rhona Smith, Ms Ratana Ly, Ms Chantevy Khourn, Dr Yasmine Nahlawi and Mr Matthew Gillett.

Over the years I have also benefited from research visits carried out at the Netherlands Institute of Human Rights (Utrecht University – Professor Jenny Goldschmidt/Professor Antoine Buyse), T.C.Beirne School of Law/Centre for Public, International and Comparative Law (Queensland University – Professor Suri Ratnapala, Professor Anthony Cassimatis and Dr Jennifer Corrin), Law School (Tübingen University – Professor Martin Nettesheim), Human Rights Centre (Ghent University – Professor Yves Haeck/Professor Johan Vande Lanotte), European Academy of Bolzano (Dr Roberta Medda) and Law School (Trento University – Professor Giuseppe Nesi), as well as from the support offered by my own institution, Newcastle University, through research leave and funding. I would also like to thank Dr Ann Sinclair for excellent research assistance, Ms Catherine Dale and Mrs Alison Judd for excellent library support and the wonderful team of Routledge, in particular Ms Katherine Carpenter, Ms Mary Del Plato, Ms Olivia Manley, Ms Helen Baxter and Ms Lucy Buchan, for making this process as smooth as possible. Finally, I remain eternally indebted to my Ph.D. supervisor Professor Colin Warbrick for his support over the years.

On a more personal note, I would like to thank my husband, Professor Nikolaos P. Proukakis, for his encouragement and support, my wonderful daughter Ioanna Proukaki, to whom this book is dedicated, for 'allowing me' to stay longer at work to finish the book, and my brother Nicos Katsellis for his love. Finally, I would like to thank my parents, Andrea and Yiannoulla Katselli who, in spite of losing everything as a result of their forcible displacement, managed through their hard work and sacrifices to rebuild our lives. Special mention should be made to my mother for her never eroding commitment and determination to secure the best possible education for me and who has always believed that education is the only thing that cannot be taken away, not even with forcible displacement.

Elena Katselli Proukaki

List of contributors

Elena Katselli Proukaki, Newcastle University, United Kingdom
Elena Katselli is Senior Lecturer in Law at Newcastle Law School, Newcastle University where she teaches and researches issues of public international law and international human rights. She holds a degree in Law (Πτυχίον) from the University of Athens, as well as a Master of Laws in International and European Legal Studies and a PhD in Public International Law (with full scholarship) both from Durham University, UK. She is also a qualified advocate (Supreme Court of Cyprus). Her monograph entitled *The Problem of Enforcement in International Law: Countermeasures, the non-injured state and the idea of international community* (Routledge) was nominated for the Paul Guggenheim Prize 2011 (Institut de Droit, Geneva), while her article entitled 'Holding the Security Council Accountable for Human Rights Violations' published in *Human Rights & International Legal Discourse* (2007) was re-produced in M.P. Malloy, *Economic Sanctions* (Edward Elgar Publishing Ltd, 2015). Over the years she has held several Visiting academic positions including at the University of Trento, Italy; the European Academy of Bolzano, Italy; the Human Rights Centre, Ghent University, Belgium; the University of Tübingen, Germany; the T.C. Beirne School of Law/Centre for Public, International and Comparative Law, University of Queensland, Australia; and the Netherlands Institute of Human Rights, Utrecht University, The Netherlands.

Vassilis Tzevelekos, University of Liverpool, United Kingdom
Vassilis Tzevelekos is a general international law lawyer with a special interest in human rights protection. Currently he is Senior Lecturer in Law at the University of Liverpool, School of Law and Social Justice. He holds a PhD on Public International Law from the European University Institute, where he also did a Master on Legal Research. Before that he studied European Politics at the College of Europe (MA in European Politics) and Public International Law at Paris 1 Panthéon-Sorbonne (DEA). Vassilis did his main studies in Law (undergraduate) at the University of Athens and is qualified with the Athens' Bar. In the past, he has been a visiting scholar at Columbia Law School and a Grotius Fellow for one academic year at the University of Michigan Law School. He is the co-editor of, *inter alia*, *Beyond Responsibility to Protect: Generating Change in International Law* (R.A. Barnes, V.P. Tzevelekos (eds.), Intersentia, 2016).

Eleni Meleagrou

Eleni Meleagrou is a Solicitor, member of the Law Society of England and Wales, and a US Attorney at Law, currently practising law in Cyprus. She has specialised in European human rights first at the AIRE Centre in London and later representing applicants at the ECtHR and advising clients in her practice in Cyprus. She has contributed to a number of articles, expert opinions and pamphlets on issues relating to the rights to property and home and is currently working on a book with Dr Costas Paraskeva on Cyprus at the ECtHR.

Costas Paraskeva, University of Cyprus, Cyprus

Costas Paraskeva is an Assistant Professor of Public Law at the University of Cyprus, an advocate and a member of the Council of Europe Committee for the Prevention of Torture (CPT). He has established himself as an expert in the area of the protection of human rights, under the European Convention on Human Rights (ECHR), both as an academic and as a practitioner. Costas regularly represents applicants before the European Court of Human Rights and provides legal consultations on diverse aspects of ECHR litigation. He is the author of a number of books, articles and chapters on various human rights issues and has conducted training on the ECHR for the Council of Europe, the OSCE and for various NGOs. His areas of research include the European system of protection of human rights, the effective enforcement and implementation of human rights norms and the right of access to justice and redress.

Nicolás Carrillo-Santarelli, La Sabana University, Colombia

Nicolás Carrillo-Santarelli holds a PhD in International Law from the Autónoma de Madrid University, an LLM in Human Rights from Alcalá University and is Professor of International Law at La Sabana University, Colombia. He has conducted research and published on non-state actors and international legal issues; has worked in Colombian and Spanish Universities, at the Colombian Constitutional Court; and has been an intern in international NGOs.

Rhona Smith, Newcastle University, United Kingdom

Rhona Smith is Head of the School of Law and Professor of International Human Rights at Newcastle University, UK. In 2015, the UN Human Rights Council appointed her UN Special Rapporteur on the situation of human rights in Cambodia. She was previously a visiting professor in Cambodia, teaching human rights and working with various universities and institutes developing human rights research and teaching capacity.

Ratana Ly, Royal University of Law and Economics, Cambodia

Ratana Ly is a researcher at the Center for the Study of Humanitarian Law, based at the Royal University of Law and Economics, Phnom Penh, Cambodia. Her primary research interests lie in the fields of refugee law, international criminal law and international human rights law. She provides training on these subjects to legal professionals as well as teaching university students at various Cambodian universities. Ratana has also presented her work at national and international conferences. Ratana has also studied overseas, obtaining a master's degree of law in international law from Nagoya University, Japan, in 2013.

Chantevy Khourn, Actionaid, Cambodia
Chantevy Khourn currently serves as women's rights team leader at Actionaid Cambodia. She manages Safe Cities for Women Cambodia Project, which aims to end violence against women in the public space and demands gender responsive public services. Chantevy is also part time professor at Pannasastra University of Cambodia where she teaches gender studies including women's rights law, political sciences, sociology and social research. She has conducted research on women's participation in politics in Cambodia and intimate partner violence. Her research interests are women's empowerment in leadership and economic and gender based violence.

Yasmine Nahlawi, Rethink Rebuild Society
Yasmine Nahlawi is Research and Policy Coordinator for Rethink Rebuild Society, which specialises on the ongoing Syrian conflict. She obtained both her PhD in Public International Law and her LLM in International Legal Studies from Newcastle University and her BSc in Political Science from Eastern Michigan University. Her research interests pertain to the 'responsibility to protect' (R2P) doctrine and its applicability to the 2011 Syrian and Libyan conflicts.

Matthew Gillett, International Criminal Tribunal for the former Yugoslavia/ Mechanism for International Criminal Tribunals
Matthew Gillett is a Legal Officer in the Office of the Prosecutor of the ICTY/ MICT and has worked on several cases involving war crimes, crimes against humanity and genocide, including Hadzic, Mladic, Lukic and Lukic, Popovic et al. and Prlic et al. In 2016, he worked as a Human Rights Officer for the United Nations in Afghanistan. Previously he worked at the International Criminal Court in the Immediate Office of the Prosecutor and in New Zealand as a criminal defence barrister and as a legal officer at the High Court. He has written several articles on international criminal law, including on crimes against the environment, and was a member of the New Zealand delegation to the Review Conference of the ICC in Kampala in 2010, where the amendments on the crime of aggression were adopted.

Table of cases

Permanent Court of International Justice

Exchange of Greek and Turkish Populations, PCIJ (1925) Ser. B, No. 11, 6.
Case Concerning the Factory at Chorzow (Claim for Indemnity) (Merits), PCIJ (1928), Judgment No 13, Series A, No. 17, 47.
The Greco-Bulgarian 'Communities' (Advisory Opinion), PCIJ (1930), Series B, No 17, July 31, 21.
Panevezys Saldutiskis Railway Case (Estonia v Lithuania), PCIJ (1939) Series AB, Judgment, 28 February 1939, 4, 16.

International Court of Justice

Asylum Case (Colombia v Peru), ICJ Reports (1950) 266.
North Sea Continental Shelf Cases (Federal Republic of Germany v Denmark and The Netherlands), ICJ Reports (1969) 3.
Case Concerning Military and Paramilitary Activities in and against Nicaragua (Nicaragua v United States of America), Merits, Judgment 27 June 1986, ICJ Reports (1986) 14.
Frontier Dispute, Judgment, ICJ Reports (1986), 554.
Legality of the Threat or Use of Nuclear Weapons, Advisory Opinion, ICJ Reports (1996), 226.
LaGrand Case (Germany v United States of America), Judgment, ICJ Rep. (2001) 466.
Legal Consequences of the Construction of a Wall in the Occupied Palestinian Territory, Advisory Opinion, ICJ Reports (2004) 136.
Case Concerning Armed Activities on the Territory of the Congo (Democratic Republic of the Congo v Uganda), Judgment, ICJ Reports (2005) 168.
Case Concerning Application of the Convention on the Prevention and Punishment of the Crime of Genocide (Bosnia and Herzegovina v Serbia and Montenegro), Judgment, ICJ Reports (2007), 43.

International Arbitral Awards

Eritrea Ethiopia Claims Commission, Partial Award, Civilians Claims, Eritrea's Claims 15, 16, 23, 27–32, 17 December 2004, Reports of International Arbitral Awards, Vol. XXVI, 195–247.

Eritrea Ethiopia Claims Commission, Partial Award, Civilians Claims, Ethiopia's Claim No. 5, 17 December 2004, https://pcacases.com/web/sendAttach/756.

Eritrea Ethiopia Claims Commission, Partial Award, Western Front, Aerial Bombardment and Related Claims Eritrea's Claims 1, 3, 5, 9–13, 14, 21, 25 & 26, 19 December 2005, https://pcacases.com/web/sendAttach/757.

In the Matter of the Chagos Marine Protected Area Arbitration (The Republic of Mauritius v The United Kingdom of Great Britain and Northern Ireland), Permanent Court of Arbitration, 18 March 2015.

European Court of Human Rights

Loizidou v Turkey (preliminary objections) (1995) App no. 15318/19, *ECHR*, Series A no. 310.

Loizidou v Turkey (merits) (1996) App no. 15318/19, *ECHR*, 1996-VI.

Loizidou v Turkey (just satisfaction) (1998) App no. 15318/19, *ECHR*, IV.

Cyprus v Turkey, Application no. 25781/94 (1997) 23 EHRR 244.

Cyprus v Turkey (Application no. 25781/94) Judgment, 10 May 2001, *ECHR*, IV.

Cyprus v Turkey (Application no. 25781/94), Judgments (Just Satisfaction) 12 May 2014.

Demopoulos and Others v Turkey (Decision), Application Nos 46113/99, 3843/02, 13751/02, 13466/03, 10200/04, 14163/04, 19993/04 and 21819/04), ECHR 2010-I.

Chagos Islanders v United Kingdom (Application No. 35622/04), Decision, 11 December 2012.

Sargsyan v Azerbaijan (decision), Application no. 40167/06, 16 June 2016.

Doğan and others v Turkey (Application nos 8803-8811/02, 8813/02 and 8815-8819/02), (2004).

Hassan v United Kingdom (App no. 29750/09), 16 September 2014.

Chiragov and others v Armenia (2015) App no. 13216/05, *ECHR*.

Saghinadze and others v Georgia (2010) Application no. 18768/05, 27 May 2010, *ECHR*.

Saghinadze and Others v Georgia (Just Satisfaction), Application no. 18768/05, 13 January 2015.

Assanidze v Georgia [GC] (2004) App no. 71503/01, *ECHR*, II.

Broniowski v Poland (merits), Application no. 31443/96, ECHR 2004-V.

Brumarescu v Romania (just satisfaction) (2001) App no. 28342/95, *ECHR*.

Chrysostomos, Papachrysostomou and Loizidou v Turkey (admissibility) (1991) App nos 15299/89 15300/89 15318/89, *ECmHR*.

Xenides-Arestis v Turkey (admissibility) (2005) App no. 46347/99, 14 March 200, *ECHR*.

Xenides-Arestis v Turkey (merits) (2005) App no. 46347/99, 22 December 2005, *ECHR*.

Xenides-Arestis v Turkey (just satisfaction) (2006) App no. 46347/99, 7 December 2006, *ECHR*.

Dacia S.R.L. v Molodova (just satisfaction) (2009) App no. 3052/04, 24 February 2009, *ECHR*.

Demades v Turkey (merits and just satisfaction), Application no. 16219/90, 31 July 2003, *ECHR*.

Eugenia Michaelidou Developments Ltd and Michael Tymvios v Turkey, Application no. 16163/90, 31 July 2003, *ECHR*.

Former King of Greece and others v Greece (merits) (2000) App no. 25701/94, *ECHR*, XII.

Former King of Greece and others v Greece (just satisfaction) [GC] (2002) App no. 25701/94, *ECHR*.

Hassan v United Kingdom [GC] (2014) App no. 29750/09, *ECHR*.

Ireland v The United Kingdom (1978) App no. 5310/71, *ECHR*, Series A no. 25.

James and others v the United Kingdom (1986) App no. 8793/79, *ECHR*.

Meleagrou and others v Turkey (decision on admissibility) (2013) App no. 14434/09, 2 April 2013, *ECHR*.

Orphanides v Turkey, Application no. 36705/97, 20 January 2009, *ECHR*.

Orphanides v Turkey (just satisfaction), Application no. 36705/97, 26 October 2010.

Papamichalopoulos and others v Greece (just satisfaction) (1995) App no. 14556/89, 31 October 1995, *ECHR*.

Scozzari and Giunta v Italy [GC], Application nos. 39221/98 and 41963/98, 2000-VI.

Selçuk and Asker v Turkey' (merits and just satisfaction) (1998) App nos 23184/94 and 23815/94, *ECHR*, II.

Verein gegen Tierfabriken Schweiz (VgT) v Switzerland (No. 2) (2009) App no. 32772/02, *ECHR*.

Zwierzyński v Poland (just satisfaction) (2002) App no. 34049/96, *ECHR*.

Airey v Ireland (merits), Application no. 6289/73, 9 October 1979.

Marckx v Belgium, Application no. 6833/74, (1980) 2 EHRR 330.

Silver v The United Kingdom, Application nos 5947/72, 6205/73, 7052/75, 7061/75, 7107/75, 7113/75, 7136/75 (1983) 5 EHRR 347.

Oleksandr Volkov v Ukraine, Application no. 21722/11, 9 January 2013.

Sedjovic v Italy, Application no. 56581/00, 01 March 2006.

Guiso-Gallisay v Italy (just satisfaction) [GC], Application no. 58858/00, 22 December 2009.

Salduz v Turkey, Application no. 36391/02, 27 November 2008.

Raicu v Romania, Application no. 28104/03, 19 October 2006.

Gavriel v Turkey, Application no. 41355/98, 20 January 2009.

Ioannou v Turkey, Application no. 18364/91, 27 January 2009.
Evagorou Christou v Turkey, Application no. 18403/91, 27 January 2009.
Michael v Turkey, Application no. 18361/91, 27 January 2009.
Nicola v Turkey, Application no. 18404/91, 27 January 2009.
Hadjiprocopiou and Others v Turkey, Application no. 37395/97, 22 September 2009.
Kyriakou v Turkey, Application No. 18407/91, 27 January 2009.
Hapeshis and Hapeshi-Michaelidou v Turkey, Application No. 35214/97, 22 September 2009.
Hadjithomas and Others v Turkey, Application No. 39970/98, 22 September 2009.
Saveriades v Turkey, Application No. 16160/90, 22 September 2009.
Diogenous and Tseriotis v Turkey (just satisfaction), Application no. 16259/90, 26 October 2010.
Zavou and Others v Turkey (just satisfaction), Application no. 16654/90, 26 October 2010.
Saveriadis v Turkey (just satisfaction), Application no. 16160/90, 26 October 2010.
Epiphaniou and Others v Turkey (just satisfaction), Application no. 19900/92, 26 October 2010.
Ramon v Turkey (just satisfaction), Application no. 29092/95, 26 October 2010.
Gavriel v Turkey (just satisfaction), Application no. 41355/98, 26 October 2010.
Papayianni and Others v Turkey (decision), Application nos 479/07, 4607/10 and 10715/10, 6 July 2010.
Fieros and Others v Turkey (decision), Application nos 53432/99, 54086/00, 57899/00, 58378/00, 63518/00, 66141/01, 77752/01, 10192/02, 25057/02, 35846/02, 5 October 2010.
Zavou and Others v Turkey (decision), Application no. 16654/90 ECHR, 26 September 2002.
Varnava and Others v Turkey [GC], Application nos. 16064/90, 16065/90, 16066/90, 16068/90, 16069/90, 16070/90, 16071/90, 16072/90 and 16073/90, ECHR 2009-V.
Loizou v Turkey, Application no. 50646/2015, ECHR (communicated) 14 December 2015.
Joannou v Turkey (App no. 532440/2015) ECHR (communicated) 19 November 2015.
Sufi and Elmi v The United Kingdom, Applications nos. 8319/07 and 11449/07, Judgment, 28 June 2011 (Final 28/11/2011).
Oršuš and others v Croatia, Application no. 15766/03, Judgment, 16 March 2010.
N. v Sweden, Application no. 23505/09, Judgment, 20 July 2010 (Final 20/10/2010).
Ilaşcu and Others v Moldova and Russia (App no. 48787/99) ECHR 8 July 2004.

European Commission on Human Rights

Cyprus v Turkey (Commission decision), Application Nos 6780/74 and 6950/75, 26 May 1975.
Cyprus v Turkey (Commission Report), Application nos 6780/74 and 6950/75, 10 July 1976.
Cyprus v Turkey (Commission Report), Application No. 8007/77, 4 Oct. 1983.
Cyprus v Turkey Commission Report, Application No. 25781/94, 4 June 1999.

Inter-American Court of Human Rights

Yakye Axa Indigenous Community v Paraguay, Series C, No. 125 (17 June 2005).
Case of Expelled Dominicans and Haitians v Dominican Republic, Judgment of 28 August 2014 (Preliminary objections, merits, reparations and costs).
Bamaca Velasquez v Guatemala, Judgment of 25 November 2000.
Case of Human Rights Defender et al. v Guatemala, Preliminary Objections, Merits, Reparations and Costs, Judgment of August 28, 2014, Series C No. 283.
Case of the Afro-descendant communities displaced from the Cacarica River Basin (Operation Genesis) v Colombia, Preliminary Objections, Merits, Reparations and Costs. Judgment of November 20, 2013, Series C No. 270.
'Other treaties' subject to the consultative jurisdiction of the Court (Art. 64 American Convention on Human Rights), Advisory Opinion OC-1/82 of September 24, 1982, Series A No. 1.
Case of 'The Last Temptation of Christ' (Olmedo-Bustos et al.) v Chile, Merits, Reparations and Costs, Judgment of February 5, 2001, Series C No. 73.
Case of Atala Riffo and Daughters v Chile, Merits, Reparations and Costs, Judgment of February 24, 2012. Series C No. 239.
Case of Chitay Nech et al. v Guatemala, Preliminary Objections, Merits, Reparations, and Costs, Judgment of May 25, 2010. Series C No. 212.
Case of Rodríguez Vera et al. (The Disappeared from the Palace of Justice) v Colombia, Preliminary Objections, Merits, Reparations and Costs, Judgment of November 14, 2014, Series C No. 287.
Case of the 'Mapiripán Massacre' v Colombia, Merits, Reparations and Costs, Judgment of September 15, 2005, Series C No. 134.
Case of the 'Street Children' (Villagrán-Morales et al.) v Guatemala. Merits. Judgment of November 19, 1999, Series C No. 63.
Case of the Ituango Massacres v Colombia, Preliminary Objection, Merits, Reparations and Costs, Judgment of July 1, 2006, Series C No. 148.
Case of the Moiwana Community v Suriname, Preliminary Objections, Merits, Reparations and Costs, Judgment of June 15, 2005, Series C No. 124.
Case of the Plan de Sánchez Massacre v Guatemala, Reparations. Judgment of November 19, 2004, Series C No. 116.
International Responsibility for the Promulgation and Enforcement of Laws in Violation of the Convention (Arts. 1 and 2 of the American Convention on

Human Rights), Advisory Opinion OC-14/94 of December 9, 1994, Series A No.14.
Juridical Condition and Human Rights of the Child, Advisory Opinion OC-17/02 of August 28, 2002, Series A No.17.
Juridical Condition and Rights of the Undocumented Migrants, Advisory Opinion OC-18/03 of September 17, 2003, Series A No. 18.
Rights and Guarantees of Children in the Context of Migration and/or in Need of International Protection, Advisory Opinion OC-21/14 of August 19, 2014, Series A No.21, [31].
The Right to Information on Consular Assistance in the Framework of the Guarantees of the due Process of Law, Advisory Opinion OC-16/99 of October 1, 1999, Series A No.16.
Control de Convencionalidad: Cuadernillo de Jurisprudencia de la Corte Interamericana de Derechos Humanos No. 7, 2015.

Inter-American Commission on Human Rights

Report on the Situation of Human Rights of a Segment of the Nicaraguan Population of Miskito Indians, Doc. 10, Rev. 3 (1983) 114.
Access to Justice as a Guarantee of Economic, Social, and Cultural Rights: A Review of the Standards Adopted by the Inter-American System of Human Rights, OEA/Ser.L/V/II.129, Doc. 4, 7 September 2007.

European Court of Justice

Case C 420/04, *Apostolides v Orams* [2009] I-03571.

African Commission on Human and People's Rights

Sudan Human Rights Organisation and Centre on Housing Rights and Evictions (COHRE) v Sudan, Communication No. 279/03–296/05 (27 May 2009).

Human Rights Committee (International Covenant on Civil and Political Rights)

Stewart v Canada, CCPR/C/58/D/538/1993 16 December 1996.
Madafferi v Australia, Communication No. 1011/2001, CCPR/C/81/D/1011/2001, 26 August 2004.
Stefan Lars Nystrom v Australia, Communication No. 1557/2007, CCPR/C/102/D/1557/2007.

International military tribunals

Trial of the Major War Criminals (1947), *Military Legal Resources*, https://www.loc.gov/rr/frd/Military_Law/NT_major-war-criminals.html.

Trial of Ulrich Greifelt and others, United States Military Tribunal, Nuremburg, 10 October 1947 – 10 March 1948 in Law Reports of the Trials of War Criminals. United Nations War Crimes Commission. Vol. XIII. London: HMSO, 1949, https://www.loc.gov/rr/frd/Military_Law/pdf/Law-Reports_Vol-13.pdf.

Greiser case, Judgment, 7 July 1946, Supreme National Tribunal at Poznan, Poland.

Krupp case, Judgment, 30 June 1948, US Military Tribunal at Nuremberg.

List (Hostages Trial) case, Judgment, 19 February 1948, Military Tribunal at Nuremberg.

Von Lewinski, Annual Digest and Reports of Public International Law Cases (1949) No. 192, 509.

International Criminal Tribunal for the former Yugoslavia

Prosecutor v Tadić, IT-94-1-AR72, Decision on the Defence Motion for Interlocutory Appeal on Jurisdiction, 2 October 1995.

Prosecutor v Krnojelac case, Judgment, IT-97-25-T, 15 March 2002.

Prosecutor v Krnojelac (Judgment) IT-97-25-A (17 September 2003).

Prosecutor v Stakić, IT-97-24-T, Trial Chamber II, Judgment, 31 July 2003.

Prosecutor v Stakić, IT-97-24-T, Appeals Chamber, Judgment, 22 March 2006.

Prosecutor v Milosevic, Decision on Motion for Judgment of Acquittal, IT-02-54-T, 16 June 2004.

Prosecutor v Krajisnik, IT-00-39-T, Trial Chamber I, Judgment, 27 September 2006.

Prosecutor v Krajisnik, IT-00-39-A, Appeals Chamber, Judgment, 17 March 2009.

Prosecutor v Gotovina et al., Trial Chamber, IT-06-90-T, 15 April 2011.

Prosecutor v Gotovina et al., Appeal Chamber, IT-06-90-A, 16 November 2012.

Prosecutor v Krstic, Judgment, IT-98-33-T, 2 August 2001.

Prosecutor v Krstic, Appeal Chamber, IT-98-33-A, 19 April 2004.

Prosecutor v Popovic, Judgment, Trial Chamber, IT-05-88-T, 10 June 2010 (Public Redacted).

Prosecutor v Tolimir, IT-05-88/2-A, 8 April 2015.

Prosecutor v Karadžić (Judgment) IT-95-5/18-T (24 March 2016).

Prosecutor v Blagojević and Jokić (Judgment) IT-02-60-T (17 January 2005).

Prosecutor v Naletilić and Martinović (Judgment) IT-98-34-T (31 March 2003).

Prosecutor v Simić, Tadić, and Zarić (Judgment) IT-95-9-T (17 October 2003).

Prosecutor v Kunarac, Kovac and Vukovic, IT-96-23& IT-96-23/1-A, AC, 12 June 2002.

Prosecutor v Đorđević, App. Ch., IT-05-87/1-A, 27 January 2014.

Prosecutor v Stanisic and Zupljanin, IT-08-91-T, 27 March 2013.

Prosecutor v Stanisic and Zupljanin, IT-08-91-A, 30 June 2016.

Prosecutor v Prlic et al., IT-04-74-T, 29 May 2013, Vol.1.

Prosecutor v Kordić and Čerkez, IT-95-14/2-A, Judgment, 17 December 2004.

Prosecutor v Brdjanin, IT-99-36.

Prosecutor v Delalić, Mucić, Delić, and Landžo, IT-96-21-A, Judgment, 20 February 2001 (*Čelebići* Appeal Judgment).
Prosecutor v Milutinovic et. al., IT-05-87-T, Trial Judgment, 26 February 2009, Vol.2.

International Criminal Tribunal for Rwanda

Prosecutor v Akayesu, Judgment, ICTR-96-4-T, September 2, 1998.

International Criminal Court

Prosecutor v Ruto and Sang, Ch. II, ICC-01/09-01/11-373, 23 January 2012.
Prosecutor v Bosco Ntaganda, Decision on Defence preliminary challenges to Prosecution's expert witnesses, 9 February 2016, ICC-01/04-02/06.
Decision Pursuant to Article 61(7)(a) and (b) of the Rome Statute on the Charges of the Prosecutor Against Bosco Ntaganda, 9 June 2014.
Prosecutor v Katanga, ICC-01/04-01/07, 7 March 2014, Judgment pursuant to article 74 of the Statute.
Prosecutor v Thomas Lubanga Dyilo, Judgment pursuant to Article 74 of the Statute, 14 March 2012, ICC-01/04-01/06.
Prosecutor v Omar Hassan Ahmad Al Bashir, Judgment on the appeal of the Prosecutor against the 'Decision on the Prosecution's Application for a Warrant of Arrest against Omar Hassan Ahmad Al Bashir', 3 February 2010, ICC-02/05-01/09-73.

Judgments of national courts

Constitutional Court of Colombia, Decision T-227 of 1997.
Constitutional Court of Colombia, T-025 of 2004, Judgment, 22 January 2004.
Constitutional Court of Colombia, T-602 of 2003, Judgment, 23 July 2003.
Eichmann case, Judgment, 12 December 1961, District Court of Jerusalem, Israel.
Hass v Commander of the IDF Forces in the West Bank, Israel High Court of Justice, HCJ 10356/02, 58(3) PD 443.
Ajuri v The Commander of IDF Forces in the West Bank, Israel, High Court of Justice 7015/02, Judgment, September 2002, 56 (6) PD, 352.
Affo and Others, Judgment, 10 April 1988, High Court, Israel.
Leo Handel et al. v Andrija Artukovic on behalf of himself and as representative of the Independent Government of the State of Croatia, US District Court for the Central District of California US 601 f. Supp. 1421 judgment of 31 January 1985.
Kenyan High Court, *Ibrahim Sangor Osman and Others v the Hon. Minister of State for Provincial Administration & Internal Security and Others*, Constitutional Petition No. 2 of 2011 (16 November 2011).

Preface

Armed conflict, whether between states or between states and non-state actors, has catastrophic results for those caught in it. Alongside the economic, political, societal and security challenges that it leads to, armed conflict has direct long-standing detrimental effects on its victims. As the ongoing conflict in Syria demonstrates, it is mostly innocent civilians who suffer as a result of serious human rights violations and atrocities associated with the conflict and committed by either state or non-state actors, or both. To escape such conflict and the abuse and devastation which this brings, civilians are coerced to abandon their homes, their lands and all their possessions seeking safety elsewhere either in other parts of their country as internally displaced or in other states as refugees. Armed conflict is not, however, the only reason that drives people into displacement. Discriminatory practices and gross human rights violations, other than those that are development driven or the result of economic and social factors or environmental disasters, are also driving forces behind forcible displacement.

This volume addresses the involuntary and arbitrary displacement of individuals that results from armed conflict and gross human rights violations and shows that such displacement constitutes not only a serious violation of international law itself but also of fundamental community interests. To this effect, the chapters included in this volume provide a critical legal analysis of the contemporary international framework permeating forcible displacement in these circumstances and explore the rights that individuals possess with specific focus on their right not to be displaced and, where this fails, their rights to return home and to property restitution. In doing so, and while the analysis and case studies considered here are far from exhaustive, the chapters expose some of the legal challenges that individuals encounter in being protected from forcible displacement, as well as the legal obstacles that persist in ensuring the return of and the recovery of property by those already displaced. It is true that the case studies examined in the various chapters present significant differences such as, for instance, in relation to the actors forcing the uprooting of individuals. In the context of Colombia and Syria, for example, individuals are or have been forced into displacement as a result of protracted conflict between state authorities and non-state actors. By contrast, displacement in Cyprus has been driven as a result of foreign state invasion and occupation. Nevertheless, despite these differences and irrespective of whether an international border has been crossed or not, this volume draws on a wealth of sources, international legal theory as well as state practice to identify some common principles and norms safeguarding the rights of individuals in the context of forcible displacement by armed conflict and serious human rights violations.

In this respect, this volume, quite innovatively, marries together international humanitarian, international human rights, international criminal law as well as the law on state responsibility in a quest to see whether, and if so how and to what extent, contemporary international law recognises the right not to be displaced, to return home and to property restitution. At the same time, the case studies chosen for this volume aim to shed light into some less explored situations of forcible displacement, such as is the case relating to forcible displacement in Cambodia, the effects of which persist to the present day. Furthermore, the case studies discussed in the following chapters present significant legal challenges due to the magnitude of displacement such as in Colombia and Syria or due to contested international jurisprudence, which, arguably, impedes the fundamental rights of the displaced, particularly in relation to return and restitution such as in the case of Cyprus. Other situations, such as displacement in the former Yugoslavia and Palestine are discussed as part of the broader legal analysis advanced in the various chapters.

The ever increasing number of those forced to abandon their homeland because of conflict, violence and serious human rights violations makes this study both of continuing relevance and of compelling importance. There is, however, an additional driving force behind the conception of this volume. As an internally displaced person herself, and having experienced at first hand the devastating effects that forcible displacement has, the editor of this volume aims to show that individuals are no longer pawns in the hands of powerful states, but, rather, that they enjoy a fundamental right not to be displaced, to return home and to recover their property.

It is hoped that this analysis will contribute towards a stronger and more effective legal protection of those threatened with, or affected by, forcible displacement.

Elena Katselli Proukaki
September 2017

1 The right not to be displaced by armed conflict under international law

Elena Katselli Proukaki

1 Introduction

With 38 million persons currently displaced by armed conflict, violence and serious human rights violations,[1] and with the conflict in Syria still unfolding with increased intensity and gravity forcing people out of their homes,[2] it is not difficult to see that forcible displacement caused by armed conflict and serious human rights violations presents a significant moral and legal challenge. It is because of the 'enormous injustice'[3] that forcible displacement causes that the Colombian Constitutional Court described it as 'a problem of humanity'.[4] In addition to this, forcible displacement has a domino effect on the enjoyment of a web of fundamental human rights well protected under customary and conventional law. Such is the magnitude of devastation that it brings both on its victims and international peace and security that it is imperative to prevent its occurrence and when this is unavoidable to remedy its aftermath effects. Nevertheless, and as Stavropoulou highlighted 20 years ago, 'The failure of international law to address the issue of displacement in a comprehensive manner results in undeniable gaps in the international protection system.'[5] Despite the significant developments since then, including the adoption of the Guiding Principles on Internal Displacement[6] and the Principles on Housing and Property Restitution

1 Report of the Special Rapporteur on the Human Rights of Internally Displaced Persons, A/HRC/32/35, 29 April 2016, 7.
2 'Mid-Year Trends 2015', UNHCR, 3, http://www.unhcr.org/56701b969.html#_ga=1.238359107.297000490.1455875838
3 de Zayas A.M. (1975), 'International Law and Mass Population Transfers', *HILJ*, Vol. 16, 207, 208, fn 12.
4 Colombian Constitutional Court, Decision T-227 of 1997, per Justice Alejandro Martinez Caballero quoted in Colombian Constitutional Court, Decision T-025 of 2004, 15.
5 Stavropoulou M. (1994), 'The Right not to be Displaced', *AUILR*, Vol. 9, No. 3, 689–749, 738–739.
6 Guiding Principles on Internal Displacement, E/CN.4/1998/53/Add.2, 11 February 1998. Prepared by UN SG's Representative on internally displaced persons Mr Francis Deng, 1998.

for Refugees and Displaced Persons (Pinheiro Principles),[7] these gaps continue to prevail today as evident from the growing wave of forcibly displaced persons across the world. While currently the main attention is placed on solutions following the uprooting of individuals, there is weaker emphasis on the prohibition of displacement. Importantly, the notion of an individual *right* not to be displaced under international law has been neglected. This is so even though according to Principle 5 of the Pinheiro Principles, 'Everyone has the right to be protected against being arbitrarily displaced from his or her home, land or place of habitual residence.'[8] This is because the Pinheiro Principles are not legally binding, presenting a legal vacuum in the prohibition of displacement as a fundamental human *right*.[9] The existing international legal standards have therefore proved inadequate and too fragmented to effectively protect individuals from such uprooting. This has even encouraged states to wrongly perceive the question of forced displacement as a matter that falls within their sovereign powers that can be negotiated, through, for instance, peace agreements.

This chapter fills this gap by establishing that contemporary international law recognises an individual right to be protected from forced displacement that results from armed conflict, whether between states (inter-state) or between a state and non-state actors (internal), and serious human rights violations.[10] As it will be shown, such right, albeit not absolute, has its grounding in international human rights law (IHRL), international humanitarian law (IHL) and international criminal law (ICL) and it is now well embedded in international customary law.

The significance of recognising an autonomous individual right not to be displaced by armed conflict lies in the fact that such right cannot be disposed of – including through peace agreements – save in exceptional circumstances recognised by international law, hence restricting considerably the powers of the parties involved in the conflict. Moreover, the existence of a right not to be displaced, as with all human rights, burdens states with negative and positive obligations to protect individuals from being displaced, including by taking all necessary measures to protect them from the conduct of non-state actors.[11] While

7 UN Principles on Housing and Property Restitution for Refugees and Displaced Persons, http://globalinitiative-escr.org/wp-content/uploads/2013/05/Pinheiro-Principles-Publication.pdf. Developed by Special Rapporteur on Housing and Property Restitution for Refugees and Internally Displaced Persons Paulo Sergio Pinheiro, adopted by UN Sub-Commission on the Promotion and Protection of Human Rights, 2005.

8 Ibid.

9 'The Human Rights Dimensions of Population Transfers including the Implantation of Settlers', Preliminary Report prepared by A.S. Al-Khasawneh and R. Hatano, E/CN.4/Sub.2/1993/17 6 July 1993, [372] (Al-Khasawneh/Hatano report).

10 An inter-state armed conflict comes to an end with the 'general conclusion of peace' whereas an internal armed conflict comes to an end with the conclusion of a peaceful settlement. *Prosecutor v Gotovina et al.*, TC, IT-06-90-T, 15 April 2011, [1676].

11 n5, 738; Sassoli M. (2002), 'State Responsibility for Violations of International Humanitarian Law', *IRRC*, Vol. 84, 401, 411.

this is not sufficient to eliminate forced displacement, the recognition that individuals cannot be displaced as of right can nevertheless increase the pressure on states and non-state actors to prevent or end its occurrence, fill existing legal gaps and strengthen the protection afforded to those threatened by it. Moreover, and while, of course, the existence of such a right does not in itself presume capacity to bring a claim before national or international (judicial or other) bodies, or enforcement, as discussed in Section 7, it nevertheless means that the individual affected by violation of the right not to be displaced can make a legal demand for the respect of their right and for the cessation of the wrongful act. To this effect, and quite fundamentally, the right not to be displaced can have one obvious and very significant advantage. It can provide the people who are in danger of being displaced with a claim that can assist them in drawing attention to a serious human rights problem that encapsulates a whole range of human rights abuses. The issue of empowerment is therefore of paramount importance in the realization of human rights such as is the case in this instance.[12]

In this regard, establishing a strong legal framework not only on the obligation not to displace in armed conflict or as a result of serious human rights violations but also on a corresponding, autonomous human right not to be displaced is an essential step towards ensuring protection against displacement in these circumstances, alongside effective mechanisms and access to remedies such as is the case with other serious violations of human rights.[13] This, in turn, has significant ramifications on the legal consequences that arise from the violation of such right, such as the right to restitution and the right of those displaced to return home, which are discussed in detail in the next chapter.

For a new human right to exist, however, it will have, among other things, to 'reflect a fundamentally important social value', attract 'a very high degree of international consensus'; and 'be sufficiently precise as to give rise to identifiable rights and obligations'.[14] The analysis in this chapter demonstrates that these conditions are satisfied rendering strong support for the existence of the right not to be displaced.

For the purposes of this chapter, forcible displacement is given effect through forcible transfer of population within the borders of a specific state or deportation that occurs when a national border is crossed. It may be part of planned policies for acquiring new territory, for creating ethnically homogenous areas or even for the destruction of a certain part of the population as part of a broader genocidal plan. It is also inflicted on its victims under duress leaving them no other option but to flee.[15] One must not, however, neglect the simple fact that individuals often

12 n5, 745.
13 n3, 227.
14 Alston P. (1984), 'Conjuring Up New Human Rights: A Proposal for Quality Control', *AJIL*, Vol. 78, 607, 615; also see analysis in n5, 694.
15 *Prosecutor v Krstic case*, Judgment, IT-98-33-T, 2 August 2001, [521]–[523].

'choose' to abandon their homes and land to protect themselves and their families from death and other serious human rights violations.[16] Hence, displacement is pursued by the victims themselves as the lesser of two evils. This could not be truer as evident from the mass exodus of populations, such as that currently experienced in the context of the Syrian conflict, in search of security elsewhere. Protection against displacement, as advanced in this chapter, is not intended to prevent the exercise of other rights such as the right to seek and enjoy asylum.[17] Nevertheless, the fact that individuals should be allowed to leave must not overshadow the primary obligation of states and non-state actors to ensure the protection of civilians from displacement by respecting their obligations under IHL and IHRL, as well as the right of individuals to remain in their homes under conditions of safety.[18] Accordingly, the term 'forced' or 'forcible displacement' is used in this chapter to indicate lack of genuine choice on the part of the individuals concerned because of conflict and human rights violations.[19] At the same time, however, forced displacement is distinguished from *temporary* protective measures taken during conflict to evacuate the civilian population for their own safety and, hence, forced displacement is associated with action that is not justified under international law. This issue is further addressed in detail below.

It is further important to clarify that this chapter is concerned with the forced displacement, 'through expulsion or other coercive means'[20] of those who lawfully reside within the territory from which they are expelled, without making a distinction between nationals and non-nationals. Even though different people within a state may have different legal status and hence may be covered by different international rules, such as for instance enemy aliens, the deportation of whom during armed conflict is arguably permitted under international law,[21] this chapter will not focus on these distinctions. Neither will the chapter draw a distinction between the internally displaced and refugees. This is because forced displacement caused by armed conflict and serious human rights violations has severe repercussions on those affected by it irrespective of nationality and whether an international border has been crossed. To this effect, the chapter will consider the existence of the right not to be displaced as a matter of a general rule. Finally, this

16 Zapater J., 'Prevention of Forced Displacement: The Inconsistencies of a Concept' (UNHCR: Policy Development and Evaluation Service) Research Paper No 186, April 2010, 3, http://www.unhcr.org/uk/research/working/4bbb2a199/ prevention-forced-displacement-inconsistencies-concept-josep-zapater.html?query=forced displacement.

17 Executive Committee of the High Commissioner's Programme, Note on International Protection, 31 August 1993, A/AC.96/815, [37].

18 Phuong C. (2005), *The International Protection of Internally Displaced Persons* (Cambridge University Press) 124.

19 n16, 18.

20 *Popovic case*, Judgement, IT-05-88-T, 10 June 2010, [891].

21 Eritrea Ethiopia Claims Commission, Partial Award, Civilians Claims, Eritrea's Claims 15, 16, 23, 27–32, 17 December 2004, Reports of International Arbitral Awards, Vol. XXVI, 195–247.

chapter does not address displacement caused because of natural or environmental disasters, development or economic migration, which, albeit important, do not fall within the scope of this examination.

Having explained what forced displacement is and why the recognition of a stand-alone right not to be displaced by armed conflict and serious human rights violations is essential, Section 2 examines how forced displacement was addressed – if at all – by international law at the rise of the 20th century. Sections 3, 4 and 5 focus on how the law on forced displacement evolved following the end of World War II (WWII), arguing that a stand-alone right not to be displaced by armed conflict and serious human rights violations exists in light of international humanitarian, international criminal and international human rights law. Section 6 assesses further evidence of state practice and *opinio juris* in support of the right not to be displaced in the circumstances under consideration whilst Section 7 discusses the significance of having such a right and a remedy under international law. Section 8 concludes this analysis.

2 Displacement and dispossession in the early 20th century

To assist us in understanding how forced displacement is regulated today, this section examines how international law responded to specific events that led to the forced displacement of populations in the early 20th century. In doing so, it provides a forum for a comparative discussion of whether, and if so to what extent, contemporary international treaty and customary law evolved towards establishing a right not to be displaced by armed conflict and serious human rights violations.

The prohibition of forced displacement through deportation found recognition in Article 23 of the Lieber Code,[22] while population transfer, a more recently evolved concept,[23] was prohibited under customary law.[24] While the 1907 Hague Convention respecting the Laws and Customs of War on Land (1907 Hague Convention) concerning inter-state conflict and still in force today does not expressly prohibit forced displacement,[25] Articles 42–56 regulating belligerent occupation have been construed as impliedly protecting against this practice.[26] Of particular relevance is Article 43, which obliges the occupying power 'to restore, and ensure, as far as possible, public order and safety, while respecting, unless absolutely prevented, the laws in force in the country'.[27] For its part, Article 46 provides that: 'Family honour

22 The Lieber Code (Washington D.C., 24 April 1863) in Friedman L. (ed.) (1973), *The Law of War, a Documentary History* (Random House) Vol. I.

23 Bassiouni M.C. (2011), *Crimes against Humanity: Historical Evolution and Contemporary Application* (Cambridge University Press) 380.

24 n3, 213.

25 This was because deportations were already prohibited under international law. See ibid, 211.

26 Ibid, 212.

27 Quigley observes that the English translation is wrong and that in fact Article 423requires the occupying power to 'maintain *la vie public*', meaning the preservation of 'general safety

and rights, the lives of persons and private property, as well as religious convictions and practices must be respected.' This, together with Articles 47–53, which prohibit among other things pillage and collective punishment against the population,[28] could be interpreted as inferring a duty not to move the civilian population from territory.[29]

Despite this, forced population transfers and deportations were common practices following the end of the Balkan Wars and World War I (WWI),[30] such as the transfers that took place between Bulgaria and Greece, and Bulgaria and Turkey.[31] Significantly, with the conclusion of the Convention Concerning the Exchange of Greek and Turkish Populations of 30 January 1923, more than 1 million Greeks were forced to leave their homes in Minor Asia and Eastern Thrace and were transferred to territories then controlled by Greece. Similarly, between 350,000 and 500,000 Muslims were transferred to Turkey.[32] Those transferred were prevented from returning to their homes, while receiving unsatisfactory compensation.[33] As Article 1 of the Convention provided, 'as from May 1st, 1923, there shall take place a compulsory exchange of Turkish nationals of the Greek Orthodox religion established in Turkish territory, and of Greek nationals of the Moslem religion established in Greek territory. These persons shall not return to live in Turkey or Greece respectively without the authorization of the Turkish government or of the Greek government respectively.'[34] The immovable property of the exchanged populations would be liquidated and passed to the state, while both the population exchange and the liquidation would be monitored by a Mixed Commission set up for this purpose.[35] The right to remain or to return and to enjoy full rights including the right to property was limited to those inhabitants of districts that were exempted from such transfers, such as for instance the 'established' inhabitants of Constantinople. At the same time, however, under the Declaration Relating to Moslem Properties in Greece, the Greek government undertook to restore the property rights of those Muslims who did not fall within

and social functions and ordinary transactions which constitute daily life'; Quigley J. (1998), 'Displaced Palestinians and a Right to Return', *HILJ*, Vol. 38, 171, 198, fn 154.

28 Convention (IV) respecting the Laws and Customs of War on Land and its annex: Regulations concerning the Laws and Customs of War on Land. The Hague, 18 October 1907 in 2 *AJIL* (1908) 90 (Supp) 1. Also see Convention (II) with Respect to the Laws and Customs of War on Land and its annex: Regulations concerning the Laws and Customs of War on Land. The Hague, 29 July 1899; (Al-Khasawneh/Hatano report), n9, [154].

29 n23, 381–382.

30 See i.e. Article 14, Treaty of Peace with Turkey signed at Lausanne, 24 July 1923.

31 See i.e. Annex to the Peace Treaty of Constantinople on 15 November 1913.

32 n3, 222.

33 Wolff S., 'Can Forced Population Transfers Resolve Self-determination Conflicts? A European Perspective', http://www.stefanwolff.com/files/ethniccleansing.pdf.

34 Convention Concerning the Exchange of Greek and Turkish Populations, Lausanne, January 30, 1923 in 18 *AJIL* (Apr 1924) No 2, Supplement, 84–90.

35 Ibid, Articles 9 and 11.

the Convention on the exchange of populations and who had left Greece before 1912.[36]

It seems from the Convention Concerning the Exchange of Greek and Turkish Populations that the forcible population exchange aimed at the creation of religiously 'pure' territories 'eliminating' the perceived problems arising from the existence of minorities, which caused political unrest. This explains why the right to return and the right to property were retained for some but not for other populations in the aftermath of WWI. This situation, which was given legitimacy through treaty law, presented a paradox since forced deportations, through population exchanges, were endorsed in parallel with treaties that aimed to protect the rights of minorities and their link to territory.[37] The issues relating to the compulsory exchange of populations in this instance were brought before the Permanent Court of International Justice (PCIJ) in the *Exchange of Greek and Turkish Populations Case* in which the Court, while not considering the lawfulness of such transfer, did not challenge it.[38] In this way, as Bassiouni notes, the Court 'implicitly' accepted the legality of such transfer.[39] This was despite the fact that as a result of the transfers those affected were left homeless and destitute.[40] As de Zayas observes, 'state interests were given preference over the interests of humanity.'[41]

By contrast, and while such forced exchanges and deportations were embedded in several treaties following WWI, the deportation of civilians that was carried out by Germany and its allies during the war was considered by the Commission on the Responsibilities of the Authors of the War and the Enforcement of Penalties as a crime against the laws of humanity.[42] In its report, the Commission concluded that the deportation of 1 million Armenians and 400,000 Greeks living in Thrace and in Minor Asia, both carried out by Turkish authorities, as well as the deportation of 1 million Greek-speaking Turks living in Turkey by Turkish and German authorities constituted such crimes.[43] This was so irrespective of whether such acts were directed against nationals (crimes against the laws of humanity) or against non-nationals (war crimes).[44] Yet, these crimes were left unpunished because the United States opposed the Commission's report on the ground that

36 Declaration Relating to Moslem Properties in Greece in 18 *AJIL* (Apr 1924) No. 2, Supplement, 95–96.

37 Weitz E.D. (2008), 'From the Vienna to the Paris System: International Politics and the Entangled Histories of Human Rights, Forced Deportations, and Civilizing Missions', *AHR*, Vol. 113, No. 5, 1313 –1343; n27, 206.

38 *Exchange of Greek and Turkish Populations*, PCIJ (1925) Ser. B, No. 11, 6.

39 Bassiouni M.C. (1999), *Crimes against Humanity in International Criminal Law* (Kluwer Law International) 321.

40 McM W. (1953), 'In Memoriam: Allen T Burns', *SSR*, Vol. 27, No. 2, 218.

41 n3, 222.

42 Report by the Commission on the Responsibilities of the Authors of War and on Enforcement of Penalties, 14 *AJIL* (Jan–Apr, 1920) No. 1/2, 95, 114.

43 n39, 321.

44 Ibid, 321 and 322.

the concept of crimes against the laws of humanity did not at that time have international legal basis.[45] Significantly, the Treaty of Sevres which required the prosecution of Turkish officials and the return of those deported to their homes was never ratified, while the Treaty of Lausanne offered amnesty for such crimes.[46] Such amnesty not only failed to punish those responsible for such acts, but it also endorsed them.[47] This set 'a very bad precedent in international law, in that it approved the first compulsory transplanting of peoples from lands where their ancestors had lived for many hundred years'.[48] Even so, it becomes evident from this analysis that while states condemned deportations carried out by Germany and Turkey during WWI, the Peace Agreements authorised deportations carried out by Allied powers. Such population exchanges are unlawful under contemporary international law,[49] an issue discussed in detail below.

Exchanges of populations were also authorised under the Convention of Neuilly between Greece and Bulgaria of 27 November 1919, which provided for 'the reciprocal emigration of the racial, religious and linguistic minorities in Greece and Bulgaria'.[50] In its Advisory Opinion in *The Greco-Bulgarian 'Communities'*, the PCIJ emphatically reiterated that the very aim of the Convention was 'that the individuals forming the communities should respectively make their homes permanently among their own race, the very mentality of the population concerned.'[51] This, however, presents an endorsement of a policy of arbitrary discrimination driving those not belonging in the majority out of such territories and depriving individual members of such communities of their fundamental rights such as the peaceful enjoyment of their possessions, their right to home and their right to family life. This is in spite of the fact that unlike the exchange of Greek and Turkish populations, Article 1 of the Convention of Neuilly provided for the voluntary emigration of those desiring to do so rather than their forced transfer.[52] One can of course question whether such population exchanges are genuinely voluntary.[53] Concerning the property of those who decided to leave, Article 7 provided that any real property belonging to them would be liquidated. The amount obtained from the value of the property would then be transferred to the owners of the property. However, as the PCIJ stressed, only those who decided to emigrate would be able to benefit from the liquidation of property that

45 n42, 149.
46 n39, 314.
47 Ibid.
48 Ibid, 314.
49 n3, 222.
50 Convention Between Greece and Bulgaria Respecting Reciprocal Emigration, 14 *AJIL* (Oct, 1920) No. 4, Supplement, 356–360.
51 *The Greco-Bulgarian 'Communities'* (Advisory Opinion), PCIJ, Series B, No. 17, July 31 1930, 21.
52 According to Nestor, a compulsory exchange of populations would be a breach of fundamental human rights. Nestor S. (1962), 'Greek Macedonia and the Convention of Neuilly (1919)' *BS*, 169–184, 181.
53 Al-Khasawneh/Hatano report, n9, [118].

belonged to the dissolved community.[54] In this instance too, the emigration and liquidation process would be observed by a Mixed Commission.

From the analysis above, it is clear that practice in relation to displacement through deportations and population transfers during and following WWI was inconsistent and, in many cases, conflicting. This was so in spite of the protections, albeit restricted to situations of occupation, afforded under the 1907 Hague Convention and customary international law discussed above. In fact, such practice reveals that states considered forced displacement given effect to 'homogenise' the newly created or expanded states as a desirable political, ethnic, racial and religious objective, which would put an end to the problems surrounding the existence of minorities. This may be explained by the lack of express prohibition of forced displacement and lack of recognition of the right not to be displaced. Such absence is owed to the predominantly state-centred nature of the international legal order at the time under consideration whereby individuals had no recognised international legal standing or personality and were subjected to the absolute, and often abusive, power of the state.[55] The evolution of human rights and the idea that individuals possess inherent fundamental rights and freedoms by virtue of being human were embodied in international law at a much later stage following the devastating effects of WWII. It therefore comes as no surprise that issues relating to displacement fell within the exclusive power of states. As the analysis in this section demonstrates, states could decide through the conclusion of international agreements to force entire communities outside specific territories, in a move that today would be considered a violation of international law.[56]

This being said, forced displacement was also a common phenomenon during and after WWII. It is, for instance, estimated that after the war 15 million people – mainly Germans – were expelled from their homes to create ethnically 'pure' regions to avoid future conflict.[57] This was in spite of the fact that the deportation of civilians from occupied territory was recognised as a war crime and a crime against humanity under Article 6 (c) of the International Military Tribunal (IMT) Charter,[58]

54 n51, 26 and 31.

55 Bugnion F. (2004–2005), 'Refugees, Internally Displaced Persons and International Humanitarian Law', *FInte'lLJ*, Vol. 28, 1397, 1406.

56 n27, 224.

57 n33; also see Korn D.A. (1999), *Exodus Within Borders: An Introduction to the Crisis of Internal Displacement* (Brookings Institution Press) 7–9; de Zayas A.M. (1993), *The German Expellees: Victims in War and Peace* (Palgrave Macmillan).

58 Article 6, United Nations, *Charter of the International Military Tribunal - Annex to the Agreement for the prosecution and punishment of the major war criminals of the European Axis ('London Agreement')*, 8 August 1945, http://www.unhcr.org/refworld/docid/3ae6b39614.html. Also see Trial of the Major War Criminals (1947), *Military Legal Resources*, https://www.loc.gov/rr/frd/Military_Law/NT_major-war-criminals.html; Affirmation of the Principles of International Law Recognized by the Charter of the Nuremberg Tribunal, G.A. Res. 95(1), UN. Doc A/64/Add.l, (1946) 188; Henckaerts J.M. (2009), 'The Grave Breaches Regime as Customary International Law', *JICJ*, Vol. 7, No. 4, 683–701, 689–690.

the 1945 Allied Control Council Law No. 10,[59] the 1946 IMT Charter (Tokyo) and the Nuremberg Principles.[60] Indeed, one of the charges against those accused before the IMT was the assimilation of occupied territories by the occupied power and their alienation from their former ethnic, national, economic, cultural character through the forcible deportation of the civilian population and the settlement of nationals of the occupying power.[61] In the *Case of Greifelt and others*, for instance, the accused faced prosecution for crimes against humanity and war crimes for population evacuations from native land occupied or otherwise controlled by Germany and resettlement of own population, expulsions and population transfers as well as for confiscations and plundering of public and private property with no compensation offered.[62] Such measures intended to Germanise the population as well as the territories annexed or occupied by the Nazis and were carried out through 'intimidation, deceit or mere force'.[63] Evacuees were often given little time to collect their personal belongings, while families were split up hence severing family ties.[64] Often such measures took place as part of genocidal plans.[65]

Hence it is surprising that while deportation was prosecuted as a war crime and a crime against humanity, at the same time it was used as the object of international agreements concluded at the end of the war.[66] Such is the Potsdam Agreement with which the United States, the United Kingdom and the Union of Soviet Social Republics agreed 'the transfer to Germany of German populations, or elements thereof, remaining in Poland, Czechoslovakia and Hungary' even though such transfers were to be carried out 'in an orderly and humane manner'.[67] This move was considered essential to 'de-nazify' the defeated German state.[68] Hence, one cannot but notice the differentiated treatment towards the population transfers

59 Article II, Allied Control Council No. 10: Punishment of Persons Guilty of War Crimes, Crimes against Peace and against Humanity, Berlin, 20 December 1945.

60 Article 5 (c) Charter of the International Military Tribunal for the Far East, Tokyo, 19 January 1946, amended on 26 April 1946; Report of the International Law Commission on the Work of its Second Session, U.N. GAOR, 5th Sess., Supp. No. 12, Principle 6(c), U.N. Doc. A/1316 (1950), in *YbILC*, Vol. 2, 374 (1950).

61 2 IMT 57, Count 3, J discussed in n39.

62 Trial of Ulrich Greifelt and others, United States Military Tribunal, Nuremburg, 10 October 1947–10 March 1948 in Law Reports of the Trials of War Criminals. UN War Crimes Commission. Vol. XIII. London: HMSO, 1949, 3 and 25– 26, https://www.loc.gov/rr/frd/Military_Law/pdf/Law-Reports_Vol-13.pdf.

63 Ibid, 20.

64 Ibid.

65 Ibid, 25. On deportations and forcible transfer also see *Greiser case*, Judgment, 7 July 1946, Supreme National Tribunal at Poznan, Poland; *List (Hostages Trial) case*, Judgment, 19 February 1948, Military Tribunal at Nuremberg, USA; *Eichmann case*, Judgment, 12 December 1961, District Court of Jerusalem, Israel.

66 Al-Khasawneh/Hatano report, n9, [11].

67 Article XII, The Berlin (Potsdam) Conference, 17 July—2 August 1945, Protocol of the Proceedings, August l, 1945, http://avalon.law.yale.edu/20th_century/decade17.asp.

68 n3, 233.

agreed by Allied powers resulting in the expulsion of 15 million Germans.[69] Bassiouni is of the belief, however, that the IMT missed the opportunity to draw a distinction between population transfers resulting from territorial adjustments and those carried out for discriminatory reasons or for the extermination of the transferred population.[70] However, this author is not convinced that transfers carried out as part of territorial re-arrangements, or even as a result of peace agreements are not problematic, as they themselves raise issues relating to discrimination while such distinction can be open to abuse. This was recognised by the International Law Institute in 1952, according to which 'international population transfer is never a means to protect human rights' and that 'To suggest that population transfer somehow works to the advantage of the affected populations, then, is to fail to make the important distinction between the interest of the individual and the interest of the State.'[71] As rightly put, '[l]' intérêt de la communauté internationale ne peut pas justifier la violation du Droit.'[72] To this effect, the forced displacement of the population, either through population transfers or other means, is today legally contested as the populations and individuals concerned should be allowed to remain in their homes unless otherwise authorised under international law.[73]

The preceding analysis has therefore shown that following WWI and WWII practice on forced population transfers, and in effect forced displacement, was inconsistent.[74] While such transfers were criminalised in the context of occupation, they were encouraged under peace agreements.[75] Nevertheless, the legal developments that followed the end of WWII through the development of IHL, ICL and IHRL not only restrain, but in fact also prohibit altogether the power of the state to 'homogenise' or 'purify' territory through displacement, whether this is carried out during armed conflict or occupation or as a result of peace agreements or discriminatory practices.[76] At the same time, a right not to be forcibly displaced has indeed evolved in contemporary international law, the legal basis of which is discussed in detail in the next sections. The examination will start with an analysis of the rules of IHL and then proceed to an analysis of how individuals are protected against displacement under ICL and IHRL.

69 Brownlie I. (1963), *International Law and the Use of Force* (Oxford University Press) 408. For a critique of such expulsions also see de Zayas A. (1988), *Nemesis at Potsdam: The Expulsions of the Germans from the East* (Bison Books).

70 n39, 315.

71 Al-Khasawneh/Hatano report, n9, [362].

72 G Scalle in 44/2 Annuaire (1952) 180 in n3, 226.

73 In support see Al-Khasawneh/Hatano report, n9, [43]; also see in this regard n 3, 250; n27, 224.

74 For further analysis on WWII forced expulsions, Al-Khasawneh/Hatano report, n9, [128]–[137].

75 On population transfers following WWII, see n3, 207.

76 For brief analysis, see 'Exchange of Populations', http://www.globalsecurity.org/military/world/war/exchange-of-population.htm; Ullom V. (2000–2001), 'Voluntary Repatriation of Refugees and Customary International Law', *DJIL&P*, Vol. 29, 115, 116.

3 The legal basis of the right not to be displaced under international humanitarian law

3.1 Introduction

Armed conflict is the armed force between states or protracted armed violence between states and organised non-state groups or between non-state groups within a state.[77] As well known, armed conflict engages the rules of IHL which regulate the means and methods of warfare and protect those caught in armed conflict, whether civilians or those no longer taking part in hostilities from the acts of states and non-state actors.[78] Armed conflict is therefore an essential requirement for the invocation of IHL, whose rules are embodied in international agreements and customs.[79] As the analysis below demonstrates, IHL has a wealth of treaty and customary rules aimed at protecting civilians from displacement.[80] It is violation of these rules, such as, for instance, indiscriminate attacks against civilians prohibited under Article 51 of Additional Protocol I (API),[81] that force civilians to abandon their homes.[82] As Bugnion correctly points out, 'If they are upheld, these provisions – which protect all civilian persons – eliminate the main reasons people are uprooted in times of war. They kick in before refugee law does, protecting civilians against forcible transfers and the threat of uprooting, whose devastating effects are all too familiar, and hence from the risk of becoming refugees or displaced persons.'[83] As it will be argued, these rules support the claim that an individual right not to be displaced exists.

3.2 Prohibition of forced displacement under the Geneva law

Unlike the Hague Regulations, and in significant progression of international law, the Geneva Conventions of 1949 and their additional protocols expressly prohibit the forced displacement of populations in inter-state and internal armed conflict, hence recognising the devastating effects of displacement and the necessity

77 *Prosecutor v Tadić*, Decision on the Defence Motion for Interlocutory Appeal on Jurisdiction, 2 October 1995, [70].
78 See n55, 1400 and 1404; Commentary of 1958, IV Geneva Convention Relative to the Protection of Civilian Persons in Time of War of 12 August 1949, 37.
79 Greer J.L., 'Critique of the ICRC's Customary Rules Concerning Displaced Persons: General Accuracy, Conflation, and a Missed Opportunity', 1, https://www.nottingham.ac.uk/hrlc/documents/publications/ hrlcommentary2007/acritiqueoficrcscustomaryrulesondisplacedpersons.pdf; n55, 1402.
80 n55 1404; Zegveld L. (2003), 'Remedies for Victims of Violations of International Humanitarian Law', *IRRC*, Vol. 85, No. 851, 501.
81 Protocol Additional to the Geneva Conventions of 12 August 1949 and Relating to the Protection of Victims of International Armed Conflicts (Protocol I), 8 June 1977, 1125 *UNTS* 3.
82 n55, 1420.
83 Ibid, 1407.

of preventing and ending it as a serious violation of international law. Importantly, the express prohibition of forced displacement, including deportation and forcible transfer, is in essence recognition of the *individual right* not to be displaced. As the International Criminal Tribunal for the former Yugoslavia (ICTFY) emphasised, 'the *legal values* protected by deportation and forcible transfer are the "right of the victim to stay in his or her home and community and the right not to be deprived of his or her property by being forcibly displaced to another location".'[84]

Article 49 of the Fourth Geneva Convention (IV GC), which applies in inter-state conflict, prohibits individual or mass forcible transfer and deportation from occupied territory irrespective of the reasons behind such act.[85] This prohibition is absolute and may not be deviated from even in 'the most compelling security considerations'.[86] Nevertheless, Article 49 allows 'the total or partial evacuation of a given area if the security of the population or imperative military reasons so demand'. Yet, such evacuation is subject to restrictions since the persons concerned must not be transferred 'outside the bounds of the occupied territory except when for material reasons it is impossible to avoid such displacement', neither may they be transferred to a country in which they may fear persecution.[87] Importantly, Article 49 stipulates that those evacuated 'shall be transferred back to their homes as soon as hostilities in the area in question have ceased'.[88] It becomes clear from the differentiated terms chosen that forcible transfer and deportation are to be distinguished from evacuations that are intended as temporary measures for the safety of the population concerned.[89] The temporary character of such evacuations is reinforced in Article 58 API according to which the removal of civilians from military targets is subject to the obligations arising under Article 49 IV GC. Finally, Article 49 prohibits in absolute terms the occupying power from transferring its own population into the occupied territory. This obligation allows no exceptions or restrictions and hence no military necessity may justify such population transfer. This issue is further discussed below as it is relevant both for the right not to be displaced as well as the rights to return home and to property restitution examined in the next chapter.

Such is the significance of Article 49 that it 'applies not only to mass deportations but to the deportation of individuals as well and that the prohibition was intended

84 *Prosecutor v Milosevic*, Decision on Motion for Judgment of Acquittal, IT-02-54-T, 16 June 2004, [63] (emphasis added).

85 Article 49 (1) IV Geneva Convention Relative to the Protection of Civilian Persons in Time of War of 12 August 1949. Also see analysis in n79.

86 Dinstein Y. (2009), *The International Law of Belligerent Occupation* (Cambridge University Press) 161; Margalit A., Hibbin S. (2010), 'Unlawful Presence of Protected Persons in Occupied Territory? An Analysis of Israel's Permit Regime and Expulsions from the West Bank under the Law of Occupation', *YbIHumL*, Vol. 13, 245, 256.

87 See Article 45 (4), n85; n55, 1405–1406.

88 n10, [1740].

89 n78, 280.

to be total, sweeping and unconditional'.[90] There is also consensus that the prohibitions entailed in Article 49 have become binding through custom.[91]

Both the terms 'transfer' and 'deportation' imply an intentional act, even though these may be carried out through positive and negative action.[92] Importantly, Article 49 prohibits forcible transfer and deportation from 'occupied territory'.[93] Occupation is established when a territory comes under the *de facto* authority of the enemy power[94] and for as long as it exercises governmental functions, even if such functions are transferred to another authority, such as a puppet 'state'.[95] The stationing of troops, or mere presence, is not sufficient to satisfy the element of occupation.[96] In this respect, Article 49 does not seem to protect from forced displacement carried out before such occupation is established, which can be very problematic as often the population is forced to abandon their homes and lands as a result of advancing enemy troops or shelling, attacks, bombardments and crimes committed elsewhere. This interpretation presents a significant legal gap concerning forced displacement that occurs outside the context of occupation, highlighting why the recognition of a general right not to be displaced by armed conflict and serious human rights violations is imperative. In any event, while Section III of the Convention, to which Article 49 falls, regulates the regime of occupation, Article 2 IV GC ensures that the Convention – in its entirety – applies 'from the outset of any conflict or occupation'. In this respect: 'The relations between the civilian population of a territory and troops advancing into that territory, whether fighting or not, are governed by the present Convention. There is no intermediate period between what might be termed the invasion phase and the inauguration of a stable regime of occupation.'[97] This aims to prevent any legal loopholes towards the protected persons and this must also be understood in the context of forced displacement.

Another difficulty that Article 49 presents is that it appears at first sight to be too narrow to encompass displacement that is forced not because of direct attacks[98] but rather indirect coercive acts. For example, forced displacement may be caused

90 See Justice Bach, *Affo and Others*, Judgment, 10 April 1988, High Court, Israel.

91 Meron T. (1989), *Human Rights and Humanitarian Norms as Customary Law* (Clarendon Press) 48–49.

92 Such transfers can be deliberate or result from 'malign neglect': 1993 Preliminary Report of the Sub-Commission on Prevention of Discrimination and Protection of Minorities relating to Population Transfers; Al-Khasawneh/Hatano report, n9, [15].

93 n3, 210.

94 n78, 273.

95 Article 6, n85. Also see n81.

96 Article 42, Hague Convention 1907, n28; *Legal Consequences of the Construction of a Wall in the Occupied Palestinian Territory*, Advisory Opinion, ICJ Reports (2004) 136, 167, [78] (Wall Advisory Opinion); *Case Concerning Armed Activities on the Territory of the Congo (Democratic Republic of the Congo v Uganda)*, Judgment, ICJ Reports (2005) 168, [172] (*DRC v Uganda case*).

97 n78, 59.

98 n10, [1743].

through confiscation of land, deprivation of means of subsistence or adverse economic conditions as is the situation resulting from Israel's construction of the wall in the occupied Palestinian territory.[99] It may also result from discriminatory measures[100] and restrictions to rights such as freedom of movement, which, in turn, have negative ramifications on access to healthcare or to schools such as in the case of enclaved Greek Cypriots who were eventually forced to abandon their homes in that part of Cyprus occupied by Turkey.[101] As Article 49 was not intended to prohibit voluntary transfers,[102] the distinction between 'forcible' and 'voluntary' transfer becomes legally significant. While voluntary transfer is restricted to situations that 'might up to a certain point have the consent of those being transferred', with specific reference to situations in which ethnic or political minorities which have been subjected to discrimination or persecution may wish to leave the country,[103] it is also clear that civilians are particularly vulnerable during conflict. This casts doubts as to whether denunciation of their rights protected under the IV GC, such as not to be displaced, can result from genuinely free will.[104] In clarifying what amounts to 'forced' displacement, the ICTFY in *Stakic* highlighted that this 'is not to be limited to physical force but includes the threat of force or coercion, such as that caused by fear of violence, duress, detention, psychological oppression or abuse of power against such person or persons or another person, or by taking advantage of a coercive environment'.[105] As further pointed out by Jordan concerning Israel's wall construction in occupied Palestinian territory,

> [I]t is sufficient that the Occupying Power should adopt practices which are intended to drive the local inhabitants from their territory, or which may be reasonably foreseen to have that result. . . . a transfer will be 'forcible' if the measures adopted by the Occupying Power are such as in practice to leave the affected local population no realistic alternatives but to leave the territory. Even if such a movement of the local inhabitants is not the purpose behind the construction of the wall it is nevertheless a clear consequence, and Article 49 makes it clear that transfers of the local population are prohibited 'regardless of their motive'.[106]

99 Wall Advisory Opinion, n96, 191–192, [133]–[134].
100 Al-Khasawneh/Hatano report, n9, [37].
101 For violations against enclaved Greek Cypriots see *Cyprus v Turkey* (Application no. 25781/94), Judgments (Just Satisfaction) 12 May 2014.
102 n78, 279; also see Article 35, n85.
103 Article 49, n78, 279.
104 Article 8, n78, 75.
105 *Prosecutor v Stakić*, IT-97-24-T, AC, Judgement, 22 March 2006, [281]; n10, [1738] and [1739]; n84, [63].
106 Written Statement submitted to the ICJ, *Legal Consequences of the Construction of a Wall in the Occupied Palestinian Territory*, 30 January 2004, [5.137]–[5.138].

Nevertheless, ambiguity exists relating to those who flee due to a general fear related to armed conflict and mistrust towards the approaching army. In *Gotovina*, for instance, the ICTFY did not find that forcible displacement had been established since there were no geographical or temporal links to the shelling attacks that were carried out elsewhere.[107] However, this finding is challenged since it is often the case that civilians are forced to abandon their homes even if they have not witnessed any violence themselves due to fear or information about atrocities taking place elsewhere. As pointed out by the ICTFY in an earlier decision, 'A lack of genuine choice may be inferred from, *inter alia*, threatening and intimidating acts that are calculated to deprive the civilian population of exercising its free will, such as the shelling of civilian objects, the burning of civilian property, and the commission of – or the threat to commit – other crimes "calculated to terrify the population and make them flee the area with no hope of return".'[108] Moreover, in the subsequent case of *Karadjic*, the Trial Chamber found that civilians were displaced as a result of fear caused by violence and other crimes committed against non-Serbs.[109] Stavropoulou further argues that displacement in the context of general fear of violence may have been incorporated in Article 17 APII concerning internal armed conflict ('otherwise compelled').[110] Forced displacement in anticipation of a coercive environment is also recognised in the introduction of the Guiding Principles on Internal Displacement.[111] The issue is of legal significance as it relates to what constitutes forced displacement, irrespective of whether this occurs in occupied territory in which Article 49 IV GC applies or not.

Not only is forced displacement prohibited under Article 49 IV GC however, but also the 'unlawful deportation or transfer . . . of a protected person' constitutes a grave breach under Article 147 IV GC and hence a war crime giving rise to both individual criminal and state responsibility under Articles 146 and 148 from which states cannot be absolved.[112] It is also a grave breach under Article 85 (4) API GC applicable to inter-state conflicts.[113] This article, which also prohibits as grave breach the transfer of the occupying power's own population in the occupied territory, was adopted by consensus[114] demonstrating the fundamental

107 n10, [1762]; Eritrea Ethiopia Claims Commission, Partial Award, Western Front, Aerial Bombardment and Related Claims Eritrea's Claims 1, 3, 5, 9–13, 14, 21, 25 & 26, 19 December 2005, [135], https://pcacases.com/web/ sendAttach/ 757.

108 n84, [74].

109 *Prosecutor v Karadjic*, IT-95-5/18-T, 24 March 2016, [2468].

110 n5, 727.

111 Kalin W. (2008), 'Guiding Principles on Internal Displacement: Annotations' (American Society of International Law and The Brookings Institution) 5; also see n27, 225; n6.

112 n78, 211; 'Land and Human Rights: Standards and Applications', UNOHCR, 2015, HR/PUB/15/5/Add.1, 88.

113 n81.

114 Diplomatic Conference on the Reaffirmation and Development of International Humanitarian Law Applicable in Armed Conflicts, *Official Records*, Vol. VI, CDDH/SR. 44, 30 May 1977, 291.

character of the prohibition entailed herewith. Crucially however, it is today well accepted that the provisions concerning grave breaches embodied in the Geneva Conventions constitute part of customary international law[115] and require states to prosecute, through legislation, individuals responsible for such breaches.[116] As pointed out, 'these rules are not simply "technical" rules but are "fundamental to the respect of the human person and [humanity]"'.[117]

Furthermore, such is the importance of the interests protected under IHL that states cannot evade their obligations, especially when grave breaches are concerned. Sassoli notes in this regard that 'a State cannot consent to a violation of the rules of IHL that protect victims' rights'.[118] Neither may the rights of protected persons be compromised or derogated from through the conclusion of special agreements between the states parties to the conflict.[119] Article 7 IV GC explicitly restricts this power. Hence, 'Article 7 is a landmark in the progressive renunciation by States of their sovereign rights in favour of the individual and of a higher juridical order.'[120] This renders further support to the argument advanced in this chapter that a right not to be displaced by armed conflict exists in international law.

At the same time, under the Geneva Conventions all its parties have an obligation to ensure compliance with them.[121] This entitles member states to invoke the responsibility of the wrongdoing state or even to make a claim on behalf of the beneficiaries in accordance with Article 48 of the 2001 Final Articles on State Responsibility.[122] With particular reference to IV GC, it has been stressed that the 'correct application of the Convention is not a matter for the belligerents alone; it concerns the whole community of States and nations bound by the Convention',[123] hence confirming the *erga omnes* character of the provisions entailed in the Convention. Protected persons are further safeguarded as Article 8 stipulates that the Convention protections are inviolable and may not be renounced. While respecting the free will of protected persons such as their right to leave the territory

115 ICRC, Working paper on war crimes submitted to the Preparatory Committee for the Establishment of an International Criminal Court, 14 February 1997, [1 (a) (vi)] and [3 (xiii)]; Al-Khasawneh/Hatano report, n9, [172]

116 First report on crimes against humanity, Special Rapporteur Mr Sean D. Murphy, A/CN.4/680, 17 February 2015, [70].

117 Henckaerts, n58, 683 and 687. Henckaerts also notes that the Geneva Conventions in their totality reflect customary rules of international law, evidenced by the universal acceptance of the Conventions supported by state practice.

118 n11, 414 and 419.

119 Article 7, n85. This provision would extend to the 1975 agreements between Greek Cypriots and Turkish Cypriots following the Turkish invasion which provided for population movement and relocation of the displaced. See *Cyprus v Turkey* (Application No 25781/94), Report of the European Commission on Human Rights, 4 June 1999, [246].

120 Commentary, n78, 70; Sassoli, n11, 414.

121 Article 1, n85; also see Al-Khasawneh/Hatano report, n9, [114]; Wall Advisory Opinion, n96, [159]; also see n91, 48–49.

122 Draft articles on Responsibility of States for Internationally Wrongful Acts, with commentaries, *YbILC*, 2001, vol. II, Part Two; Sassoli, n11, 419.

123 Commentary, n78, 72.

under Article 35 IV GC, Article 8 aims to shield those concerned from state abuse.[124] Article 8, in fact, demonstrates the peremptory character of the protections afforded under the Convention. As a consequence of this, and in accordance with Article 41 2001 Final Articles on State Responsibility, states have an obligation not to render any aid or assistance to the state that commits serious violations of peremptory norms, not to recognise the unlawful act and to cooperate to bring the violation to an end.[125] This also opens up the possibility of countermeasures by non-injured states.[126]

The peremptory nature of the interests protected under the IV GC does not run counter to the temporary evacuations permitted under Article 49 or the assigned residence a protected person may be subjected to by the occupying power under Article 78. Such restrictions are only allowed 'for imperative reasons of security' or 'imperative military necessity'.[127] What constitutes imperative military necessity for the purposes of Article 49 is therefore important for the lawfulness of population removals.

Article 47 IV GC is another important provision as it makes the rights of protected persons in occupied territory inviolable which cannot be compromised, '*in any case or in any manner whatsoever*', by changes introduced as a result of the occupation, agreements between the occupying power and the authorities of the occupied territories, or by annexation of the territory concerned.[128] The absolute nature with which this provision is stipulated provides further evidence of the fundamental nature of the protections entailed in the IV GC, including those relating to forcible transfer and deportation and the rights of civilians.[129] This is because the drafters of the Convention aimed to prevent a wrongdoing party from benefiting from its wrongful acts, including through the conclusion of agreements that would concretise the illegality of the situation brought by its acts.

Notably, states have a due diligence obligation to take all necessary measures to protect civilians from forced displacement whether this is carried out by state or non-state actors. During foreign occupation, for instance, the occupying power has an obligation to exercise vigilance and to ensure respect of international human rights law and IHL by its own troops and other non-state actors. This

124 Article 8, ibid.

125 Draft Articles, n122.

126 For analysis see Katselli Proukaki E. (2010), *The Problem of Enforcement in International Law: Countermeasures, the Non-Injured State and the Idea of International Community* (Routledge).

127 This flows from the Nuremburg trials, which distinguished between evacuations ordered for protecting the populations and those carried out because of their military advantage. While the former were acceptable the latter were not. See in this regard *List et al. (Hostages trial)* Ann Dig (1948) No 15, 632, 8 *War Crimes Reports* (1949) 34; *Von Lewinski*, Annual Digest and Reports of Public International Law Cases (1949) No 192, 509, 521 discussed in n3, 219.

128 Article 47, n85.

129 See analysis in Takkenberg L. (1998), *The Status of Palestinian Refugees in International Law* (Oxford University Press) 220.

position was confirmed by the ICJ, which held Uganda responsible for failing to prevent ethnic conflict between the Hema and Lundu communities in the Ituri district in the DRC. According to the ICJ's findings, Ugandan troops encouraged the taking of land from Lundu by Hema and failed to prevent the violence that led to the death of thousands of civilians and the displacement of 50,000 people.[130]

The right not to be displaced may also be inferred from Article 27 IV GC. This applies irrespective of whether occupation exists and provides that 'protected persons are entitled, in all circumstances, to respect for their persons, their honour, their family rights, their religious convictions and practices, and their manners and customs. They shall at all times be humanely treated, and shall be protected especially against all acts of violence or threats thereof.'

In addition to these provisions, individuals are also protected against displacement that occurs in internal armed conflict. Article 17 Additional Protocol II (APII) expressly prohibits the displacement of the population except where necessary for the safety of the population or for imperative military reasons. Article 17 further stipulates that civilians 'shall not be compelled to leave their own territory for reasons connected with the conflict'[131] and it protects civilians from the acts of all parties engaged in the conflict, whether state or non-state actors.[132] This provision was adopted by consensus.[133] Moreover, common Article 3 of the Geneva Conventions stipulates the duty of 'each Party' to a non-international conflict to treat all those persons not taking part in hostilities humanely without adverse discrimination on grounds of race, colour, religion or faith, sex, birth or wealth or any other similar criteria. This provision is relevant as it may be argued that forced displacement does constitute treatment in violation of this obligation.[134] In addition to these conventional rules, the conduct of parties engaging in internal armed conflict is also regulated through customary law.[135]

Furthermore, there is a growing body of state practice that condemns forced displacement as a war crime and a crime against humanity for which both individual and state responsibility may arise, reinforcing in this way the argument in support of the right not to be displaced.[136] Of particular relevance for the purposes of this examination constitutes Chapter 38 of the Study of the International Committee of the Red Cross (ICRC Study) on customary IHL concerning displacement.[137]

130 DRC v Uganda case, n96, [179] and [209].
131 Protocol Additional to the Geneva Conventions of 12 August 1949 and relating to the protection of victims of non-international armed conflicts (Protocol II), Geneva, 8 June 1977, 1125 UNTS (1979) 609.
132 For the obligations of individuals and other non-state actors, see n5, 725.
133 n114, 144.
134 Al-Khasawneh/Hatano report, n9, [168].
135 n55, 1403.
136 For analysis see Henckaerts J.M., Doswald-Beck L. (eds) (2005), *Customary International Humanitarian Law: Volume II: Practice, Part 2* (Cambridge University Press) 2928–2942.
137 The Study is available on the International Committee for the Red Cross' Database on Customary international humanitarian law, https://www.icrc.org/customary-ihl/eng/docs/home.

According to Rule 129, customary law prohibits parties to an international conflict to deport or to forcibly transfer the civilian population of an occupied territory, while parties to a non-international conflict may not order the displacement of the civilian population. In both cases, such conduct may only be allowed for the security of civilians or for imperative military reasons.[138] The ICRC Study has been criticised, however, for failing to distinguish between different categories of displaced such as refugees and those internally displaced.[139] More specifically, Greer argues that the ICRC Study should have taken into consideration the fact that refugees have stronger legal protection under IHRL, IHL and refugee law in comparison to IDPs. According to him: 'By mixing duties to and rights of refugees with those of a less-protected legal status, the ICRC Study diluted the Rules pertaining to displaced persons.'[140] Nevertheless, the ICRC Rules do not aim to compromise rights already established under international law but rather to strengthen the protection concerning those who are forced to leave their home because of conflict, irrespective of whether they are crossing an international border or not. More importantly, it is because of this fragmented international legal protection that Greer refers to that the recognition of an autonomous right not to be displaced considered in this chapter becomes compelling.

It becomes clear from the preceding analysis that IHL, and the Geneva law and its additional protocols particularly, prohibit forced displacement and that such prohibition aims to safeguard the individual right not to be displaced. Not only is forced displacement prohibited under this law, but violation of such international norms infringes fundamental interests of the international community as a whole.

In parallel with those rules, however, which expressly prohibit forced displacement, individuals are also protected from other acts that force them to abandon their homes. This is examined next, although not exhaustively, with the focus on how property is protected under IHL and on settlements established by occupying powers.

3.3 Protection of property and prohibition of population transfers in occupied territory

Property provides a safe refuge without which people are exposed to serious violations of their fundamental rights. Its importance is recognised in the 1907 Hague Convention, which protects both enemy property from being destroyed or seized unless necessitated by war (Article 23) while safeguarding the rights of the nationals of the hostile party; and private property from confiscation as well as pillage during occupation. Such protection is not subject to restrictions (Articles 46 and 47)[141] and it was in light of Article 46 that the Nuremburg Tribunal in the

138 Ibid.
139 n79, 1.
140 Ibid, 6 and 7.
141 Hague Convention 1907, n28.

Krupp case held that transactions based on discriminatory laws that affect private property rights are unlawful.[142]

The protection of property is now also embodied in Geneva law. More specifically, Article 33 IV GC prohibits the pillage of property as well as reprisals against the property of protected persons whether in occupied territory or in the territory of belligerent parties.[143] This provision is a recognition of the serious impact that destruction of property bears for the victims,[144] which, in fact, may lead to their displacement. Article 46 IV GC concerning aliens in the territory of a belligerent party provides that restrictive measures towards protected persons must end as soon as hostilities have ended, including those concerning property.[145] Article 53 IV GC regulates the conduct of an occupying power in relation to property, whether private or belonging to the state, according to which such property is immune from destruction unless such destruction is 'absolutely necessary' for military operations. Such necessity was not found by the ICJ to exist in relation to Israel's construction of the wall in the Palestinian occupied territories.[146] Moreover, Article 147 IV GC stipulates that extensive destruction and appropriation of property that is not justified by military necessity and which is carried out unlawfully and wantonly constitutes a grave breach subject to universal jurisdiction.[147] This is also recognised in Rules 50 and 51 of the ICRC Study as well as under customary international law. Rule 52 further provides that pillage is prohibited in both inter-state and internal conflict. Moreover, the prohibition of arbitrary or illegal seizure of property not justified by war necessities constitutes a general principle of law,[148] violation of which may constitute a war crime.[149] Rule 133 further stipulates that the property rights of the displaced must be respected.

The Statute of the ICTFY (ICTFY Statute) itself prohibits in Article 2 extensive destruction and appropriation of property not justified by military necessity and carried out unlawfully and wantonly as a grave breach of the Geneva Conventions. Furthermore, Article 3 prohibits as a war crime the plunder of public or private property including unlawful and intentional appropriation not justified by military necessity, especially when this is carried out on discriminatory grounds. The aim of this provision is to protect fundamental values whose violation has grave consequences for the victim, particularly if the violation is widespread.[150] A similar prohibition is embodied in Article 8 of the Rome Statute, which also prohibits as war crimes attacks directed against civilians and their property.

142 *Krupp case,* Judgment, 30 June 1948, US Military Tribunal at Nuremberg.
143 See n21, 235, [126].
144 Commentary, n78, 226.
145 Ibid, 271.
146 Wall Advisory Opinion, n96, 192, [135].
147 n85; n79, 1.
148 n137.
149 'Land and Human Rights', n112, 88.
150 n10, [1672], [1779], [1821].

The ICJ for its part has found that Uganda's looting and bombing of Congolese property in the Ituri region was in breach of both IHL and IHRL,[151] although, disappointingly, the ICJ did not specifically address the issue of forced displacement that was caused because of the conflict in DRC. While pillage and the destruction and appropriation of property during conflict are violations themselves, it is quite clear that such acts are often used with intent to force civilians out of their homes or they indirectly lead to forced displacement. Prohibition of such acts provides further evidence in support of the existence of the right not to be displaced, as well as the rights to return home and to property restitution, which are discussed in the next chapter.

Alongside these prohibitions, Article 49 IV GC prohibits an occupying power from transferring its own population into occupied territory. Such transfers aim to alter the demography and legal status of occupied territory by concretising control over it and by creating an intended humanitarian crisis causing instability and animosity among the competing populations.[152] International law stands firm in this regard and no attempt that deviates from this clear prohibition should be accepted through, for instance, peace agreements. The significance of this prohibition is also illustrated in the European Court of Human Rights' (ECtHR) judgment in *Loizidou*. The case concerned an individual complaint against Turkey as occupying power for preventing the applicant from peacefully enjoying her property as safeguarded under Article 1 Protocol 1 of the European Convention on Human Rights (ECHR). Although the ECtHR was not called to examine Turkey's actions in light of IHL, the ECtHR refused to accept that the need to rehouse displaced Turkish Cypriots satisfied the requirement of necessity for lawfully interfering with the applicant's right.[153] Such finding, however, is to be contrasted with the subsequent disappointing, and arguably flawed,[154] judgment in *Demopoulos*, in which the ECtHR in effect accepted the realities created because of the Turkish occupation at the expense of the property and other fundamental rights of those forcibly displaced.[155] This brings *Demopoulos* into variance with both IHRL and IHL.[156] To this effect, the rights of the displaced must take prevalence over potentially competing human rights claims,[157] while the wrongdoing state must bear responsibility for undoing the illegality it has brought about.

As pointed out, 'these [population transfer and demographic manipulation] practices make more difficult the process of reaching a constructive outcome. The

151 DRC v Uganda case, n96, 241, [211].

152 Al-Khasawneh/Hatano report, n9, [35].

153 *Loizidou v Turkey* (Application no. 15318/89) Judgment 18 December 1996, [35] and [64].

154 See Tzevelekos, Chapter 3, and Meleagrou and Paraskeva, Chapter 4, of this volume.

155 In this case, the ECtHR in effect undermined the rights of the displaced in favour of settlers. *Demopoulos and Others v Turkey*, ECHR Reports 2010; EHRR SE 14, [116]. For a critique of this decision, see Katselli Proukaki E. (2014), 'The Right of Displaced Persons to Property and to Return Home after *Demopoulos*', *HRLR*, Vol. 14, No. 4, 701–732.

156 Also see Katselli Proukaki, ibid.

157 Ibid, 721.

practices involved should be recognized as having a character of their own and deserving a clearer profile as a wrong to international public order.'[158] Indeed, such a serious violation constitutes a war crime and a grave breach as set out in Article 85 (4) (a) AP I and it is accepted as a prohibition embedded in customary law.[159] It is also prohibited under Article 8 (2) (b) (viii) of the Rome Statute. Such transfers in occupied territory have been described as having no legal validity by the Security Council[160] and breach international law.[161] The transfer of settlers is also prohibited under Rule 130 of the ICRC Study on Customary International Humanitarian Law. Such prohibition also reinforces both the right not to be displaced and the rights to return home and to property restitution, as it prevents states from benefiting from the fruits of their own unlawful conduct.

3.4 Concluding remarks on the right not to be displaced

The preceding analysis demonstrates that forced displacement constitutes a serious violation of IHL. Under this law, the removal of the population from their homes and lands can only be justified as a temporary measure in exceptional circumstances necessitated by the conflict or the safety of the population. At the same time, it becomes clear that expulsion can never be used as a form of punishment or in retaliation of other wrongful acts.[162] As pointed out: 'A mass expulsion is a Draconian conception that has absolutely no place in the modern world.'[163] Importantly: 'Displacement of persons carried out pursuant to an agreement among political or military leaders, or under the auspices of the ICRC or another neutral organization, does not necessarily make it voluntary.'[164] The preceding analysis also demonstrates that civilians are often induced to flee as a result of unlawful destruction or appropriation of property or settlements.

One of the main questions relevant to this examination, however, is whether individuals are afforded *rights* that they can invoke either at national or international level. This is a question of predominant significance for the protection against forced displacement in light of the state-centric character of international law according to which international norms create obligations and rights towards and/or between states. This position was, in effect, reflected in the *Panevezys Saldutiskis Railway Case (Estonia v Lithuania)* in which the Permanent Court of International Justice (PCIJ) affirmed that, by bringing an international claim on behalf of its nationals, the state was, in reality, asserting its own right to ensure

158 Brownlie I. (1990), 'The Problem of Demographic Manipulation in International Law', Paper delivered at human rights conference, Nicosia, 21 May 1990, 8.
159 n137.
160 UNSC Resolution 446 (1979) 22 March 1979.
161 Wall Advisory Opinion, n96, 184, [120].
162 n3, 240.
163 Ibid.
164 n10, [1739].

the compliance of another state with international rules.[165] However, international law has evolved to recognise that an international treaty between states may, in fact, confer rights on individuals. This is the position taken in *LaGrand* where the rights of the individuals that, in that instance emanated from the Vienna Convention on Consular Relations,[166] co-existed with the rights of the state emanating from that same treaty. Indeed, the fact that international rules, whether embodied in treaties or in customary rules may award rights to individuals is now a well-established position, particularly in IHRL.[167] This extends to IHL, which, going beyond imposing certain obligations on states or parties to the conflict on what their conduct should be during armed conflict, is intended to protect individuals, even if by doing so the state also protects its own interests and rights. At the end of the day, similarly with IHRL, norms under this legal regime aim to alleviate the pain and suffering of individuals, whether wounded enemy combatants or civilians. The perception that IHL regulates the conduct between states[168] and that it cannot be relied on by individuals neglects the significant transformation of contemporary international legal thinking whereby individuals are proper subjects with international rights and obligations.[169] International humanitarian law should therefore be understood as not only setting out obligations on states but also as affording rights to those it aims to protect,[170] otherwise the significance of the protections entailed under this body of law would be devoid of any meaning. To ensure the effective protection of the individual as intended under IHL, it is necessary to interpret the rights embodied in that field of law broadly, while any exceptions or restrictions must be narrowly construed.[171] Moreover, the increasing significance of individuals advocates an interpretation of IHL in compliance with fundamental human rights standards.[172] As Zegveld points out, the concept of 'rights' is not unknown in the Geneva Conventions themselves[173] and, in any

165 *Panevezys Saldutiskis Railway Case (Estonia v Lithuania)*, PCIJ (1939) Series AB, Judgment, 28 February 1939, 4, 16.

166 *LaGrand Case (Germany v United States of America)*, Judgment, ICJ Rep. (2001) 466, 482–483.

167 Clapham A. (2010), 'The Role of the Individual in International Law', *EJIL*, Vol. 21, No 1, 25–30, 27–8.

168 n80, 503.

169 In support of this argument, see Lopes C., Quenivet N. (2008), 'Individuals as Subjects of International Humanitarian Law and Human Rights Law' in Arnold R., Quenivet N. (eds.), *International Humanitarian Law and Human Rights Law: Towards a New Merger in International Law* (BRILL) 207–244. Also see n11, 401.

170 Zegveld, n80, 503; Sassoli, n11, 419.

171 For analysis on principle of effectiveness under the ECHR, see Rietiker D. (2010), 'The Principle of "Effectiveness" in the Recent Jurisprudence of the European Court of Human Rights: Its Different Dimensions and Its Consistency with Public International Law – No Need for the Concept of Treaty *Sui* Generis', *NJIL*, Vol. 79, No. 2, 245–277.

172 For a similar argument, see Zegveld, n80, 505.

173 Ibid, 503. Also see Final Record of the Diplomatic Conference of Geneva of 1949, Vol. II (A), 821 which refers to 'individual rights'.

event, it is essential that treaties which protect fundamental community interests are interpreted as 'living instruments' that are subject to evolution for the effective protection of those which they were set up to protect in the first place.[174] Importantly, and as the Commentary to Article 8 IV GC reveals, 'it is the first time that a set of international regulations has been devoted not to State interests, but solely to the protection of the individual.'[175]

The preceding analysis makes clear that IHL supports the existence of an individual right not to be displaced by armed conflict. Nevertheless, it also becomes clear that the fact that different legal rules and regimes apply depending on whether displacement is carried out in inter-state or internal armed conflict or during occupation undermine clarity and legal certainty and weaken the protection afforded to individuals. The recognition of an independent right not to be displaced, as advanced in this chapter, aims to fill these gaps and to protect the individual from forced displacement in a more unitary and integral manner. The next section turns to ICL and whether, and if so how, the individual is protected against forced displacement.

4 The legal basis of the right not to be displaced under international criminal law

The trials that followed the end of WWII exercised significant influence on the development of ICL as a tool that imposes individual criminal responsibility for violations of IHL and widespread or systematic serious human rights abuses such as forced displacement. Indeed, following WWII deportation of individuals who shared the same nationality as the perpetrators was punished as a crime against humanity. Today, this concept evolved to encapsulate grave violations of international law committed in war or in peacetime that affect not only the victims themselves but also mankind as a whole.[176] At the same time, ICL has significantly influenced the development of the right not to be displaced as explained below.

In recent legal developments, forced displacement is prohibited as a grave breach of the Geneva Conventions under Article 2 (g) of the ICTFY Statute and as a crime against humanity under Article 5 (d),[177] although the content of the offence remains the same in each instance.[178] Article 5 does not make a distinction between internal or inter-state armed conflict[179] and punishes forced displacement that

174 In support, see n171, 267.

175 Article 8,Commentary, n78, 77.

176 n116, [27].

177 Articles 2 and 5, ICTFY Statute, http://www.icty.org/x/file/Legal%20Library/Statute/statute_sept09_en.pdf; also see n10, [1738].

178 *Prosecutor v Krnojelac case*, Judgment, IT-97-25-T, 15 March 2002, [473]. Also see ICRC Study, n137, Practice Relating to Rule 129. The Act of Displacement, https://ihl-databases.icrc.org/customary-ihl/eng/docs/v2_rul_rule129.

179 n109, [471].

occurs through expulsion or other coercive means.[180] If carried out on discriminatory grounds, it is punished as persecution and, hence, a crime against humanity in violation of Article 5 (h). As the ICTFY jurisprudence reveals, for forcible transfer and deportation to be established as crimes against humanity, it is not necessary to establish actual control or occupation over the territory under consideration.[181] This is consistent with Article I (b) of the Convention on the Non-Applicability of Statutory Limitations to War Crimes and Crimes Against Humanity according to which 'eviction by armed attack *or* occupation' is a crime against humanity.[182] Moreover, displacement may be the result of severe living conditions that force civilians to move.[183] These may include dismissal from employment, house searches and the cutting off of water or electricity supply.[184] Forced displacement as a crime against humanity can also take the form of preventing return, which is often achieved through discriminatory legislative restrictions to reclaiming abandoned property.[185] Furthermore, while the ICTFY has accepted that evacuation may be permitted in exceptional circumstances, it has refused to relieve an individual from international criminal responsibility when the displacement carried out for humanitarian reasons was the result of the unlawful activity of the accused.[186] Hence, it becomes clear that forcible displacement is significantly restricted, with the ICTFY jurisprudence illuminating the situations in which it was given effect without grounds under international law.

In its recent judgment in the *Karadzic* case, the Trial Chamber found that the accused took part in a joint criminal enterprise to forcibly remove Bosnian non-Serbs (Croats and Muslims) from the territory claimed by Bosnian Serb forces in the Municipalities in violation of Article 5 ICTFY Statute. Significantly however the Trial Chamber found Karadzic guilty for participating in a joint criminal enterprise the aim of which was to 'eliminate the Bosnian Muslims in Srebrenica', first, by forcibly removing the women, children and the elderly and then by killing the men and boys.[187] According to the Trial Chamber, the circumstances of the forcible removal were such as to demonstrate intent to inflict serious physical and mental suffering and amounted to persecution[188] and it was satisfied that the killings demonstrated intent to destroy the Muslims of Srebrenica and hence genocide.[189] This is a landmark judgment, which, together

180 Ibid, [488].
181 n10, [1750].
182 Adopted and opened for signature, ratification and accession by UNGA resolution 2391 (XXIII), 26 November 1968.
183 *Prosecutor v Krajisnik*, IT-00-39-A, AC, Judgment, 17 March 2009, [308]
184 *Prosecutor v Krajisnik*, IT-00-39-T, TC I, Judgment, 27 September 2006, [729].
185 n10, [2061], [2098], [2310] and [2312]. Also see [1756] and [1758].
186 *Prosecutor v Stakic*, IT-97-24-T, TC II, Judgment, 31 July 2003, [287].
187 n109, [5998].
188 Ibid, [5740].
189 Ibid, [5830]. Also see *Prosecutor v Tolimir*, IT-05-88/2-A, 8 April 2015, [208] et seq.

with *Tolimir*, showcases that forced displacement may, in certain circumstances, lead to very serious human rights violations such as genocide.

Similarly to Article 5 ICTFY Statute, Article 3 (d) of the 1994 Statute of the International Criminal Tribunal for Rwanda (ICTR Statute) prohibits systematic or widespread deportation on national, ethnic, religious or political grounds as a crime against humanity. However, the ICTFY and ICTR Statutes do not distinguish between lawful and unlawful displacement although the ICTFY has accepted that forced displacement must be caused without grounds permitted under international law.[190] This was interpreted as meaning that protection from forced displacement is extended irrespective of whether an individual satisfies the legal requirements of residence or immigration so as to protect 'those who have, for whatever reason, come to "live" in the community – whether long term or temporarily', including IDPs who have established temporary homes elsewhere. The only exception from such protection relates to those who occupy houses or premises unlawfully or illegally.[191]

Controversy has, however, been sparked concerning what amounts as unlawful conduct forcing displacement. In *Gotovina*, for instance, forced displacement was linked to the unlawfulness of the attack[192] holding that artillery attacks carried out within a range of 200 metres from a military objective were lawful attacks whereas attacks beyond this distance were indiscriminate and hence unlawful.[193] On this basis, the Trial Chamber found the two accused liable for participating in a joint criminal enterprise whose purpose was to permanently remove the Serbs of Krajina by force or threat of force.[194] This standard was subsequently rejected by the Appeals Chamber in its much criticised acquittal judgment[195] without, however, providing guidance with which a distinction between lawful and unlawful attacks could be made. As Clark points out, in reality the Trial Chamber had taken into consideration the fear caused by the shelling as a factor that forced people to leave. As a consequence: 'It is not the case . . . as the judgement of the Appeals Chamber incorrectly asserts, that the Trial Chamber "considered unlawful attacks the core indicator that the crime of deportation had occurred".'[196] To this effect, the Appeal Chamber's over-reliance on the 200-metre standard as an error made by the Trial Chamber was not justified as it overlooked other significant evidence in support of a finding of forced displacement involving the accused's

190 For instance, n183, [723].

191 n20, [900].

192 *Prosecutor v Gotovina et al.*, AC, IT-06-90-A, 16 November 2012.

193 However, the TC used this standard as guidance for case-by-case determination of unlawfulness of attack. Clark J.N. (2013), 'Courting Controversy: The ICTY's Acquittal of Croatian Generals Gotovina and Markac' *JICJ*, Vol. 11, 399, 408.

194 n10, [2314].

195 n193, 411; *Prosecutor v Gotovina and Markac*, AC, IT-06-90-A, 16 November 2012, Dissenting Opinion of Judge Carmel Agius and Dissenting Opinion of Judge Fausto Pocar.

196 n10, [409].

responsibility.[197] In this respect, the ICTFY missed an important opportunity to challenge the forced removal of approximately 200,000 ethnic Serbs from Krajina, few of whom have been able to return home.[198]

Unlawful deportation or transfer committed in international armed conflict and displacement not justified by the need to protect civilians or imperative military reasons in internal armed conflict are prohibited under Article 8 of the Rome Statute as war crimes. Forced displacement without grounds permitted under international law is also prohibited as a crime against humanity under Article 7 Rome Statute.[199] Article 7 encompasses coercive measures such as death threats, destruction of property or obstacles in accessing employment or education[200] if carried out on a widespread and systematic basis with knowledge of the attack, while it may also encompass violations committed by non-state actors.[201] According to the Elements of Crime: 'The term "forcibly" is not restricted to physical force, but may include threat of force or coercion, such as that caused by fear of violence, duress, detention, psychological oppression or abuse of power against such person or persons or another person, or by taking advantage of a coercive environment.'[202] Article 7 also prohibits persecution, namely the 'intentional and severe deprivation of fundamental rights contrary to international law' on racial, ethnic, political, national, cultural or religious grounds, which is often the case in forced displacement.[203] Distinguishing between grounds permitted under international law and those that are not also becomes significant in this context. For instance, Bassiouni argues that deportations or transfers that arise from a treaty concerning territorial changes fall outside the protection scope of Article 7 Rome Statute.[204] However, as already argued in Section 2, forced displacement, carried out either during war or in light of peace agreements or territorial arrangements continues to be a

197 *Prosecutor v Gotovina and Markac*, n 195, Dissenting Opinion of Judge Fausto Pocar, [17]; n193, 413.

198 n193, 401 and 403.

199 Rome Statute of the International Criminal Court, Rome, 17 July 1998, 2187 UNTS; see analysis in n23, 394; Boot M. (2002), *Genocide, Crimes against Humanity, War Crimes: Nullum Crimen Sine Lege and the Subject Matter Jurisdiction of the International Criminal Court* (Intersentia) 504, fn 177.

200 Hall C.K. (1999), 'Crimes against Humanity' in O. Triffterer (ed.), *Commentary on the Rome Statute of the International Criminal Court* (Nomos Verlagsgesellschaft), 162.

201 'Attack' is not restricted to a military attack but it may also encompass discriminatory policies and other measures which coerce the population to abandon their homes. *Prosecutor v Akayesu*, Judgment, ICTR-96-4-T, September 2, 1998, [581]. Also see n116, [147].

202 Elements of Crimes, International Criminal Court, fn 12, https://www.icc-cpi.int/NR/rdonlyres/336923D8-A6AD-40EC-AD7B-45BF9DE73D56/0/ElementsOfCrimesEng.pdf?.

203 Such other examples of forcible transfers/expulsions, see 'Iraq: Forcible Expulsion of Ethnic Minorities', March 2003, Vol. 15, No. 3,https://www.hrw.org/reports/2003/iraq0303/index.htm#TopOfPage.

204 n23, 394. Also see Droege C., 'Developments in Legal Protection of Internally Displaced Persons: 10 Years of Experience since the Guiding Principles', 4, https://www.icrc.org/eng/assets/files/other/09-2008-icrc-c-droege-guiding-principles.pdf.

serious violation of international law. In fact, it is not clear why an international agreement would render forced displacement as lawful, particularly when such displacement is premised on violation of other rules of international law such as the law prohibiting armed force, or violation of fundamental human rights, including prohibition from discrimination and the right not to be displaced. Any restriction of rights, whether safeguarded under IHRL or IHL, needs to be justified as necessary and proportionate and as fulfilling a legitimate aim. In the author's view, the forcible uprooting of people especially when carried out on discriminatory grounds can never be justified as pursuing a legitimate aim.

Finally, forced displacement 'by expulsion or other coercive acts from the area in which they are lawfully present, without grounds permitted under international law' is recognised as a crime against humanity under Article 3 of the ILC's Draft Articles on Crimes Against Humanity,[205] as well as under Article 18 ILC Draft Code of Crimes against the Peace and Security of Mankind.[206] 'Eviction by armed attack or occupation' is also recognised as a crime against humanity in the 1968 Convention on the Non-Applicability of Statutory Limitations to War Crimes and Crimes against Humanity while states parties are called to criminalise such acts domestically and to remove any statutory provisions that prevent prosecution of such crimes.[207] Finally, it is a crime against humanity under international customary law either when committed in an inter-state or an internal armed conflict.[208] Fundamentally, forced displacement violates obligations *erga omnes*[209] whose prohibition falls within the body of peremptory norms of international law.[210] To this effect, in addition to the obligation not to force people out of their homes, states have a well-established duty to prevent crimes against humanity[211] whether these occur within or outside their territory.[212]

The prohibition of forced displacement as an international crime, whether committed during war or as part of widespread or systematic practice, as established

205 ILC, Crimes Against Humanity, 67th Session, A/CN.4/L.853, 2 June 2015.

206 Draft Code of Crimes against the Peace and Security of Mankind, Report of the ILC on the work of its forty-eighth session, YbILC, 1996, Vol. II (Part Two), 17.

207 n182.

208 ICRC Database on Customary international humanitarian law, https://www.icrc.org/customary-ihl/eng/docs/home. Also see n3, 221. For a critique see Greer, n79, 3.

209 n116, [29].

210 Commentary on Article 26, [5], n122; Fragmentation of International Law: Difficulties Arising from the Diversification and Expansion of International Law, Report of the Study Group of the ILC, U.N. Doc. A/CN.4/L.682, [374] (Apr. 13, 2006), as corrected by U.N. Doc. A/CN.4/L.682/Corr.1 (Aug. 11, 2006) (finalized by Martti Koskenniemi); n116, [39].

211 n205; Principles of international co-operation in the detection, arrest, extradition and punishment of persons guilty of war crimes and crimes against humanity, UNGA resolution 3074 (1973), [3]; Basic Principles and Guidelines on the Right to a Remedy and Reparation for Victims of Gross Violations of International Human Rights Law and Serious Violations of International Humanitarian Law, UNGA 60/147, Annex, (Dec. 16, 2005), [3 (a)] (Principles on Remedy).

212 n116, [85].

here is further evidence in support of the right not to be displaced under these circumstances. The next section turns to the question of whether international human rights law renders further support on the existence of such right.

5 The legal basis of the right not to be displaced under international human rights law

Forced displacement does not only constitute a violation of IHL and ICL, but it is first and foremost a human rights issue. As pointed out:

> The fundamental premise is that the displacement of a person from his place of residence and his forcible assignment to another place seriously harms his dignity, his liberty and his property. A person's home is not merely a roof over his head, but it is also a means for the physical and social location of a person, his private life and his social relationships . . . Several basic human rights are harmed as a result of an involuntary displacement . . . even if this assigned residence does not involve him crossing an international border.[213]

Similarly, the ICTFY highlighted that:

> The prohibition against forcible displacements aims at safeguarding the right and aspiration of individuals to live in their communities and homes without outside interference.[214]

Truly, forced displacement exposes the displaced population to serious threats to life and to physical and psychological integrity,[215] significantly interfering with the right not to be subjected to torture or to inhuman or degrading treatment or punishment, to family and private life including the right to respect one's home, to peaceful enjoyment of possessions as well as freedom of movement and settlement in one's own country. These are protected in various human rights treaties including the International Covenant on Civil and Political Rights (ICCPR) and the European Convention on Human Rights (ECHR).[216] In *Loizidou*, for example, the ECtHR refused to accept that the irreversible expropriation of property and the complete negation of the applicant's right to peaceful enjoyment of her possessions as safeguarded under Article 1 Protocol 1

213 *Ajuri v The Commander of IDF Forces in the West Bank*, Israel, High Court of Justice 7015/02, Judgment, September 2002, 56 (6) PD, 352, [14].

214 n84, [69].

215 Commentary of 1958, n78, 278–279.

216 n5, 736 and 737; also see UN Sub-Commission on Human Rights, Special Rapporteur on the Human Rights Dimensions of Population Transfer, including the Implantation of Settlers and Settlements, Final Report, UN Doc. E/CN. 4/Sub.2/1997/23, 27 June 1997, [15], [16], [64] and [70].

of the ECHR, and which resulted from the Turkish occupation of Cyprus, could be justified under necessity.[217] Importantly, the European Commission on Human Rights had early on affirmed that population movements carried out in the context of humanitarian efforts are not sufficient to remove the forcible, and hence unlawful, nature of such movements. As noted: 'Even those who leave the northern area under the humanitarian transfer arrangements are left no other choice than unconditionally abandoning their homes, there being no possibility for a reconsideration of their cases if they should eventually wish to return.'[218]

Of particular relevance for the purposes of this examination is Article 12 ICCPR, which provides that 'Everyone lawfully within the territory of a State shall, within that territory, have the right to liberty of movement and freedom to choose his residence' and that 'No one shall be arbitrarily deprived of the right to enter his own country.' While this provision does not expressly provide for the right not to be displaced, the Human Rights Committee (HRC), the ICCPR's monitoring body, interpreted the right to choose one's residence as including 'protection against all forms of forced internal displacement'.[219] Moreover, 'the right of a person to enter his or her own country recognizes the special relationship of a person to that country. The right has various facets. It implies the right to remain in one's own country.'[220] Notably, so significant is the right not to be displaced that the HRC, in considering the scope of Article 4 ICCPR in relation to derogations in times of public emergency, pointed out that acts amounting to crimes against humanity cannot provide justification for such derogations. As pointed out, 'deportation or forcible transfer of population without grounds permitted under international law, in the form of forced displacement by expulsion or other coercive means from the area in which the persons concerned are lawfully present, constitutes a crime against humanity.'[221] Accordingly, a state party may not derogate its obligations under Article 12 ICCPR safeguarding freedom of movement if the restrictions imposed are the result of the commission of a crime against humanity.

While freedom of movement in the context of forced displacement is explored in detail in the following chapter, it is worth pointing out the close connection between the right not to be displaced and respect of freedom of movement. This was recognised by the African Commission on Human and People's Rights, according to which states have a duty to adopt measures to prevent displacement.[222] At the same time, the ICJ, in its Advisory Opinion in the *Wall case* concluded that

217 n153, [64].

218 *Cyprus v Turkey*, n119, [267].

219 General Comment No. 27, CCPR/C/21/Rev.1/Add.9, 2 November 1999, [7].

220 Ibid, [19]; Joseph S., Schultz J., Castan M. (2000), *The International Covenant on Civil and Political Rights: Cases, Materials and Commentary* (Oxford University Press) 259; Nowak M. (2005), *U.N. Covenant on Civil and Political Rights: CCPR Commentary* 2nd ed. (N.P. Engel Publisher) 266.

221 General Comment No. 29, CCPR/C/21/Rev.1/Add.11, 31 August 2001, [13 (d)].

222 *Sudan Human Rights Organisation and Centre on Housing Rights and Evictions (COHRE) v Sudan*, Communication No. 279/03–296/05 (27 May 2009), [188]–[189].

destruction or confiscation of property, restrictions on freedom of movement and other rights that resulted from the construction of the wall were not proportionate or the least intrusive and, hence, they were unlawful.[223]

Moreover, forced displacement deprives its victims of essential means for their survival including housing, employment, education and healthcare, which are safeguarded under the International Covenant on Economic, Social and Cultural Rights (ICESCR).[224] It also violates people's right to self-determination including through denial of disposing of their natural resources[225] and has detrimental consequences on communities with special attachment to their land for their cultural development.[226] Forced displacement is also often based on discrimination, which is a breach of international law. For example, Article 1 of the Convention on the Elimination of Discrimination of All Forms of Racial Discrimination outlaws 'any distinction, exclusion, restriction or preference based on race, colour, descent, or national or ethnic origin' intended to interfere with equal access to 'the political, economic, social, cultural or any other field of public life', including the right to own property and to housing.[227] The Convention on the Suppression and Punishment of the Crime of Apartheid is also relevant here as it prohibits legislative and other measures intended to deny members of a targeted group of their right to leave and return to their country and their freedom of movement, as well as the expropriation of property along racial lines.[228] Relatedly, so significant is the prohibition of apartheid that it is well established as a peremptory norm of international law giving rise to obligations *erga omnes*.

As Verdross pointed out it is clear that:

> [L]es individus ne sont plus des simples objets des Etats, mais des personnes qui ont des droits propres qui doivent être reconnus et protégés par les Etats. De cela découle que les Etats ne peuvent plus disposer d'eux comme du bétail: Un transfert de populations contre la volontue des individus intéresés me semble donc exclu.[229]

223 Wall Advisory Opinion, n96, 193, [137].

224 See analysis in Colombian Constitutional Court, Decision T-025 of 2004, 24. For the significance of land rights, see 'Land and Human Rights', n112, 1; Mandate of the Special Rapporteur on the human rights of internally displaced persons, 32/11, A/71/53, [6], adopted 1 July 2016 at 43rd meeting without a vote; 'Al-Khasawneh/Hatano report, n9, [235]. International Covenant on Economic, Social and Cultural Rights, 993 *UNTS*. The ICESCR currently has 165 states parties.

225 'Land and Human Rights' n112, 58; Wall Advisory Opinion, n96, 184, [122]; Al-Khasawneh/Hatano report, n9, [203] and [204].

226 See, for instance, *Yakye Axa Indigenous Community v Paraguay*, IACtHR, Series C, No. 125 (17 June 2005), [131].

227 Articles 1 and 5, Convention on the Elimination of Discrimination of All Forms of Racial Discrimination, 660 *UNTS* 195.

228 International Convention on the Suppression and Punishment of the Crime of Apartheid, 1015 *UNTS*, I 14861.

229 Verdross A., quoted in n3, 225.

This analysis, albeit non-exhaustive, shows that the right not to be displaced against one's will emanates from several legally binding human rights provisions.[230] At the same time, and as the next section establishes, the right not to be displaced has its own independent standing as part of customary law.

6 The right not to be displaced by armed conflict as part of customary international law

This section will show that not only is forced displacement prohibited, but also that there is a corresponding individual right not to be displaced under international customary law. To achieve this, the analysis will focus on evidence from state practice and ***opinio juris*** by reliance on a variety of sources. These include legally binding and 'soft' law instruments, the jurisprudence and the literature all of which establish the existence of general, continuous, repetitive and consistent practice as well as legal belief that such right is the law.[231]

To begin with, the prohibition and the need to end systematic displacement of civilians during armed conflict have been the focus of the 2000 Cairo Declaration, in which African and EU states participated,[232] and of the 1992 Declaration on Humanitarian Assistance and Gradual Repatriation of Temporary Refugees and Displaced Persons from the War in Bosnia and Herzegovina and in Croatia.[233] The right not to be forcibly removed from their lands or territories is also recognised in Article 10 of the UN Declaration on the Rights of Indigenous People. As the provision stipulates, any relocation requires the free, prior and informed consent of the indigenous people, just and fair compensation and the option of return where possible.[234] The forced removal of people from the lands they occupy is also prohibited under Article 16 of 1989 Indigenous and Tribal Peoples Convention.[235]

Significantly, the Guiding Principles on Internal Displacement stipulate that: 'All authorities and international actors shall respect and ensure respect for their obligations under international law, including human rights and humanitarian law, in all circumstances, so as to prevent and avoid conditions that might lead to displacement of persons.'[236] Principle 6 is of compelling significance as it stipulates

230 Report of the Representative of the Secretary-General, Mr. Francis M. Deng, submitted pursuant to Commission resolution 1997/39. Addendum: Guiding Principles on Internal Displacement, 11 February 1998, E/CN.4/1998/53, [9].

231 On analysis of each of these requirements, see *Asylum Case (Colombia v Peru)*, ICJ Reports (1950) 266; *North Sea Continental Shelf Cases (Federal Republic of Germany v Denmark and The Netherlands)*, ICJ Reports (1969) 3; *Military and Paramilitary Activities in and against Nicaragua (Nicaragua v United States of America)*, Merits, ICJ Reports (1986) 14, [186]; also see analysis in n126, 201 et seq.

232 Cairo Declaration, Africa-Europe Summit under the Aegis of the OAU and the EU, [61].

233 Ljubljana, 2 July 1992.

234 Declaration adopted by Human Rights Council, Resolution 2006/2.

235 Indigenous and Tribal Peoples Convention, 1989 (No. 169).

236 Principle 5, n6.

the right of every human being to be protected from arbitrary displacement from their home or place of habitual residence, including displacement that results from discriminatory practices and ethnic cleansing that aims to alter the ethnic, religious or racial composition of the affected population and when used as collective punishment. Principle 7 further stipulates that displacement should be a means of last resort and that all other alternative means should be explored 'in order to avoid displacement altogether'.[237] Although the Guiding Principles are not legally binding, they 'reflect and are consistent with international human rights and humanitarian law and analogous refugee law'.[238] Such is the impact of the Guiding Principles that they exercised significant influence on the Pinheiro Principles, which they also entail the right to be protected from displacement, and were incorporated into the Protocol on the Protection and Assistance to Internally Displaced Persons adopted by the International Conference on the Great Lakes Region, an inter-governmental organisation consisting of 12 African states.[239] This provides an excellent example of state practice and *opinio juris* in support of the principles entailed therein, including the right not to be displaced.

The Protocol commits states parties to prevent and eliminate root causes of arbitrary displacement through prevention. In Article 4 member states undertake to adhere to the general principles of IHL and IHRL and to the Guiding Principles on Internal Displacement concerning the rights of IDPs. The Protocol provides a legal platform whereby a non-legally binding instrument, in this instance the Guiding Principles, is given legal effect through a binding agreement.[240] The Guiding Principles have also inspired the conclusion of the Kampala Convention, the first legally binding instrument on internal displacement, which imposes an obligation on states parties to prevent and put an end to arbitrary displacement caused by both state and non-state actors. Article 3 (1) (a) provides that states parties shall '[r]efrain from, prohibit and prevent arbitrary displacement of populations'.[241] Article 4 sets out the obligation of states parties to punish under domestic law arbitrary displacement that is tantamount to genocide, war crimes and crimes against humanity. It also provides a non-exhaustive list of situations that are tantamount to arbitrary displacement, including displacement not justified for the security of civilians or military necessity or when used as a method of war or as a result of other violations of IHL. It further includes displacement that results from racial discrimination or other similar practices aimed at altering the ethnic, religious or racial composition of the

237 Principle 6, ibid.

238 Introductory Note by the Representative of the Secretary-General on Internally Displaced Persons Mr. Francis M. Deng, http://www.ifrc.org/Docs/idrl/I266EN.pdf.

239 n7 and n237.

240 This was concluded by the International Conference on the Great Lakes Region, 30 November 2006, http://www.refworld.org/pdfid/52384fe44.pdf.

241 African Union Convention for the Protection and Assistance of Internally Displaced Persons in Africa, adopted in Kampala, Uganda, 23 October 2009.

population.[242] The Kampala Convention is a landmark step in recognition of the right not to be displaced and provides further evidence of the impact and influence of the Guiding Principles on Internal Displacement.

In support of the right not to be displaced is Article 8 (1) of the Protocol for the Prevention and Punishment of the Crime of Genocide, War Crimes and Crimes Against Humanity and all forms of Discrimination, according to which: 'The Member States recognise that the crime of genocide, war crimes, and crimes against humanity are crimes under international law and are *crimes against people's rights* which they undertake to prevent and punish.'[243]

Moreover and as pointed out, 'the right to return derives from the illegality of the expulsion itself. It is generally recognised that a state cannot legally expel a population under its control. Those expelled clearly have the right to reverse an illegal act, that is, to return to their homeland.'[244] The right to return as well as the right to restitution examined in the next chapter count in support of the existence of a right not to be displaced: truly, why would one need these rights if they did not have a right not to be displaced in the first place? Moreover, there exist numerous legally and non-legally binding instruments that protect an individual's right to have access to land, either as tenant or as owner,[245] and that complement state practice and *opinio juris* in support of the right not to be displaced.

The right not to be displaced has also found expression in numerous UN General Assembly resolutions. For instance, the General Assembly has affirmed that 'civilian populations, or individual members thereof, should not be the object of . . . forcible transfers'[246] and that the destruction of dwellings and forcible eviction carried out by belligerents during military operations or in occupied territory shall be considered criminal.[247] The General Assembly has also deplored the 'evacuation, deportation, expulsion, displacement and transfer of Arab inhabitants of the occupied territories and denial of their right to return'.[248] The UN Security Council has itself affirmed

242 On the Kampala Convention, see Ojeda S. (2010), 'The Kampala Convention on Internally Displaced Persons: Some International Humanitarian Law Aspects' *RSQ*, Vol. 29, No. 3, 58–66; 'Translating the Kampala Convention into Practice: A Stocktaking Exercise', ICRC, February 2017.

243 Emphasis added. The Protocol was adopted by the International Conference on the Great Lakes Region as part of the Pact on Security, Stability and Development in the Great Lakes Region, adopted on 29 November 2006, https://www.icglr.org/index.php/en/the-pact.

244 n129, 234.

245 'Land and Human Rights', n112, 25–26.

246 'Basic Principles on the Protection of Civilian Populations in Armed Conflicts', UNGA resolution, A/RS/2675, 9 December 1970 (adopted by 109 votes in favour, none against and 8 abstentions).

247 Declaration on the Protection of Women and Children in Emergency and Armed Conflict, UNGA resolution 3318 (XXIX) of 14 December 1974 (adopted by 110 votes in favour, none against and 14 abstentions), [5].

248 UNGA resolution 36/147 C, 16 December 1981, [7 (c)]. This position was re-affirmed in UNGA resolution 37/88 C, 9 December 1982, [7 (d)]; UNGA resolution 38/79 D, 15 December 1983, [7] (d); UNGA resolution 39/95 D, 14 December 1984, [7 (E)]. Also see UNGA Resolution 55/116, A/Res/55/116 concerning the situation in Sudan.

in numerous resolutions the right not to be forcibly displaced. For instance, in Resolution 752 concerning Bosnia and Herzegovina, it called 'all parties and others concerned to ensure that forcible expulsions of persons from the areas where they live and any attempts to change the ethnic composition of the population, anywhere in the former Socialist Federal Republic of Yugoslavia, cease immediately.'[249] Although this resolution was not adopted under Chapter VII UN Charter, it provides evidence of state practice and *opinio juris* in support of the right not to be displaced. In Resolution 1009, adopted under Chapter VII, the Security Council demanded from Croatia to 'respect fully the rights of the local Serb population, including their rights to remain, leave or return in safety'.[250] A similar Chapter VII demand for cessation of forced evacuations carried out in Srebrenica was made in Resolution 819.[251] By reference to the worsening situation in the former Yugoslavia, the Security Council condemned the unlawful deportation of civilians as a 'grave violation of international humanitarian law'.[252]

The Parliamentary Assembly of the Council of Europe declared civilian expulsion as a crime against humanity[253] and deplored ethnic cleansing and civilian deportations from the territory of the former Yugoslavia.[254] Such displacement was also condemned by EU observers,[255] but also by several states as inhuman and a grave breach of IV GC.[256] It must be said, however, that this runs counter to Western efforts to bring internal territorial partition, causing more displacement, as the only perceived way to end the conflict in the country.[257] Nevertheless, many national military manuals and domestic laws prohibit civilian deportation and forcible transfer as a war crime and a grave breach of the Geneva Conventions, with some emphasising that this is so, irrespective of motive.[258] Furthermore, forced displacement as a result of occupation has been condemned by the International Conference of the Red Cross[259] and by the Gulf Cooperation

249 UNSC resolution 752, 15 May 1992, [6].
250 UN SC resolution 1009, 10 August 1995, [2].
251 UNSC, S/Res/819 (1993) 16 April 1993, [6]. UNGA, Res. 55/116; UN Commission on Human Rights, Res. 1995/77 and Res. 1996/73; United Nations Commission on Human Rights 1997, [10]; Sub- Commission resolution 1998/9, 20 August 1998.
252 UNSC resolution 1019, 9 November 1995, preamble.
253 Council of Europe, Parliamentary Assembly, Rec. 1198, 5 November 1992, [6].
254 Council of Europe, Parliamentary Assembly, Res. 994, 3 February 1993, [1].
255 See, for instance, Report by EU observers on statements about violations of the second protocol to the Geneva Conventions concerning Ilok, 1 November 1991, 3–4. For more information, see n136, 2937.
256 UK, Statement before the UN General Assembly, UN Doc. A/46/PV.89, 24 August 1992, 36; US, Former Yugoslavia: Grave Breaches of the Fourth Geneva Convention (Second Submission) annexed to Letter dated 22 September 1992 to the UN Secretary-General, UN Doc. S/24583, 23 September 1992, Annex, [4]; Council of Europe, Parliamentary Assembly, Res. 994, 3 February 1993, [1].
257 n18, 182.
258 For more analysis, see n136, 2913–2927.
259 25th International Conference of the Red Cross, Geneva, 23–31 October 1986, Res. I, preamble.

Council's Supreme Council.[260] The right not to be displaced was further affirmed by the Human Rights Council, where it called for upholding IHL and IHRL obligations in order to prevent forced displacement.[261] Moreover, according to a 1997 report of the UN Special Rapporteur on the Human Rights Dimensions of Population Transfer, including the Implantation of Settlers and Settlements, the non-consensual displacement through transfers and implantations constitute human rights violations prohibited under international law.[262] The prohibition of arbitrary displacement was reaffirmed recently by the Special Rapporteur on the Human Rights of Internally Displaced Persons.[263]

The prohibition of civilian displacement unless necessary for their security or imperative military reasons has been embodied in several agreements such as the Agreement on the Application and Implementation of International Humanitarian Law between the Parties to the Conflict in Bosnia and Herzegovina,[264] and in Articles 2 (15) and 3 (7) of the Comprehensive Agreement between the Republic of the Philippines and the National Democratic Front of the Philippines.[265] The 1993 Cotonou Agreement on Liberia obliges the parties to the conflict to end and prevent further displacement of the population and to facilitate the return of those displaced.[266] Furthermore, Article 6 of the Statute of the Extra-ordinary African Chambers[267] stipulates that deportation is a crime against humanity while Article 7 stipulates that unlawful deportation or transfer is a war crime.

It can therefore be concluded from the preceding analysis, which is by no means exhaustive, that the forced displacement of the civilian population either across or within national borders in armed conflict and as a result of serious human rights violations is prohibited under international law. Importantly, the analysis demonstrates that so deplorable is the practice of forced displacement when not justified under international law, that individuals are protected not only after

260 GCC, Supreme Council, 10th session, Muscat, 18–21 December 1989, Final Communique, annexed to Letter dated 29 December 1989 from Oman to the UN Secretary-General, UN Doc. A/45/73-S/21065, 2 January 1990, 4.
261 Mandate of the Special Rapporteur on the human rights of internally displaced persons, 32/11, A/71/53, [9], adopted 1 July 2016 at 43rd meeting without a vote.
262 UN Sub-Commission, n216, [15], [16], [64] and [70].
263 n1, 15.
264 Bosnia and Herzegovina, Agreement No. 1, 22 May 1992.
265 Comprehensive Agreement on Respect for Human Rights and International Humanitarian Law between the Government of the Republic of the Philippines and the National Democratic Front of the Philippines, http://peacemaker.un.org/sites/peacemaker.un.org/files/PH_980316_Comprehensive%20Agreement%20on%20Respect%20for%20Human%20Rights.pdf.
266 Article 18, Cotonou Agreement (Liberia), 25 July 1993, http://www.unhcr.org/refworld/docid/3ae6b5796.html.
267 Established with the Agreement on the Establishment of the Extraordinary African Chambers within the Senegalese Judicial System, Senegal-African Union, Aug. 22, 2012, 52 I.L.M. 1024 (2013); Agreement on the Statute of the Chambers, Senegal-African Union, Jan. 30, 2013, 52 I.L.M. 1028.

displacement has taken place but also before such displacement occurs. To this effect, both state practice and *opinio juris* and specific treaty law support the existence of the right not to be displaced by armed conflict and serious human rights violations.

7 Individual rights and remedies under international law

The preceding analysis established that forced displacement is prohibited under international law and that individuals have the right not to be displaced. Nevertheless, the fact that individuals possess international rights, whether under human rights or humanitarian law, is markedly distinct from the existence of remedies that will enable the injured individuals (victims)[268] to *exercise* as well as to give effect to such rights. It is therefore not sufficient that states possess obligations that give rise to specific individual rights, since these must also be accompanied by remedies, a position that was also stipulated during the Diplomatic Conference that was held in 1949.[269] In spite of this, international humanitarian law is particularly marked by the fact that there may be a right that is, however, not matched by individual remedy.[270] For instance, according to the Commentary to Article 29 IV GC, the Convention does not empower individuals with a right to claim compensation as the Convention sets out a state to state mechanism.[271] Despite this, the commentary to IV GC leaves the door open to individuals bringing a claim against their state of origin for any violations they may have suffered as a result of agreements concluded with the belligerent state, 'in those countries at least in which individual rights may be maintained before the Courts'.[272] Importantly, however, the Convention enables protected persons 'to employ any procedure available, however rudimentary, to demand respect for the Convention's terms'.[273] Article 30 IV GC, for instance, provides that protected persons 'shall have every facility for making an application to Protecting Powers', absence of which would render any protection afforded under the Convention devoid of meaning.[274] Moreover, it has been argued that Article 3 of the 1907 Hague Convention extends the right to compensation to individuals and not merely states, while Article 91 API also provides for compensation for violations of the Geneva Conventions.[275] At the same time, the Basic Principles and Guidelines on the Right to a Remedy and Reparations for Victims of Violations

268 Understood here as those who have suffered specific harm. See n 80, 502; Principle 8, Principles on Remedy, n211.
269 Final Record, n173, 822.
270 Zegveld, n80, 502 and 507.
271 Commentary of 1958, n78, 211 and 212.
272 Article 8, ibid, 79.
273 Ibid, 79.
274 Article 30, ibid, 214.
275 n80, 506 and 512.

of International Human Rights and Humanitarian Law, albeit not legally binding[276] provide for the right to a remedy through 'equal and effective access to justice', 'adequate, effective and prompt reparation for harm suffered' and reparation including restitution, compensation and satisfaction.[277]

Equally problematic in international law is the absence of international judicial or other enforcement mechanisms through which victims of international humanitarian law violations can *claim* their rights.[278] The legal gap that this presents is particularly noticeable in situations of serious violations committed on a widespread scale, such as forced displacement. Nevertheless, individuals have increasingly been able to seek some remedy for such violations through international human rights judicial and other monitoring bodies such as the Inter-American Court of Human Rights, the HRC, the African Court on Human and Peoples Rights and the ECtHR but only to the extent that such violations breach one of the rights entailed in their respective treaties.[279] This is because jurisdictional considerations restrict the ability of such bodies to implement international humanitarian law directly. Moreover, even where the individual can rely on other legal regimes for wrongdoing they suffered as a result of international humanitarian law violations, this provides an indirect way for the affected individual to obtain a remedy for a violation *that has already occurred*. This also means that victims of violations can only seek such remedy if the state concerned is a party to that treaty. In addition to this, international bodies, such as the ECtHR are sometimes unwilling, as the decision in *Demopoulos* reveals,[280] or even unable to deal with massive human rights violations. Nevertheless, the significance of this, albeit limited and indirect, access to protection for international humanitarian law violations, should not be underestimated.[281] To this effect, it has been noted that: 'Whereas the applicability of humanitarian law will end with the cessation of hostilities, human rights obligations remain applicable in peacetime.'[282] The significance of this lies in the fact that IHRL may offer protection for continuing effects of armed conflict such as is the case with forced displacement, and particularly the right not to be displaced, to return and to property restitution

276 Principles on Remedy, n211.

277 Principles 7, 8 and 9, ibid.

278 See, for instance, Cassese A. (2005), *International Law*, 2nd ed. (Oxford University Press) 145; n80, 514.

279 For a discussion on remedies available to individuals under international human rights law, see Report of the ILC, 58th session (1 May–9 June and 3 July–11 August 2006), UN Doc. A/61/10, 87–88; also see Shelton D. (1999), *Remedies in International Human Rights Law* (Oxford University Press).

280 *Demopoulos and Others v Turkey*, n155, [69] and [114], whereby the ECtHR was not willing to apply the ECHR in relation to the rights of those forcibly displaced as a result of Turkey's illegal occupation of Cyprus any differently; also see analysis by Katselli Proukaki, n155.

281 Greenwood C. (2000), 'International humanitarian law' in Kalshoven F. (ed.), *The Centennial of the First International Peace Conference: Reports and Conclusions* (Kluwer Law International) 240.

282 A/HRC/5/5, [56]–[57] quoted in 'Land and Human Rights', n112, 91.

examined in the next chapter. Moreover, 'seeking reparation for violations of human rights might be easier than for violations of international humanitarian law'[283] particularly in relation to identifying the bearer of the obligation. This is because IHL violations may be committed by non-state actors or foreign states. As pointed out in this regard:

> [I]t may be impossible to obtain redress and seeking compensation may be complicated by issues of jurisdiction and the general settlement of claims in peace agreements between States. Proving a violation of international humanitarian law may also be more difficult than proving a violation of human rights law . . . On the other hand, the non-fulfilment of a human right is fairly straightforward, easily observable and thus easier to prove.[284]

At the same time, access to international mechanisms needs to be distinguished from domestic remedies that may be available to victims of IHL violations, although in situations of forced displacement by another state, victims may encounter significant difficulties in claiming their rights particularly in relation to their right not to be displaced or to return home. Indeed, access to domestic remedies very much depends on whether the domestic legal system in question allows individuals to rely on rights conferred on them through international rules, customary or conventional. Domestic courts have been generally reluctant to allow individual claims for violations occurring during armed conflict, as evident from Japanese courts' rejection of individuals claims brought in relation to sexual slavery of women during WWII.[285] Opening the door to millions of individuals whose rights have been violated during armed conflict presents a significant challenge that domestic courts are not always prepared to deal with.[286] This is despite the fact that Principle 2 Basic Principles and Guidelines on the Right to a Remedy and Reparations for Victims of Violations of International Human Rights and Humanitarian Law requires states to take necessary domestic measures to prevent violations and to provide victims with effective access to justice and remedies.[287]

There is no doubt that effectively exercising the right not to be displaced by armed conflict and claiming a remedy for its violation remains distant from reality. It is, however, for this reason that the recognition of a right not to be displaced by armed conflict as advanced in this chapter becomes significant as it will enable the development of mechanisms to ensure the effective protection of the

283 Ibid.

284 Ibid.

285 Zegveld, n80, 508.

286 See analysis ibid, 508–509. Zegfeld refers to a judgment of a US District Court concerning claims brought by Jews for IHL violations that occurred in Croatia during WWII: *Leo Handel et al. v Andrija Artukovic on behalf of himself and as representative of the Independent Government of the State of Croatia*, US District Court for the Central District of California US 601 f. Supp. 1421 judgment of 31 January 1985.

287 Principles on Remedy, n211.

individual. Without the existence of a right there can be no violation and without a violation there can be no remedy. At the same time, the reverse is true: '[T]o assert that a person has a right is to say that he possesses ways and means of having that right respected, and that any violation thereof entails a penalty.'[288]

These goals will arguably be better achieved through the adoption of an international convention on forced displacement caused by armed conflict and serious human rights violations. In fact, it is submitted that the time has now ripened for the adoption of such a convention, without prejudicing other circumstances of forced displacement that, however, as explained earlier, do not fall within the scope of the present discussion. While such a convention would not eliminate the problem of forced displacement, it would strengthen the existing legal framework.[289] The Kampala Convention shows the way for a cross-continent agreement that will prohibit and prevent forced displacement and safeguard the rights of the victims of such violations. Such convention would need to provide clarity regarding the rights of individuals concerning displacement and establish appropriate remedies in case of violation of the right not to be forcibly removed from one's home and land. Such a convention would need to strengthen the regime of legal protection rather than compromise already existing legal standards regarding forced displacement.[290] This is not the first time that a call for codification of the rules concerning forced displacement is made. More specifically, the UN Sub-Commission on Human Rights called in 1993 for an instrument that would 'provide for an express reaffirmation of the unlawfulness of population transfer and the implantation of settlers; define State responsibility in the matter of unlawful population transfer, including the implantation of settlers; provide for the criminal responsibility of individuals involved in population transfer, whether such individuals be private or officials of the State'.[291] The Special Rapporteur for his part suggested the adoption of a declaration that would re-affirm everyone's right to remain in their home, land and country and which would prohibit displacement, a violation of which would give rise to both state responsibility and criminal prosecution of the perpetrator.[292] Rather than a call for a declaration, however, this contribution argues that it is now necessary to have a legally binding instrument to this effect.

8 Conclusion

This chapter has demonstrated that the forcible uprooting of individuals from their lands and homes as the direct or indirect consequence of armed conflict and serious human rights violations has not only diminished but it continues to

288 Article 8, n78, 77.
289 n3, 258.
290 For a similar concern see n116, [17].
291 n216, [15], [16], [64] and [70].
292 Ibid, Annex II, Draft Declaration on Population Transfer and the Implantation of Settlers, Articles 4 and 9.

increase. This is despite the significant evolution of international law in the last century whereby the individual possesses fundamental human rights and the state no longer enjoys absolute sovereignty. This demonstrates that the existing international legal system has been inadequate to prevent and end the displacement of people against their will, which is still often intentionally pursued to achieve territorial gains or 'homogeneity' along ethnic, racial and religious lines.

This chapter has exposed some of the challenges that forced displacement because of armed conflict and serious human rights violations presents as a phenomenon with devastating repercussions on its victims and as a serious violation of international law itself. To this effect, it has been shown that forced displacement is the breaking of an individual's link with their land and home that is the result of lack of free choice. Such coerced breakage has a dramatic impact on the well-being of the uprooted and the dispossessed as land, property and home encompass something more fundamental than merely an economic material value: a sense of refuge, security, belonging and identity[293] where the individual can develop and prosper in conditions of stability and free from arbitrary interference.

Nevertheless, in spite of the significance of protection against forced displacement, the international legal framework has been unable to effectively protect individuals from being unlawfully displaced, particularly during armed conflict and as a result of other serious human rights violations that remain one of the biggest drivers of such displacement. This chapter has shown that while forced displacement is prohibited under IHL, ICL and IHRL and that it may amount to a war crime and a crime against humanity under certain circumstances, failure to match such prohibition with an express general right not to be displaced as a fundamental individual right – applicable in both war and peacetime – has undermined efforts for effective and consistent protection.[294] The preceding analysis has showcased that the international legal framework on forced displacement is still very much fragmented with different rules applicable in different contexts such as occupation, inter-state or internal armed conflict, during peace, or even depending on the circumstances under which such forced displacement takes place. At the same time, this analysis showed that the practice following WWI and WWII was inconsistent according to which while forcible displacement through deportations and forcible transfers was punished as an international crime in some contexts, it was encouraged in others and was given effect through population transfers embodied in international peace agreements. Such population transfers were very much driven by the desire to ensure peace and security, even though the lawfulness or even the justification for such transfers is, as submitted in this chapter, subject to dispute.

More recently, the Guiding Principles on Internal Displacement contributed significantly to addressing the fragmented protection against forced displacement

293 Fox O'Mahony L., Sweeney J. (2011), 'The Idea of Home in Law: Displacement and Dispossession' in Fox O'Mahony L., Sweeney J. (eds.), *The Idea of Home in Law: Displacement and Dispossession* (Ashgate) 11.

294 n230, [9].

by outlining the framework governing forced displacement as arising from different legal contexts as mentioned above.[295] Nevertheless, the non-legal character of the Guiding Principles as well as the fact that they are restricted to the displacement of those who have not crossed an international border, presents its own legal limitations. To address this legal gap, this chapter provided detailed evidence in support not only of an indirect recognition of the right not to be displaced through norms prohibiting forced displacement, but also its direct recognition as a right embodied in international customary law through state practice and *opinio juris*. Importantly, the preceding analysis has demonstrated that the right not to be displaced by force does indeed qualify as a fundamental human right as it aims to safeguard the individual from the arbitrary interference of the state as well as to protect fundamental community values.[296] As also highlighted in the preceding analysis, the significance that the recognition of such right bears lies in the ability of the individual to make a legal claim against the party that violates its international obligations. While truly the effectiveness of such legal claim depends heavily also on the ability of the individual concerned to have access to appropriate mechanisms and remedies, it nevertheless provides them a legal empowerment to demand respect of their rights from all parties concerned, whether states or non-state actors and to be protected from forced displacement, before such displacement is given effect. Surely, and as Stavropoulou points out, 'if the patchwork of international law currently in force leads to "chronic lack of implementation," then it may be time to rethink seriously on the lack of protection from displacement.'[297] Recognition of the right not to be displaced aims to 'define explicitly what is now only implicit in international law'.[298] While there is no illusion that recognition of the right not to be displaced will eliminate human suffering, it is an important step towards a coherent and consistent protection from forced displacement that occurs as a result of armed conflict or other serious human rights violations.

Bibliography

Books

Bassiouni M.C. (1999), *Crimes against Humanity in International Criminal Law* (Kluwer Law International).

Bassiouni M.C. (2011), *Crimes against Humanity: Historical Evolution and Contemporary Application* (Cambridge University Press).

Boot M. (2002), *Genocide, Crimes against Humanity, War Crimes: Nullum Crimen Sine Lege and the Subject Matter Jurisdiction of the International Criminal Court* (Intersentia).

295 n111, 7.
296 n5, 748.
297 Ibid.
298 n230, [10].

Brownlie I. (1963), *International Law and the Use of Force* (Oxford University Press).

Cassese A. (2005), *International Law*, 2nd ed. (Oxford University Press).

de Zayas A. (1988), *Nemesis at Potsdam: The Expulsions of the Germans from the East* (Bison Books).

de Zayas A.M. (1993), *The German Expellees: Victims in War and Peace* (Palgrave Macmillan).

Dinstein Y. (2009), *The International Law of Belligerent Occupation* (Cambridge University Press).

Friedman L. (ed.) (1973), *The Law of War, a Documentary History Vol. I* (Random House).

Henckaerts J.M., Doswald-Beck L. (eds.) (2005), *Customary International Humanitarian Law: Volume II: Practice, Part 2* (Cambridge University Press).

Joseph S., Schultz J., Castan M. (2000), *The International Covenant on Civil and Political Rights: Cases, Materials and Commentary* (Oxford University Press).

Kalin W. (2008), 'Guiding Principles on Internal Displacement: Annotations' (American Society of International Law and The Brookings Institution).

Katselli Proukaki E. (2010), *The Problem of Enforcement in International Law: Countermeasures, the Non-Injured State and the Idea of International Community* (Routledge).

Korn D.A. (1999), *Exodus Within Borders: An Introduction to the Crisis of Internal Displacement* (Brookings Institution Press).

Meron T. (1989), *Human Rights and Humanitarian Norms as Customary Law* (Clarendon Press).

Nowak M. (2005), *U.N. Covenant on Civil and Political Rights: CCPR Commentary* 2nd ed. (N.P. Engel Publisher)

Phuong C. (2005), *The International Protection of Internally Displaced Persons* (Cambridge University Press).

Shelton D. (1999), *Remedies in International Human Rights Law* (Oxford University Press).

Takkenberg L. (1998), *The Status of Palestinian Refugees in International Law* (Oxford University Press).

Book chapters

Fox O'Mahony L., Sweeney J. (2011), 'The Idea of Home in Law: Displacement and Dispossession' in Fox O'Mahony L., Sweeney J. (eds.), *The Idea of Home in Law: Displacement and Dispossession* (Ashgate).

Greenwood C. (2000), 'International Humanitarian Law' in Kalshoven F. (ed.), *The Centennial of the First International Peace Conference: Reports and Conclusions* (Kluwer Law International).

Hall C.K. (1999), 'Crimes against Humanity' in O Triffterer (ed.), *Commentary on the Rome Statute of the International Criminal Court* (Nomos Verlagsgesellschaft), 162.

Lopes C., Quenivet N. (2008), 'Individuals as Subjects of International Humanitarian Law and Human Rights Law' in Arnold R., Quenivet N. (eds.), *International Humanitarian Law and Human Rights Law: Towards a New Merger in International Law* (BRILL).

Journal articles

Alston P. (1984), 'Conjuring Up New Human Rights: A Proposal for Quality Control', *American Journal of International Law*, Vol. 78, 607.

Brownlie I. (1990), 'The Problem of Demographic Manipulation in International Law', Paper delivered at human rights conference, Nicosia, 21 May 1990.

Bugnion F. (2004–2005), 'Refugees, Internally Displaced Persons and International Humanitarian Law', *Fordham Inte'l L. J*, Vol. 28, 1397.

Clapham A. (2010), 'The Role of the Individual in International Law', *European Journal of International Law*, Vol. 21, No. 1, 25–30.

Clark J.N. (2013), 'Courting Controversy: The ICTY's Acquittal of Croatian Generals Gotovina and Markac' *Journal of International Criminal Justice*, Vol. 11, 399.

de Zayas A.M. (1975), 'International Law and Mass Population Transfers', *Harvard International Law Journal*, Vol. 16, 207.

Henckaerts J.M. (2009), 'The Grave Breaches Regime as Customary International Law', *Journal of International Criminal Justice*, Vol. 7, No. 4, 683–701.

Katselli Proukaki E. (2014), 'The Right of Displaced Persons to Property and to Return Home after *Demopoulos*', *Human Rights Law Review, Vol. 14,* No. 4, 701–732.

Margalit A., Hibbin S. (2010), 'Unlawful Presence of Protected Persons in Occupied Territory? An Analysis of Israel's Permit Regime and Expulsions from the West Bank under the Law of Occupation', *Yearbook of International Humanitarian Law*, Vol. 13, 245.

McM W. (1953), 'In Memoriam: Allen T Burns', *Social Service Review*, Vol. 27, No. 2, 218.

Nestor S. (1962), 'Greek Macedonia and the Convention of Neuilly (1919)', *Balkan Studies*, 169–84.

Ojeda S. (2010), 'The Kampala Convention on Internally Displaced Persons: Some International Humanitarian Law Aspects', *Refugee Survey Quarterly*, Vol. 29, No. 3, 58–66.

Quigley J. (1998), 'Displaced Palestinians and a Right to Return', *Harvard International Law Journal*, Vol. 38, 171.

Rietiker D. (2010), 'The Principle of "Effectiveness" in the Recent Jurisprudence of the European Court of Human Rights: Its Different Dimensions and Its Consistency with Public International Law – No Need for the Concept of Treaty *Sui* Generis', *Nordic Journal of International Law*, Vol. 79, No. 2, 245–277.

Sassoli M. (2002), 'State Responsibility for Violations of International Humanitarian Law', *International Review of the Red Cross*, Vol. 84, 401.

Stavropoulou M. (1994), 'The Right not to be Displaced', *American University International Law Review*, Vol. 9, No. 3, 689–749.

Ullom V. (2000–2001), 'Voluntary Repatriation of Refugees and Customary International Law', *Denver Journal of International Law & Policy*, Vol. 29, 115.

Weitz E.D. (2008), 'From the Vienna to the Paris System: International Politics and the Entangled Histories of Human Rights, Forced Deportations, and Civilizing Missions', *American Historical Review*, Vol. 113, No. 5, 1313–43.

Zegveld L. (2003), 'Remedies for Victims of Violations of International Humanitarian Law', *IRRC*, Vol. 85, No. 851, 501.

2 The right to return home and the right to property restitution under international law

Elena Katselli Proukaki

1 Introduction

In a landmark resolution adopted on 22 June 2017, the UN General Assembly decided to request an Advisory Opinion from the International Court of Justice (ICJ) on the legal consequences of the separation of the Chagos Archipelago from Mauritius in 1965.[1] The dispute relates to the United Kingdom's (UK) 1965 decision to separate the Chagos Archipelago islands from Mauritius, which was at the time a British colony,[2] to forcibly move 1700 Chagossians out of the islands[3] and to subsequently lease the biggest of the islands, Diego Garcia, to the United States to use as a military base. The forcible removal of the Chagossians was given effect with the 1971 Immigration Ordinance according to which '[n]o person shall enter the Territory or, being in the Territory, shall be present or remain in the Territory' unless authorised.[4] In 1982 Mauritius and the UK concluded an agreement according to which the UK undertook to pay monetary compensation to Mauritius as a 'full and final settlement of all claims [arising from the removal or resettlement of the population of the Chagos Archipelago]'.[5] It was on the basis of this agreement that the European Court of Human Rights (ECtHR) dismissed as inadmissible the Chagossians' claim that they had been the victims of violations under the European Convention on Human Rights (ECHR). According to the ECtHR, 'in settling their claims . . . and in accepting and receiving compensation, those applicants have effectively renounced further use of these remedies.'[6]

1 UNGA, A/Res/71/292, 22 June 2017.
2 *In the Matter of the Chagos Marine Protected Area Arbitration (The Republic of Mauritius v The United Kingdom of Great Britain and Northern Ireland)*, PCA, 18 March 2015, [1]–[2].
3 Ibid, [88].
4 Ibid, [90]. Also see [521]. While the PCA in this case refused to engage with issues relating to the sovereignty over the Chagos Archipelago as a matter falling outside its jurisdiction, it recognised Mauritius' legal right over the 'eventual' return to it of the islands, as well as its fishing rights in the area.
5 Ibid, [92].
6 *Chagos Islanders v UK* (Application No. 35622/04), Decision, 11 December 2012.

It is in this background that the ICJ is requested to provide its Advisory Opinion on the lawfulness of the separation of the Chagos Archipelago from Mauritius and the legal consequences arising from UK's continued denial to resettle those forcibly moved back to the islands. These questions fall at the heart of this book and this chapter as they invite consideration of, among other things, the lawfulness of the forcible removal of the Chagos Archipelago's inhabitants and of their continuing inability to return home. Therefore, the request for an Advisory Opinion raises compelling legal questions pertaining to the rights not to be forcibly displaced examined in the previous chapter and to return home and to property restitution, which are the focus of this chapter. Importantly, it raises questions regarding whether monetary compensation is sufficient to 'wipe off' these rights.

This case illustrates that past injustices – in addition to new ones – continue to affect millions of people who have been forced out of their homes, either by armed conflict or other serious human rights violations and to deny them the possibility of return and property restitution. How does then contemporary international law respond to these legal challenges?

The focus of this chapter is on the rights of those forcibly displaced as a result of armed conflict or serious human rights violations to return home and to property restitution. While not every person who was forced to abandon home and property will want to return, especially due to security concerns,[7] for many the desire to return never fades. Since, as demonstrated in the previous chapter, forced displacement is prohibited under international law and individuals have the right not to be forcibly displaced, it must be true that such displacement must come to an end to reverse the illegality and to return the *status quo ante*. To this effect, it has been pointed out that 'the right to return derives from the illegality of the expulsion itself. It is generally recognised that a state cannot legally expel a population under its control. Those expelled clearly have the right to reverse an illegal act, that is, to return to their homeland.'[8] Not only, however, is return the legal consequence that arises from an internationally wrongful act, namely unlawful forced displacement, but it is also an independent right as the analysis in this chapter shows. The significance of this lies in the fact that states do not have, as a matter of general rule, discretion as to what means they can choose to remedy forced displacement such as is the case with the Chagos islands, neither can such right be restricted unconditionally. The right to return should therefore be a viable option for those who want to do so but for this to be achieved it is necessary to ensure security, economic development as well as the protection of property.[9] Indeed, the restitution of property is an essential requirement for the return of those forcibly uprooted since without such restitution return is

7 Ullom V. (2000–2001), 'Voluntary Repatriation of Refugees and Customary International Law', *DJIL&P*, Vol. 29, 115, 116.

8 See analysis in Takkenberg L. (1998), *The Status of Palestinian Refugees in International Law* (Oxford University Press) 234.

9 See Colombian Constitutional Court, Decision T-025 of 2004, 33.

hampered.[10] Accordingly, and while restitution is well established as a secondary norm of international law, the restitution of property of those forcibly displaced by armed conflict and serious human rights violations is significant in its own right for 'helping people to both restore their lives in their communities but also to have that valuable asset back',[11] as well as for peace building.[12]

Nevertheless, these rights are not uncontested. First of all, there is no codified universal obligation to accept back those displaced,[13] neither is there an express reference to the right to return home or to property restitution in the Universal Declaration of Human Rights (UDHR), the International Covenant on Civil and Political Rights (ICCPR) or the ECHR. Second, a conflict exists between the view that supports the implementation of a non-absolute right of return and the view in support of a 'categorical right of return'.[14] Disagreement also exists as to whether there exists a right to property restitution as evident in the ECtHR's decision in *Demopoulos*.[15] Finally, while some authors have argued that there is an emerging customary international norm imposing an obligation on states to accept the voluntary repatriation of refugees,[16] others have conditioned this on the nationality of those displaced and as an obligation that burdens the state of nationality of the displaced.[17] This last view, however, leaves unprotected those whose return is dependent on a foreign state, such as in the case of foreign occupation, e.g. Cyprus, as well as those who do not have the nationality of the state from which they were displaced, e.g. Palestinians. Moreover, some authors have cast doubt on whether there exists a right to return in cases of mass exodus.[18]

The following analysis demonstrates that the right to return home and the right to property restitution are well established under conventional as well as customary international law and that such rights, which extend to situations of mass displacement,[19] are not dependent on nationality. Importantly, 'demographic

10 Phuong C. (2005), *The International Protection of Internally Displaced of Persons* (Cambridge University Press) 61–62.

11 Stanley V., Senior Rural Development Specialist, World Bank Group, http://www.worldbank.org/en/news/ feature/2015/12/02/the-power-of-sharing-knowledge-helps-countries-tackle-forced-displacement.

12 Mdontswa T., Deputy Chief Land Claims Commissioner, South Africa Commission on Restitution of Land Rights, http://www.worldbank.org/en/news/feature/2015/12/02/the-power-of-sharing-knowledge-helps-countries-tackle-forced-displacement.

13 Ullom, n7, 116.

14 Helton A. (2004–2005), 'End of Exile: Practical Solutions to the Palestinian Refugee Question: Refugees and the Right of Return', *FordhamInt'lLJ*, Vol. 28, 1325, 1327.

15 *Demopoulos and Others v Turkey*, ECHR Reports 2010; EHRR SE 14.

16 See analysis in Takkenberg, n8, 232.

17 Ullom, n7, 117 and 118; Lapidoth R. (1986), 'The Right of Return in International Law, with Special Reference to the Palestinian Refugees', *IYbHR*, Vol. 16, 103, 114.

18 Benvenisti E., Zamir E. (1995), 'Private Claims to Property Rights in the Future Israeli-Palestinian Settlement', *AJIL*, Vol. 89, 295, 325.

19 See analysis in Quigley J. (1998), 'Displaced Palestinians and a Right to Return', *HILJ*, Vol. 38, 211–212.

security' which aims to retain 'ethnically pure' areas is not in compliance with international law, which prohibits discrimination on ethnic, racial or religious grounds. As Quigley rightly points out: 'No arguable legal principle permits a denial of repatriation to those so entitled on the basis of their ethnicity.'[20]

Section 2 discusses how the rights to return home and to property restitution are protected under international humanitarian law (IHL), while Section 3 analyses such protection under the spectrum of international human rights law (IHRL). Section 4 examines how these two fields of law interrelate when it comes to the protection of those forcibly displaced through critical evaluation of existing legal gaps. Section 5 analyses further evidence of state practice and *opinio juris* in support of the existence of the rights to return home and to property restitution as independent rights, while Section 6 concludes.

2 The legal basis of the rights to return and to property restitution under international humanitarian law

International humanitarian law, as codified in the Hague Regulations and the Geneva Conventions and as reflected in customary international law, safeguards the rights to return home and to property restitution. For instance, the right to return, which must be understood as the right to return to one's home and land, and the right to property restitution are safeguarded under the Hague Regulations,[21] according to which an occupying power has the obligation to 'maintain *la vie public* in the occupied territory'.[22] The rights to return and to property restitution are also embedded in the Geneva Conventions, which restrict the ability of parties to a conflict to denounce the rights entailed therewith 'until peace has been concluded, and until after operations connected with the release, *repatriation* and re-establishment of the persons protected by the present Convention have been terminated'.[23] This is further safeguarded under the Fourth Geneva Convention (IV GC), most relevant for protecting civilians from forced displacement in international armed conflict, which sets out minimum standards of treatment and dignity[24] and restricts the power of states parties to the conflict

20 Ibid, 229.
21 Convention Respecting the Laws and Customs of War on land, Oct. 18, 1907, Annex: Regulations Respecting the Laws and Customs of War on Land.
22 Quigley, n19, 198.
23 Article 63, Geneva Convention for the amelioration of the condition of the wounded and sick in armed forces in the field (I GC), 75 *UNTS* 970; Article 62, Geneva Convention for the amelioration of the condition of the wounded, sick and shipwrecked members of the armed forces at sea (II GC), 75 *UNTS* 971; Article 142, Geneva Convention relative to the treatment of prisoners of war (III GC), 75 *UNTS* 972; Article 158, Geneva Convention Relative to the Protection of Civilian Persons in Time of War of 12 August 1949 (IV), 75 *UNTS* 973 (emphasis added). See analysis in Takkenberg, n8, 232; Wright Q. (1968), 'Legal Aspects of the Middle East Situation', *L&Cont.Problems*, Vol. 33, 5, 19; and Quigley, n19, 197.
24 Commentary of 1958, IV Geneva Convention Relative to the Protection of Civilian Persons in Time of War of 12 August 1949, 70 and 76.

to compromise the rights of protected persons entailed therein either through the conclusion of special agreements or through renunciation.[25] Moreover, Article 27 IV GC safeguards respect for the person and in effect, for fundamental rights that are 'inseparable from the human being' and continue even during foreign occupation.[26] This includes protection of freedom of movement, which is relevant to the right to return home, and protection of family rights, including the family home, from arbitrary interference.[27] Moreover, and as pointed out in the Commentary of the IV GC, the state in breach of its obligations under the Convention must provide reparation that includes restitution, unless this is impossible, or compensation.[28]

Importantly, the rights to return and to property restitution find express recognition in Article 49 IV GC, which provides that persons evacuated for their safety or for imperative military reasons 'shall be transferred back to their homes as soon as hostilities in the area in question have ceased'. While return may require a lot of time to be given effect, well after the conclusion of hostilities,[29] such return must not be delayed beyond what is absolutely necessary for the safety of those concerned. Furthermore, the prohibition of settlements and population transfers into occupied territory as embodied in Article 49 IV GC aims to safeguard both the property as well as the return of the displaced. The unlawfulness of such policies, which are given effect through expulsions and denial of the right of the populations affected to return, was highlighted in the report of the UN Special Rapporteur on the Human Rights Dimensions of Population Transfer, including the Implantation of Settlers and Settlements.[30] It is clear that states that engage in such unlawful implantation of settlers aim to solidify their control over occupied territory by making it difficult to reverse the *status quo* and by creating a humanitarian crisis[31] that places the displaced at an equal footing with those who commit internationally wrongful acts.

The prohibition of settlements is reaffirmed in Rule 130 Study of the International Committee of the Red Cross (ICRC Study), while the principle of voluntary return is stipulated in Rule 132 ICRC Study, both of which are reflective of customary international law.[32] The significance of property is also recognised in Rule 133 ICRC Study, which provides that: 'The property rights

25 Articles 7 and 8, IV GC, n23.
26 Commentary of 1958, n24, 202.
27 Ibid.
28 Ibid, 210.
29 Eritrea Ethiopia Claims Commission, Partial Award, Western Front, Aerial Bombardment and Related Claims Eritrea's Claims 1, 3, 5, 9–13, 14, 21, 25 & 26, 19 December 2005, [127-28], https://pcacases.com/web/ sendAttach/757.
30 'The Human Rights Dimensions of Population Transfers including the Implantation of Settlers', Preliminary Report prepared by AS Al-Khasawneh and R Hatano, E/CN.4/Sub.2/1993/17 6 July 1993, [35] (Al-Khasawneh/Hatano report).
31 Ibid.
32 ICRC Study on Customary International Humanitarian Law, https://www.icrc.org/customary-ihl/eng/docs/v1_rul_rule132.

of displaced persons must be respected.' The ICRC Study drew support from the reaffirmation of this principle and condemnation of its violation in various contexts such as in the conflicts of the former Yugoslavia, Colombia and Cyprus and the conclusion of agreements calling for the respect of the property rights of the displaced.[33]

It needs to be noted that while forced displacement is also prohibited in the context of internal armed conflict, Article 17 of Additional Protocol II (AP II) does not entail a provision similar to that in Article 49 IV GC on the return of those displaced. Nevertheless, according to the ICRC Study the rights to return home and to property extend to all those forcibly displaced irrespective of the nature of the conflict.[34]

While IHL protects civilians including those displaced from the effects of armed conflict,[35] its guarantees apply only to the territory of the parties to the conflict. This means that not all IHL provisions continue to apply once individuals flee such territory. However, the provisions concerning the return of the displaced and the protection of property continue to apply. At the same time, and as will be discussed in Section 4, IHL does not preclude the application of other relevant rules such as those under IHRL, which continues to apply in armed conflict and irrespective of the existence of occupation.[36] How IHRL supports the claim that those forcibly displaced have a right to return home and to property restitution is considered in the next section.

3 The legal basis of the rights to return home and to property restitution under international human rights law

The analysis in this section aims to establish the legal basis of the rights to return home and to property restitution under IHRL.

The Universal Declaration of Human Rights, albeit non-legally binding, guarantees the right not to be arbitrarily subjected to exile (Article 9 UDHR) as well as freedom of movement and residence within the borders of each state and the right to return to one's own country (Article 13). These principles subsequently found legally binding expression in Article 12 ICCPR, which protects freedom of movement and to choose one's residence and freedom to leave one's country while prohibiting arbitrary deprivation of the right to enter one's country. These rights, as all ICCPR rights, constitute fundamental interests that every state party has a legal interest in their protection.[37] Article 12 is particularly relevant in

33 Ibid.

34 Ibid.

35 Bugnion F. (2004–2005), 'Refugees, Internally Displaced Persons and International Humanitarian Law', *FordhamInte'lLJ*, Vol. 28, 1397, 1408.

36 Ibid, 1409. Also see 'Land and Human Rights: Standards and Applications', UNOHCR, 2015, HR/PUB/15/5/Add.1, 89 (Land and Human Rights).

37 General Comment No. 31, The Nature of the General Legal Obligation imposed on States Parties to the Covenant, CCPR/C/21/Rev.1/Add. 13, 26 May 2004, [2].

situations in which individuals are forced to leave their home and lands, either as refugees or internally displaced, as it protects both the right not to be displaced as argued in the previous chapter, as well as the right to return home as argued in this chapter. While some states have disputed that freedom of movement is a fundamental right,[38] its significance is highlighted by others according to whom freedom of movement 'constituted an important human right and one which was an essential part of the right to personal liberty'.[39] As Stavropoulou rightly states, 'the right to remain, or the right to stay, or even the right to return, are expressions of the freedom of movement.'[40]

The first paragraph of Article 12 guarantees freedom of movement and freedom to choose one's residence to everyone lawfully within the territory of that state. The Human Rights Committee (HRC), the ICCPR's human rights monitoring body, stressed that Article 12 (1) extends to the entire territory of a state and is not dependent on any reasons of why a person wishes to move or reside to that part of the state.[41] It is clear that nationals of a state are lawfully within the territory of that state[42] as a result of which they 'have a *de facto* absolute *right of residence* in the territory of this State'.[43] It is equally clear, however, from the wording of Article 12 (1) that the guarantees safeguarded therein are not restricted to nationals.[44]

Freedom of movement and freedom of residence are not however absolute. Rather, Article 12 (3) sets out the circumstances under which they can be restricted, balancing the individual's rights with the state's vital interests such as protection of national security and public order. Although during the drafting of this provision, there was suggestion to include a list of potential limitations, a more general wording was favoured in the end.[45] From the discussions during the drafting of this article, it appears that there was concern by some states regarding potential abuse particularly through law.[46] Interestingly, however, one of the proposals was to restrict movement and residence 'where it is necessary in the interests of peace and good government to proclaim reserved areas in favour of the different sections of the population, and to restrict and control the free

38 See analysis in Nowak M. (2005), *U.N. Covenant on Civil and Political Rights: CCPR Commentary*, 2nd ed. (N.P. Engel Publisher) 260.
39 Quoted in Bossuyt M.J. (1987), *Guide to the 'Travaux Preparatoires' of the International Covenant on Civil and Political Rights* (Martinus Nijhoff Publishers) 253.
40 Stavropoulou M. (1994), 'The Right not to be Displaced', *AUILR*, Vol. 9, No. 3, 689–749, 739.
41 General Comment No. 27, Article 12 (Freedom of Movement), CCPR/C/21/Rev.1/Add.9, 2 November 1999, [5] and [7].
42 Ibid, [4]; and in Joseph S., Schultz J., Castan M. (2000), *The International Covenant on Civil and Political Rights: Cases, Materials and Commentary* (Oxford University Press) 246.
43 Nowak, n38, 263 [emphasis in the original]. Also see *Prosecutor v Gotovina et al.*, TC, IT-06-90-T, 15 April 2011, [1747].
44 CCPR General Comment No. 15, The Positions of Aliens under the Covenant, 11 April 1986, [7].
45 See Bossuyt, n39, 252.
46 Ibid, 252–259.

movement and free choice of residence on the part of individuals belonging to different sections of the population'.[47] It comes as no surprise that such proposal (which was rejected) was put forward by the then racist regime of South Africa. What *is* surprising, however, is the fact that similar discriminatory proposals were put forward in the Comprehensive Settlement of the Cyprus Problem introduced by the then UN Secretary General Kofi Annan in 2004.[48] Such proposals were in breach of the freedoms safeguarded in Article 12 ICCPR. In the case of both South Africa and Cyprus, one could argue that such restrictions were justified as they pursued a legitimate aim, namely that of protecting public order and peace. One needs, however, to be extremely cautious when human rights are being sacrificed to ensure that the strict, specific, and free from discrimination restrictions, when allowed, are indeed justified. To this effect, while freedom of movement and freedom of residence are subject to restrictions, these must not 'nullify' the essence of the interests protected[49] and must satisfy at least one of the reasons stipulated in Article 12 (3), including the protection of national security, which is more relevant in situations of armed conflict. However, it is not sufficient that the restriction to the right serves a national security interest, but rather, it must also be necessary to achieve this objective. Furthermore, according to the HRC, such restrictions 'must be provided by law, must be necessary in a democratic society for the protection of these purposes and must be consistent with all other rights recognized in the Covenant'.[50] Necessity is satisfied if the restrictions are a response to 'a pressing public and social need', they pursue a 'legitimate aim' and they are 'proportionate to that aim'.[51] Moreover, proportionality is essential to ensure that the restrictions are appropriate to protect the interests under consideration and they bring about the least intrusion to achieve the intended result.[52] It is in this respect that restriction of freedom of movement and residence on discriminatory grounds, as that imposed in South Africa and that intended to be imposed in Cyprus, does not satisfy these conditions. This is because discrimination that deprives one section of the population or a particular group of fundamental human rights on grounds of race or ethnicity and in pursuance of political or territorial claims cannot in these circumstances serve a legitimate aim, neither necessary in a democratic society. Quite the contrary, such discrimination is a well-established prohibition in international law. Moreover, in the 21st century it is through respect of human rights that the peaceful co-existence of different groups can be achieved, and not through denial of such rights.

47 Ibid, 253.

48 For a critique of the Plan, see Katselli Proukaki E. (2014), 'The Right of Displaced Persons to Property and to Return Home after *Demopoulos*', 14 *HRLR* (2014) No. 4, 701–732, 711.

49 General Comment No. 27, n41, [2] and [13].

50 Ibid, [11]. Quite interestingly, Article 12 (3) does not include the terms 'democratic society'.

51 Article 6 (c) of the Draft Declaration on freedom and non-discrimination in respect of the right of everyone to leave any country, including his own, and to return to his country, by Mubanga-Chipoya, E/CN.4/Sub.2/1987/10 quoted in Nowak, n38, 275.

52 General Comment No. 27, n41, [14].

Article 12 is also subject to derogations under Article 4 ICCPR. Nevertheless, derogations must comply with other international law obligations, including those arising from the Geneva Conventions regarding both the prohibition of forced displacement and the obligation to allow the return of those temporarily evacuated.[53] Importantly, derogations must be temporary measures. Derogations do not provide a carte blanche on the state to act arbitrarily and without legal restraint; rather, derogations must meet the conditions of legality and must be justified as exceptional and necessary measures to tackle a serious situation. While such derogations may be justified during armed conflict or unrest for as long as hostilities continue, they are not justified in situations in which there are no longer such hostilities and the exigencies of the situation are no longer in place. That would be the case in the occupied part of Cyprus, for instance, whereby Turkey still refuses to allow the return and restitution of property to displaced Greek Cypriots.[54] To this effect, regimes of prolonged and continuing foreign occupation or indefinite restrictions to human rights, including freedom of movement and residence, *cannot* be justified.[55] The more extensive the period under which derogations apply, the more ambivalent their necessity is. This is in accordance with HRC conclusions in relation to Israel's prolonged state of emergency. As pointed out, the necessity for such derogation must be reviewed with the aim to limit 'as far as possible its scope and territorial applicability and the associated derogation of rights'.[56]

On a separate but related point, Article 12 (1) guarantees are not set aside in situations of foreign occupation. On the contrary, and as seen earlier, the law of occupation requires the occupying power to 'maintain *la vie public* in the occupied territory'.[57] As we know already, occupation does not alter the legal status of the occupied territory, which continues *de jure* to be part of the territory of the state under occupation.[58] Moreover, freedom of movement and residence are not attached to an individual in relation to a specific state but rather in relation to a specific territory within which they are lawfully present. Occupation does not, therefore, reverse the lawfulness of such presence. It is in this context that the HRC has often expressed concerns over Israel's unjustified restrictions of freedom of movement against Palestinians as a result of the construction of the Wall as well as its policies of expulsion of long-term residents from the West Bank to the Gaza

53 On the right to return in situations of derogation, see analysis in Stavropoulou, n40, 740. Also see IACommHR, Report on the Situation of Human Rights of a Segment of the Nicaraguan Population of Miskito Indians, Doc. 10, Rev. 3 (1983) 114.

54 Report of HRC, Cyprus, CCPR A/32/44 (1977), [384].

55 Quigley, n19, 204–205; Report of HRC, Supplement No. 40, A/34/40 (1979), 20.

56 Consideration of reports submitted by states parties under Article 40 of the Covenant, Concluding observations of HRC, Israel, CCPR/C/79/Add. 93, 18 August 1998, [11]. Also see Consideration of reports submitted by states parties under Article 40 of the Covenant, Concluding observations of HRC, Israel, CCPR/C/ISR/CO/3, 3 September 2010, [7].

57 Quigley, n19, 198.

58 *Loizidou v Turkey* (Application no. 15318/89) Judgment 18 December 1996, [44] and [46].

Strip and settlements in the occupied Palestinian territories.[59] The HRC has also condemned the punitive destruction of homes and property and the discriminatory housing policy that denied Palestinians permit to construct houses, as well as interference with their right to return to their country as being in violation of Articles 12, 17 and 26 ICCPR.[60] This demonstrates that while IHL regulates the conduct of parties during armed conflict and occupation, IHRL also continues to apply in these situations. As the HRC has stressed: 'While, in respect of certain Covenant rights, more specific rules of international humanitarian law may be specially relevant for the purposes of the interpretation of Covenant rights, both spheres of law are complementary, not mutually exclusive.'[61] To this effect, even if it is necessary to restrict freedom of movement and residence, such as in relation to accessing military zones,[62] such restrictions should be given effect as exceptional measures that must be construed narrowly and must not undermine the essence of the freedom protected under Article 12 (1).[63] Neither does occupation justify restrictions to Article 12 (1), which are based on discriminatory grounds such as ethnicity, nationality or religion,[64] as is the case of Turkey's restrictions imposed against Greek Cypriots in the occupied northern part of Cyprus. The position that human rights extend to occupied territories is now well established and has been confirmed, among other comments, in the ICJ Advisory Opinion on the *Legality of the Threat or Use of Nuclear Weapons* according to which the ICCPR does not cease in times of war except when a state derogates from its obligations in times of emergency.[65] This was subsequently further developed in the *Wall case*[66] and in the *Case Concerning Armed Activities on the Territory of the Congo*,[67] which confirmed that human rights protection extends to situations of belligerent occupation and that the actions of occupying powers are tested towards their compliance with human rights standards.[68] In the *Wall case*, in particular, where Israel was found to have violated its obligations under the ICCPR, the International Covenant on Economic, Social and Cultural Rights (ICESCR) and the Convention

59 Concluding observations of HRC, Israel, 2010, n56, [8], [14] and [16].
60 Concluding observations of HRC, Israel, 1998, n 6, [13], [22] and [24]; Consideration of reports submitted by states parties under Article 40 of the Covenant, Concluding observations of HRC, Israel, CCPR/CO/78/ISR, 21 August 2003, [12].
61 General Comment No. 31, n37, [11]; Concluding observations of HRC, Israel, 2010, n56, [5].
62 n41, [16].
63 Nowak, n38, 275; General Comment No. 31, n37, [6].
64 General Comment No. 27, n41, [18].
65 *Legality of the Threat or Use of Nuclear Weapons*, Advisory Opinion, ICJ Reports 1996, 226, [25] (Nuclear Weapons AO).
66 *Legal Consequences of the Construction of a Wall in the Occupied Palestinian Territory*, Advisory Opinion, ICJ Reports (2004) 136 (Wall AO).
67 *Case Concerning Armed Activities on the Territory of the Congo (Democratic Republic of the Congo v Uganda)*, Judgment, ICJ Reports (2005) 168.
68 Gross A.M. (2007), 'Human Proportions: 'Are Human Rights the Emperor's New Clothes of the International Law of Occupation?', *EJIL*, Vol. 18, No. 1, 1–35, 3.

on the Rights of the Child (CRC),[69] the ICJ emphasised that human rights obligations burden the state even for violations that occur extra-territorially but that still fall within its jurisdiction.[70] According to the Court, some rights may be regulated under IHL, others under international human rights law and others still may be regulated under both branches of international law.[71]

One could, of course, question whether the use of unlawful armed force and the unlawful occupation of territory satisfy either the conditions for the restriction of rights such as in Article 12 (3) or the conditions for derogations as in Article 4 ICCPR. Arguably, the unlawful character of a conduct should have a bearing as to whether a state may temporarily suspend/restrict its international obligations so as to prevent a state from benefiting from its own unlawful conduct. Since the purpose of derogations and restrictions is to protect the fundamental interests of the state that is under threat, it becomes evident that a state that uses unlawful force and occupies another state is not threatened; rather it is itself a threat to other states, the international community and individuals. This factor of unlawfulness should in fact be taken into consideration when assessing whether any restrictions or derogations are justified. It is accordingly submitted that the legality of state action, under for instance the *jus ad bellum*, which is relevant for the purposes of this examination, does influence the obligations or potential rights – such as in the context of restrictions and derogations – that the state has under other legal regimes such as IHL or IHRL. Such position is justified under the necessity to see different legal regimes as complementing one another and as strengthening the unity of international law but also for strengthening the protection towards those mostly affected by armed conflict, namely individuals.

Furthermore, like all human rights norms, Article 12 (1) imposes on states parties both a negative and a positive obligation. While the negative obligation requires the state to refrain from conduct that will breach the right, the positive obligation requires the state to adopt all necessary, legislative and other measures to ensure that the right is also protected from the acts of private parties.[72] Dispossession, settlements as well as allowing private parties, such as, for instance, estate agencies to exploit the abandoned properties of the displaced, such as those carried out against Greek Cypriot homes and properties in the northern part of Cyprus,[73] involve violations both of the negative and positive obligations of the state.

In addition to the protection of freedom of movement and freedom of residence, Article 12 (4) also safeguards the individual right to enter one's country and, in effect, the right to return. According to Saideman, the wording of Article 12 (4) suggests the existence of an individual right rather than a collective one the significance of which lies in the fact that any agreement concluded enabling

69 Wall AO, n66, [106].
70 Ibid, [108].
71 Ibid, [106].
72 General Comment No. 27, n41, [6].
73 Case C 420/04, *Apostolides v Orams* [2009] I-03571.

the return of some but not all of those displaced could be challenged as being in violation of this provision.[74] Nevertheless, and in spite of views to the contrary,[75] the recognition of an individual right of return does not set aside claims of return in cases of mass displacement.[76]

Since Article 12 (4) prohibits arbitrary interference with the right to enter one's country, its application seems to extend to refugees who have crossed an international border but not to internally displaced persons who would nevertheless be protected under Article 12 (1). An arbitrary interference is not limited to situations in which specific law has been violated but it also includes refusal of entry that is incompatible with the objective of the protection.[77] Moreover, the right to enter one's country is not subject to the restrictions of Article 12 (3).[78] This interpretation is consistent with the *travaux preparatoires* according to which: 'The general consensus was, however, that, while the right was not absolute, it should not be made subject to the same kind of restrictions as the other rights defined in paragraphs 1 and 2 of the same article.'[79] This is further supported by the HRC according to which 'there are few, if any, circumstances in which deprivation of the right to enter one's own country could be reasonable.'[80]

Article 12 (4) opens the question of how 'one's own country' is understood and who is entitled to protection under this provision. The fact that this provision does not refer to a right to return but rather to a right to enter suggests that it is not intended to be restricted to those individuals who lived in the state of origin as opposed to individuals who never lived there.[81] The HRC stated in this regard:

> The right of a person to enter his or her own country recognizes the special relationship of a person to that country. The right has various facets. It implies the right to remain in one's own country. It includes not only the right to return after having left one's own country; it may also entitle a person to come to the country for the first time if he or she was born outside the country . . . The right to return is of the utmost importance for refugees seeking voluntary repatriation. It also implies prohibition of enforced population transfers or mass expulsions to other countries.[82]

But how about aliens? Is the right restricted to nationals or is it also enjoyed by non-nationals? While some states such as Canada conditioned such right on the

74 Saideman L. (2004), 'Do Palestinian Refugees Have a Right of Return to Israel? An Examination of the Scope of and Limitations on the Right of Return', *VJIL*, Vol. 44, 829, 834.
75 Benvenisti and Zamir, n18, 325.
76 Quigley, n19, 211–212.
77 Hannum H. (1987), *The Right to Leave and Return in International Law and Practice* (Martinus Nijhoff Publishers) 44–45.
78 For a different view, see Ullom, n7, 121.
79 Bossuyt, n39, 262.
80 General Comment No. 27, n41, [21]; Nowak, n38, 262 and 283; Quigley, n19, 201.
81 Hannum, n77, 56.
82 General Comment No. 27, n41, [19]. Nowak, n38, 266.

existence of a nationality link between the state and the individual exercising their right to return/enter their country,[83] the right to enter as safeguarded under Article 12 (4) is not restricted to the territory of the state of nationality.[84] Indeed, what matters is the effectiveness of the links that an individual has with the said country. As pointed out: 'A person's "country" is that to which he is connected by a reasonable combination of such relevant criteria as race, religion, language, ancestry, birth and prolonged domicile. Governments come and go, and their political fluctuations should not affect the fundamental right of human beings, such as the right to return to one's own country and to have a homeland.'[85] The HRC seems to accept that nationality is not an essential condition although it does seem to restrict the scope of those who can exercise it.[86] To this effect, the right extends to 'an individual who, because of his or her special ties to or claims in relation to a given country, cannot be considered to be a mere alien. This would be the case, for example, of . . . individuals whose country of nationality has been incorporated in or transferred to another national entity.'[87] This would apply to population transfers or expulsion such as those carried out in the aftermath of World Wars I and II (WWI /WWII) as discussed in the previous chapter, as well as to 'peoples on land occupied belligerently by another State, such as the Palestinians of the Gaza strip'.[88] Nevertheless, the HRC appears in this case to have taken a restrictive approach later criticised by the dissenting opinion in *Stewart v Canada*. As noted there, 'For the rights set forth in article 12, the existence of a formal link to the State is irrelevant; the Covenant is here concerned with the strong personal and emotional links an individual may have with the territory where he lives and with the social circumstances obtaining it.'[89]

Bringing non-nationals under the scope of Article 12 (4) is not, according to Hannum, supported by the ICCPR's *travaux preparatoires*. Moreover, if such a broad scope were accepted it would 'imply a right to "return" or "enter" to any number of persons who seek to return "home"'. According to him: 'There is no evidence that mass movements of groups such as refugees or displaced persons were intended to be included within the scope of article 12 of the Covenant by its drafters, particularly where those seeking to return are not nationals of the state of destination.'[90] Instead, such mass displacement, such as that which occurred in the aftermath of WWI and WWII, is a matter of self-determination or national

83 Hannum, n77, 56.
84 Ibid, 57 and 59.
85 Muzzawi quoted in Hannum, ibid, 58.
86 See, for instance, *Madafferi v Australia*, Communication No. 1011/2001, CCPR/C/81/D/1011/2001, 26 August 2004, [9.6].
87 Joseph, Schultz, Castan, n42, 267.
88 General Comment No. 27, n41, [18].
89 *Stewart v Canada*, CCPR/C/58/D/538/1993 16 December 1996; also see Joseph, Schultz, Castan, n42, 258; Nowak also expresses reservations about the correctness of this case law: Nowak, n38, 286–287.
90 Hannum, n77, 59–60.

sovereignty and not a matter that falls within the protective scope of the right to enter or to return or human rights standards.[91] This interpretation is, in fact, challenged by the HRC itself, which makes express reference to the relevance of Article 12 to refugees and those forcibly displaced.[92] It is also challenged by the *travaux preparatoires*, according to which the phrase 'country of which he is a national' was replaced by the phrase 'his own country',[93] although, at a later session held in 1959, 'his own country' was accepted as meaning 'the country of which the individual concerned was a national or a citizen'.[94] Nevertheless, in *Stefan Lars Nystrom v Australia*, the HRC departs from its findings in *Stewart v Canada*, holding that 'one's own country' is broader than the country of nationality. To this effect, the HRC accepted that this phrase encompasses not just formal nationality links but also the individual's 'special ties to or claims in relation to a given country' as well as 'close and enduring connections between a person and a country, connections which may be stronger than those of nationality' including long standing residence, close family ties and absence of ties elsewhere.[95]

The issue of nationality gains prominence in the context of the Palestinian problem. According to one view, those Palestinians who were forcibly displaced in 1948 and 1967 and who took up the nationality of another state may no longer claim the right to return.[96] This would prevent a large proportion of those forcibly displaced from returning. There is also the view that if a refugee loses her rights under the Geneva Convention on Refugees because she acquired new nationality, then she is not entitled to return as she can no longer rely on Article 12 ICCPR, since she is not prevented from returning to her 'own country' ('own' understood here as the new state).[97] However, this interpretation is wrong because the Geneva Convention on Refugees grants refugees specific rights when in a country outside their own and it is not intended to abolish rights that they may be entitled to under other rules of international law such as those under the ICCPR. The two treaties have different objectives and should be seen as complementing each other rather than as the one prevailing over the other as suggested. To claim otherwise would contravene the aims and objectives of each of these treaties and would significantly weaken the position of the individual in international law.[98] It is accordingly submitted that the right to return, detached from nationality, is enjoyed by all inhabitants of the territory they were forced to flee, including their descendants,[99]

91 Ibid, 59–60.
92 General Comment No. 27, n41, [7] and [19].
93 Bossuyt, n39, 261.
94 Ibid, 262.
95 *Stefan Lars Nystrom v Australia*, Communication No. 1557/2007, CCPR/C/102/D/1557/2007, [7.4]–[7.6]; Nowak, n38, 286; Saideman, n74, 849.
96 See analysis in Saideman, ibid, 833 and 859.
97 Ibid, 863.
98 Ibid, 865. Quigley is of the view that taking up another nationality does not prevent or abolish the right to return. Quigley, n19, 216–217.
99 Saideman, ibid, 857 and 859.

irrespective of change of sovereignty, acquisition of territory by another state, establishment of a new state (such as, in this instance, Israel), acquisition of new nationality or termination of refugee status.[100]

Other international legal instruments that support the right to return home include the ECHR, which, in Article 2 (1) Protocol 4, safeguards freedom of movement and residence. At the same time, Article 3 Protocol 4 prohibits individual or collective expulsions from the territory of the state of which the individual is a national as well as deprivation of entry in the territory of nationality. Unlike freedom of movement and residence, which is subject to restrictions, the protection in Article 3 is set out in absolute terms. While Article 3 in effect recognises the prohibition of forced displacement as well as the right to return, it nonetheless restricts these rights to nationals, hence providing a narrower protection than the one under Article 12 ICCPR. Article 22 (5) of the American Convention on Human Rights (ACHR) uses similar unequivocal language to prohibit the expulsion of an individual from the territory of the state of which they are a national. The same provision also dictates in strict language that no one shall be refused entry in the territory of the state of which they are a national. Article 22 ACHR also protects freedom of movement and residence albeit subject to limitations. Such is the significance attached to freedom of movement and residence that the American Court of Human Rights stressed that this 'is an essential condition for the free development of the person'.[101] The African Charter on Human and Peoples' Rights also recognises in Article 12 every individual's freedom of movement and residence while paragraph 2 recognises every individual's right to return to their country, a right that may only exceptionally be limited.

The right to return home is further safeguarded under Article 17 ICCPR and Article 8 ECHR, which provide for respect of the 'home'. With reference to Turkey's continuing policy of denying the right of the displaced persons in Cyprus to return to their homes and given effect through 'tight restrictions', denial of reoccupation of their homes and physical prevention 'from even visiting them' (let alone returning to them), the ECtHR held that such 'complete denial of the right of displaced persons to respect for their homes' was not justified under Article 8 ECHR.[102] Denial of the right to return is aggravated if this is based on discriminatory grounds, an issue, however, which the ECtHR has disappointingly refrained from touching on.[103]

The right of those forcibly displaced to return is also safeguarded under Article 1 Protocol 1 of the ECHR, which protects the peaceful enjoyment of possessions. In *Sargsyan v Azerbaijan*, it was held that the failure of the respondent

100 For detailed analysis, see Quigley, n19, 205 et seq.; Saideman, ibid, 848 and 863, citing Takkenberg.

101 *Case of Expelled Dominicans and Haitians v Dominican Republic*, IACtHR, Judgment, 28 August 2014 (Preliminary objections, merits, reparations and costs), [385].

102 *Cyprus v Turkey* (Application no. 25781/94) Judgment, 10 May 2001, [172]–[175].

103 See, for instance, ibid, [199].

state to allow the applicant to access his property and 'to restore his property rights or to provide him with compensation for his loss of their enjoyment' was a continuing breach of that provision.[104] The ECtHR also found that prevention of return violated both the right to home as well as the right to private life.[105] In *Dogan and others v Turkey*, the ECtHR referred to the Guiding Principles on Internal Displacement to stress that 'the authorities have the primary duty and responsibility to establish conditions, as well as provide the means, which allow the applicants to return voluntarily, in safety and with dignity, to their homes or places of habitual residence, or to resettle voluntarily in another part of the country.'[106] This case related to the forced eviction by Turkish security forces of the applicants, who were ethnic Kurds. The applicants complained that their forced eviction as well as their prevention from returning home amounted to a violation of Article 1 Protocol 1 and Article 8, a claim that the ECtHR accepted.[107] The ECtHR concluded that the measures taken by the respondent government for the return of the displaced were ineffective and inadequate.[108] Moreover, in its just satisfaction judgment on the same case the ECtHR concluded that allowing the return of the displaced applicants as well as compensation for the losses they suffered as a result of denial of access to their homes and lands were appropriate remedies that 'would put the applicants as far as possible in a situation equivalent to the one in which they would have been if there had not been a breach of Article 1 of Protocol No. 1 and Article 8 of the Convention.'[109]

The preceding analysis is far from exhaustive. It has, however, demonstrated that IHRL has several provisions that protect the right of those forcibly displaced to return home as well as to property restitution. The next section turns to examine whether the protection afforded to the displaced under both international human rights and humanitarian law is symbiotic, before continuing with further evidence of state practice and *opinio juris* in support of the existence of an independent individual right to return home and to property restitution as part of customary international law in Section 5.

4 The relationship between international humanitarian and international human rights law and the rights to return home and to property restitution

The previous two sections concentrated on how IHL and IHRL protect the rights to return home and to property restitution. While it was shown that human rights continue to apply in times of war, the relationship between IHL and IHRL

104 *Sargsyan v Azerbaijan* (Application no. 40167/06), (2015), [257].
105 Ibid.
106 *Doğan and others v Turkey* (Application nos 8803-8811/02, 8813/02 and 8815-8819/02), (2004), [154].
107 Ibid, [143] and [159].
108 Ibid, [154].
109 Ibid, [48].

continues to give rise to legal challenges. Some authors have argued for instance that the 'convergence' of these two bodies of international law undermines the protection afforded especially to those living under occupation.[110] Gross, in particular, notes that this convergence places the occupied on equal footing with the occupier, in disregard of the special protection the former enjoy under IHL.[111] In doing so, occupation becomes a dispute between individuals or between individuals and governments, hence, 'obscuring the occupation context and "privatising" political issues'.[112] Moreover, as the argument goes, the wide scope of restrictions allowed under international human rights law, as opposed to the narrow security interest required under international humanitarian law, may be used as a justification for curtailing the rights of the occupied in favour of the citizens of the occupying power.[113] Even more worryingly, if one accepts that protecting the security of settlers is a human rights issue then this is not but 'a typical dimension of "righting" the law of occupation' through convergence of IHL and IHRL, which, in effect, weakens the protection afforded to the occupied.[114] While IHL makes a clear distinction between the occupied and the occupying power, IHRL does not, in spite of the 'structural inequality between the status of the settlers and that of the protected persons.'[115] Another parameter that this convergence does not take into consideration is the scope of proportionality, which differs in IHL and IHRL. While under the former, proportionality is assessed in light of military necessity, in the latter, it is assessed in light of the legitimate aim to be pursued by the restriction of rights. Since, however, occupation creates an anomalous situation, proportionality cannot be assessed within human rights parameters.[116]

The dangers from converging IHL and IHRL can be illustrated in the context of the Israeli–Palestinian conflict, whereby Israel's High Court of Justice (HCJ), in relying on 'competing' human rights norms, justified restrictions imposed against Palestinians in the occupied Palestinian territories. More specifically, by equalising Palestinians' human rights with those of settlers, and by accepting security concerns as a valid ground for restricting human rights, the HCJ ignored aspects of the protections afforded under IHL concerning occupied territories.[117] In *Hass*, for instance, the HCJ balanced the settlers' freedom of movement and worship with the property rights of the Palestinians and gave prevalence to the rights of the settlers.[118] The case concerned a complaint against the destruction of Palestinian property for the purpose of widening the road that led to the Cave

110 Gross, n68, 1 and 2.
111 Ibid, 5.
112 Ibid, 7.
113 Ibid, 7 and 19.
114 Ibid, 8.
115 Ibid.
116 Ibid, 9 and 18.
117 Ibid, 10.
118 HCJ 10356/02, *Hass v Commander of the IDF Forces in the West Bank*, 58(3) PD 443.

of the Patriarchs. Such finding does not sit well with the Hague Regulations and IV GC, where the destruction of occupied property is only allowed if 'imperatively demanded by the necessities of war' or 'absolutely necessary by military operations'. Exercise of freedom of worship cannot be said to qualify as such reason.[119] As Gross rightly points out, 'this supposed balancing act is in fact an imbalance, since it places the burden of the settlers' security on the people living under occupation, conceptualises the need for balance between the rights involved as if they were the rights of equal parties, and allocates the rights to be balanced in a way that predetermines the results.'[120] The decision in *Hass* disregards the obligations that the occupying power has in relation to the occupied territory and its inhabitants, including the prohibition of settlements under Article 49 IV GC.[121] While, as Gross points out: 'Protecting human rights for all and the universality of human rights are noble and attractive goals . . . the price of attaining them is abstraction and imbalance rather than a balance of rights and, ultimately, a possibly unwarranted consequence.'[122] To this effect, one needs to be cautious since: 'The new framing of those conflicts in human rights terms may turn IHRL into the emperor's new clothes of the law of occupation.'[123]

Gross's word of caution is correct. Similar unjustified results were reached by the ECtHR in *Demopoulos*, whereby the Court, departing from its own case law and well-established principles of international law, responded to the applicants' claim concerning the properties occupied by settlers as follows:

> [I]t would be unrealistic to expect that . . . these applicants obtain access to, and full possession of, their properties, irrespective of who is now living there or whether the property is allegedly in a military sensitive zone or used for vital public purposes.[124]

Similarly, the HRC found Cyprus in violation of its obligations under Article 12 ICCPR for impeding all residents', including Turkish settlers', freedom of movement by preventing their crossing onto the free parts of the island.[125] By doing so, the HRC disregarded the question of whether settlers can be regarded as lawfully residing within the territory of Cyprus and put aside the applicable rules of IHL.

Nevertheless, these specific examples demonstrate not that the complementary existence of IHL and IHRL is problematic, but rather that their rules have been

119 Gross, n68, 16.
120 Ibid, 16.
121 Ibid, 18.
122 Ibid, 19.
123 Ibid, 26.
124 *Demopoulos and Others v Turkey*, n 15, [111]–[112]; also see critique in Katselli Proukaki, n48.
125 Concluding observations on the fourth periodic report of Cyprus, CCPR/C/CYP/CO/4, 30 April 2015, [17].

selectively misapplied by courts.[126] Indeed, the inter-active existence between these two fields of law has been described by Meron as 'the "humanisation" of international law'.[127] Such 'humanisation' must necessarily mean that the provisions entailed in each regime are interpreted in a harmonious manner for offering the strongest possible protection to the individual affected by conflict and occupation.[128] This is justified by the compelling significance of human rights both in war and in peace.[129] Having said this, IHRL cannot be seen in isolation of other rules of international law including IHL, state responsibility, international criminal law and even the law of armed conflict. Moreover, and while IHRL permits in certain instances the restriction of rights, such restrictions must still be regarded as exceptional measures and must be narrowly construed.[130] Importantly, when a conflict between the rights of those displaced or those living under occupation and the rights of settlers arises, the former should prevail. The earlier jurisprudence of the ECtHR as embodied, for instance, in *Loizidou* reflects the successful 'marriage' between IHL and IHRL[131] and how these two bodies of law can strengthen rather than undermine those in need of protection. That was well before the intrusion of *real politik* in the thinking and decision-making of the ECtHR.[132]

While it is necessary to interpret IHRL in accordance with IHL such as in situations of forced displacement discussed above, legal challenges arise when, in fact, the scope of protection afforded under IHL is weaker than that offered under IHRL. This becomes evident in the ICJ's Advisory Opinion on the *Legality of Use or Threat of Nuclear Weapons*, in which it concluded that the question of whether deprivation of life resulting from the use of nuclear weapons and in violation of human rights standards is arbitrary must be determined in the light of IHL as *lex specialis*.[133] Nevertheless in *Hassan*, the ECtHR took a different approach. The case concerned a complaint that the UK had violated Article 5 (1) ECHR protecting

126 Gross also concedes to this conclusion: Gross, n68, 25.

127 Meron T. (2000), 'The Humanisation of Humanitarian Law', *AJIL*, Vol. 94, 239. For the debate on the relationship between IHL and IHRL, also see Teitel R.G. (2001–2002), 'Humanity's Law: Rule of Law for the New Global Politics', *CILJ*, Vol. 35, 359; Doswald-Beck L. (2004), 'Human Rights and Humanitarian Law: Are there Some Individuals Bereft of all Legal Protection?', *ASILP*, Vol. 98, 353; Verdirame G. (2008), 'Human Rights in Wartime: A Framework for Analysis' *EHRLR*, Vol. 6, 689; Ben Naftali O., Shavy Y. (2003–2004), 'Living in Denial: The Application of Human Rights in the Occupied Territories', *ILR*, Vol. 37, 17.

128 Verdirame, ibid, 692.

129 See, e.g., Hannum, n77, 23 on interpreting human rights restrictions in the most favourable way to the individual. Also see conclusions of the Eritrea Ethiopia Claims Commission, Partial Award, Civilians Claims, Ethiopia's Claim No 5, 17 December 2004, [28], https://pcacases.com/web/sendAttach/756.

130 Hannum, ibid, 23.

131 *Loizidou v Turkey,* n58; Gross, n68, 30–31.

132 Katselli Proukaki, n48, 710.

133 Nuclear Weapons AO, n65, [25]; also see Gross, n68, 31.

the right to liberty by detaining the applicant's brother in Iraq on security grounds. Article 5 (1) protects individual liberty, save in specifically defined circumstances of lawful arrest and detention, none of which includes arrest or detention for security grounds during armed conflict. Hence the Court faced a dilemma: either to hold, as the UK argued, that it lacked jurisdiction to adjudicate a matter that is regulated by IHL, namely detention during armed conflict on grounds of security; or to assess the lawfulness of such detention in light of both IHRL and IHL. The Court proceeded on the position that the application of IHL did not deprive it of jurisdiction to consider the compliance of the respondent state with its ECHR obligations.[134] In determining, however, as to whether the UK had violated its Article 5 (1) obligations by detaining the individual concerned on grounds other than those expressly provided for in the relevant provision and in the absence of a derogation under Article 15 ECHR, the Court provided an interpretation which allowed it to 'adjust' Article 5 (1) in light of IHL. To this effect, rather than conceding to the position that IHL prevailed as *lex specialis* putting aside IHRL or that Article 5 (1) did provide for security detention in international armed conflict, it accepted that detention in such circumstances does not violate the ECHR. This was done in spite of the divergence of the scope of protections afforded under IHRL and IHL particularly in relation to international armed conflict and occupation in an effort to read the ECHR consistently with other rules of international law.[135] Although the ECtHR's judgment has been described as offering a 'symbiotic'[136] interpretation of the relevant rules of IHRL and IHL applicable to the case under consideration, its correctness is subject to debate. This is particularly because it 'watered down' the strict requirements of deprivation of liberty under Article 5 (1) ECHR, but importantly because of allowing states to introduce restrictions other than those expressly provided under the ECHR outside the context of derogations.[137] Insisting on states invoking the derogation regime provided under Article 15 ECHR would ensure not a free ride, but rather, it would subject the state to scrutiny over the justification relied on for such derogations.

While the application of IHL and IHRL by international law has been problematic rather than 'symbiotic', there is compelling need for a coherent and complementary application of both fields of law. This relates to the absence of international monitoring or judicial bodies to ensure compliance with IHL. This is because in the limited circumstances in which international mechanisms were set up to address violations of IHL, these were set up either through a mandatory Security Council resolution such as in the case of the UN Compensation Commission established following the Iraq war in the 1990s or a peace agreement

134 *Hassan v United Kingdom* (App no. 29750/09), 16 September 2014, [77].

135 Ibid, [104]; Borelli S. (2015), '*Jaloud v Netherlands* and *Hassan v United Kingdom*: Time for a Principled Approach in the Application of the ECHR to Military Action Abroad', *QIL*, Vol. 16, 25–43, 30.

136 Hill-Cawthorne L. (2014), 'The Grand Chamber Judgment in *Hassan v UK*', EJIL: Talk!, https://www.ejiltalk.org/the-grand-chamber-judgment-in-hassan-v-uk/.

137 Borelli, n135, 39.

such as the Eritrea Ethiopia Claims Commission.[138] The availability of such mechanisms is therefore quite restricted.[139] This gap is rectified, to some degree, by IHRL, which provides more opportunities for the individual to bring claims regarding violation of their rights, even those that occur as a result of conflict or military occupation.[140] It is therefore no surprise that the ECtHR has been flooded in recent years with individual applications concerning alleged violations that occurred during armed conflict. While one can be critical about the correctness of some of the decisions of international human rights bodies and courts such as in *Demopoulos* and *Meleagrou*, the alternative, namely the impossibility to bring a claim for violation of human rights resulting from conduct during armed conflict, is even more devastating. This bears tremendous legal significance, particularly for those victims of armed conflict, such as those forcibly uprooted from their homes and lands who still fight for justice and for their right to return home and to claim their property back. An international human rights body requested to look at violations of rights that result from conduct regulated under a different body of international law would not be overriding its legal mandate emanating from the treaty establishing it, but rather, it would be interpreting such treaty in the light of other relevant international legal instruments.[141]

Relatedly, in determining whether the rights of the displaced have been violated, particularly their freedom of movement, their right to return home and their right to peaceful enjoyment of possessions under the ICCPR and the ECHR, it will be necessary for the relevant international human rights bodies to take into consideration relevant rules of IHL including Article 49 IV GC. Setting aside or disregarding such other relevant rules risks, the fragmentation of the international legal system and, quite significantly, creates a legal void and deepens the injustice towards those forcibly displaced. While acknowledging the differences between these two bodies of law and the advantages and disadvantages of each one of them is necessary, the harmonious application of their rules with the aim to secure the strongest protection to victims of armed conflict is a goal that needs to be pursued.[142]

Having discussed some of the conceptual difficulties arising from the existence of parallel legal regimes, the next section turns to state practice and *opinio juris* to determine whether international customary law recognises the rights to return and to property restitution.

138 Zegveld L. (2003), 'Remedies for Victims of Violations of International Humanitarian Law', *IRRC*, Vol. 85, No. 851, 521. Also see UNSC Resolution 687 (1991) 8 April 1991, [6]; Article 5, Agreement between Eritrea and Ethiopia to be signed in Algier and the Government of the Federal Democratic Republic of Ethiopia (Algiers Peace Agreement), 2000.

139 Zegveld, ibid, 523.

140 Verdirame, n127, 691.

141 *Bamaca Velasquez v Guatemala*, IACtHR, Judgment, 25 November 2000; Zegveld, n138, 516–518.

142 In support of such conclusion, see Verdirame, n127, 705.

5 The rights to return home and to property restitution under international customary law

The analysis that follows builds on further evidence from state practice and *opinio juris* concerning the rights of those forcibly displaced to return home and to claim their property back. While some of this evidence focuses on property and subsequently the right to property restitution, other evidence focuses on the right to return. Nevertheless, both rights are closely connected in the sense that the restitution of property cannot be achieved without return, while return often cannot be given effect without such restitution.

To begin with, a brief reference to some early examples in support of the rights under consideration in this chapter is useful. The significance of property can be traced for instance in Article 33 of the Treaty of Lausanne signed by Turkey following the territorial and population re-arrangements that took place at the end of WWI. Despite the criticism it has attracted as discussed in the previous chapter, Article 33 of the Treaty provides that those who transferred their place of residence elsewhere in accordance with the treaty 'will be entitled to retain their immovable property in the territory of the other State where they had their place of residence before exercising their right to opt'.[143] Article 65 unequivocally requires the restoration of the 'property, rights and interests which still exist' to their legitimate owners, extending the application of this provision both to property in territory which remained under Turkish control as well as property in territory controlled by the Allies. Significantly, under Article 66, the right of the legitimate owner to property restoration/restitution prevails over third party claims over such property. It is, however, quite oxymoronic that the Treaty protects property but at the same time it encompasses the (forced) population exchanges imposed after WWI, which deprived communities of their right to remain or to return home. Even so, and in clear contravention of the terms of the Lausanne Treaty, Turkey, through legislation, confiscated as 'abandoned' property left by Armenians when they were forced out of Turkey in 1921–22.[144] Diplomatic efforts focused on the award of compensation, which, however, was met with resistance as such compensation would prevent the return of those who were forced to leave their homes.[145] Indeed, under the Ankara Convention of 27 October 1932 only a very small percentage of Armenians were able to claim their property.[146] The similarities of this practice with Turkey's legislative policies in the northern part of Cyprus with which it has taken the property of forcibly displaced Greek Cypriots are striking.

143 Treaty of Peace with Turkey signed at Lausanne, July 24, 1923.

144 Tachjian V., Theriault H. (2014), 'An Attempt to Recover Armenian Properties in Turkey through the French Authorities in Syria and Lebanon in the 1920s', *ICLR*, Vol. 14, No. 2, 343–357, 344.

145 Ibid, 349–350.

146 Ibid, 353–355.

Another relevant agreement concluded after WWII is the Convention on the Settlement of Matters Arising out of the War and the Occupation between the United Kingdom of Great Britain and Northern Ireland, France, the United States of America and the Federal Republic of Germany,[147] which in Chapter III provided for the restitution of property of Nazi victims as well as the establishment of a Supreme Restitution Court.

The continuing plight of Palestinians for statehood and their right to return home offers another example of how compliance with international law is far from materialising. Since 1948 Palestinians have endured uprooting through bombings, intimidation, expulsions, destruction of property and other restrictive measures on their fundamental rights and freedoms.[148] Israel's position has been and continues to be that the massive exodus of Palestinians was not coerced or that such displacement is necessary for protecting its vital security interests as well as for accommodating Jewish immigrants.[149] The fate of the displaced gained, although unsuccessfully, prominence from the beginning of the Israeli–Palestinian conflict. As pointed out:

> [N]o settlement can be just and complete if recognition is not accorded to the right of the Arab refugee to return to the home. . . . It would be an offence against the principles of elemental justice if these innocent victims of the conflict were denied the right to return to their homes while Jewish immigrants flow into Palestine, and, indeed, at least offer the threat of permanent replacement of the Arab refugees who have been rooted in the land for centuries.[150]

Moreover, General Assembly Resolution 181 (II) 1947, which was adopted following the partition of Palestine, prohibited the expropriation of property.[151] The Palestinians' right to return was affirmed in UN General Assembly (UNGA) Resolution 194, according to which 'refugees wishing to return to their homes and live at peace with their neighbours should be permitted to do so at the earliest practicable date, and that compensation should be paid for the property of those

147 Bonn, May 26, 1952, http://treaties.fco.gov.uk/docs/fullnames/pdf/1959/TS0013%20(1959)%20CMND-656%201952%2026%20MAY,BONN%3BCONVENTION%20ON%20SETTLEMENT%20OF%20MATTERS%20ARISING%20OUT%20OF%20WAR&THE%20OCCUPATION%20BETWEEN%20NI,FRANCE,USA&FEDERAL%20REPUBLIC%20OF%20GERMANY_1.pdf?.

148 Report of the independent international factfinding mission to investigate the implications of the Israeli settlements on the civil, political, economic, social and cultural rights of the Palestinian people throughout the Occupied Palestinian Territory, including East Jerusalem, A/HRC/22/63, 7 February 2013.

149 Quigley, n19, 184.

150 Progress Report of the United Nations Mediator on Palestine, U.N. GAOR, Supplement No. 11, A/648 (1948), 14.

151 UNGA Resolution 181 (II) (1947), 137.

choosing not to return and for loss of or damage to property which, under principles of international law or in equity, should be made good by the Governments or authorities responsible.'[152] Contrary to some authors' view that Resolution 194 did not affirm a right to return,[153] the resolution did ascertain both the right to return home and the right to remain in one's land.[154] While UNGA resolutions are not legally binding per se, they provide evidence of state practice and *opinio juris* in support of the existence of a customary norm. To this effect, it is particularly important that the *inalienable* right of Palestinians to return home was re-affirmed in numerous subsequent GA resolutions,[155] as well as by other bodies such as UN Secretary General Thant[156] and the UN Commission on Human Rights.[157] The UN Committee on the Exercise of the Inalienable Rights of the Palestinian People further stressed that the right to return 'should be absolute for every Palestinian and must have priority over any other form of substitute arrangements, such as compensation'.[158]

The principles of return and restitution are also embedded in the PCIJ's findings in the *Chorzow Factory case*. According to these reparation 'must, as far as possible, wipe out all the consequences of the illegal act and reestablish the situation which would, in all probability, have existed if that act had not been committed', placing restitution in kind as the primary form of reparation. [159]

Applying this principle in the *Wall case*, the ICJ held that 'Israel is accordingly under an obligation to return the land, orchards, olive groves and other immovable property seized from any natural or legal person for purposes of construction of the wall in the Occupied Palestinian Territory.' Israel's obligation to offer compensation comes only 'in the event that such restitution should prove to be materially impossible'.[160]

The rights to property restitution and to return have been affirmed not only in the context of the Palestinian–Israeli conflict but also in several other situations and by several international bodies. They have been, for instance, affirmed in relation to those forcibly displaced in Cyprus,[161] in Sudan[162] and in

152 UNGA Res. 194, U.N. GAOR, 3d Sess., 11, U.N. Doc. A/810 (1948), [11].
153 Lapidoth, n17, 116; Saideman, n74, 836.
154 Quigley, n19, 193.
155 See, for instance, UNGA Resolution A/Res/3236(XXIX) (1974).
156 Introduction to the Annual Report of the Secretary-General on the Work of the Organization, U.N. GAOR, Supplement No. 1A, A/6701/Add.1 (1967) 7.
157 Commission on Human Rights, Report on the 43rd session, Resolution 1987/4, E/1987/18 (1987).
158 Report of the Committee on the Exercise of the Inalienable Rights of the Palestinian People U.N. SCOR, U.N. Doc. S/12090 (1976) 8.
159 *Case Concerning the Factory at Chorzow (Claim for Indemnity)* (Merits), Judgment No 13, 1928, PCIJ, Series A, No. 17, 47.
160 Wall AO, n66, [153].
161 See, for example, UNGA Res. 37/253, U.N. GAOR, Supplement No. 51, U.N. Doc. A/37/51 (1983) 48; S/RES/365 (1974).
162 UNGA Resolution 55/116, A/Res/55/116 (Sudan).

Namibia.[163] They have also been affirmed by the UN Security Council (UNSC) in several resolutions. While UNSC Resolutions 361 (Cyprus), 726 (Palestine/Israel), 779 (Croatia),[164] 820 (Bosnia–Herzegovina), 874 (Azerbaijan/Armenia),[165] 896, 906,[166] 993[167] and 1036 (Georgia),[168] 999 (Tajikistan)[169] and 1078 (Great Lakes)[170] have not been adopted under Chapter VII of the UN Charter, they all encompass/urge/request/endorse/reaffirm/recognise/reiterate/call/demand the speedy and voluntary return of those displaced. Despite the varied language used in each of these resolutions, the voluntary return of the displaced holds a significant place. In addition to this, UNSC Resolutions 859 (Bosnia and Herzegovina)[171] and 947 (Croatia) were adopted under Chapter VII and affirmed the right to voluntary return of those displaced. While it has been argued that these resolutions do not create customary law and are only binding in relation to the specific situations for which they were adopted,[172] as Quigley rightly points out, these resolutions refer to return in accordance with international law, implying that return is, in fact, required by international law.[173] Moreover, UNSC resolutions can, in fact, be relied on as providing evidence for the existence of state practice and *opinio juris* in support of a rule of customary international law as is the case in this instance with regards to the right of those forcibly displaced to return home.[174] It has also been argued that the UNSC's omission to affirm the right of Palestinians to return[175] reflects lack of state practice and *opinio juris* in support of such rights. However, such omission is rather a reminder of the politicised and often double standard policy followed by the UNSC rather than a denial of the right of return. Furthermore, according to Quigley, the UNSC has not differentiated between internal or international wars, or between those expelled and those otherwise displaced, corroborating the view that: 'Anyone displaced as a result of hostilities would seem to enjoy a right to return.'[176]

The HRC has also called for the resettlement and the sustainable return of those displaced in Bosnia and Herzegovina following the conflict in the country between 1992 and 1995.[177] The HRC also expressed concern over the extent of

163 S/RES/385 (1976).
164 S/Res/779 (1992).
165 S/Res/874 (1993).
166 S/Res/906 (1994); S/Res/896 (1994).
167 S/Res 993 (1995).
168 S/Res/1036 (1996).
169 S/Res/999 (1995).
170 S/Res/1078 (1996).
171 S/Res/859 (1993).
172 Saideman, n74, 845.
173 Quigley, n19, 215.
174 In support of the argument that these resolutions reveal state practice and *opinio juris* in support of a right to return home, see ibid.
175 Saideman, n74, 845.
176 Quigley, n19, 216.
177 Concluding observations on the second periodic report of Bosnia and Herzegovina, adopted by the Committee at its 106th session (15 October–2 November) 2012, CCPR/C/BIH/

displacement in Colombia and requested the state to set up mechanisms that will enable the restitution of land.[178] Following the HRC's recommendation, Colombia has returned and relocated 44,000 families in light of legislation that guarantees the right of those forcibly displaced to return or to relocate if they so desire. Article 22 Law 387 of 1997 (Colombia) for instance provides that one of the objectives of the National Fund for the Comprehensive Assistance of the Population Displaced by Violence is return. Land restitution is also safeguarded under Act No. 1448 of 2014, which applies to those who owned or possessed land but were forced into uprooting. Significantly, the Colombian Constitutional Court held that the state has an obligation not to prevent the displaced from voluntarily returning to their habitual place of residence, which constitutes a protected right under the Charter of Basic Rights developed by law.[179]

Several other international bodies have also ascertained the right to return. The UN Sub-Commission on Prevention of Discrimination and Protection of Minorities relied on Article 12 (4) ICCPR to stress that 'practices of forcible exile, mass expulsions and deportations, population transfer, "ethnic cleansing" and other forms of forcible displacement of populations within a country or across borders deprive the affected populations of their right to freedom of movement.'[180] The Committee on the Elimination of Racial Discrimination, condemning the displacement of Bosnian Muslims by Serbs and the attempts to change the demographic composition of specific areas demanded the return of those displaced 'to the places they inhabited before the beginning of the conflict.'[181] Indeed, refusal to allow an individual to return to their country on grounds of race, colour, nationality or ethnicity are prohibited under the International Convention on the Elimination of All Forms of Racial Discrimination.[182] The Convention has 177 states parties and provides further support to the argument that there exists a customary rule recognising the right to return.[183]

CO/2, [16]; Consideration of reports submitted by States Parties under Article 40 of the Covenant, Concluding observations of HRC, Bosnia and Herzegovina, 22 November 2006, CCPR/C/BIH/CO/1, [20].

178 Consideration of reports submitted by states parties under Article 40 of the Covenant, Concluding observations of HRC, Colombia, CCPR/C/COL/CO/6, 4 August 2010, [23].

179 Colombian Constitutional Court, Decision T-025 of 2004, 58 and 64; Consideration of reports submitted by States Parties under Article 40 of the Covenant, Seventh periodic reports of States parties due in 2014, Colombia, CCPR/C/COL/7, 7 April 2015, [110]–[111].

180 UN Subcommission on Prevention of Discrimination and Protection of Minorities, Res. 1995/13, U.N. ESCOR, 50th Sess., 20, U.N. Doc. EICN.4Sub.2119951L.11Add.3 (1995); also see Quigley, n19, 213.

181 Report of the Committee on the Elimination of Racial Discrimination, U.N. GAOR, 50th Sess., Supp. No. 18, 219, U.N. Doc. A/50/18 (1995) 26; also see Quigley, ibid, 214.

182 660 *UNTS* 195.

183 Information acquired from the Office of the High Commissioner for Human Rights, http://indicators.ohchr.org/; also see Ullom, n7, 122.

The Parliamentary Assembly of the Council of Europe, drawing on the close co-relation between return and property restitution condemned any measures such as property destruction that breached the rights of the dispossessed and made reconciliation and peace-building more difficult. To this effect, the Parliamentary Assembly highlighted property restitution as essential for the restoration of the rights of the displaced and the rule of law and as 'the optimal response to the loss of access and rights to housing, land and property', since it facilitates return to one's home.[184] With reference to the Pinheiro Principles, among others, the Parliamentary Assembly stressed the need to restore 'safe physical access to, and possession of, such property', calling for compensation only where restitution was impossible.[185] In another resolution concerning displacement in Armenia, Azerbaijan and Georgia, the Parliamentary Assembly called for prioritising the return of the displaced 'even before an overall settlement'.[186] A similar call to allow and speed up return was made in relation to displaced Kurds in Turkey.[187] Furthermore, the Committee of Ministers of the Council of Europe emphasised that internally displaced persons 'have the right to repossess their property' and that compensation should only be preferred in circumstances of deprivation of property.[188] The right to return was further incorporated in the Basic Principles for a peaceful settlement of the Nagorno-Karabakh conflict adopted by the Organisation on the Security and Cooperation in Europe.[189] At the same time, the EU, through its institutions, has also affirmed the right to return. As noted: 'The European Commission and its partner organisations, in particular UNHCR, have an important role in advocating for and enabling durable solutions for refugees and IDPs, especially with regard to fulfilling the right of return to their countries of origin or habitual residence.'[190]

There are also a number of international agreements that ascertain freedom of movement as well as more explicitly the right to return, such as the Agreement on the Resolution of the Conflict in the Republic of South Sudan, which prohibits restriction of movement, safeguards the right of refugees and internally displaced to return, and sets up a Hybrid Court empowered, among other things, to order

184 'Solving property issues of refugees and displaced persons', Parliamentary Assembly Resolution 1708 (2010), [4].

185 Ibid, [10.2]; also see *Sargsyan v Azerbaijan*, n104, [98].

186 'Refugees and displaced persons in Armenia, Azerbaijan and Georgia', Parliamentary Assembly Resolution 1497 (2006), [12.4].

187 'Humanitarian situation of the displaced Kurdish population in Turkey', Parliamentary Assembly of the Council of Europe, Recommendation 1563 (2002), 29 May 2002.

188 Recommendation of the Committee of Ministers to member states on internally displaced persons, Rec (2006)6 100 also quoted in *Sargsyan v Azerbaijan*, n104, [100].

189 Basic principles for a peaceful settlement of the Nagorno-Karabakh conflict, Madrid, 29 November 2007, http://www.deutscharmenischegesellschaft.de/wp-content/uploads/2016/04/Madrid-Principles-%E2%80%93-Full-Text-20071129.pdf.

190 European Commission, 'Forced Displacement – Refugees and Internally Displaced People', ECHO Fact Sheet, June 2016, http://ec.europa.eu/echo/files/aid/countries/factsheets/thematic/refugees_en.pdf.

the return of property acquired unlawfully to their legitimate owner;[191] and the Comprehensive Agreement between the Republic of the Philippines and the National Democratic Front of the Philippines.[192] Moreover, the Rampouillet Accords recognise freedom of movement of all persons in Kosovo, the right of all persons to return home and the right 'to reoccupy their real property, assert their occupancy rights in state-owned property and recover their other property and personal possessions'.[193] Moreover, the Accords provide that the international community will provide assistance for the return of the displaced to their former homes, indicating the significance of the right to return home and to property restitution.[194] Recognising the significance of return for the settlement of the conflict in Bosnia and Herzegovina, Article 1 of the 1995 Dayton Peace Agreement provides for the right of all refugees and displaced persons for voluntary return to their homes of origin.[195] Moreover, the Agreement on Refugees and Displaced Persons annexed to the Dayton Peace Agreement safeguards the right to property restoration and, where such restoration is not possible, the right to compensation. Under this agreement, an independent Commission for Real Property Claims of Displaced Persons and Refugees was set up with the purpose of determining property claims in Bosnia and Herzegovina relating to property abandoned as a result of the conflict. A similar Commission was set up to deal with property claims in Kosovo. While problems persist with the implementation of the obligations under agreements relating to the rights of those displaced in the former Yugoslavia, as evident, for instance, from the legislative time restrictions imposed by Croatia

191 Addis Ababa, 17 August 2015, Chapter II, Article 1.7. 1, Chapter III, Article 1.1 and Chapter V Article 2.2 respectively; and Ceasefire Agreement between the Government of Sudan and the Justice and Equality Movement-Sudan, 10 February 2013, http://peacemaker.un.org/sites/peacemaker.un.org/files/SD_130210_ CeasefireGoSJEMSudan.pdf; Agreement between the Government of the Republic of Sudan and the Sudan People's Liberation Movement on Temporary Arrangements for the Administration and Security of the Abyei Area, 20 June 2011, http://peacemaker.un.org/sites/peacemaker.un.org/files/SD_110620_AgreementTemporary ArrangementsAbyeiArea.pdf. Also see 'The Roadmap for Return of IDPs and Implementation of Abyei Protocol', 8 June 2008, http://peacemaker.un.org/sites/peacemaker.un.org/files/ SD_080608_Roadmap%20for%20Return%20of%20IDPs%20and%20Implementation%20of%20Abyei%20Protocol.pdf.

192 Comprehensive Agreement on Respect for Human Rights and International Humanitarian Law between the Government of the Republic of the Philippines and the National Democratic Front of the Philippines, Article 2 (14), http://peacemaker.un.org/sites/peacemaker.un.org/files/PH_980316_Comprehensive%20Agreement% 20on%20Respect%20for%20Human%20Rights.pdf.

193 Chapter 1, Article II (3), Chapter 2, Article I, Interim Agreement for Peace and Self-government in Kosovo, S/1999/648, 7 June 1999, http://peacemaker.un.org/sites/peacemaker.un.org/files/990123_ RambouilletAccord.pdf.

194 Chapter 4 A [3], Interim Agreement for Peace and Self-government in Kosovo, S/1999/648, 7 June 1999, http://peacemaker.un.org/sites/peacemaker.un.org/files/990123_RambouilletAccord.pdf.

195 Dayton Peace Agreement, Annex 7, Article 1 (1995).

for the return of those displaced,[196] these agreements constitute examples of state practice and *opinio juris* in support of the right to property restitution and to return home.[197]

The speedy return of the displaced 'to their original environments' is recognised as a necessity in Article 6 of the Peace Agreement of the Democratic Republic of the Congo and Le Congres National pour la Defense du Peuple.[198] Article 8 of the Agreement on Cessation of Hostilities between Eritrea and Ethiopia endorsed by the Organisation of African Unity and the UN also provides for the return of the population.[199] Return of the displaced was also provided in Article 59 of the Panmunjom Armistice Agreement.[200]

In addition to these situation-specific agreements, there exist other international agreements that recognise the rights of those displaced concerning movement, residence, return and restitution. The Protocol on the Protection and Assistance to Internally Displaced Persons provides for respect of freedom of movement and choice of residence and that any restrictions are necessary, justified and proportionate for protecting public order, health and security.[201] The OAU Convention Governing the Specific Aspects of Refugee Problems in Africa recognises the right of voluntary repatriation of refugees.[202]

The 2006 Pact on Security, Stability and Development in the Great Lakes Region signed by 11 of the Great Lakes Region states establishes in Article 12 the duty to protect and assist IDPs especially by adopting the UN Guiding Principles on Internal Displacement, which, in turn, provide for the right not to be displaced and the right to return home. In addition to this, the Pact provides in Article 13 that the member states undertake to legally protect the property of refugees and IDPs in their countries of origin and to ensure recovering of such property on their return and to set up legal mechanisms for the resolution of disputes regarding such property. The Pact places emphasis on the rights of the legitimate owners.[203] The property rights of the displaced persons is further recognised in the Protocol on the Property Rights of Returning Persons.[204] The Protocol, by reference to the Pinheiro Principles, protects property from pillage and destruction during armed

196 ICRC Study, n32.

197 Helton, n14, 1349.

198 23 March 2009, http://peacemaker.un.org/sites/peacemaker.un.org/files/CD_090323_Peace%20Agreement% 20between%20the%20Government%20and%20the%20CNDP.pdf.

199 Agreement on Cessation of Hostilities between the Government of the Federal Democratic Republic of Ethiopia and the Government of the State of Eritrea, 18 June 2000, Volume 2138, I-37273.

200 The Korean War Armistice Agreement, Panmunjom, Korea, 27 July 1953, http://www.usfk.mil/Portals/ 105/Documents/SOFA/G_Armistice_Agreement.pdf.

201 30 November 2006, http://www.refworld.org/pdfid/52384fe44.pdf.

202 Adopted 10 September 1969, *UNTS* No. 14691, Article V.

203 14 and 15 December 2006, http://peacemaker.un.org/sites/peacemaker.un.org/files/061215_ PactonSecurityStabilityDevelopmentGreatLakes.pdf.

204 30 November 2006, https://www.icglr.org/images/Pact%20ICGLR%20Amended%2020122.pdf.

conflict as well as from illegal and arbitrary appropriation, use or occupation. It also imposes an obligation on member states to assist those displaced to recover the property they had to abandon and receive compensation if recovery is not possible. The emphasis here is again on restitution rather than compensation. Member states are only exceptionally allowed to expropriate the property of the displaced in compelling and overwhelming circumstances justified by general interest and only under procedures prescribed by law.[205]

Significantly, Article 9 of the Kampala Convention, while guaranteeing the right of individuals to seek safety and the voluntariness of any return, safeguards the right of internally displaced persons to movement and residence subject to necessary, justified and proportionate restrictions for the safety of those displaced or public security, public order and public health. Article 9 also imposes an obligation on the state parties to protect the property of those displaced while Article 11 imposes an obligation on state parties to enable voluntary return, to set up appropriate mechanisms for the resolution of property disputes and to restore, to the extent that this is possible, 'lands of communities with special dependency and attachment to such lands upon the communities' return, reintegration, and reinsertion'.[206] Article 12 also stipulates the obligation of state parties to provide effective remedies such as compensation and reparations for damage they have incurred as a result of their displacement.

The right of return has also been affirmed in various declarations, which, albeit non-legally binding, contribute to state practice and *opinio juris* in support of the existence of a customary rule relating to the right to return. Article VI of the Bangkok Principles on the Status and Treatment of Refugees makes express reference to the right of refugees and their dependents to voluntarily return irrespective of whether displacement from the habitual place of residence was caused by foreign domination, external aggression or occupation.[207] This is, indeed, very important since the 'natural', as stipulated in the Principles, right to return as indeed property restitution must be fulfilled by governments or authorities in control of the places of habitual residence. The Nairobi Declaration on the Effective Implementation and Operationalization of the Protocol on Property Rights of Returning Persons in the Great Lakes Region recognises the strong linkage between property or land repossession with the right to return home.[208] The Declaration and Concerted Plan of Action in Favour of Central American Refugees, Returnees and Displaced Persons safeguards the voluntary return of the displaced

205 Adopted by the International Conference on the Great Lakes Region, 30 November 2006, https://www.icglr.org/images/Pact%20ICGLR%20Amended%2020122.pdf.

206 African Union Convention for the Protection and Assistance of Internally Displaced Persons in Africa, 23 October 2009.

207 Bangkok Principles on the Status and Treatment of Refugees, 31 December 1966 (adopted by the Asia-African Legal Consultative Committee).

208 23 April 2015, http://icglr.org/images/Declaration-Ministers%20in%20charge%20of%20 lands% 20issues%20April%202015.pdf.

persons.[209] That the right to return to one's country is not subject to fees, taxes or visa requirements is safeguarded under Article 11 of the Declaration on the Right to Leave and the Right to Return[210] and under Article 6 (c) of the Strasbourg Declaration on the Right to Leave and Return[211] respectively. Finally, the right of refugees to return was included in the 2000 Declaration between Bosnian Serbs and Croats.[212]

The right to return has also been recognised by the African Commission on Human and People's Rights. According to the Commission, because freedom of movement and residence is a fundamental right, states have a duty to take all necessary measures to prevent displacement.[213] The ECtHR itself has said that 'the right of displaced persons to return voluntarily and in safety to their homes or places of habitual residence as soon as the reasons for their displacement cease to exist, [which] is regarded as a rule of customary international humanitarian law applying to all territory whether "occupied" or "own".'[214]

The ICRC Study also concludes that the right to return forms part of customary law. It draws evidence from military manuals, official statements, national legislation and international agreements.[215]

Nevertheless, and while the right to property restitution is entailed in Principle 2 of the Pinheiro Principles, which prevails over the right to compensation as 'a key element of restorative justice' and as 'a distinct right', as well as under Principle 29 (2) of the Guiding Principles on Internal Displacement, these remain non-legally binding instruments.[216] With particular reference to the latter, Phuong, writing in 2005 concluded that:

> It may still be too early today to conclude that a right to restitution of property lost as a result of displacement or compensation for such a loss has been firmly established in international law. Nevertheless, the Guiding Principles may contribute to the development of the law in the area, and increasing international attention is now being paid to the issue of housing and property restitution in the context of the return of refugees and internally displaced persons.[217]

209 CIREFCA 89/13/Rev.1, 30 May 1989.

210 Adopted by the Uppsala Colloquium, Uppsala, Sweden 21 June 1972.

211 Adopted on 26 November 1986.

212 'State Setting of the Present-day Bosnia-Herzegovina', Information Bulletin, Center for Constitutional Studies and Democratic Development.

213 *Sudan Human Rights Organisation and Centre on Housing Rights and Evictions (COHRE) v Sudan*, Communication No. 279/03–296/05 (27 May 2009) [187]–[189].

214 *Sargsyan v Azerbaijan*, n104, [232]. In support of the customary character of such rights, see Henckaerts J.M., Doswald-Beck L. (2005), *Customary International Humanitarian Law*, (ICRC/Cambridge University Press).

215 ICRC Study, n32.

216 Phuong, n10, 61–62.

217 Ibid, 64–65. Also see Land and Human Rights, n36, 4.

Nevertheless, it is evident from the analysis above that the Guiding Principles on Internal Displacement and the Pinheiro Principles have exerted significant influence in the development of legally binding treaties protecting individuals from displacement and safeguarding the right to return and to property restitution,[218] as well as in international jurisprudence.[219]

Moreover, the Special Rapporteur on the human rights of internally displaced persons has recently stressed the need for property restitution but also voluntary return as means for addressing the difficulties arising from internal displacement.[220]

The wealth of voluntary repatriation programmes also demonstrates that the right to return to one's country holds great significance in international law. Repatriation programmes have taken place in the context of Ethiopia, Guinea and Uganda,[221] as well as in Afghanistan, Cambodia, Mozambique, Namibia, Nicaragua, Salvador and Guatemala.[222] The UN has also facilitated the return of the displaced in conditions of safety such as the return of 6000 displaced persons in Mutarule, Democratic Republic of Congo.[223] As pointed out: 'While UN bodies have not always made it clear whether they acted on the basis of human rights law or humanitarian law, language in UN documents indicates that the nations based their calls for return on the understanding of an international legal obligation to repatriate.'[224]

Restitution of the *status quo ante* concerning housing and land from which a community was forcibly evicted was considered as the proper remedy by the Kenyan High Court in *Ibrahim Sangor Osman and Others v the Hon. Minister of State for Provincial Administration & Internal Security and Others*.[225]

The analysis in this section has brought together a wide range of sources and materials in support of the main argument supported in this chapter that, indeed, there exists a customary rule of international law that protects the individual rights to return home and to property restitution, particularly in situations in which forced displacement is the product of armed conflict.[226] Nevertheless, some authors have disputed the legal value of such evidence, arguing for instance that only states affected by refugee problems can contribute through state practice and *opinio juris*

218 For example, Pact on Security, Stability and Development in the Great Lakes Region signed by 11 of the Great Lakes Region states; Kampala Convention.

219 For example, *Chiragov and others v Armenia* (Application no. 13216/05) (2015); *Saghinadze and others v Georgia* (Application no. 18768/05) (2010).

220 Mandate of the Special Rapporteur on the human rights of internally displaced persons, 32/11, A/71/53, [6] and [7], adopted 1 July 2016 at 43rd meeting without a vote.

221 Report of UNHCR to the Economic and Social Council, UN Doc.E/1985/62 (1985) 16–18. Also see Hannum, n77, 110.1

222 Helton, n14, 1335–1336.

223 'Mutarule's Displaced Start Returning Home', 20 August 2015, https://monusco.unmissions.org/en/ mutarule%E2%80%99s-displaced-starts-returning-home.

224 Ullom, n7, 122 quoting Quigley.

225 Constitutional Petition No. 2 of 2011 (16 November 2011); 'Land and Human Rights: Standards and Applications', n36, 30.

226 For a thorough analysis of state practice and opinion juris on this matter, see Ullom, n7, 115; Quigley, n19,185–186.

to the development of customary rules. This is the case, for instance, in relation to the principle of equidistance according to which only coastal states can contribute to its development.[227] However, this argument is not convincing. Even if a state is not affected by a situation at the time of the development of a customary rule this does not preclude the possibility of being affected by such situation in the future. A land-locked state, for instance, may become a coastal state through merger with another state. Yet, there is even a stronger case to be made in support of every state's interest in developing rules concerning forced displacement. As the waves of refugees currently flooding Europe and other parts of the world show, the problems associated with internal or external forced displacement affect every state in the international community as well as international peace and security. Hence, every state has a legal interest not only in the prohibition of such displacement, as argued in the previous chapter, but also in countering the effects of such displacement through return and restitution. Significantly, states develop international legal standards which consider necessary for the regulation of inter-state affairs and the promotion of specific individual or community interests irrespective of whether those states are specially affected by a certain situation. To this effect, the customary rules on the prohibition of armed force, torture or genocide have emerged through state practice and *opinio juris* of states without a distinction being made as to which state was affected by such practice. By developing these legal standards states have accepted that they are also bound by them.[228]

Neither does the argument that, in some instances, the return of the displaced was forced through military action or sanctions and therefore do not count as state practice and *opinio juris* stand merit.[229] Such was, for instance, the US bombing campaign against Kosovo, which was justified on coercing the return of the displaced.[230] Setting aside the lawfulness or unlawfulness of such action, such practice lends support to the argument that the right to return is a customary rule of international law. How such rule is given effect is a different matter of legal analysis, which differs from the position advanced in the previous section that the unlawfulness of a situation should influence the determination of whether a derogation or a restriction to such rights is justified or not.

In light of the preceding analysis, it is submitted that customary international law recognises the right to return home and to property restitution failure to comply with engages the international responsibility of the wrongdoing state.[231] In fact, it has been shown that there is sufficient practice that is continuous and consistent, general and repetitive even if it is not uniform[232] and even if some states

227 Saideman, n74, 843 quoting Radley; Ullom, n7, 127.
228 On the distinction between other states' duty to repatriate their nationals, see Ullom, ibid, 126.
229 Saideman, n74, 844.
230 Saideman, ibid, 844.
231 Ullom, n7, 117–118.
232 *Asylum Case (Colombia v Peru)* Judgment 20 November 1950, ICJ Reports (1950) 266, 277; *North Sea Continental Shelf cases (Federal Republic of Germany v Denmark and the*

continue to deny these rights. As in the ICJ judgment in the *Nicaragua case*, such conduct must be treated as violation of the existing rules. It is, however, necessary that state practice is also accompanied by the required belief that return and property restitution are required by law or are becoming law.[233] As the analysis in this chapter demonstrates, the psychological element is based on numerous legally binding as well as other instruments/sources that lend support to the argument that, in fact, today, the rights to return home and to property restitution are recognised as international customary norms.

The significance of the argument advanced in this chapter that international law recognises the rights of the displaced to return home and to property restitution lies in the legal ramifications that this entails and, more specifically, in the restriction of the powers of the state. In this respect, states are no longer able to authorise through agreements forcible population transfers such as those carried out after WWI and WWII since, according to Quigley, the right to return is a peremptory norm of international law.[234] Neither is such return conditional on a final settlement or a peace agreement between the disputing parties.[235]

6 Conclusion

To say that forced displacement has detrimental impact on the lives of those affected by it, whatever the circumstances that caused it, is an understatement. This is because displacement severs the ties an individual has with their home, land and property and interferes with the right to life, the right not to be subjected to inhuman or degrading treatment or punishment, the right to private and family life, the peaceful enjoyment of possessions, freedom of movement and residence, the right to remain and the right to return to one's country and the right to self-determination. This does not include the numerous economic and social rights that are significantly compromised/denied as a result of forcible uprooting exposing the victims of such displacement to poverty and other violations. While some may be fortunate enough, after overcoming a mountain of obstacles, to re-build their lives for them and their families elsewhere, the majority of victims endure continuing devastating effects for generations to come as a result of their uprooting, especially when this is caused by conflict and human rights violations. For all, however, their forced

Netherlands), ICJ Reports (1969) 3, [74]; *Case Concerning Military and Paramilitary Activities in and against Nicaragua (Nicaragua v United States of America)*, Merits, Judgment 27 June 1986, ICJ Reports (1986) 14, 98, [186].

233 *Case Concerning Military and Paramilitary Activities in and against Nicaragua*, ibid, 108–109, [207]. On the conditions required for the development of international customs, see analysis in Katselli Proukaki E. (2010), *The Problem of Enforcement of International Law* (Routledge) 202 et seq.

234 Quigley, n19, 219.

235 Ibid, 185–186.

displacement becomes 'the single most defining feature of their lives', which they want to be 'acknowledged and accepted'.[236]

Nevertheless, acknowledgment and acceptance are not enough. Instead, for many displaced persons across the globe the desire to return to their lands and properties never burns out[237] – even for those who, like the author, were born after the displacement occurred or even for those who choose not to return because of security or other concerns. This is very much owing to the fact that the concepts of home, land and property represent more than just a material commodity that can be easily replaced. Instead, they are associated with the very existence and being of the displaced and their link with the country, the community, the family, the self. In this respect, return and property restitution become significant for restoring the fundamental rights of the displaced but also for restoring international justice since both return and property restitution are an essential attribute of individual autonomy and self-determination.[238] Moreover, and as has rightly been argued: 'A state that violates rights is required under international law to restore the situation as it was before the illegal act. Repatriation is the remedy that comes closest to restoring the status quo ante, even after the passage of decades and changes in the demography of the areas in question.'[239] Truly, with the increased significance of individual human rights, the state no longer enjoys absolute sovereign rights either in peace or in war. Neither can the international community disregard the rights of those 38 million persons who have been forced out of their homes as a result of armed conflict and human rights violations. Indeed, the continuing displacement of people in Palestine, Colombia, the former Yugoslavia and Cyprus, to name but a few examples is not justified under international law.

For this purpose, this chapter focused on how contemporary international law reacts to forced displacement and how it protects those already displaced, not prejudicing, of course, the right not to be displaced considered in the previous chapter. This analysis is important because irrespective of whether the forcibly displaced have been able to break the chains of their predicament and to re-build their lives, their displacement remains a haunting stain on the incompetence and ineffectiveness of the international legal system to prevent such displacement, but also to enable the return of those displaced and the restoration of their property rights. This examination was able to conclude that there exists sufficient evidence in support of the argument, advanced in this chapter, that the rights to return home and to property restitution are well recognised norms of international law. Not only, however, are these rights essential elements of freedom of movement

236 For an excellent empirical work on the impact of forced displacement, see Cohen R., 'Listening to the Voices of the Displaced: Lessons Learned', Brookings-Bern Project on Internal Displacement, September 2008, 9, https://www.brookings.edu/wp-content/uploads/2016/06/09_internal_displacement_cohen.pdf.

237 Ibid, 28.

238 See Hannum, n77, 4 for the significance of the right to return home.

239 Quigley, n19, 299.

and residence and the rights to remain and to return to one's country as embodied for instance in the ICCPR, the ECHR and the ACHR, but they are rights with their own merit. In the absence of an international, as opposed to regional, agreement that expressly recognises the rights to return home and to property restitution in cases of forcible displacement,[240] the analysis was informed by a wealth of legally binding as well as other sources of international law such as multilateral and bilateral agreements, UN Security Council resolutions, judgments and decisions of international and national courts, as well as 'soft' law such as UN General Assembly resolutions, the Guiding Principles on Internal Displacement and the Pinheiro Principles, the influence of which is constantly increasing and the literature. Based on this evidence, it is ascertained that state practice and *opinio juris* reflect the common recognition by states and other international and national actors that return and restitution are essential ways to remedy forced displacement.

The significance of this finding lies in the recognition that forced displacement *is* a human rights violation and as such it 'should give entitlements' to those displaced such as their right to return and restitution.[241] To this effect, states have an obligation to reverse the status quo and bring back legality.[242] This obligation is not erased by the lapse of time.[243] As further pointed out:

> Immediately following a period of conflict, ensuring the right to an effective remedy for human rights violations and abuses is crucial for the consolidation and maintenance of peace. Peace cannot be achieved unless the population is confident that redress for grievances and human rights violations and abuses, including those arising from land disputes or deprivation of access to land, can be obtained through legitimate structures for the peaceful settlement of disputes and the fair administration of justice.[244]

This is precisely what is hoped to be achieved through the recognition of the rights to return home and to property restitution.

Bibliography

Books

Bossuyt M.J. (1987), *Guide to the 'Travaux Preparatoires' of the International Covenant on Civil and Political Rights* (Martinus Nijhoff Publishers).

240 For a discussion on the advantages and disadvantages of such a treaty, see Bugnion, n35, 1410–1411.

241 Report of the Representative of the Secretary-General on the human rights of internally displaced persons, W Kälin, Mission to Colombia, UN Doc. A/HRC/4/38/Add.3, 24 January 2007 in Cohen, n236, 19.

242 Quigley, n19, 219.

243 Saideman, n74, 829.

244 Land and Human Rights, n36, 27.

Hannum H. (1987), *The Right to Leave and Return in International Law and Practice* (Martinus Nijhoff Publishers).

Henckaerts J.M., Doswald-Beck L. (2005), *Customary International Humanitarian Law* (ICRC/CUP).

Joseph S., Schultz J., Castan M. (2000), *The International Covenant on Civil and Political Rights: Cases, Materials and Commentary* (Oxford University Press).

Katselli Proukaki E. (2010), *The Problem of Enforcement of International Law* (Routledge).

Nowak M. (2005), *U.N. Covenant on Civil and Political Rights: CCPR Commentary*, 2nd ed. (N.P. Engel Publisher).

Phuong C. (2005), *The International Protection of Internally Displaced of Persons* (Cambridge University Press).

Takkenberg L. (1998), *The Status of Palestinian Refugees in International Law* (Oxford University Press).

Journal articles

Ben Naftali O., Shavy Y. (2003–2004), 'Living in Denial: The Application of Human Rights in the Occupied Territories', *Israel Law Review*, Vol. 37, 17.

Benvenisti E., Zamir E. (1995), 'Private Claims to Property Rights in the Future Israeli–Palestinian Settlement', *AJIL*, Vol. 89, 295.

Borelli S. (2015), '*Jaloud v Netherlands* and *Hassan v United Kingdom*: Time for a Principled Approach in the Application of the ECHR to Military Action Abroad', *QIL*, Vol. 16, 25–43.

Bugnion F. (2004–2005), 'Refugees, Internally Displaced Persons and International Humanitarian Law', *Fordham International Law Journal*, Vol. 28, 1397.

Doswald-Beck L. (2004), 'Human Rights and Humanitarian Law: Are there Some Individuals Bereft of all Legal Protection?', *American Society of International Law Proceedings*, Vol. 98, 353.

Gross A.M. (2007), 'Human Proportions: 'Are human Rights the Emperor's New Clothes of the International Law of Occupation?', *EJIL*, Vol. 18, No. 1, 1–35.

Helton A. (2004–2005), 'End of Exile: Practical Solutions to the Palestinian Refugee Question: Refugees and the Right of Return', *Fordham Int'l LJ*, Vol. 28, 1325.

Katselli Proukaki E. (2014), 'The Right of Displaced Persons to Property and to Return Home after *Demopoulos*', 14 *Human Rights Law Review*, No. 4, 701–732.

Lapidoth R. (1986), 'The Right of Return in International Law, with Special Reference to the Palestinian Refugees', *Israel Yearbook on Human Rights*, Vol. 16, 103.

Meron T. (2000), 'The Humanisation of Humanitarian Law', *AJIL*, Vol. 94, 239.

Quigley J. (1998), 'Displaced Palestinians and a Right to Return', *Harvard International Law Journal*, Vol. 38, 171.

Saideman L. (2004), 'Do Palestinian Refugees Have a Right of Return to Israel? An Examination of the Scope of and Limitations on the Right of Return', *Virginia Journal of International Law*, Vol. 44, 829.

Stavropoulou M. (1994), 'The Right not to be Displaced', *American University International Law Review*, Vol. 9, No. 3, 689–749.

Tachjian V., Theriault H. (2014), 'An attempt to Recover Armenian Properties in Turkey through the French Authorities in Syria and Lebanon in the 1920s', *International Criminal Law Review*, Vol. 14, No. 2, 343–357.

Teitel R.G. (2001–2002), 'Humanity's Law: Rule of Law for the New Global Politics', *Cornell International Law Journal*, Vol. 35, 359.
Ullom V (2000–2001), 'Voluntary Repatriation of Refugees and Customary International Law', *Denver Journal of International Law & Policy*, Vol. 29, 115.
Verdirame G. (2008), 'Human Rights in Wartime: A Framework for Analysis', *European Human Rights Law Review*, Vol. 6, 689.
Wright Q. (1968), 'Legal Aspects of the Middle East Situation', *Law & Contemp. Problems*, Vol. 33, 5.
Zegveld L. (2003), 'Remedies for Victims of Violations of International Humanitarian Law', IRRC September, Vol. 85, No. 851, 521.

3 Reparation of the rights to property and home of displaced persons arising from armed conflict under the European Convention of Human Rights

Falling short of the exigencies of international law and the humanistic purpose of human rights?

*Vassilis P. Tzevelekos**

1 Introduction

People may involuntarily leave their homes for a variety of reasons. This can be a means of protection from natural disasters or the result of a lawful expropriation by competent public authorities for general interest purposes, such as the construction of a public hospital or to facilitate economic development that will benefit the entire community. But people may also be forcibly separated from their family, possessions, home and homeland because they fear persecution or to seek refuge from violence, armed conflict and gross human rights violations. According to the United Nations Refugee Agency, a total 65.3 million people were forcibly displaced at the end of 2015.[1] Forced displacement causes affected persons to experience vulnerability and destitution. It challenges a wide range of human rights, including the rights to home and property, which are the focus of this chapter, as these are guaranteed by the European Convention on Human Rights (ECHR, the Convention) and interpreted by the European Court of Human

* Senior Lecturer in Law, University of Liverpool School of Law and Social Justice. I am thankful to Judge Christos Rozakis, Dr Vaios Koutroulis and Dr Antal Berkes for our discussions and for materials they provided, and to the volume's editor, Dr Elena Katselli Proukaki, for her constructive feedback. I am honoured by the invitation to contribute to this volume, especially because its editor allowed me to treat a topic that she has extensively researched and analysed in her scholarly work (cited in n38). The usual disclaimer applies.

1 Edwards A. (2016) 'Global forced displacement hits record high', www.unhcr.org/uk/news/latest /2016/6/5763b65a4/global-forced-displacement-hits-record-high.html.

Rights (ECtHR, the Court) in cases of displacement caused by armed conflict (leading, in most of the cases discussed in this chapter, to occupation).

Part 2 of the chapter discusses the relevant case law of the ECtHR. To avoid repetitions and overlaps with other studies contained in the present volume, analysis is limited to selected cases that demonstrate how the Court departed from its earlier case law, shifting from restitution to compensation for the loss of property. However, as a conclusion, this is far from generalizable. It rather needs to be taken with a pinch of salt as it only concerns one particular case study, i.e. the Cyprus issue. The ECtHR case law on comparable situations is not yet rich enough. Part 3 argues that in cases of forced displacement, restitution is the appropriate form of reparation. Analysis in that part of the study follows two different courses. The first refers to general international law. The argument made in that respect is that the case law at issue is not aligned with general international law. This concerns both primary law and the rules on state responsibility (i.e. secondary law) and, in particular, its rules on the legal consequences of internationally wrongful acts. Yet, this does not necessarily imply unlawfulness. Especially in the case of secondary rules, the regime of the ECHR may be interpreted as containing *lex specialis* that applies in lieu of the rules of general international law on state responsibility and, in particular, on the reparation of international wrongs.[2] Nevertheless, the Court may be reproached for disregarding general international law, failing to harmoniously integrate the ECHR into the broader environment of the international legal order and growing characteristics of self-containment when these are not justified by the special aim and purpose of human rights law.[3] Thereby, it might be –unnecessarily – contributing to the fragmentation of international law. The second path taken in Part 3 to argue in favour of restitution instead of compensation for loss of property in the case of forced displacement concerns human rights law. Analysis explains why, given the humanistic teleology of that area of law, it is necessary to consider the context of each case and the particular circumstances of forced displacement when assessing the permissibility of a limitation and its reparation. *In principle*, when displacement is the result of unlawful military occupation (as is the case in most of the judgments of the ECtHR examined in this chapter), it should not be remedied through compensation – unless this is mutually agreed through a friendly settlement of the

2 On *lex specialis* in the context of the law of responsibility, see Simma B., Pulkowski D. (2006) 'Of Planets and the Universe: Self-contained Regimes in International Law', *EJIL*, Vol. 17, 483–529, 485. More generally, see United Nations, International Law Commission, 'Fragmentation of International Law: Difficulties Arising from the Diversification and Expansion of International Law, Report of the Study Group of the International Law Commission on the Work of its 58th Session', 1 May–9 June 2006 and 3 July–11 August 2006, UN Doc A/CN.4/L.682, [46] and following, http://legal.un.org/docs/?symbol=A/CN.4/L.682.

3 On the origins of the term, see Simma B. (1985) 'Self-contained Regimes', *NYbIL*, Vol. 16, 111–136. See also n2 and A/CN.4/L.682 (n2) 65 and following, [123] and following and, especially regarding human rights, 85–87, [161]–[164].

case between a displaced person and the responsible state or part of a (human rights friendly)[4] agreement between the states involved in the conflict that led to displacement. Part 4 concludes.

2 Highlights from the case law of the ECtHR on the reparation of the rights of forcibly displaced people: from restitution to compensation?

2.1 The original position

The starting point of the analysis cannot be other than the seminal case of *Loizidou v Turkey*,[5] concerning the Cyprus issue, in the aftermath of the Turkish military invasion of 1974 (as a reaction to a military coup in Cyprus by the Greek dictatorship) and the consequent occupation[6] leading to loss of control by the government of Cyprus over part of its territory. The case raises a considerable number of interesting legal questions spanning from extraterritoriality and attribution[7] to the inter-relationship between human rights law and humanitarian law[8] and the validity of reservations in human rights treaties,[9] but the limited scope of this study requires that analysis focuses on the question of reparation of the violations of Articles 8 and, especially, 1 of Protocol 1 ECHR. Before tackling the applicant's claims under these two provisions of the Convention, the Court dealt with a number of preliminary questions, to conclude (*inter alia*) that the self-proclaimed Turkish Republic of Northern Cyprus (TRNC) is not recognised as a state[10] and that the alleged violations are attributable to the respondent state, i.e. Turkey.[11]

4 See discussion towards the end of Section 3.2 and n151.

5 *Loizidou v Turkey* (1995) App no. 15318/89, *ECHR*. The Court delivered judgments on the preliminary objections raised by the respondent state (*Loizidou v Turkey* (preliminary objections) (1995) App no. 15318/19, *ECHR*, Series A no. 310), on the merits (*Loizidou v Turkey* (merits) (1996) App no. 15318/19, *ECHR*, VI) and on former Article 50 (*Loizidou v Turkey* (just satisfaction) (1998) App no. 15318/19, *ECHR*, IV).

6 *Loizidou* (preliminary objections, n5), [63].

7 The literature is vast, but see Tzevelekos V.P. (2015) 'Reconstructing the Effective Control Criterion in Extraterritorial Human Rights Breaches: Direct Attribution of Wrongfulness, Due Diligence, and Concurrent Responsibility', *MJIL*, Vol. 36, 129–178, 152–157, especially 135–142.

8 The literature is vast. For a concise overview, see Tomuschat C. (2010) 'Human Rights and International Humanitarian Law', *EJIL*, Vol. 21(1), 15–23; Orakhelashvili A. (2008) 'The Interaction between Human Rights and Humanitarian Law: Fragmentation, Conflict, Parallelism, or Convergence?', *EJIL*, Vol. 19(1), 161–182. The ECtHR has repeatedly dealt with this issue. See, e.g., the seminal judgment in *Hassan v United Kingdom* [GC] (2014) App no. 29750/09, *ECHR*.

9 The literature is very rich. For a critical analysis of the ILC work on the topic, see Ziemele I., Liede L. (2013) 'Reservations to Human Rights Treaties: From Draft Guideline 3.1.12 to Guideline 3.1.5.6', *EJIL*, Vol. 24(4), 1135–1152.

10 *Loizidou* (merits, n5) [44].

11 *Loizidou* (preliminary objections, n5), [63].

As to the merits of the case, the applicant complained that her property in the northern part of the island was inaccessible to her[12] and that the right to respect for her home had been breached.[13] With its judgment on the merits, the Court confirmed that the applicant remained the legal owner of the property at issue in northern Cyprus[14] and that the interference with her property rights was a continuous one.[15] This continuous denial of access to possessions in the occupied part of Cyprus amounts to an interference with the rights protected by Article 1 Protocol 1 ECHR[16] and, in particular, with the first of the three rules contained in that provision,[17] namely the right to peacefully enjoy property.[18] After rejecting the arguments of the respondent state as to the reasons justifying the interference with the said right, the Court concluded that 'there has been and *continues to be* a breach of Article 1 of Protocol No. 1.'[19] Finally, as to the right to home under Article 8, the Court held that, because the applicant's home was not on the land in question, no interference/violation could be found in that respect.[20]

The key point in the Court's judgment in the *Loizidou case* is that the applicant's legal title of ownership remained unaffected by the Turkish military invasion and consequent occupation. The violation of the right to peaceful enjoyment of property started with the invasion but is a continuous one – allowing the Court to exercise its competence *ratione temporis*.[21] That violation will last for as long as the applicant has no access to her property. As to how the diagnosed violation can be remedied, the Court, after reminding that the applicant remains the legal owner of the property at issue, adjudicated (*inter alia*) a pecuniary compensation 'in respect of losses directly related to *this* violation', as of the date of the acceptance by Turkey of its (i.e. the Court's) compulsory jurisdiction.[22] The compensation specifically concerns the particular aspect of the right to property that the Court declared as breached (i.e. the first rule contained in Article 1 Protocol 1, concerning the peaceful enjoyment of the property)[23] and only covers the period between the

12 *Loizidou* (merits, n5), [48].
13 Ibid, [65].
14 Ibid, [46], [47] and [62].
15 Ibid, [41].
16 Ibid, [63].
17 The Court has analysed Article 1 of Protocol 1 as comprising three rules. The first (in the first sentence of the first paragraph) is general and enunciates the principle of peaceful enjoyment of property. The second (in the second sentence of the first paragraph) concerns deprivation of possessions. The third (in the second paragraph) recognises that states are entitled to control the use of property in accordance with general interest. These three rules are interconnected: the second and third need to be construed in the light of the general principle of the first rule. See *James and others v the United Kingdom* (1986) App no. 8793/79, *ECHR*, [37].
18 *Loizidou* (merits, n5) [63].
19 Ibid, [64] (emphasis added).
20 Ibid, [66].
21 *Loizidou* (preliminary objections, n5) [102–105] and (merits, n5) [39–47].
22 *Loizidou* (just satisfaction, n5) [33] (emphasis added).
23 See n17.

delivery of the judgment and the date of the recognition of the Court's competence by the respondent state. Finally, as is discussed in more detail in Part 3 of the chapter, the payment of compensation by the respondent state amounts to partial execution of the Court's judgment, as it only covers the pecuniary dimension of the reparation. This does not eradicate the inner causes of the violation. Thus, it only offers an imperfect remedy. Given that the occupation left unaffected the property titles of the applicant, Turkey cannot remedy the violation diagnosed by the Court, unless it ceases to obstruct the access to the property at issue and the enjoyment of it by its owner and offers guarantees of non-repetition. Full compliance with the judgment requires addressing these dimensions too. But these are questions that are examined in more detail in the next part of the chapter.

The ramifications of the *Loizidou* judgment are wide, expanding beyond the confines of that specific case. First, to repair the violation found by the Court, Turkey ought to allow the owners of property that it occupies to access and enjoy it. Such enjoyment runs counter to the very essence of occupation. Second, next to Mrs Loizidou, there are as many other victims (i.e. people who find themselves in a similar situation to that of Mrs Loizidou) as the owners of property in northern Cyprus that is inaccessible to them because of the military occupation. *Loizidou* is part of and representative of a broader, systemic problem. This is reflected in the inter-state case of *Cyprus v Turkey*,[24] but also in the individual complaints that the Court received from Greek-Cypriots against Turkey after *Loizidou* (some of which are discussed below).

Starting with the interstate case, the Court held that 'there has been a continuing violation of Article 8 of the Convention by reason of the refusal to allow the return of any Greek-Cypriot displaced persons to their homes in northern Cyprus.'[25] As far as property is concerned, the Court confirmed that the Greek-Cypriots remain the legal owners of their property in the occupied part of the island[26] and concluded that there is a continuous[27] violation of the Convention, as 'both its reasoning and its conclusion in the *Loizidou* judgment (*merits*) apply with equal force to displaced Greek-Cypriots who, like Mrs Loizidou, are unable to have access to their property in northern Cyprus'.[28]

2.2 TRNC's immovable property commission

Nevertheless, the post-*Loizidou* individual applications resulted in a gradual departure from the prototypical *Loizidou*. The first noticeable – but still inconsequential in terms of standards of substantive protection – reconsideration came

24 *Cyprus v Turkey* [GC] (2001) App no 25781/94, *ECHR*, IV. This is the fourth interstate case between Cyprus and Turkey for the Cyprus issue, but the first examined by the ECtHR.
25 Ibid, (merits) [175].
26 Ibid, [186].
27 Ibid, [189].
28 Ibid, [187].

with *Xenides-Arestis v Turkey*.[29] In that case, the respondent government invited the Court to refrain from examining the merits of the case as the applicant had failed to exhaust local remedies by resorting to the 'compensation commission' that law 49/2003 of the TRNC established for displaced people in Cyprus.[30] The Court scrutinised the remedy provided by Turkey[31] and found it, for a variety of reasons (for instance, it was vague as to its temporal application and limited to immovable property, whereas it only provided for pecuniary compensation), to fall short of the standards of the ECHR. Thus, the domestic remedy provided by Turkey was found to be inadequate and ineffective. Therefore, applicants should not be expected to have their complaints examined by that commission (i.e. exhaust the local remedies) before soliciting the Court's involvement.[32] Consequently, the Court rejected the admissibility objection raised by Turkey.

In essence, with its decision on the admissibility of *Xenides-Arestis*, the ECtHR provided guidance to the respondent as to how it should establish its domestic remedy to satisfy the ECHR. The logic behind this approach is that of pilot judgments,[33] as this is reflected in the Grand Chamber's judgment in the case of *Broniowski v Poland*.[34] The latter presents similarities with the *Xenides-Arestis case* to the extent that it was raising issues of respect of property and compensation by the Polish state for persons repatriated from territories that no longer formed part of Poland. Most importantly, both cases, i.e. *Xenides-Arestis* and *Broniowski*, concerned problems of a systemic nature and proportions that affected a large number of people. With this in mind, the Court asked Poland in *Broniowski* to effectively address at the domestic level the issues raised by that case, through measures that would 'remedy the systemic defect underlying the Court's finding of a violation so as not to overburden the Convention system with large numbers of applications deriving from the same cause'.[35] For that purpose, i.e. to protect itself from the backlog of thousands of similar cases, the Court decided to limit the discretion states traditionally enjoy and proceeded with 'indicat[ing] the type of measure that might be taken by the Polish State in order to put an end

29 *Xenides-Arestis v Turkey* (2005) App no. 46347/99, *ECHR*. The Court delivered a decision on the admissibility of the case (*Xenides-Arestis v Turkey* (admissibility) (2005) App no. 46347/99 *ECHR*), and judgments on the merits (*Xenides-Arestis v Turkey* (merits) (2005) App no. 46347/99, *ECHR*) and on just satisfaction (*Xenides-Arestis v Turkey* (just satisfaction) (2006) App no. 46347/99 *ECHR*).

30 Ibid, (admissibility).

31 The committee established by TRNC is seen as a remedy provided by Turkey. *Cyprus v Turkey*, (merits, n24) [102] and [92].

32 *Xenides-Arestis*, (admissibility, n29).

33 For a comprehensive introduction and list with relevant cases, see the Court's factsheet on pilot judgments, Council of Europe, *Pilot Judgments* (2017) www.echr.coe.int/Documents/FS_Pilot_judgments_ENG.pdf. See also, Haider D. (2013) *The Pilot-Judgment Procedure of the European Court of Human Rights* (Leiden: Nijhoff); Leach P.R. *et al.* (2010) *Responding to Systemic Human Rights Violations. An Analysis of 'Pilot Judgments' of the European Court of Human Rights and their Impact at National Level.* (Antwerp: Intersentia).

34 *Broniowski v Poland* (merits) [GC] (2004) App no. 31443/96. *ECHR*, V, [189].

35 Ibid, [193].

to the systemic situation identified' in *Broniowski*.[36] *Mutatis mutandis*, with its judgment on the merits of *Xenides-Arestis*, the Court ordered Turkey (under Article 46 ECHR) to 'introduce a remedy which secures the effective protection of the rights laid down in Article 8 of the Convention and Article 1 of Protocol No. 1 in relation to the present applicant *as well as in respect of all similar applications pending before the Court*'[37] and explicitly invited that state to design its domestic remedy in line with the Court's admissibility decision on *Xenides-Arestis*.[38] In a nutshell, the Court gave the necessary instructions that would allow the respondent state to address domestically the issue of the property and home rights of displaced persons.

As to the substance of the claims by *Xenides-Arestis*, the Court followed *Loizidou* (and similar cases[39] that it had examined before *Xenides-Arestis*) regarding property,[40] but (unlike *Loizidou*), it also found a violation of Article 8, as the applicant had her home in the occupied northern part of the island.[41] This way, the Court reinforced its previous case law and insisted on its interpretation of the ECHR and the standards of substantive protection that should prevail for displaced people. However, because of the systemic dimension of the case and the big number of affected persons, the Court shifted, in a sense, from the international level of protection to the national level. To this effect, it apparently maintained for itself the role of the last word adjudicator that may ultimately scrutinise the practice of the commission operating in TRNC (Immovable Property Commission, IPC), and sanction it for any failure to follow its (i.e. the ECtHR's) previous interpretation of the ECHR and meet the standards set by its case law.

In the aftermath of *Xenides-Arestis*, Turkey (acting through TRNC) enacted law 67/2005, the aim of which was to improve the local remedy (i.e. the IPC) established by the previous law (i.e. 49/2003) and address the issues raised by the Court in the *Xenides-Arestis* admissibility decision.[42] The IPC was given (among other competences) the power to decide about the restitution of immovable property and offer exchange or compensation. The Court expressed its satisfaction with the Turkish remedy in its judgment on compensation (just satisfaction) in

36 Ibid, [194].

37 *Xenides-Arestis* (merits, n29), conclusive part of the judgment, entitled '[f]or these reasons', conclusion 5 (emphasis added).

38 Ibid, [40]. On the compatibility of such a domestic remedy with international law, see Katselli Proukaki E. (2014) 'The Right of Displaced Persons to Property and to Return Home after Demopoulos', *HRLR*, Vol. 14, 701–732, 716. See also 723 on the practice of that domestic remedy. For a critical overview of the powers and practice of the remedy in TRNC, see Hadjigeorgiou N. (2016) 'Remedying Displacement in Frozen Conflicts: Lessons from the Case of Cyprus', *CYbELS*, Vol. 18, 152–175.

39 *Demades v Turkey*, (2003) App no. 16219/90, *ECHR*; *Eugenia Michaelidou Developments Ltd and Michael Tymvios v Turkey*, (2003) App no. 16163/90, *ECHR*.

40 *Xenides-Arestis* (merits, n29), [32].

41 Ibid, [19]–[22]. See also *Demades* (n39), [21]–[37].

42 The law is accessible in English in *Demopoulos*, [35]–[37]. *Demopoulos and others v Turkey* (admissibility) [GC] (2010) App nos 46113/99 3843/02 *et al.*, *ECHR*.

Xenides-Arestis,[43] but mainly dealt with it (sitting as a Grand Chamber) in the admissibility decision of the *Demopoulos and others v Turkey case*.[44]

2.3 From restitution to compensation and the (sociolegal) rationale behind the shift

In *Demopoulos*, the Court departed from *Loizidou*, shifting from restitution to compensation for loss of property. According to the former Vice President of the Court, the Greek judge, Professor Rozakis, the Court allowed the complaints by displaced persons to be treated 'in the same way as if they concerned simple expropriation of property by a State'.[45] The Court concluded that the domestic remedy offered by Turkey satisfies the exigencies of the ECHR and made it a requirement for displaced people to seek reparation before it – alternatively, they (i.e. displaced people) should/could wait for a potential political settlement of the dispute.[46] Before reaching that conclusion, the Court clarified that, using the commission at issue, in no way signified an indirect recognition of TRNC, as the Republic of Cyprus remains the sole legitimate government of Cyprus.[47] The very purpose of the remedy provided in TRNC is to enable Turkey to correct its wrongs and avoid a vacuum in human rights protection.[48] The Court then confirmed its earlier case law, repeating that the legal titles of displaced people remained unaffected and that the breach of property and home rights was a continuous one, to conclude that the judgments at issue only concerned 'pecuniary damage for loss of use of [the applicants'] properties, not compensation for the loss of the properties themselves of which they continued to be regarded as the legal owners'.[49]

However:

> At the present point, many decades after the loss of possession by the then owners, property has in many cases changed hands, by gift, succession or otherwise; those claiming title may have never seen, or ever used the property in question. The issue arises to what extent the notion of legal title, and the

43 *Xenides-Arestis* (just satisfaction, n29), [37]. Concluding, however, that the applicant should not be expected to go through the TRNC Commission since the Court had already decided the merits of the case. This was consistently followed in similar cases: e.g., *Orphanides v Turkey* (2009) App no. 36705/97, *ECHR*, [24], rejecting the objection of non-exhaustion of domestic remedies as it was raised after declaring the application admissible.

44 *Demopoulos*, n42.

45 Rozakis C.L. (2015), 'The Rights of Displaced Persons under Article 1 Protocol 1 and 8 of the European Convention of Human Rights' in Casadevall J. *et al.* (eds.), *Liber Amicorum Dean Spielmann. Mélanges en l'honneur de Dean Spielmann / Essays in Honour of Dean Spielmann* (Netherlands: Wolf Legal Publishers), 561.

46 *Demopoulos* (n42), [128].

47 Ibid, [96], [100] and [108].

48 Ibid, [96].

49 Ibid.

> expectation of enjoying the full benefits of that title, is realistic in practice. The losses thus claimed become increasingly speculative and hypothetical.[50]

Furthermore:

> [I]t would be unrealistic to expect that as a result of these cases the Court should, or could, directly order the Turkish Government to ensure that these applicants obtain access to, and full possession of, their properties, irrespective of who is now living there or whether the property is allegedly in a militarily sensitive zone or used for vital public purposes.[51]

Therefore, if restitution of property proves to be impossible, the alternative is to pay compensation.[52] This is a decision to be made by Turkey (i.e. the occupying power), which shall enjoy discretion in that respect.[53] Implying subsidiarity:

> [T]he Court maintains its view that it must leave the choice of implementation of redress for breaches of property rights to Contracting States, who are in the best position to assess the practicalities, priorities and conflicting interests on a domestic level even in a situation such as that pertaining in the northern part of Cyprus.[54]

Another thing the Court appears to imply is the possibility to lawfully limit non-absolute human rights for purposes of general interest or for the protection of the rights of thirds. This involves proportionality. Thus, according to the Court, it is 'necessary to ensure that the redress applied to those old injuries does not create disproportionate new wrongs'.[55] Life goes on after military interventions and occupations. Hence, the rights of Greek-Cypriots need to be balanced against the rights of those who now live in what used to be their homes. Therefore:

> It cannot be within this Court's task in interpreting and applying the provisions of the Convention to impose an unconditional obligation on a Government to embark on the forcible eviction and rehousing of potentially large numbers of men, women and children even with the aim of vindicating the rights of victims of violations of the Convention.[56]

This conclusion primarily owes to the time that has lapsed between the 1974 invasion and the time when the Court examined *Demopoulos*,[57] and the new status

50 Ibid, [111].
51 Ibid, [112].
52 Ibid, [114].
53 Ibid, [114].
54 Ibid, [118].
55 Ibid, [117].
56 Ibid, [116].
57 Ibid, [113].

quo this has established, having consequences for the lives of people in both parts of the island. Yet, it can also be read as owing to the failure (one could argue, especially after the rejection by Greek-Cypriots of the UN Secretary General's 'Annan Plan')[58] of the involved parties to reach an agreement that would settle their long-standing dispute in a mutually acceptable manner. Thus, in a rather lyrical fashion, the Court explains that:

> [S]ome thirty-five years have elapsed since the applicants lost possession of their property in northern Cyprus in 1974. Generations have passed. The local population has not remained static. Turkish Cypriots who inhabited the north have migrated elsewhere; Turkish Cypriot refugees from the south have settled in the north; Turkish settlers from Turkey have arrived in large numbers and established their homes. Much Greek Cypriot property has changed hands at least once, whether by sale, donation or inheritance.[59]

The result is that:

> [T]he Court finds itself faced with cases burdened with a political, historical and factual complexity flowing from a problem that *should have been resolved by all parties assuming full responsibility for finding a solution on a political level.*[60]

But this might also be revealing of the fact that, outside any genuine reasons of human rights protection and the need to balance through proportionality the right to property of the displaced people with the rights and interests of the new inhabitants, Court's decision to shift from restitution to compensation is (also) aiming at protecting its own interests. *Demopoulos* is clearly a judgment of disengagement from the Cyprus issue. First, the Court wishes to protect its own authority and the effectiveness of its judgments. Therefore, although it 'eschew[s] any notion that military occupation should be regarded as a form of adverse possession by which title can be legally transferred to the invading power',[61] it

58 On a referendum held on 24 April 2004, 65% of Turkish Cypriots approved the Plan. 76% of the Greek Cypriots rejected it. See *Cyprus 'spurns historic chance'* (2004), http://news.bbc.co.uk/1/hi/world/ europe/3656753.stm. On the Annan Plan (and links to the official texts), see The UK Parliament, House of Commons (2005) *Cyprus, Session 2004–05* (HC 2004-05 113-I), Foreign Affairs Committee Publications, www.publications.parliament.uk/pa/cm200405/cmselect/cmfaff/113/11305.htm. As to why time should not affect restitution of property in case of displacement and occupation, see Veraart W. (2009) 'Redressing the Past with an Eye to the Future: The Impact of the Passage of Time on Property Rights Restitution in Post-Apartheid South Africa', *NQHR*, Vol. 27, 45–60, especially 46; Lawand K. (1996) 'The Right to Return of Palestinians in International Law', *IJRL*, Vol. 8, 532–568, 555–557. Cf. Paglione P.G. (2008) 'Individual Property Restitution: From Deng to Pinheiro – and the Challenges Ahead', *IJRL*, Vol. 20, 391–412, 409–412.

59 *Demopoulos* (n42), [84].

60 Ibid, [85] (emphasis added).

61 Ibid, [112].

admits, as already mentioned, that 'it would be *unrealistic* to expect that [. . .] the Court should, or could, directly order the Turkish Government to ensure that these applicants obtain access to, and full possession of, their properties.'[62] Second, the Court wishes to avoid the burden of the thousands of cases that it might be asked to deal with. As it very honestly admits, its previous case law on the property of displaced Greek-Cypriots that focused on the inaccessibility of property rather than favouring the logic of compensation for its loss (i.e. expropriation) means that, 'in theory, [displaced Greek-Cypriots may] come to the Court periodically and indefinitely to claim loss of rents until a political solution to the Cyprus problem is reached.'[63]

For these reasons, namely proportionality and protection of the rights established because of the prolonged period of occupation, on the one hand, but also to protect the Court's self-interests and authority from backlog and delivery of judgments that are unlikely to produce real effects and be fully (in the sense of restitution) implemented, on the other, the Court decided to disregard the cause of the interference with the rights of the applicants (that is, use of force and military occupation), to conclude that:

> While it goes without saying that Turkey is regarded by the international community as being in illegal occupation of the northern part of Cyprus, *this does not mean that when dealing with individual applications concerning interference with property, the Court must apply the Convention any differently.*[64]

After all, the Court reminds us, property is merely a material commodity, the loss of which can be compensated for.[65] Property 'cannot be used as a vehicle for the vindication of sovereign rights or findings of breaches of international law between Contracting States'.[66] This is how restitution receded in favour of compensation for the loss of property, with the latter possibly becoming the rule and the former the exception.

2.4 Beyond the Cyprus issue

Moving from Cyprus to Nagorno-Karabakh, interestingly, although the relevant case law is rather limited, thus less developed and elaborated, the impression given is that the Court's approach is not the same as in *Demopoulos* (i.e. the Court is not shifting from restitution to compensation). Moving then from the dispute between Cyprus and Turkey to that between Azerbaijan and Armenia, the Court delivered on the same day two cases stemming from that conflict, one against each involved state.

62 Ibid (emphasis added).
63 Ibid, [111].
64 Ibid, [114].
65 Ibid, [115].
66 Ibid.

To begin with Armenia, *Chiragov and others*[67] is in many respects similar to the *Loizidou*-type of cases. The self-proclaimed Nagorno-Karabakh Republic (NKR) is not recognised as a state, but as part of the territory of Azerbaijan, which is effectively controlled by Armenia. NKR's conduct is attributable to the latter. The victims are displaced Azerbaijanis who have no access to their homes and possessions in NKR. The Grand Chamber of the Court held that the fact that, several years after the ceasefire agreement between the involved states, the applicants have not been able to return to Nagorno-Karabakh amounts to a continuous violation of their right to access and enjoy their property.[68] Furthermore, the ECtHR found no effective domestic remedies in either Armenia or in NKR.[69] As in the case of the Cyprus issue, the Court pointed to the direction of the establishment of a property claims mechanism at the domestic level. Yet, unlike Cyprus, the Armenian mechanism's purpose would be to allow 'the applicants and others in their situation to have their property rights restored and to obtain compensation for the loss of their enjoyment'[70] –not for the loss of property. Moreover, the Court avoided making this mechanism a requirement of compliance with its judgment for the respondent state, as it had done in *Xenides-Arestis*.[71]

Moving to the case against Azerbaijan, *Sargsyan*[72] differs from *Chiragov* as the case raises no issues of extraterritoriality and mainly concerns the positive dimension of the human rights at stake, i.e. the duty of the respondent state to proactively protect them. The applicant is an Armenian who used to live in Azerbaijan. He had to flee his home during the Nagorno-Karabakh conflict. The interference with the right to property was found by the Court to be a continuous one,[73] raising an issue of lack of enjoyment of property and not of deprivation of it.[74] The Court decided to consider the claim regarding property from the perspective of the positive obligations[75] of the respondent state and examined (in the light of proportionality) whether a fair balance had been maintained between the duty of the state to protect the rights of the applicant and its aims to protect public interest. Furthermore, the Court examined whether Azerbaijan ought to provide to the applicant access to his home (i.e. restitution) and/or a compensation for the loss of its use.[76] Given the circumstances of the case and the fact that access to the property at issue was not possible for reasons of safety and protection of

67 *Chiragov and others v Armenia* [GC] (2015) App no. 13216/05, *ECHR*.
68 Ibid, [195]–[196].
69 Ibid, [194].
70 Ibid, [199].
71 *Xenides-Arestis* (merits, n29), conclusive part of the judgment, entitled '[f]or these reasons', conclusion 5.
72 *Sargsyan v Azerbaijan* [GC] (2015) App no. 40167/06, *ECHR*.
73 Ibid, [215], [242], [259]–[261].
74 Ibid, [218].
75 Ibid, [220]–[226].
76 Ibid, [228].

human life (as this was a mined area of military activity),[77] the Court concluded that the respondent state, irrespective of whether it was responsible for the displacement or not, was under a duty to take alternative measures to secure property rights.[78] Such a measure would be the establishment of an internal mechanism whose task would be to restore property and compensate for the loss of the enjoyment of it.[79] Having found no reasons justifying the negligence of the state to protect the rights of the applicant, the Court diagnosed a violation of Article 1 Protocol 1[80] and, for the same reasons, Article 8 of the ECHR.[81]

Sargsyan presents similarities with an earlier judgment of the Court in the case of *Doğan and others v. Turkey*.[82] Therefore, it is no surprise that it repeatedly refers to that case law,[83] which concerned internally displaced people in Turkey because of the conflict in its south-east provinces between its security forces and sections of the Kurdish population in favour of autonomy. The Court found that the facts of the case raised issues from the perspective of the right to use (i.e. enjoy) property, but not of dispossession[84] and, while examining proportionality, held that:

> [State] authorities have the primary duty and responsibility to establish conditions, as well as provide the means, which allow the applicants to return voluntarily, in safety and with dignity, to their homes or places of habitual residence, or to resettle voluntarily in another part of the country.[85]

3 Why not shift from restitution to compensation for displacement because of occupation?

This brief, albeit selective, *tour d'horizon* allows us to draw some conclusions about the ECtHR's stance vis-à-vis forced displacement, but also raises some important questions. Starting with the conclusions, one may safely argue that the Court classifies consistently forced displacement as an issue falling under the first general rule of Article 1 Protocol 1 and not as an issue of dispossession. In principle, the victims of displacement remain the owners of the home/property they were forced to abandon. Furthermore, irrespective of the role played by state authorities in the conditions that led a victim to leave her home, states exercising jurisdiction are entrusted with the responsibility to provide remedies. Ideally, remedies should be provided at the domestic level. The ECtHR's role is subsidiary. Its case law sets the standards that should prevail and serves as a benchmark for

77 Ibid, [233].
78 Ibid, [234].
79 Ibid, [238].
80 Ibid, [241]–[242].
81 Ibid, [260]–[261].
82 *Doğan and others v Turkey* (2004) App nos 8803-8811/02 *et al.*, *ECHR*.
83 *Sargsyan* (n72), e.g. [179], [213], [222].
84 *Doğan* (n82), [146].
85 Ibid, [154].

authorities at the domestic level to address systemic issues that concern a large number of persons who, in the absence of domestic remedies, would be entitled to reach the ECtHR directly and contribute this way to the backlog of applications it experiences. But next to these common elements, *Demopoulos* (as the crucial 'chapter' in the Cyprus saga before the ECtHR) allows identifying a rupture in the way the Court approaches displacement: although, in principle, occupation does not justify deprivation ('expropriation') of possessions (and especially of home), restitution might recede in favour of alternatives, such as compensation for the loss of property.

Moving then to the questions raised by the case law discussed earlier, the first question is whether the decline from restitution to compensation concerns the Cyprus issue exclusively. Moreover, is it because of the particular features of the Cyprus issue (i.e. the argument by the Court regarding the time that has lapsed and the new reality established after so many years, in the light especially of the rejection by the Greek-Cypriots of the UN-promoted solution) that displaced persons in that specific context should lose their homes? Finally, what criteria may lawfully justify the payment of compensation instead of restitution?

Unfortunately, up to the present time, the ECtHR case law has not offered any comprehensive answers to these questions. With this in mind, rather than endeavouring to speculate what the Court's answers would be, the purpose of this study is to argue that, in *Demopoulos*, the Court erred. *In principle*, restitution is the appropriate form of reparation in case of forced displacement. To support this position, the paper employs two different lines of reasoning in the two subsections that follow. First, it is argued that international law favours restitution. The second strand of analysis argues that, from the perspective of human rights, in principle, restitution is the optimal solution – given the causes of the interference with the rights to property and home in cases of forcible displacement because of occupation.

3.1 The ECHR and international law

3.1.1 Primary norms

Starting with the former, to be fair to the Court, the truth is that it often strives to interpret the ECHR in the light of and in conformity with international law. Its efforts are also discernible in the cases discussed earlier. For instance, in *Sargsyan*, the Court refers repeatedly[86] to the rules of international humanitarian law and, in particular to the Fourth Geneva Convention,[87] but also to international customary law, by reference to the scholarly work by the International Committee of the Red Cross (ICRC) on customary humanitarian law.[88] In similar terms, both *Sargsyan*

86 *Sargsyan* (n72), [95] (relevant law), [229]–[232].
87 Ibid, [231].
88 Ibid, [232].

and *Chiragov* (to give just one more example) refer in a number of instances[89] to a UN soft law instrument, namely:

> The 'Principles on Housing and Property Restitution for Refugees and Displaced Persons' (Commission on Human Rights, Sub-Commission on the Promotion and Protection of Human Rights, 28 June 2005, E/CN.4/Sub.2/2005/17, Annex), [which] are the most complete standards on the issue. They are also known as the Pinheiro principles. The aim of these principles, which are grounded within existing international human rights and humanitarian law, is to provide international standards and practical guidelines to States, UN agencies and the broader international community on how best to address the complex legal and technical issues surrounding housing and property restitution.[90]

The argument in this study is that, had the Court wished to give the appropriate weight to restitution in the context of the Cyprus issue, it could have achieved it through this very same technique, namely the interpretation of the ECHR in the light of other relevant rules of international law,[91] on the basis of Article 31(3)(c) of the 1969 Vienna Convention on the Law of Treaties (VCLT).[92] To give a few examples that reinforce this argument, starting with displacement in general, Article 2 of the aforementioned Pinheiro Principles reads:

89 For instance, *Chiragov* (n67), [136], [199]–[200].

90 Ibid, [98]. On the evolution within the UN system of soft law on property restitution and displacement, see Thiele B. (2000) 'Housing and Property Restitution in the Context of the Return of Refugees and Internally Displaced Persons: Developments at the United Nations', *NQHR*, Vol. 18, 283–288. See also Paglione (n58) 397–403.

91 But, as Katselli Proukaki argues, the Court should have also examined the issue in the light of other rules of international human rights law and especially the principle of non-discrimination. Katselli Proukaki (n38) 719 and 729–730.

92 Article 31(3)(c) establishes a rule of treaty interpretation requiring interpreters to consider, together with the context, '[a]ny relevant rules of international law applicable in the relations between the parties'. Initially, it was associated with inter-temporality in treaty interpretation, but scholarship and the ILC linked it with the systemic integration method of interpretation. On systemic integration, see ILC, UN Doc A/CN.4/L.682 (n2) [410–480] and Merkouris P. (2015) *Article 31(3)(c) VCLT and the Principle of Systemic Integration. Normative Shadows in Plato's Cave* (Leiden: Brill). For a critical overview of systemic integration within human rights law and, in particular, the ECHR, see, among others, Pitea C. (2013), 'Interpreting the ECHR in the Light of "Other" International Instruments: Systemic Integration or Fragmentation of Rules on Treaty Interpretation?' in Boschiero N. *et al.* (eds.), *International Courts and the Development of International Law. Essays in Honour of Tullio Treves* (Netherlands: Asser Press), 545–559; Rachovitsa A. (2015) 'Fragmentation of International Law Revisited: Insights, Good Practices, and Lessons to be Learned from the Case Law of the European Court of Human Rights', *LJIL*, Vol. 28, 863–885; Tzevelekos V.P. (2010) 'The Use of Article 31(3)(C) of the VCLT in the Case Law of the ECtHR: An Effective Anti-Fragmentation Tool or a Selective Loophole for the Reinforcement of the Teleology of Human Rights? Between Evolution and Systemic Integration', *MJIL*, Vol. 31, 621–690.

2. The right to housing and property restitution.

   2.1 All refugees and displaced persons have the right to have restored to them any housing, land and/or property of which they were arbitrarily or unlawfully deprived, or to be compensated for any housing, land and/or property that is factually impossible to restore as determined by an independent, impartial tribunal.

   2.2 States shall demonstrably prioritize the right to restitution as the preferred remedy for displacement and as a key element of restorative justice. The right to restitution exists as a distinct right, and is prejudiced neither by the actual return nor non-return of refugees and displaced persons entitled to housing, land and property restitution.[93]

Moving then to humanitarian law, the Fourth Geneva Convention is explicit in its Article 49(2), providing that:

> Persons thus evacuated shall be transferred back to their homes as soon as hostilities in the area in question have ceased.[94]

In similar terms, Rule 132 of the ICRC Customary Law Study confirms the right of displaced persons to:

> [V]oluntary return in safety to their homes or places of habitual residence as soon as the reasons for their displacement cease to exist.[95]

93 See, UN Commission on Human Rights, Sub-Commission on the Promotion and Protection of Human Rights, *Housing and property restitution in the context of the return of refugees and internally displaced persons. Principles on housing and property restitution for refugees and displaced persons*, 28 June 2005, E/CN.4/Sub.2/2005/17. For a commentary, see Hassine K., Leckie S. (2016) *The United Nations Principles on Housing and Property Restitution for Refugees and Displaced Persons ('The Pinheiro Principles'): A Commentary* (Leiden: Brill), 17–21. See also Principle 29(2) of the UN Guiding Principles on Internal Displacement, E/CN.4/1998/53/Add.2, that reads: 'Competent authorities have the duty and responsibility to assist returned and/or resettled internally displaced persons to recover, to the extent possible, their property and possessions which they left behind or were dispossessed of upon their displacement. When recovery of such property and possessions is not possible, competent authorities shall provide or assist these persons in obtaining appropriate compensation or another form of just reparation.' See also n90, UN Economic and Social Council, Commission on Human Rights, *Guiding Principles on Internal Displacement*, E/CN.4/1998/53/Add.2, www.ohchr.org/EN/Issues/IDPersons/Pages/Standards.aspx, and Weiss T.G., Korn, D.A. (2006) *Internal Displacement. Conceptualisation and its Consequences* (London: Routledge).

94 Convention Relative to the Protection of Civilian Persons in Time of War (Fourth Geneva Convention) (1950) 75 *United Nations Treaty Series* 287, 163–228, https://ihl-databases.icrc.org/ihl/INTRO/380. See also n144 on Article 53 and Article 46(2), reading: 'Restrictive measures affecting the [. . .] property [of protected persons] shall be cancelled, in accordance with the law of the Detaining Power, as soon as possible after the close of hostilities.'

95 International Committee of the Red Cross, Customary IHL *Rule 132. Return of Displaced Persons*, https://ihl-databases.icrc.org/customary-ihl/eng/docs/v1_rul_rule132. For a

Last but not least, Article 46 of the 1907 Hague Convention, the breach of which may be said to correspond to a war crime,[96] provides that:

> Family honour and rights, the lives of persons, and private property, as well as religious convictions and practice, must be respected. Private property cannot be confiscated.[97]

From its side, the International Court of Justice has noted that Article 46 of the 1907 Hague Convention does not contain any qualifying provision that would enable mitigating its effects as a means to facilitate military exigencies in occupied territories.[98]

In *Demopoulos*, the ECtHR explicitly explains that it aims to interpret the ECHR in harmony with international law.[99] However, it chose to disregard the examples of *lex specialis*[100] that were just given. These would have allowed it to corroborate (through systemic integration)[101] the symbiotic relationship between human rights and humanitarian law. Instead, it prioritised the 'special character'[102]

critical overview, see Greer J.L. (2007) 'A Critique of the ICRS's Customary Rules Concerning Displaced Persons: General Accuracy, Conflation, and a Missed Opportunity', *MilLR*, Vol. 192, 116–126, 120–121.

96 Article 8(2)(b)(XIII), *Rome Statute of the International Criminal Court* (Rome Statute) (2002). Entry into force 1 July 2002.

97 Hague Convention (IV) *Respecting the Laws and Customs of War on Land and Its Annex: Regulations Concerning the Laws and Customs of War on Land* (The Hague Convention) (1907). Entry into force 26 January 1910.

98 *Legal Consequences of the Construction of a Wall in the Occupied Palestinian Territory* (Advisory opinion) (2004) *International Court of Justice*, Judgment of 9 July 2004, [135], www.icj-cij.org/files/case-related/131/131-20040709-ADV-01-00-EN.pdf.

99 *Demopoulos* (n42), [115].

100 *Legality of the Threat or Use of Nuclear Weapons* (Advisory Opinion) (1996) *International Court of Justice*, Judgment of 8 July 1996, [25], www.icj-cij.org/files/case-related/131/131-20040709-ADV-01-00-EN.pdf. Yet, it must be underlined that the interrelationship between the two branches of international law, i.e. human rights and humanitarian law, is complicated and goes beyond *lex specialis*. See also n8

101 See n92.

102 The ECHR's specialty is linked to the idea of European public order. Thus, 'it is clear from the Preamble to the Convention that the High Contracting Parties in concluding the Convention intended [. . .] to take steps for the collective enforcement of the rights and [. . .] that the purpose [. . .] was to establish a common public order of the free democracies of Europe': *Chrysostomos, Papachrysostomou and Loizidou v Turkey*' (admissibility) (1991) App nos 15299/89 *et al.*, *ECmHR*, [20]. Human rights' specialty transforms the ECHR into a regional 'constitutional' instrument. *Chrysostomos, Papachrysostomou and Loizidou*, [22] and *Loizidou* (preliminary objections, n 5), [75]. From the perspective of international law, the specialty of human rights law translates into a special class of obligations, i.e. *erga omnes* (*partes*) that benefit from collective enforcement. The ECtHR has recognised this since its early days: 'Unlike international treaties of the classical kind, the Convention comprises more than mere reciprocal engagements between contracting States. It creates, over and above a network of mutual, bilateral undertakings, objective obligations which, in the words of the Preamble, benefit from a "collective enforcement"': *Ireland v The United Kingdom* (1978) App no. 5310/71, *ECHR*, Series A no. 25, [239].

of the ECHR.[103] Yet, it did so, not to offer higher standards of human rights protection,[104] but to shift from restitution to satisfaction and (to a certain degree) protect its own interests.

3.1.2. Secondary norms

According to the International Law Commission's (ILC) Articles on the Responsibility of States for Internationally Wrongful Acts (ARSIWA), both restitution[105] and compensation[106] amount to forms of reparation of a wrong.[107] But compensation is owed for the damage caused, 'insofar as such damage is not made good by restitution'.[108]Restitution is the principal form of reparation, with compensation following if restitution is unavailable or inadequate.[109] By restitution is meant the duty of the internationally responsible state to re-establish the situation that existed before the wrongful act (i.e. return to the *status quo ante*),[110] unless this is materially impossible and does not involve a burden out of all proportion to the benefit deriving from restitution instead of compensation.[111] According to the ILC, the (narrow) conception of restitution it opts for might require 'to be complemented by compensation in order to ensure full reparation for the damage caused'.[112] Furthermore, it is an established principle that, between the various forms of reparation, restitution is the primary one.[113] However, the text of ARSIWA makes it clear that the duty to restitute a wrong may be limited if it is materially impossible or disproportionate. As to the former case (i.e. material impossibility) the ILC explains that '[t]his would apply where property to be restored has been permanently lost or destroyed, or has deteriorated to such an extent as to be valueless.'[114] But even if the home of a displaced person has been

103 The ECtHR appears to be cognizant of the 'special' nature of its instrument when it interprets it against extraneous to the ECHR rules of international law. *Loizidou* (preliminary objections, n5), [93] and *Demopoulos* (n42), [115].

104 Especially when relevant, but extraneous to the ECHR rules of international law complement (rather than conflicting with) its text, systemic integration allows 'absorbing' these rules and expanding the semantic field of the ECHR rights. See Tzevelekos (n92), 640–664.

105 Article 35, ILC (2001) *Draft Articles on Responsibility of States for Internationally Wrongful Acts, with commentaries* (ARSIWA) Supplement No. 10 (A/56/10) chp.IV.E.1, Yearbook of ILC, Vol. II, Part Two, http://legal.un.org/ilc/texts/instruments/english/commentaries/9_6_2001.pdf.

106 Ibid, Article 36.

107 Ibid, Article 34.

108 Ibid, Article 36.

109 ILC (2001) *Draft Articles on Responsibility of States for Internationally Wrongful Acts, with commentaries* (ARSIWA), Yearbook of ILC, Vol. II, Part Two, http://legal.un.org/ilc/texts/instruments/english/commentaries/ 9_6_2001.pdf, 96, 99.

110 Ibid, 96.

111 Article 35, ARSIWA (n105).

112 ARSIWA Commentary (n109), 96.

113 Ibid, 96–97.

114 Ibid, 98.

destroyed, the restitution of the land on which that home was built is meaningful. Full reparation can be achieved through compensation *complementing* restitution. As far as is concerned the limitation pertaining to the disproportionate nature of the benefit gained through restitution, this only applies in case of grave disproportionality between the burden on the responsible state and the benefit of the injured party, the criteria being equity and reasonableness.[115] Therefore, any limitation needs to be equitable. Besides, as the ILC explains in its commentaries to ARSIWA, particularly in the case of occupation, 'ancillary measures (the return of persons or property seized in the course of the invasion) will be required as an aspect either of cessation or restitution.'[116]

That last sentence reminds that reparation is just one of the legal consequences of an internationally wrongful act. The wrongdoer is under an obligation to offer guarantees of non-repetition[117] and cease wrongfulness.[118] Otherwise, the state continues to be responsible for as long as wrongfulness lasts.[119] Besides, the legal consequences of an internationally wrongful act, including the duty to repair the wrong, 'do not affect the continued duty of the responsible State to perform the obligation breached'.[120]

The practice of the ECHR system as a whole – and especially of the Court in *Demopoulos* – falls short of the standards of international law on state responsibility and in particular of its rules on reparation. Unfortunately, this concerns not only *Demopoulos* and the cases after it, but also the judgments on the Cyprus issue prior to *Demopoulos*. The Committee of Ministers (CM), which is entrusted under Article 46(2) ECHR with the supervision of the execution of the judgments of the Court, declared that it had exercised its functions when the respondent state paid the compensation awarded by the Court to Mrs Loizidou.[121] That resolution of the CM remains silent as to restitution and return of property. However, on the same day, the CM delivered a second resolution on *Loizidou*, deciding to resume consideration of the execution of the judgment at a later time.[122] To date, almost 20 years after its delivery by the Court, *Loizidou* remains in the list with the cases monitored by the CM, under 'enhanced supervision'.[123]

115 Ibid.
116 Ibid.
117 Article 30(b), ARSIWA (n105).
118 Ibid, Article 30(a).
119 Ibid, Article 14(2).
120 Ibid, Article 29.
121 Council of Europe, Committee of Ministers (2003) *Resolution ResDH(2003)190 concerning the judgment of the European Court of Human Rights of 28 July 1998 in the* Loizidou *case against Turkey*, Resolution ResDH(2003)190 (2 December 2003), http://hudoc.echr.coe.int/eng?i=001-71910.
122 Council of Europe, Committee of Ministers (2003) *Resolution ResDH(2003)191 concerning the judgment of the European Court of Human Rights of 18 December 1996 in the* Loizidou *case against Turkey*, Resolution ResDH(2003)191 (2 December 2003), http://hudoc.echr.coe.int/eng?i=001-71908.
123 See http://hudoc.exec.coe.int/eng#{"fulltext":["loizidou"],"EXECDocumentTypeCollection":["CEC"]}.

Moreover, *Demopoulos* has had a strong impact on *Loizidou* – even if the latter was decided many years before the former. The Memorandum prepared by the Secretariat of the Department for the Execution of Judgments of the ECHR about the cases of displaced Greek-Cypriots makes it clear that the establishment of the IPC in TRNC amounts to a satisfactory general measure of compliance, but also that it is the right avenue for applicants whose cases have been adjudicated by the Court before *Demopoulos* to the extent that it can provide individualised remedies specifically on their case[124] – including, apparently, compensation for loss of property instead of restitution. Judgments before *Demopoulos* cannot be affected as far as the compensations adjudicated by the ECtHR are concerned (*res judicata*), but when it comes to the broader issue of individualised measures adopted by the respondent state to remedy the violations diagnosed, these are to be decided by the IPC, whose practice may then be scrutinised by the ECtHR.[125]

In the ECHR system, if a violation has been found, the conclusive part of the judgment declares its existence. The Court might also adjudge pecuniary compensation under Article 41 of the Convention, which provides for the adjudication of just satisfaction, if only partial reparation is possible. '[T]he purpose of awarding sums by way of just satisfaction is to provide reparation solely for damage suffered by those concerned to the extent that such events constitute a consequence of the violation *that cannot otherwise be remedied*.'[126] In exceptional circumstances, the Court had, in the past, included in the conclusive part of its judgment an obligation for states to act in a certain way by taking specific measures, such as releasing detained persons.[127] But, outside what is in the conclusive part of a judgment, i.e. what the Court may explicitly request states to do as a remedy of a violation states have a duty to adopt individual measures that will remedy any violation found by the Court.[128] If wrongfulness is ongoing, such individual

124 Council of Europe, Committee of Ministers (2010) Memorandum prepared by the Secretariat of the Department for the Execution of Judgments of the ECHR (Directorate General of Human Rights and Legal Affairs), *Cases examined by the Committee of Ministers concerning the property rights and homes of displaced Greek Cypriots. Consequences of the inadmissibility decision adopted by the European Court on 5 March 2010 in the case of* Demopoulos v Turkey and 7 other cases, CM/Inf/DH(2010)21, parts II and III, https://search.coe.int/cm/Pages/result_details.aspx?ObjectId=09000016805af4da.

125 Ibid, part III. Cf. *Meleagrou and others v Turkey* (decision on admissibility) (2013) App no. 14434/09, *ECHR*, [13]–[16]. The Court declared inadmissible the claims as the applicants had only sought before the IPC restitution of the property and not exchange of it or compensation for its loss. According to the Court, the applicants did not make proper use of the available domestic remedies.

126 *Scozzari and Giunta v Italy* [GC] (2000) App nos 39221/98 and 41963/98, *ECHR*, VIII, [250] (emphasis added).

127 For instance, *Assanidze v Georgia* [GC] (2004) App no. 71503/01, *ECHR*, II, conclusive part of the judgment, conclusion 14(a).

128 See Council of Europe, *The supervision process,* www.coe.int/en/web/execution/the-supervision-process. See also Zwaak L. (2006) 'The Supervisory Task of the Committee of Ministers' in Hoof P.V. *et al.* (eds.), *Theory and Practice of the European Convention on Human Rights*, 4th edn. (Cambridge: Intersentia), 301–308.

measures encompass the duty to cease it. Next to individual measures, states are under an obligation to take general measures as well that will be addressing the causes of the problem diagnosed.[129] This may be seen as corresponding to the duty under general international law to offer guarantees of non-repetition. The aim is to prevent similar human rights violations in the future. In that sense, guarantees of non-repetition may be said to fall under the duty of states to demonstrate due diligence.[130] Consequently, the Court's judgments develop a broader effect, requiring states to do more than what they are explicitly asked in the conclusive part of the judgment.[131] States are under a duty to pay any compensation adjudicated by the Court *and* strive for 'substantial' compliance consisting in putting an end to wrongfulness, remedying it and eliminating its causes so that this is not repeated.[132] The principle is that the means of compliance are to be decided by the state.[133] This is a sign of respect for state sovereignty, but also an expression of the principle of subsidiarity. Therefore, in principle, states shall enjoy discretion in choosing the means for preventing the repetition of their wrongs and repairing them, but only as long as and to the extent that restitution is impossible.[134]

129 See *The supervision process* (n128); Zwaak (n128), 308–317.

130 See, e.g., International Law Association (2014) *Study Group on Due Diligence in International Law, First Report by Duncan French (Chair) and Tim Stephens (Rapporteur)*, Report of the Seventy-Sixth Conference, Washington: International Law Association, 14–22, https://olympereseauinternational.files.wordpress.com/2015/07/due_diligence_-_first_report_2014.pdf.

131 Outside compensation (i.e. just satisfaction), and individual and general measures aiming at remedying and preventing breaches, ECtHR's case law develops a broader authority/effect beyond the respondent state against which a breach has been diagnosed. 'The principle of solidarity implies that the case-law of the Court forms part of the Convention, thus extending the legally binding force of the Convention *erga omnes* (to all the other parties). This means that the states parties not only have to execute the judgments of the Court pronounced in cases to which they are party, but also have to take into consideration the possible implications which judgments pronounced in other cases may have for their own legal system and legal practice.' Council of Europe, Parliamentary Assembly (2000) *Execution of judgments of the European Court of Human Rights*. Resolution 1226, [3], http://assembly.coe.int/nw/xml/XRef/Xref-DocDetails-EN.asp?FileID=16834&lang=EN.

132 *Scozzari and Giunta* (n126), [249]. Zwaak (n128), 295–296. Cohen-Jonathan G. (1995) 'Quelques considérations sur l'autorité des arrêts de la Cour européenne des Droits de l'Homme' in Berger V. (ed.), *Liber amicorum Marc-André Eissen* (Bruxelles: Bruylant), 49–50.

133 Zwaak (n128) 298. This explains why, when in *Assanidze* (n127) the Court requested the applicant's release, it felt obliged to explain that 'by its very nature, the violation found in the instant case does not leave any real choice as to the measures required to remedy it.' [202].

134 *Selçuk and Asker v Turkey* (merits and just satisfaction) (1998) App nos 23184/94 and 23815/94, *ECHR*, II, [125]. According to the Court 'a judgment in which it finds a breach imposes on the respondent State a legal obligation to put an end to the breach and make reparation for its consequences in such a way as to restore as far as possible the situation existing before the breach (*restitutio in integrum*). However, if *restitutio in integrum* is in practice impossible, the respondent States are free to choose the means whereby they comply'.

The purpose of this brief reminder of the effects developed by the judgments of the ECtHR is not to make an abstract, theoretical comparison between the rules of general international law on state responsibility and those of the ECHR (the way they have been shaped by the competent Council of Europe institutions).[135] The point to make is that the shift from restitution to compensation for loss of property runs counter to general international law (both primary and secondary), but also to the Convention system itself. Seen from the perspective of international law, *Demopoulos* and its effects fail to contribute to the ECtHR's declared intention to take into account when interpreting the ECHR the relevant rules of international law. Hence, in that case, the Court cannot pride itself that it is harmoniously integrating its regime into the system of international law.

The counterargument is that there is nothing preventing the ECHR regime from containing or developing its own 'custom-made' *lex specialis*[136] that will be fit for the purpose of the reparation of violations in the special area of human rights protection. Additionally, the ECtHR is the last word, authentic interpreter of the ECHR and its regime may not always be aligned with other rules (or/and their interpretation) of international law. Admittedly, this may lead to the fragmentation of international law, but, in a sense, this is inherent to that legal order. Besides, the ECtHR is an effective and influential 'player' within the system of international law that co-shapes its rules and standards. Moreover, from the perspective of human rights law (and under a cost-benefit logic) fragmentation might be a side effect that the system of international law should suffer to allow a regional system for the protection of human rights to offer higher standards than those that apply in other regions or worldwide. But this is not the case in the present instance. Shifting from restitution to compensation for loss of property in the context of military occupation is neither aligned with international law, nor does it promote human rights protection. *Demopoulos* is in manifest misalignment not only with international law but also with the humanistic teleology and the very *raison d'être* of human rights protection at the international level. The reasons supporting the latter aspect of this claim are explained below.

3.2 Restitution of property as a matter of human rights

The right to property is not absolute. It may be limited for reasons of public interest or to protect the rights of third persons. Provided that compensation is paid, one may be deprived of her possessions and, in a sense, 'sacrifice' her rights for the benefit of the society or of third individuals whose interests/rights are

135 See, e.g., *Verein gegen Tierfabriken Schweiz (VgT) v Switzerland* (No. 2) (2009) App no. 32772/02, *ECHR*, [86], where the Court explicitly refers to Article 35 ARSIWA and interprets the ECHR in its light.

136 Just satisfaction, instead of full satisfaction, is an example of a special rule within the ECHR regime that departs in that respect from general international law and ARSIWA. See also Simma, Pulkowski (n2).

found to be weightier in the light of the particular circumstances of a given case. That being explained, the question to be asked is why then to exclude compensation for loss of property in the case of displaced persons?

The first argument in that respect is that in the cases examined in this chapter the Court has consistently held that the applicants remained the lawful owners of the possessions they have been forced to abandon and that their cases raised no issues of dispossession, but of inability to access and enjoy their property/home. Approving the payment of compensation for loss of property in this context amounts to a miscalibration between the violation found and its remedy. The reparation of a wrong needs to be fit for purpose, that is to say, in alignment with the violation of the rule found. By allowing the payment of compensation (instead of restitution) in the case of forced displacement as a result of occupation, the Court is in reality shifting from the first rule contained in Article 1 Protocol 1 to the second.[137]

But, to continue with a second argument, even if one treats the issues raised by these cases as a (*de facto*) expropriation, the Court has distinguished between lawful and unlawful deprivation of property – in the sense of not being prescribed by national law, i.e. incompatible with the principle of legality.[138] In case of unlawful dispossession, restitution is the optimal form of reparation.[139] When deprivation of property is found to have a basis in the law, the Court proceeds with assessing the legitimacy and the necessity of the reasons allegedly justifying it. For a lawful dispossession to meet the ECHR criteria, (some) compensation is owed.[140] But compensation needs not to be full, if reasons of public interest justify

137 See n17.

138 *Former King of Greece and others v Greece* (merits) [GC] (2000) App no. 25701/94, *ECHR*, XII, [90].

139 *Papamichalopoulos and others v Greece* (just satisfaction) (1995) App no. 14556/89, *ECHR*, [36], [38]. The case concerned *de facto* expropriation. The Court explained that the unlawfulness of dispossession affects the criteria for remedying the wrong and referred to the Permanent Court of International Justice's judgment of 13 September 1928 in the case concerning the factory at Chorzów. Cf. *Brumarescu v Romania* (just satisfaction) (2001) App no. 28342/95, *ECHR*. Failing restitution, the respondent state was allowed to pay compensation. See also *Zwierzyński v Poland* (just satisfaction) (2002) App no. 34049/96, *ECHR* and *Dacia S.R.L. v Molodova* (just satisfaction) (2009) App no. 3052/04, *ECHR*. But see, in the context of internal displacement, *Saghinadze and others v Georgia* (2010) App no. 18768/05, *ECHR*, [160] and the conclusive part of the judgment. The Court decided that if restitution is impossible, states should provide alternative appropriate accommodation.

140 Ibid, [99]. See also Article 1 Protocol 1, prohibiting the deprivation of property 'except in the public interest and subject to the conditions provided for by law and by the *general principles of international law*' (emphasis added). As Conodorelli explains, the purpose of the reference made to 'general principles of international law' was to 'bypass' the disagreement among the drafters as to whether specific mention should be made to compensation as a precondition for the lawfulness of a dispossession. The case law of the ECtHR has now solved this issue, but, in their early practice (influenced by foreign investment law), the ECHR institutions were of the opinion that compensation was owed only for foreign property. Condorelli L. (1999) 'Premier Protocole Additionnel. Article 1'

the payment of a lower amount of money.[141] Thus, balancing the rights of an individual against general interest or third persons' rights may be seen as playing a double role in the context of the right to property. It is a tool used to assess the permissibility of a dispossession, but may also find an application as a means to evaluate the remedy owed (although these two aspects might be seen as interconnected or as two sides of the same coin).[142] The argument suggested in this chapter is that nothing justifies shifting from restitution to compensation in the case of forced displacement arising from unlawful use of force leading to occupation. In principle, such a displacement is arbitrary, i.e. lacks a normative foundation. This should prevent the Court from continuing with its habitual test. That is to say that the Court should not enter into testing proportionality. Besides (leaving aside the criterion of arbitrariness), a precondition for assessing the necessity of an interference as a means to pursue an aim is that the aim pursued is legitimate. Arguing that the maintenance of military occupation in breach of the most fundamental rules of international law amounts to a legitimate aim that would justify assessing the necessity of property misappropriation would be highly problematic. In this context – from the perspective of human rights law –, as such, expropriation cannot but be seen as pursuing an illegitimate aim.[143] This means that the interference with the property is violating the ECHR. Restitution is the preferable form of reparation for the simple reason that dispossession is arbitrary/unlawful, whereas the payment of compensation supports and deepens unlawful military occupation by offering it a façade of lawfulness. Land and property are at the very core of military occupation – and human rights are not meant to neither have they been designed to 'launder' military occupation.

But, to move to the third argument, one may claim that the justification of compensation has nothing to do with occupation. *Per se*, occupation can only very exceptionally render legitimacy to (i.e. justify) interferences with property.[144]

in Pettiti L.E. *et al.* (eds.), *La Convention européenne des droits de l'homme. Commentaire article par article* (London: Economica) 986–988. See also Kriebaum U. (2007) 'Regulatory Takings: Balancing the Interests of the Investor and the State', *JWIT*, Vol. 8, 717–744, 720.

141 *Former King of Greece and others v Greece* (just satisfaction) [GC] (2002) App no. 25701/94, *ECHR*, [78]. See also *James* (n17), [54].

142 *Former King of Greece* (n138), [89]. Kriebaum (n140), 739–743.

143 But see n144 on military necessity. Military necessity applies in case also of unlawful occupation. See Koutroulis V. (2013), 'And Yet It Exists: In Defence of the 'Equality of Belligerents' Principle', *LJIL*, Vol. 26, 449–472, 467.

144 See, e.g., Article 53 of the Fourth Geneva Convention (n 94) that reads: 'Any destruction by the Occupying Power of real or personal property belonging individually or collectively to private persons, or to the State, or to other public authorities, or to social or cooperative organizations, is prohibited, except where such destruction is rendered *absolutely necessary by military operations*' (emphasis added). This is an example of a rule of humanitarian law that allows interfering with property for reasons of military necessity. In this context, military necessity refers to the protection of the security of the occupying forces. As all exceptions, it needs to be interpreted strictly. Moreover, military necessity should not be invoked in the absence of a basis explicitly referring to it. Another precondition is the

What, however, may justify them (enabling also the shift from restitution to compensation) is the rights of those who now live in the occupied land (i.e. the rights of the secondary occupants). As it has already been discussed, this is what the Court seems to argue in *Demopoulos.*[145] Life goes on after a military invasion and, especially when the parties to the dispute fail to solve it for a large number of years, a new reality is established. People living on the occupied land develop ties with it and establish rights. The new land is their home as much as it was for the displaced persons. This makes it necessary to weigh the rights of the latter group of people against those established over time by the new occupants of the homes and properties. Human rights aim at protecting all human beings – not only displaced persons. Indeed, this path of reasoning raises issues of legitimacy and asks for the establishment of priorities in the protection.

Why then exclude compensation for deprivation of property in that case? Why not let the new occupants enjoy their ties with the property in question? As a matter of fact, these ties may be stronger as those people are actually living or working in the property at stake.[146] The answer to these questions is that human rights law needs to protect both groups as they both have legitimate claims over and links with the disputed home/property. However, it would be wrong to ignore the particular context of these cases and the circumstances that led to the situation described here. Displacement in this context has been caused by unlawful military occupation. The dilemma at issue is not merely one between displaced persons and new occupants, but also between law (that prohibits the use of force and occupation) and fact, that is to say, the new reality established by occupation. It may be that in international law effectiveness produces legal effects in certain instances, but we know that this should be squarely excluded in the case of reality generated through unlawful means. *Ex injuria jus non oritur.*[147] Therefore, one is prompted to see the bigger picture and acknowledge that this is not a usual case of conflict of interests/rights between two categories of individuals. Military occupation is not akin to 'ordinary' expropriation that can be fully remedied provided that the loss is compensated. Shifting to compensation from restitution fails to serve the purposes of deterrence. Quite the opposite, it gives incentives to

applicability of humanitarian law (n8). Finally, the chances are higher for military necessity to justify interferences with property during the early stages of an occupation. Necessity declines in case of prolonged occupation, especially when hostilities have reached an end. See Koutroulis V. (2012), 'The Application of International Humanitarian Law and International Human Rights Law in Situation of Prolonged Occupation: Only a Matter of Time?', *IRRC*, Vol. 94, 1656205, 193.

145 See also *Meleagrou* (n125).

146 The ties between displaced persons and lost property are not automatic. See Williams R.C, Gürel A. (2011) 'The European Court of Human Rights and the Cyprus Property Issue: Charting a Way Forward', Peace Research Institute, Oslo, Paper 1/2011, 18.

147 See Distefano G. (2002) *L'ordre international entre légalité et effectivité. Le titre juridique dans le contentieux territorial* (Paris/Geneva: Pedone). The author discusses the legal effects of effectiveness in territorial disputes and refers explicitly to the principles of *ex injuria jus nor oritur* and *ex factis jus oritur* in 253, and 314 and following.

the occupying power to continue with occupation, hoping that its conduct can be legitimised in the future through compensation. Moreover, it might be seen as a policy that risks encouraging ethnic, religious etc. cleansing or segregation. Outside the competing rights between the displaced old owners and the secondary occupants, displacement raises issues of public order and public interest.

In essence, both groups of people, i.e. the displaced persons and the new occupants, are victims of the same responsible state. This is the state whose powers unlawfully occupy foreign territory. It is that state's responsibility to repair the damage suffered by both groups. The displaced persons should be given the right to return to their home. In principle, their rights trump those of the new occupants.[148] Thus, *in principle*,[149] displaced persons should be allowed to peacefully enjoy their property, whereas *bona fide* secondary occupants should be compensated for the property they will have to leave.[150] Unless a (human rights friendly)[151] political

148 Leckie S. (2003) 'New Directions in Housing and Property Restitution' in Leckie S. (ed.), *Returning Home: Housing and Property Restitution Rights of Refugees and Displaced Persons* (Ardsley: Transnational Publishers) 3–6, 47–48; Phuong C. (2004), *The International Protection of Internally Displaced Persons* (Cambridge: Cambridge University Press) 194; Allen T. (2006) 'Restitution and Transitional Justice in the European Court of Human Rights', *CJIL*, Vol. 13(1), 1–46, 27.

149 Each situation calls for an *ad hoc* balancing considering its particularities (such as the personal circumstances of the old and the new occupants, the use – i.e. residential, commercial etc. – of the property or whether the new occupant acts in good faith) and seeking to produce equitable/just results. On secondary occupants' rights, see Kagan K. (2007) 'Restitution as a Remedy for Refugee Property: Claims in the Israeli-Palestinian Conflict', *FJIL*, Vol. 19, 422–489, 466–486.

150 As Leckie argues, 'adequate measures [need to be] taken to ensure that current occupants will be protected against homelessness or unreasonable relocation'. Leckie S. (2000) 'Housing and Property Issues for Refugees and Internally Displaced Persons in the Context of Return: Key Considerations for UNCHR Policy and Practice', *RSQ*, Vol. 19, 5–63, 16. See also the Pinheiro Principles (n 93), Principle 17 on the rights of secondary occupants and the critical analysis of Smit A. (2012), *The Property Rights of Refugees and Internally Displaced Persons* (London: Routledge) 167 and following.

151 In principle, any agreement solving a dispute between two or more states/actors needs to comply with human rights law. This is because of the humanistic aims of that area of law and the importance of the values it protects, but also because respect for human rights contributes to the sustainability of the solution promoted by the agreement. On the concept of 'sustainable return', see Chimni B.S. (2002) 'Post-Conflict Peace-Building and the Return of Refugees: Concepts, Practices, and Institutions' in Newman E. and van Selm J. (eds), *Refugees and Forced Displacement: International Security, Human Vulnerability, and the State* (Tokyo: United Nations University Press) 200–201. The idea of a human rights friendly solution raises a broader theoretical question concerning the limits of sovereign will (as this could be reflected for instance in a future interstate agreement solving the Cyprus issue) when conflicting with human rights. Any such agreement will inevitably favour (to a certain extent) the rights of one group of people to the detriment of the rights of another group. No such agreement can have zero cost for human rights. However, non-absolute human rights are flexible enough and may accommodate limitations that are necessary for public interest purposes. Proportionality establishes occasional priorities and is the tool to be used to assess the lawfulness of such limitations. This raises two interconnected important issues, one technical and one sociolegal.

settlement is reached that will be voluntarily accepted by the parties to the dispute or the state that has caused the displacement (which might be an occupying power) wishes to compensate for the loss of property and the displaced person prefers that solution (i.e. compensation for loss of property) instead of restitution.[152]

Admittedly, a political settlement may affect human rights and even limit them. For instance, according to the Annan Plan, only a relatively small percentage of displaced persons would return to their homes.[153] It goes without saying that the same rules and logic apply here too. Any political settlement must be compatible with human rights. Yet, with very few exceptions, most human rights are not unlimited. Proportionality and the legitimacy of an interference can only be assessed in the light of the particular circumstances of a case and, indeed, the context changes significantly in the case of a mutually acceptable solution. Not because of the agreement itself, as sovereign will is not a reason *per se* justifying human rights limitations, but because such an agreement will be destined to open a new era of peaceful co-existence between nations and facilitate the transition to that new era. Because such an agreement will be a means of prevention of future human rights violations and will contribute to peace, which is a precondition for the enjoyment of human rights, including rights that are more important than the rights to property and home, such as human life. Transitional considerations and the relativism[154] that these entail will need to be taken duly into account when assessing the permissibility of interferences by any agreement settling conflicts involving forcible displacement.

4 Instead of a conclusion

This chapter addressed the question of the reparation of the rights to property and home in the context of the ECHR, observing that the ECtHR does not exclude the payment of compensation by the responsible state for the deprivation

The technical one concerns hierarchy of rules and the establishment of occasional priorities in case of conflict between fundamental rights and an (international) agreement settling a dispute. The sociolegal one concerns the extent to which a political solution to a complex issue affecting the lives and rights of many people should be allowed to limit individual rights. Inevitably, cost-benefit analysis applies. For instance, exchange of populations is a painful policy that, *prima facie*, violates fundamental human rights. But, if these rights are not absolute, exchange of populations can be a permissible solution when, considering the specifics of a dispute, it can prevent a genocide, war crimes etc. Losing a home is less painful than life losses – and this is something that can be translated into normative (in the sense of norms as rules) prioritisation through proportionality balancing.

152 Paglione (n58) 408–409.

153 *Demopoulos* (n42) [16]. For a critique of the Annan Plan from the perspective of human rights, see Katselli Proukaki (n38), 711–712 (and the sources to which she refers).

154 On transitional relativism, see Sweeney J.A. (2013), *The European Court of Human Rights in the Post-Cold War Era. Universality in Transition* (London: Routledge) 30–37.

of property in case of military occupation. Although the case law at question is neither sufficient nor clear enough to allow drawing conclusions as to whether it only concerns displacement in the context of the Cyprus issue and what are the conditions to be met to shift from restitution to compensation for loss of property, this is what the Court has done with *Demopoulos*. The argument built in that respect in the paper is easy to summarise: downgrading from restitution to compensation goes against international law, both primary and secondary; although the human rights at issue may suffer limitations (especially if an agreement is reached between the involved states, settling the issue and establishing the condition for a new era of peaceful co-existence), limitations are difficult to be justified in the case of unlawful military occupation. The right to return home and peacefully enjoy it amounts to an essential remedy against occupation.

But, sometimes, because of its technical nature, law is not the plainest way to communicate an argument. Neither can it aptly reveal the human dimension of it. For that reason, readers are invited to watch two publically available documentaries. *This is Kiruna: How to Move a City* is a short documentary available on YouTube.[155] Kiruna is the northernmost town in Sweden. It has a population of around 20,000 people, the majority of which works for the main employer in the area, a company mining iron. Because of its activities, the ground under the town is growing increasingly unstable. As a result, a big part of the city has to be relocated two miles to the east. People's homes and immovable property are to be expropriated and Kiruna's residents may choose between a new home at the relocated part of the city or compensation. The second recommended documentary (among the several ones on the topic) is an interactive web documentary[156] in which a real estate agency markets expropriated Palestinian properties as 'Arab style'. These two documentaries tell different stories. Displacement because of occupation differs from any other reason leading to interferences with property and home rights. The law, especially human rights law, cannot disregard this. And if market and its logic may tolerate corporations using the 'Arab style' euphemism to disguise stories of individual tragedies and pain caused by displacement and alienation from one person's home and land, where she has lived part of her life and with which she is connected, the very purpose of human rights law, the very reason why that area of law exists is to show no tolerance to such phenomena. Restitution of property and voluntary return to home are the preferable ways to repair forced displacement.

155 *This is Kiruna: How to Move a City* (2016), www.youtube.com/watch?v=WKvqJ05AsPY&t=547s.

156 *Dream Homes Property Consultants* (2013), www.dreamhomespropertyconsultants.com. For a synopsis, see Handal A. (2007–ongoing) *Ciné-dérive cinema and new media production house*, www.cine-derive.com/projects/DHPC.

Bibliography

Books

Distefano G. (2002), *L'ordre international entre légalité et effectivité. Le titre juridique dans le contentieux territorial* (Paris/Geneva, Pedone).

Haider D. (2013), *The Pilot-Judgment Procedure of the European Court of Human Rights* (Leiden, Nijhoff).

Hassine K. and Leckie S. (2016), *The United Nations Principles on Housing and Property Restitution for Refugees and Displaced Persons ('The Pinheiro Principles'): A Commentary* (Leiden, Brill).

Leach P.R. *et al.* (2010), *Responding to Systemic Human Rights Violations. An Analysis of 'Pilot Judgments' of the European Court of Human Rights and their Impact at National Level* (Antwerp, Intersentia).

Merkouris P. (2015), *Article 31(3)(c) VCLT and the Principle of Systemic Integration. Normative Shadows in Plato's Cave* (Leiden, Brill).

Phuong C. (2004), *The International Protection of Internally Displaced Persons* (Cambridge, Cambridge University Press).

Smit A. (2012), *The Property Rights of Refugees and Internally Displaced Persons* (London, Routledge).

Sweeney J. A. (2013), *The European Court of Human Rights in the Post-Cold War Era. Universality in Transition* (London, Routledge).

Weiss T.G. and Korn D.A. (2006), *Internal Displacement. Conceptualisation and its Consequences* (London, Routledge).

Book chapters

Chimni B.S. (2002), 'Post-Conflict Peace-Building and the Return of Refugees: Concepts, Practices, and Institutions' in Newman E. and van Selm J. (eds.) *Refugees and Forced Displacement: International Security, Human Vulnerability, and the State* (Tokyo, United Nations University Press) 195–220.

Cohen-Jonathan G. (1995), 'Quelques considérations sur l'autorité des arrêts de la Cour européenne des Droits de l'Homme' in Berger V. (ed.), *Liber amicorum Marc-André Eissen* (Bruxelles, Bruylant).

Condorelli L. (1999), 'Premier Protocole Additionnel. Article 1' in Pettiti L.E. *et al* (eds.), *La Convention européenne des droits de l'homme. Commentaire article par article* (London, Economica).

Leckie S. (2003), 'New Directions in Housing and Property Restitution' in Leckie S. (ed.), *Returning Home: Housing and Property Restitution Rights of Refugees and Displaced Persons* (Ardsley, Transnational Publishers) 3–61.

Rozakis C.L. (2015), 'The Rights of Displaced Persons under Article 1 Protocol 1 and 8 of the European Convention of Human Rights' in Casadevall J. *et al.* (eds.), *Liber Amicorum Dean Spielmann. Mélanges en l'honneur de Dean Spielmann /Essays in Honour of Dean Spielmann* (Netherlands, Wolf Legal Publishers) 561.

Pitea C. (2013), 'Interpreting the ECHR in the Light of "Other" International Instruments: Systemic Integration or Fragmentation of Rules on Treaty Interpretation?' in Boschiero N. *et al.* (eds.), *International Courts and the Development of International Law. Essays in Honour of Tullio Treves* (Netherlands, Asser Press) 545–559.

Zwaak L. (2006), 'The Supervisory Task of the Committee of Ministers' in Hoof P.V. et al (eds), *Theory and Practice of the European Convention on Human Rights* (Cambridge, Intersentia).

Journal articles

Allen T. (2006), 'Restitution and Transitional Justice in the European Court of Human Rights', *Columbia Journal of European Law*, Vol. 13(1), 1–46.

Greer J.L. (2007), 'A Critique of the ICRS's Customary Rules Concerning Displaced Persons: General Accuracy, Conflation, and a Missed Opportunity', *Military Law Review*, Vol. 192, 116–126.

Hadjigeorgiou N. (2016), 'Remedying Displacement in Frozen Conflicts: Lessons from the Case of Cyprus', *Cambridge Yearbook of European Legal Studies*, Vol. 18, 152–175.

Kagan K. (2007), 'Restitution as a Remedy for Refugee Property: Claims in the Israeli-Palestinian Conflict', *Florida Journal of International Law*, Vol. 19, 422–489.

Katselli Proukaki E. (2014), 'The Right of Displaced Persons to Property and to Return Home after Demopoulos', *Human Rights Law Review*, Vol. 14, 701–732.

Koutroulis V. (2012), 'The Application of International Humanitarian Law and International Human Rights Law in Situation of Prolonged Occupation: Only a Matter of Time?', *International Review of the Red Cross*, Vol. 94, 165–205.

Koutroulis V. (2013), 'And Yet It Exists: In Defence of the 'Equality of Belligerents' Principle', *Leiden Journal of International Law*, Vol. 26, 449–472.

Kriebaum U. (2007), 'Regulatory Takings: Balancing the Interests of the Investor and the State', *Journal of World Investment and Trade*, Vol. 8, 717–744.

Lawand K. (1996), 'The Right to Return of Palestinians in International Law', *International Journal of Refugee Law*, Vol. 8, 532–568.

Leckie S. (2000), 'Housing and Property Issues for Refugees and Internally Displaced Persons in the Context of Return: Key Considerations for UNCHR Policy and Practice', *Refugee Survey Quarterly*, Vol. 19, 5–63.

Orakhelashvili A. (2008), 'The Interaction between Human Rights and Humanitarian Law: Fragmentation, Conflict, Parallelism, or Convergence?', *European Journal of International Law*, Vol. 19(1), 161–182.

Paglione P.G. (2008), 'Individual Property Restitution: From Deng to Pinheiro – and the Challenges Ahead', *International Journal of Refugee Law*, Vol. 20, 391–412.

Rachovitsa A. (2015), 'Fragmentation of International Law Revisited: Insights, Good Practices, and Lessons to be Learned from the Case Law of the European Court of Human Rights', *Leiden Journal of International Law*, Vol. 28, 863–885.

Simma B. (1985), 'Self-contained Regimes', *Netherlands Yearbook of International Law*, Vol. 16, 111–136.

Simma B., Pulkowski D. (2006), 'Of Planets and the Universe: Self-contained Regimes in International Law', *European Journal of International Law*, Vol. 17, 483–529.

Thiele B. (2000), 'Housing and Property Restitution in the Context of the Return of Refugees and Internally Displaced Persons: Developments at the United Nations', *Netherlands Quarterly Human Rights*, Vol. 18, 283–288.

Tomuschat C. (2010), 'Human Rights and International Humanitarian Law', *European Journal of International Law*, Vol. 21(1), 15–23.

Tzevelekos V.P. (2010), 'The Use of Article 31(3)(C) of the VCLT in the Case Law of the ECtHR: An Effective Anti-Fragmentation Tool or a Selective Loophole for the Reinforcement of the Teleology of Human Rights? Between Evolution and Systemic Integration', *Michigan Journal of International Law*, Vol. 31, 621–690.

Tzevelekos V.P. (2015), 'Reconstructing the Effective Control Criterion in Extraterritorial Human Rights Breaches: Direct Attribution of Wrongfulness, Due Diligence, and Concurrent Responsibility', *Michigan Journal of International Law*, Vol. 36, 129–178.

Veraart W. (2009), 'Redressing the Past with an Eye to the Future: The Impact of the Passage of Time on Property Rights Restitution in Post-Apartheid South Africa', *Netherlands Quarterly of Human Rights*, Vol. 27, 45–60.

Ziemele I., Liede L. (2013), 'Reservations to Human Rights Treaties: From Draft Guideline 3.1.12 to Guideline 3.1.5.6', *European Journal of International Law*, Vol. 24(4), 1135–1152.

Research papers

Williams R.C, Gürel A. (2011) *The European Court of Human Rights and the Cyprus Property Issue: Charting a Way Forward*, Peace Research Institute Oslo. Paper 1/2011.

4 The right to respect of home and enjoyment of property for Cypriot IDPs

The developing jurisprudence of the ECtHR

Eleni Meleagrou and Costas Paraskeva

1 Introduction

Under the European Convention on Human Rights ("ECHR" or "Convention") the right to respect of home is protected under Article 8[1] whereas the right to the enjoyment of property is protected under Article 1 of Protocol No. 1.[2]

The European Court of Human Rights ("ECtHR" or "Court") has applied Article 1 of Protocol No. 1 and Article 8 to the violations of these rights in the context of internal displacement and has further developed its case law to safeguard and promote the property and home rights of internally displaced persons ("IDPs"). Thus, member states found in violation of the rights to property and home of IDPs under the Convention are obligated to take the appropriate measures to remedy the violations to the extent possible in the circumstances of each case.

The very first cases concerning the violations of the rights to property and homes of displaced persons under the Convention to be heard in Strasbourg were those concerning the large numbers of Greek Cypriots displaced to the south of the island. This was the direct result of the occupation of the northern part of Cyprus by Turkey, following a Greek junta instigated coup, a Turkish invasion and war in the summer of 1974.[3]

The continuing occupation of the northern part of Cyprus by Turkey has resulted in the forceful eviction of some 210,000 Cypriots – 165,000 Greek Cypriots and 45,000 Turkish Cypriots [4]– from their homes and properties; the

1 Article 8 of the Convention for the Protection of Human Rights and Fundamental Freedoms, better known as the European Convention on Human Rights (ECHR), ETS No 5, was opened for signature in Rome on 4 November 1950 and came into force in 1953.

2 Article 1 of Protocol No. 1 to the ECHR, n1.

3 See, among others, Hitchens C. (1984), Cyprus (Quartet Books). [Revised 3rd ed. Hostage to History: Cyprus from the Ottomans to Kissinger, 1997 (Verso Books); Ker-Lindsay J. (2011), The Cyprus Problem, What Everyone Needs to Know (OUP).

4 For details on the numbers and their calculation, see Republic of Cyprus Official Gazette, 26 July 2002; Internal Displacement Monitoring Centre, http://www.internal-displacement.org/countries/cyprus.

term coined at the time regarding the Greek Cypriot displaced persons was "refugees in our own homeland".[5] The displacement continues to this day and is the longest standing one in Europe.

Shortly after the events of 1974 the Government of Cyprus applied to the European Commission of Human Rights alleging a number of human rights violations imputable to Turkey, directly resulting from war and occupation. Consequently, violations of Article 8 and Article 1 of Protocol No. 1 were initially found to be imputable to Turkey by the European Commission of Human Rights both in its 1976 Report on applications Nos. 6780/74 and 6950/75[6] and in its 1983 Report[7] on application No. 8007/77.[8] At the time, the Commission found that there were no effective remedies available[9] to the applicant Government and thus rejected Turkey's preliminary objection regarding the non-exhaustion of domestic remedies.

The stage was thus set for the "Cyprus cases" before the ECtHR during the decades that followed, coming to a seemingly abrupt end in early 2010 with the inadmissibility decision in *Demopoulos and Others v Turkey*.[10] In that decision, the ECtHR held that the remedy set up in the north of Cyprus by the

5 The term IDP is a more recent one and the distinction between refugees and IDPs not drawn at the time hence the reference to "refugees in their own country", coined by the Cypriots at the time of the displacement.

6 *Cyprus v Turkey* (Commission Report), Application nos. 6780/74 and 6950/75, 10 July 1976, [208]: "The Commission considers that the prevention of the physical possibility of the return of Greek Cypriot refugees to their homes in the north of Cyprus amounts to an infringement, imputable to Turkey, of their right to respect of their homes as guaranteed in Art. 8 (1) of the Convention. This infringement cannot be justified on any ground under para. (2) of this Article. The Commission concludes by 13 votes against one that, by the refusal to allow the return of more than 170,000 Greek Cypriot refugees to their homes in the north of Cyprus, Turkey did not act, and was continuing not to act (3) in conformity with Art, 8 of the Convention in all these cases"; and [486]: "The Commission, by 12 votes against one, finds it established that there has been deprivation of possessions of Greek Cypriots on a large scale . . . This deprivation must be imputed to Turkey under the Convention-and it has not been shown that any of these interferences were necessary for any of the purposes mentioned in Art, 1 of Protocol No 1."

7 *Cyprus v Turkey* (Commission Report), Application no. 8007/77, 4 Oct. 1983, [133]: "In the present case the Commission, again examining the issue of displaced persons under Art 8 of the Convention, confirms the finding made, at [168] of its Report on the previous applications, that displaced Greek Cypriots in the South are physically prevented from returning to the northern are as a result of the fact that the demarcation line across Cyprus ('green line' in Nicosia) is sealed off by the Turkish army"; [135]: "The Commission concludes . . . that by her continued refusal to allow over 170,000 Greek Cypriots the return to their homes in the North of Cyprus, Turkey continues to violate Art 8 in all these cases"; and [155]: "The Commission concludes . . . that Turkey has violated Article 1 of Protocol No.1."

8 See Coufoudakis V. (1982), "Cyprus and the European Convention on Human Rights: The Law and Politics of Cyprus v Turkey" HRQ, Vol. 4, 450–473.

9 *Cyprus v Turkey* (Commission decision), Application nos. 6780/74 and 6950/75, 26 May 1975, [157].

10 *Demopoulos and Others v Turkey* (Decision) [GC], Application nos. 46113/99, 3843/02, 13751/02, 13466/03, 10200/04, 14163/04, 19993/04 and 21819/04), ECHR 2010-I.

"Turkish Republic of Northern Cyprus" ("TRNC") was an effective one that had to be exhausted before taking recourse to the ECtHR.

The remedy under consideration, the Immovable Property Commission ("IPC"), was introduced in 2005, three decades after the deprivation of homes and properties suffered by the Greek Cypriot IDPs, and following the Court's indications in the pilot judgment of *Xenides-Aresti v Turkey*.[11] The IPC was established following the enactment in the TRNC of the "Law for the Compensation, Exchange and Restitution of Immovable Properties" ("Law no. 67/2005"), which entered into force on 22 December 2005.[12] Under Law 67/2005, the IPC has "the competence to decide on the restitution, exchange of properties or payment of compensation".[13]

In this chapter, we examine the main findings of the Court in these cases, trace their grounding in the Court's jurisprudence concerning, on the one hand, the requirement for individual applicants to exhaust any effective domestic remedies (Article 35.1) and, on the other, the obligations of member states to implement its judgments under Article 46 of the ECHR. The aim of this inquiry is to critically assess those remedies that are considered appropriate under the Court's own jurisprudence for the violations of the Cypriot IDPs' rights to property and homes as a result of the acts of Turkey in the north of Cyprus.

2 *Loizidou v Turkey* and the fourth interstate case of *Cyprus v Turkey*: the Court's well- settled case law

Turkey accepted the right of individual application in 1987, and recognised the compulsory jurisdiction of the Court on 22 January 1990. This made it possible for individual IDPs from Cyprus to apply to the Court alleging, among other things, violations of their rights to property and home following the occupation of the north of Cyprus and their continuing displacement from homes and ancestral lands. At the time of the *Demopoulos* decision in 2010, there were 1400 such applications, the vast majority of which had been pending for almost two decades; these were all struck off by the Court and the applicants directed to the newly established remedy in the TRNC.

The main issues decided by the Court in the handful of Cyprus cases it did hear[14] concerned continuing violations of Article 8 and Article 1 of Protocol

11 *Xenides-Arestis v Turkey* (Merits), Application no. 46347/99, 22 December 2005.

12 Turkey's subordinate administration also enacted the "Rules made under Sections 8 (2) (A) and 22 of the Law for the Compensation, Exchange and Restitution of Immovable Properties which are within the scope of sub-paragraph (b) of paragraph 1 of Article 159 of the Constitution" (Law no. 67/2005), which entered into force on 20 March 2006.

13 *Xenides-Arestis v Turkey* (just satisfaction), Application no. 46347/99, 7 December 2006, [11].

14 At the time of Demopoulos' inadmissibility decision (1/3/2010), the Court had issued judgments, both on the merits and just satisfaction in only four cases; in another 30 cases, the Court ruled first on the merits during 2009 and then on just satisfaction but after the Demopoulos inadmissibility decision in 2010.

No. 1, the imputability of these violations to Turkey, the recognition that Greek Cypriot IDPs retained legal ownership of homes and properties and the availability and/or effectiveness of remedies for the violations found as well as just satisfaction under the Court's jurisprudence.

2.1 Continuing violation of Article 1 of Protocol No. 1

In its *Loizidou* judgment,[15] the first individual application against Turkey by a Greek Cypriot IDP to be heard, the ECtHR found that the applicant having been refused access to her land since 1974, "has effectively lost all control over, as well as all possibilities to use and enjoy, her property" and that such continuous denial is an interference with the applicant's rights under Article 1 of Protocol No. 1. The interference, the ECtHR further ruled, was neither a deprivation nor control of use of property within the meaning of the first two paragraphs of Article 1 of Protocol No. 1; but it "falls within the meaning of the first sentence of that provision (P1-1) as an interference with the peaceful enjoyment of possessions. In this respect, the Court observes that hindrance can amount to a violation of the Convention just like a legal impediment".[16]

The ECtHR was not persuaded by the argument proffered by the Respondent state that the interference with the applicant's right was justified by the need to rehouse displaced Turkish Cypriots from the south and similarly rejected the argument relating to ongoing intercommunal negotiations regarding property rights as irrelevant. "In such circumstances, the Court concludes that there has been and continues to be a breach of Article 1 of Protocol No. 1 (P1-1)."[17]

In the interstate case of *Cyprus v Turkey*, the Court applied the *Loizidou* finding of a continuing violation of Article 1 of Protocol No. 1 to "all displaced Greek Cypriots", noting that no compensation has been paid to the displaced IDPs for the purported expropriation.[18] The Court further endorsed the Commission's

15 *Loizidou v Turkey* (merits), Application no. 15318/89, 1996-VI, [63–64].

16 Ibid, [63], *Airey v Ireland* (merits), Application no. 6289/73, 9 October 1979, [25].

17 *Loizidou v Turkey*, ibid, [64].

18 *Cyprus v Turkey* [GC], Application no. 25781/94, ECHR 2001-IV, [184–189]: "The Court is persuaded that both its reasoning and its conclusion in the Loizidou judgment (merits) apply with equal force to displaced Greek Cypriots who, like Mrs Loizidou, are unable to have access to their property in northern Cyprus by reason of the restrictions placed by the 'TRNC' authorities on their physical access to that property. The continuing and total denial of access to their property is a clear interference with the right of the displaced Greek Cypriots to the peaceful enjoyment of possessions within the meaning of the first sentence of Article 1 of Protocol No. 1. It further notes that, as regards the purported expropriation, no compensation has been paid to the displaced persons in respect of the interferences which they have suffered and continue to suffer in respect of their property rights. For the above reasons the Court concludes that there has been a continuing violation of Article 1 of Protocol No. 1 by virtue of the fact that Greek-Cypriot owners of property in northern Cyprus are being denied access to and control, use and enjoyment of their property as well as any compensation for the interference with their property rights."

previous findings that such interference was part of an administrative practice,[19] which even if it pursued a legitimate aim, was disproportionate to the aims put forth by Turkey,[20] which justified the interference by reference to the intercommunal negotiations and the need to rehouse Turkish Cypriot IDPs.

2.2 Imputability

The issue of the responsibility of Turkey for the interference with the applicant's rights under Article 1 of Protocol No. 1 had already been settled in the earlier judgment, *Loizidou v Turkey* (Preliminary Objections),[21] in which the Court found that under Article 1 of the ECHR a state may exercise effective control over an area outside its territory. In the subsequent judgment on the merits, the Court then ruled that the continuous denial to the applicant of access, control and enjoyment of her property was imputable to Turkey.[22] In *Cyprus v Turkey*,[23] the Court reaffirmed that Turkey was responsible for securing all substantive rights under the Convention in the occupied north of Cyprus. It pointed out that, since it found that the Cyprus Government was unable "to exercise their Convention obligations in northern Cyprus", not holding Turkey responsible for the violations of human rights alleged in the application "would result in a regrettable vacuum in the system of human-rights protection in the territory in question by removing from individuals there the benefit of the Convention's fundamental safeguards and their right to call a High Contracting Party to account for violation of their rights in proceedings before the Court".[24]

19 *Cyprus v Turkey*, Commission Report, Application no. 25781/94, 4 June 1999, [319].

20 Ibid, [320]; *Cyprus v Turkey*, n18, [188].

21 *Loizidou v Turkey* (preliminary objections), Application no. 15318/89, [1995] ECHR 10, [62]: "the responsibility of a Contracting Party may also arise when as a consequence of military action – whether lawful or unlawful – it exercises effective control of an area outside its national territory. The obligation to secure, in such an area, the rights and freedoms set out in the Convention derives from the fact of such control whether it be exercised directly, through its armed forces, or through a subordinate local administration."

22 *Loizidou v Turkey*, n15, [61]: "It is obvious from the large number of troops engaged in active duties in northern Cyprus that her army exercises effective overall control over that part of the island. Such control, according to the relevant test and in the circumstances of the case, entails her responsibility for the policies and actions of the 'TRNC'. Those affected by such policies or actions therefore come within the 'jurisdiction' of Turkey for the purposes of Article 1 of the Convention (art. 1). Her obligation to secure to the applicant the rights and freedoms set out in the Convention therefore extends to the northern part of Cyprus."

23 *Cyprus v Turkey*, n18, [77]: "Having effective overall control over northern Cyprus, [Turkey's] responsibility cannot be confined to the acts of its own soldiers or officials in northern Cyprus but must also be engaged by virtue of the acts of the local administration which survives by virtue of Turkish military and other support. It follows that, in terms of Article 1 of the Convention, Turkey's 'jurisdiction' must be considered to extend to securing the entire range of substantive rights set out in the Convention and those additional Protocols which she has ratified, and that violations of those rights are imputable to Turkey."

24 *Cyprus v Turkey*, Application no. 25781/94 (1997) 23 EHRR 244, [77]–[80].

2.3 Legal ownership

In *Loizidou*, the Court rejected[25] the arguments of the Turkish Government that the applicant had lost title to her property as a result of Article 159.1 (b) of the 7 May 1985 Constitution of the TRNC.[26] The TRNC was not recognised under international law and hence such "purported expropriation without compensation"[27] carried no validity and therefore the applicant retained legal ownership of the property. This finding was confirmed in the fourth interstate case where the Court concurred with the finding of the Commission's report[28] that "Article 159 of the TRNC Constitution", which purported to remove legal title from the applicant, was invalid; similarly, invalid was Law no. 52/1995, which gave effect to the constitutional provision. Consequently, the Court held that the displaced Greek Cypriots had not lost their ownership rights with respect to their properties in the occupied north of Cyprus.[29]

2.4 Continuing violation of Article 8

In the fourth interstate case of *Cyprus v Turkey*, the Commission concluded unanimously that, during the period under consideration, there has been a continuing violation of Article 8 of the ECHR by the refusal to allow the return of Greek Cypriot displaced persons to their homes in the occupied northern part of Cyprus.[30] The ECtHR, on its part, endorsed this conclusion holding at the same time that there was no justification under Article 8.2 for the total denial of the right of the Cypriot IDPs to respect for their home, rejecting the Turkish Government's argument that the ongoing intercommunal talks could serve as a legitimate justification.[31]

25 *Loizidou v Turkey*, n15, [44].

26 Article 159.1 (b) of the 7 May 1985 Constitution of the "Turkish Republic of Northern Cyprus" (the "TRNC") provides, where relevant, as follows: "All immovable properties, buildings and installations which were found abandoned on 13 February 1975 when the Turkish Federated State of Cyprus was proclaimed or which were considered by law as abandoned or ownerless after the above-mentioned date, or which should have been in the possession or control of the public even though their ownership had not yet been determined . . . and . . . situated within the boundaries of the TRNC on 15 November 1983, shall be the property of the TRNC notwithstanding the fact that they are not so registered in the books of the Land Registry Office; and the Land Registry Office shall be amended accordingly."

27 *Loizidou v Turkey*, n15, [64].

28 *Cyprus v Turkey*, n19, [317].

29 *Cyprus v Turkey*, n24, [186]: "The Court recalls its finding in the Loizidou judgment (merits) that that particular applicant could not be deemed to have lost title to her property by operation of 'Article 159 of the TRNC Constitution', a provision which it held to be invalid for the purposes of the Convention . . . This conclusion is unaffected by the operation of 'Law no. 52/1995'. It adds that, although the latter was not invoked before the Court in the Loizidou case, it cannot be attributed any more legal validity than its parent 'Article 159' which it purports to implement."

30 *Cyprus v Turkey*, n19, [272].

31 *Cyprus v Turkey*, n18, [172]–[175].

2.5 Availability of remedies for the violations found

In its report,[32] the Commission inquired into the status of remedies available within the TRNC for purposes of the exhaustion of domestic remedies under former Article 26 of the Convention. It observed that since it was established that the TRNC is Turkey's subordinate local administration, it follows as a "necessary corollary" that any remedies available within it are domestic remedies of Turkey. The critical importance of this finding, for the developing jurisprudence of the Court, in the Cyprus IDP cases, cannot be overstated.

As discussed below, TRNC remedies, as remedies of Turkey – the state responsible for the protection of human rights in the occupied north – will have to be considered by the Court in connection with the obligation to exhaust effective remedies before applying to the Court.

The Commission further noted that despite the fact that the TRNC was not recognised under international law, the Government of Cyprus being the only legitimate one, nonetheless it was a *de facto* regime, exercising its *de facto* authority under the overall control of Turkey. In light of the ECtHR's conclusion in *Loizidou*,[33] according to which despite the illegality of the regime "certain legal arrangements and transactions" should be recognised as valid because of their benefit to the inhabitants of such a territory,[34] the Commission went further to reason that the international unlawfulness of the TRNC regime does not on its own "deprive the remedies of their effectiveness".[35] Consequently, any effective remedies made available to the victims of human rights violations within the TRNC must be taken into account; the question of the effectiveness of such remedies is considered when it arises under the specific circumstances of each case.[36]

The Commission considered the availability of remedies to the Cypriot IDPs for the continuing violations of their rights to property and respect of their homes in the north of the island. Noting that these violations were the result of administrative practices,[37] the Commission reiterated that it was not necessary under Convention practice to exhaust domestic remedies. The Commission also concluded that the absence of effective remedies was in breach of Article 13.[38] It is noted that in reaching this finding the report does not concur with the Cyprus Government's position that TRNC laws should not be recognised as legislation.[39]

32 *Cyprus v Turkey*, n19, [122].
33 *Loizidou v Turkey*, n15, [45].
34 The Commission was here making reference to the ICJ's Advisory Opinion on Legal Consequences for States of the Continued Presence of South Africa in Namibia (South West Africa) Notwithstanding Security Council Resolution 276 (1970), [1971] International Court of Justice Reports 16, 56, [125].
35 *Cyprus v Turkey*, n19, [124].
36 Ibid, [128].
37 Ibid, [264], [313], [326].
38 Ibid, [328].
39 Ibid, [326].

The Commission's conclusions were later adopted by the Court,[40] which took the view that where a state is held responsible for acts occurring within a territory unlawfully under its control, that state should be allowed "the opportunity to try to avoid such responsibility by correcting the wrongs imputable to it in its courts". The Court pointed out a similar contradiction with the argument of the Government of Cyprus that there is no effective remedy under Article 13, while maintaining "the alleged unlawfulness of the institutions set up by the TRNC".[41] The Court's clear conclusion was that remedies available within the TRNC are for purposes of the exhaustion of domestic remedies requirement of former Article 26 "domestic remedies" of Turkey whereas their effectiveness "is to be considered in the specific circumstances where it arises".

The Court, like the Commission, concluded that there has been a violation of Article 13 of the Convention because Turkey had failed to provide to Greek Cypriot IDPs any remedies to contest interferences with their rights under Article 8 of the Convention and Article 1 of Protocol No. 1.[42]

The Court's jurisprudence, as described above, regarding the applicability of the rule of exhaustion of effective domestic remedies under Article 35.1, was applied in its *Demopoulos and Others v Turkey*[43] decision when examining the effectiveness of the remedy finally introduced by Turkey to address the alleged violations of the rights of Greek Cypriot IDPS to their homes and properties. The Court pointed out that the right of individual application under the Convention is not a substitute for any effective remedies, within a functioning judicial system, available within the TRNC, which remained under the overall control of Turkey; such a remedy should be exhausted before proceeding with an application to the Court.

It is critical to appreciate, when inquiring into the protection afforded the Cyprus IDPs under the Convention, that the *Demopoulos* decision, both as to the availability and necessity to exhaust effective domestic remedies within the TRNC, regarding the interferences with the rights of Greek Cypriot IDPs, is in accordance with the Court's jurisprudence as applied and settled in the landmark cases of *Loizidou* and *Cyprus v Turkey*. The introduction of the pilot judgment procedure in the case of *Xenides-Aresti v Turkey*,[44] was the conduit for Turkey's assumption, in fact, of responsibility for the violations and the establishment of the remedy of the Immovable Property Commission in the occupied part of Cyprus.

40 *Cyprus v Turkey*, n18, [98]–[102].

41 Ibid, [318]–[321] and [99]: "[I]t cannot be asserted, on the one hand, that there has been a violation of that Article because a State has not provided a remedy while asserting, on the other hand, that any such remedy, if provided, would be null and void."

42 Ibid, [194].

43 *Demopoulos and Others v Turkey*, n10, [96]. The Court repeated that: "The Court maintains its opinion that allowing the respondent State to correct wrongs imputable to it does not amount to an indirect legitimisation of a regime unlawful under international law."

44 *Xenides-Aresti v Turkey*, n11, [38].

In the period preceding the Demopoulos decision when Turkey was refusing to accept responsibility for the human rights violations in the occupied north, and no remedies were made available to the Greek Cypriot IDPS, the Court proceeded to rule on just satisfaction claims under Article 41 ECHR.

3 Implementation of the Court's judgments: Articles 46 and 41 of the ECHR: restitution and just satisfaction in the Court's jurisprudence

A brief outline of the Court's interpretation of the ECHR, regarding the obligation of Contracting states to remedy violations, is instructive in order to critically assess the extent to which the Court's conclusion regarding the remedy made available in the TRNC to the Greek Cypriot IDPs is sufficiently consistent with its jurisprudence on the matter.

Under Article 46 of the Convention the judgments of the Court are binding on the Contracting parties, which under the principle of subsidiarity[45] enjoy a margin of appreciation[46] in the implementation of the Convention and the judgments of the ECtHR.

Respondent Governments found in violation of any Convention rights are under a threefold obligation[47] to take steps to put an end to the violation, to adopt general measures to end similar violations and prevent future ones, and to make reparation to the affected parties for the violation[48] in order to restore to the extent possible the situation in place before the breach (*restitutio in integrum*).[49] Implementation of the Court's judgments is thus "a multifaceted

45 See High Level Conference on the future of the European Court of Human Rights, Brighton Declaration (20 April 2012), http://www.echr.coe.int/Documents/2012_Brighton_FinalDeclaration_ENG.pdf.

46 Subject to monitoring by the CoM, the Respondent state remains free to choose the means by which it will discharge its legal obligation under Article 46 of the ECHR, provided that such means are compatible with the conclusions set out in the Court's judgment. (See *Scozzari and Giunta v Italy* [GC], Application nos. 39221/98 and 41963/98, 2000-VI, [249].)

47 "In fulfilling their duty under Art.46(1) of the Convention to abide by final judgments of the Court, states have three obligations: (a) to pay just satisfaction awarded by the Court; (b) to take measures in favour of the applicant to put a stop to the violation and to erase to the maximum extent possible its consequences (individual measures); and (c) to take measures guaranteeing non-repetition of similar violations (general measures)", http://www.coe.int/t/ dghl/monitoring/execution/Presentation/About_en.asp.

48 Lambert-Abdelgawad E. (2008), The Execution of Judgments of the ECtHR, Human Rights, Files No. 19, 2nd ed. (Strasbourg: Council of Europe Publishing) 10; see also Committee of Ministers Recommendation CM/Rec(2008) 2, on efficient domestic capacity for rapid execution of judgments of the European Court of Human Rights (Adopted by the Committee of Ministers on 6 February 2008 at the 1017th meeting of the Ministers' Deputies).

49 Article 35 of the Articles on Responsibility of States for international wrongful acts, provides that a state "is under an obligation to make restitution . . . provided that restitution is not 'materially impossible' and does not involve a burden out of all proportion to the benefit deriving from restitution instead of compensation".

task"[50] and the obligation of the state goes well beyond the mere payment of damages.[51]

In particular, the obligation of member states to adopt general measures in consequence of a judgment of the ECtHR finding a violation is associated with Article 46 of the ECHR and with the requirement not to repeat the violation.[52] It is an obligation to eliminate the cause(s) of the violation so subsequent applications whose complaint arises from the same circumstances should be seen as a problem of execution.[53] It is for the member state to choose the means by which it will discharge its obligations under Article 46, as long as those are compatible with the ECHR; thus the ECtHR's judgments have traditionally been "declaratory"[54] rather than prescriptive and states retain a "wide discretion in the choice of means to be used"[55] in their implementation of the ECtHR's judgments. This approach follows from the doctrine of state sovereignty in international law and the related principle of subsidiarity, one of the main principles underpinning the ECtHR's deferential attitude to member states in its judgments.

Whenever *restitutio in integrum* is, either de jure or de facto impossible, the Respondent state can only offer partial reparation under Article 46; hence, it is for the ECtHR to afford the applicant just reparation.[56] When the ECtHR has deemed necessary to award just satisfaction, it is the state's duty to pay the applicants the relevant sums. "Just satisfaction in the sense of Article 41 of the ECHR comprises monetary compensation for moral and pecuniary damages as well as reimbursement of costs and expenses."[57]

The Court's jurisprudence on the application of Article 41 in conjunction with the principle of *restitutio in integrum* is that where the nature of the violation allows it, it is the duty of the state to afford *restitutio in integrum*, as the Court

50 Anagnostou D. and Mungiu-Pippidi A. (2009), "Why Do States Implement Differently the European Court of Human Rights Judgments? The Case Law on Civil Liberties and the Rights of Minorities (work in progress)", JURISTRAS Project, 20.

51 See, among others, *Scozzari and Giunta v Italy* [GC], Application nos. 39221/98 and 41963/98, 2000-VI, [249]: "A judgment in which the Court finds a breach imposes on the respondent state a legal obligation not just to pay to those concerned the sums awarded by way of just satisfaction, but also to choose, subject to the supervision by the Committee of Ministers, the general and/or, if appropriate, individual measures to be adopted in their domestic legal order to put an end to the violation found by the Court and to redress so far as possible the effects."

52 Lambert-Abdelgawad, n48, 20.

53 Wildhaber L. (2004), "The ECtHR in Action", RitsLRev, Vol. 21, 83, 90.

54 *Marckx v Belgium*, Application no. 6833/74, (1980) 2 EHRR 330, [58]; see also, among others, *Silver v The United Kingdom*, Application nos. 5947/72, 6205/73, 7052/75, 7061/75, 7107/75, 7113/75, 7136/75 (1983) 5 EHRR 347, [113](d); *Oleksandr Volkov v Ukraine*, Application no. 21722/11, 9 January 2013, [194].

55 *Sedjovic v Italy*, Application no. 56581/00, 01 March 2006, [127].

56 Costa J.P. (2002), "The Provision of Compensation Under Article 41 of the ECHR" in Fairgrieve D., Andenas M., Bell J. (eds.), Tort Liability of Public Authorities in Comparative Perspective (London, British Institute of International and Comparative Law) 6.

57 Polakiewicz J. (2001), "The Execution of Judgments of the ECtHR" in Blackburn R., Polakiewicz J. Fundamental Rights in Europe (OUP) 64.

itself does not have the power or the means to do so; but if such restitution is not possible, or only partially so under domestic law, then the Court has the power under Article 41 to award the injured party appropriate satisfaction.[58]

3.1 Violations of Article 1 of Protocol No. 1: restitution or compensation

For the first time in the case of *Papamichalopoulos v Greece*,[59] the Court offered the Respondent state the choice either to make *restitutio in integrum* by returning the land and buildings that had been unlawfully expropriated or to pay compensation for the pecuniary damage within six months.[60] In its judgment,[61] the Court cited the judgment of the Permanent Court of Justice in the case *Factory at Chorzow*[62] that "reparation must, as far as possible, wipe out all the consequences of the illegal act and re-establish the situation which would, in all probability, have existed if that act had not been committed. Restitution in kind or if this is not possible, payment of a sum corresponding to the value which a restitution in kind would bear."[63]

Subsequently, the ECtHR held in a number of property-related cases where it found violation of Article 1 of Protocol No. 1, that the Respondent state was either to return to the applicant the property concerned or pay damages that reflected the current value of the property.[64] In the case of *Saghinadze v Georgia*, where the

58 *Guiso-Gallisay v Italy* (just satisfaction) [GC], Application no. 58858/00, 22 December 2009, [90].

59 *Papamichalopoulos and Others v Greece*, Application no. 14556/89, 31 October 1995, [34].

60 Ibid, [39].

61 See also *Salduz v Turkey*, Application no. 36391/02, 27 November 2008, Joint Concurring Opinion of Judges Rozakis, Spielman, Ziemele, and Lazarova Trajkovska, [5]: "The principle of restitutio in integrum has its origin in the judgment of 13 September 1928 of the Permanent Court of International Justice (PCIJ) in the case concerning the Factory at Chorzów."

62 Factory at Chorzow (*Germany v Poland*), 1928 PCIJ (ser. A) No. 17 (Sept. 13). The right to reparation for loss of property as a result of the construction of the wall was similarly upheld by the ICJ in its Advisory Opinion on the *Legal Consequences of the Construction of the Wall in the Occupied Palestinian Territory* of July 9 2004, ICJ Reports (2004), 136.

63 The right to reparation for human rights violations in post-conflict situations in international law relates to state responsibility. As stressed: "[I]t is a principle of international law that any breach of an engagement involves an obligation to make reparation", Article 31 of the Articles on Responsibility of States for international wrongful acts, in UN Doc A/56/10, Report of the International Law Commission on the work of its Fifty-third session, Official Records of the General Assembly, November 2001, 43–59. Restitution is considered the preferred form (others are compensation and satisfaction), intended to restore the situation ex ante: The UN Basic Principles and Guidelines on the Rights to a Remedy and Reparation for Victims gross violations of International Human Rights Law and Serious violations of International Humanitarian Law, adopted by the United Nations on 21 March 2006, (UN Doc. / RES/60/147).

64 *Brumarescu v Romania*, Application no. 28342/95, 23 January 2001, [22]–[23]: "[R]eturn of the property . . . would put the applicant as far as possible in the situation equivalent to

applicant was an IDP, the ECtHR considered again that the most appropriate form of relief under the IDP Act in force would be for the Government to return to the applicant the cottage he had been lawfully residing in for over a decade until such time as conditions would allow his return in safety and dignity to his home in Abkhazia. The ECtHR then added that if that were not possible the Government should find alternative accommodation for such an IDP and, if that also could not be done, to award him compensation for the loss of the cottage.[65]

Thus, though according to the ECtHR's jurisprudence the preferred remedy for the finding of a violation of the right to property is *restitutio in integrum*,[66] namely return of the property, it almost always allows an alternative for the state, in directing that failing restitution a fixed sum in respect of pecuniary damage should be paid.[67]

As mentioned above, the Court's judgments have been traditionally "declaratory" in nature, still, gradually over the last decade or so the ECtHR has on several occasions given indications regarding general and/or individual measures relying mostly on Article 46, thus assuming more responsibility for the execution of its own judgments. The property-related cases discussed above reflect this exception to the rule of declaratory judgments in that the ECtHR issued specific directions in respect of the execution of those judgments underlining the appropriateness of *restitutio in integrum.*

The main category of judgments in which the ECtHR has indicated general and/or individual measures is that of pilot judgments.[68] In such judgments, the ECtHR identifies "structural or systemic problems" in the domestic legal order

the one in which he would have been if there had not been a breach of Article 1 of Protocol No. 1 . . . Failing such restitution by the respondent State within six months of the delivery of this judgment, the Court holds that the Respondent State is to pay the applicant pecuniary damage, the current value of the house"; *Dacia S.R.L. v Moldova*, Application no. 3052/04, 24/02/2009, [40], [55]: "[T]he most appropriate form of restitutio in integrum . . . is for the hotel and underlying land to be returned to the applicant company" or if that proved impossible pay the compensation in an amount "representing its current value.".

65 *Saghinadze and Others v Georgia*, Application no. 18768/05, 27 May 2010, [160]. In its subsequent judgment on just satisfaction, the ECtHR approved the government's offer of the transfer of ownership of two apartments and an amount in damages payable to the applicants. *Saghinadze and Others v Georgia* (Just Satisfaction), Application no. 18768/05, 13 January 2015, [15].

66 Article 35 of the Articles on Responsibility of States for international wrongful acts, provides that a state "is under an obligation to make restitution . . . provided that restitution is not 'materially impossible' and does not involve a burden out of all proportion to the benefit deriving from restitution instead of compensation".

67 See, for example. *Raicu v Romania*, Application no. 28104/03, 19 October 2006, [38]. The ECtHR ordered Romania to return the flat or, as the alternative, to pay the applicant a specific sum of money.

68 The pilot judgment procedure was put in place following the adoption of CoE, Committee of Ministers Resolution Res (2004) 3, On judgments revealing an underlying systemic problem, 12 May 2004.

of the state concerned which generate numerous similar cases; at the same time, it may adjourn such pending similar cases.[69]

The ECtHR's indications of measures in these cases are designed to facilitate the implementation of its judgment by the Respondent state while promoting more effective supervision by the Committee of Ministers over cases that raise structural issues and thus prevent and/or adjourn multiple similar applications, easing the ECtHR's backlog of cases.

3.2 Court awards in the Cyprus cases

In *Loizidou v Turkey* (just satisfaction),[70] the applicant had asked for loss of use only[71] and the ECtHR ruled that she was "entitled to a measure of compensation in respect of losses directly related to this violation of her rights as from the date of Turkey's acceptance of the compulsory jurisdiction of the Court, namely 22 January 1990, until the present time".[72] The Court considered that the applicant's valuation method of calculating economic loss by reference to annual ground rent, as a percentage of the market value over the relevant period, although reasonable was also speculative; it granted the applicant half the amount sought.[73]

The ECtHR also awarded the applicant non-pecuniary damages "in respect of the anguish and feelings of helplessness and frustration" experienced by the applicant over a long period of time.[74] However, the ECtHR added that the case concerned the individual applicant and not the property rights of all displaced Greek Cypriots.[75]

In addition to the inter-state case of *Cyprus v Turkey*, almost 1400 applications were submitted by displaced Greek Cypriots claiming violations of Article 1 Protocol No. 1 and Article 8, by 2004, the so called "post-*Loizidou* cases". The Court reiterated its findings regarding legal ownership of properties and continuing violations of the Convention by Turkey, first in *Demades v Turkey*[76] then in *Eugenia Michaelidou Developments Ltd and Michael Tymvios v Turkey*[77] and later

69 *Broniowski v Poland* [GC], Application no. 31443/96, ECHR 2004-V. Broniowski is considered to be the first pilot judgment: the ECtHR found a violation of Article 1 Protocol No. 1 as a result of the failure to compensate the applicant for property left behind when forced to move to Poland after World War II and considered that the individual violation "originated in a widespread problem" that was systemic and affected a large number of applicants. The ECtHR then indicated that "general measures should either remove any hindrance to the implementation of the right to numerous persons affected by the situation found to have been in breach of the ECHR or provide equivalent redress in lieu."

70 *Loizidou v Turkey* (just satisfaction), Application no. 15318/89, 28 July 1998.

71 Ibid, [20].

72 Ibid, [31].

73 Ibid, [33]–[34].

74 Ibid, [39].

75 Ibid, [40].

76 *Demades v Turkey* (merits and just satisfaction), Application no. 16219/90, 31 July 2003, [46].

77 Eugenia Michaelidou Developments Ltd and *Michael Tymvios v Turkey*, Application no. 16163/90, 31 July 2003, [31].

in *Xenides-Aresti v Turkey*.[78] Continuing violations of Article 1 of Protocol No. 1 and Article 8 were also found in a cluster of judgments issued in 2009, in which the Court reiterated its conclusions regarding the interference with the IDPs' rights imputable to Turkey and the absence of a domestic remedy;[79] at the same time it emphasised its position regarding the legitimacy of certain legal arrangements, under international law, under administrations with similar character as the TRNC and that the effectiveness of possible remedies will be examined on "a case-by-case basis." [80]

In these post-*Loizidou* judgments,[81] the Court awarded non-pecuniary damages as well as pecuniary ones in just satisfaction under Article 41 of the ECHR. Thus in *Xenides-Aresti v Turkey*,[82] the ECtHR ruled that it "is of the opinion that an award should be made under this head in respect of the anguish and feelings of helplessness and frustration which the applicant must have experienced over the years in not being able to use her property as she saw fit and to enjoy her home".[83] Using the same reasoning, the Court awarded non-pecuniary damages as well as pecuniary damages to all these applicants whose cases[84] became admissible before the *Demopoulos* inadmissibility decision in 2010.

The just satisfaction judgment in the fourth interstate of *Cyprus v Turkey*[85] was issued over a decade after the judgment on the merits due largely to the delay on

78 *Xenides-Arestis*, n11, [32].
79 See, for example, *Demades v Turkey*, n76, [46].
80 *Xenides-Arestis v Turkey* (Decision), Application no. 46347/99, 14 March 2005.
81 See, for example, *Orphanides v Turkey*, Application no. 36705/97, 20 January 2009, [39]; *Gavriel v Turkey*, Application no. 41355/98, 20 January 2009, [44]; *Ioannou v Turkey*, Application no. 18364/91, 27 January 2009, [35]; *Evagorou Christou v Turkey*, Application no. 18403/91, 27 January 2009, [31]; *Michael v Turkey*, Application no. 18361/91, 27 January 2009, [30]; *Nicola v Turkey*, Application no. 18404/91, 27 January 2009, [32]; *Hadjiprocopiou and Others v Turkey*, Application no. 37395/97, 22 September 2009, [33]; *Kyriakou v Turkey*, Application No. 18407/91, 27 January 2009, [31]; *Hapeshis and Hapeshi-Michaelidou v Turkey*, Application No. 35214/97, 22 September 2009, [33]; *Hadjithomas and Others v Turkey*, Application No. 39970/98, 22 September 2009, [40]; *Saveriades v Turkey*, Application No. 16160/90, 22 September 2009, [25]: "the house where the applicant was living qualified as a home within the meaning of Article 8 of the Convention, at the time when the acts complained of took place."
82 *Xenides-Arestis v Turkey*, n13, [47].
83 *Demades v Turkey*, n76, [29].
84 See, for example, Diogenous and *Tseriotis v Turkey* (just satisfaction), Application no. 16259/90, 26 October 2010, [36]; *Zavou and Others v Turkey* (just satisfaction), Application no. 16654/90, 26 October 2010, [43]; *Saveriadis v Turkey* (just satisfaction), Application no. 16160/90, 26 October 2010, [39]; *Epiphaniou and Others v Turkey* (just satisfaction), Application no. 19900/92, 26 October 2010, [45]; *Ramon v Turkey* (just satisfaction), Application no. 29092/95, 26 October 2010, [35]; *Orphanides v Turkey* (just satisfaction), Application no. 36705/97, 26 October 2010, [41]; *Gavriel v Turkey* (just satisfaction), Application no. 41355/98, 26 October 2010, [39]. (In these cases, the ECtHR has also taken into account in its final calculation of the awards, the offers for "loss of use" made by the compensation and restitution mechanism set up in the northern part of Cyprus following the judgment in Xenides-Arestis.)
85 *Cyprus v Turkey* (just satisfaction) [GC], 2014-II.

the part of the applicant Government to submit the relevant claims. After the inadmissibility decision in *Demopoulos*, the Government of Cyprus reserved the issue of the application of Article 41 of the Convention to the violations of Article 1 of Protocol No. 1 and Article 8 and has not yet made any claims regarding the homes and properties of the IDPs.

4 *Xenides-Aresti v Turkey* and *Demopoulos and Others v Turkey*: from pilot judgment to the establishment of a remedy

4.1 A pilot judgment for the Cyprus cases

In the pilot judgment of *Xenides-Aresti v Turkey*,[86] one of the post-*Loizidou* cases concerning the denial of the applicant's access to property and home, the Court held that the Turkish Government should introduce a remedy that would provide effective redress for everyone in a situation similar to that of the applicant. Following the Court's explicit directions,[87] Turkey, enacted the TRNC, Law 67/2005 in December 2005[88] and established under it the Immovable Property Commission in March 2006. The IPC has the competence to consider applications for restitution, compensation or exchange of properties[89] in order to address the violations of both Article 1 of Protocol No. 1 and Article 8 of the Convention[90] in the occupied northern part of Cyprus.[91] Consequently, a further 1400 European Court applications were adjourned, pending the implementation of such a system of redress.

In the admissibility decision in the case of *Xenides-Aresti v Turkey*,[92] the Court examined for the first time a specific remedy that Turkey claimed had to be exhausted before the applicant could be heard by the Court. The Court reiterated

86 *Xenides-Arestis*, n11.

87 Ibid, [38].

88 The "Law for the Compensation, Exchange and Restitution of Immovable Properties", which entered into force on 22 December 2005, and the "By-Law made under Sections 8 (2) (A) and 22 of the Law for the Compensation, Exchange and Restitution of Immovable Properties which are within the scope of sub-paragraph (b) of paragraph 1 of Article 159 of the Constitution", which entered into force on 20 March 2006.

89 The Commission is composed of five to seven members, two of whom are foreign members, Mr Hans-Christian Krüger and Mr Daniel Tarschys. It has the competence to decide on the restitution, exchange of properties or payment of compensation. A right of appeal lies to the TRNC High Administrative Court.

90 The Court in the case of Xenides-Arestis identified the dual nature of the systemic problem, which was generating the Greek Cypriot cases before the Court. It held that: "the violation of the applicant's rights guaranteed by Article 8 of the Convention and Article 1 of Protocol No. 1 originates in a widespread problem affecting large numbers of people, namely the unjustified hindrance of her 'respect for her home' and 'peaceful enjoyment of her possessions' as a matter of TRNC policy or practice": *Xenides-Arestis*, n11 [38].

91 Paraskeva C. (2009), "The Application of the 'pilot judgments procedure' to the post-Loizidou cases", AIDH, Vol. IV, 573–588.

92 *Xenides-Aresti v Turkey*, n80.

its position that the effectiveness of remedies will be considered on a case-by-case basis[93] and proceeded to do just that in connection with Law no.49/2003 enacted by the TRNC[94] in July 2003 and the compensation commission established under it. The Court concluded that the remedy under Law no. 49/2003 was neither adequate nor effective and therefore the applicant was not required to exhaust it. The Court's reasoning in rejecting the remedy was primarily that it did not provide for the possibility of restitution[95] or for non-pecuniary damage and, further, it did not address the alleged violations of Article 8 and Article 14 of the ECHR; in addition, the independence and impartiality of the members of the Commission was seriously undermined by the fact that most of them seemed to live in properties previously owned by Greek Cypriot IDPs.

In its judgment on the merits in *Xenides-Aresti v Turkey*,[96] the Court reiterated its jurisprudence under Article 46 of the Convention regarding the obligation of Contracting states to provide appropriate remedies for breaches of the Convention. In particular, concerning Turkey, the Court clearly articulated the nature of the remedy required that should redress the violations of Article 8 and Article 1 of Protocol No. 1 in relation not only to the applicant but in respect of all pending similar applications; the Court allowed Turkey three months to introduce such a remedy.

In its just satisfaction judgment in the case of *Xenides-Aresti v Turkey*,[97] the Court observed that Law no. 67/2005,[98] and the IPC established under it provided a "compensation and restitution mechanism", which, "in principle", had complied with the requirements set out by the Court in its admissibility and merits judgments. Nonetheless, the Court was not in a position to inquire into its effectiveness as the parties had not reached a settlement and the applicant did not have to exhaust it as the case was made admissible before the enactment of the new remedy. In its award of just satisfaction for pecuniary damages the Court stated that it took into account the assessment[99] of the IPC[100] as well as the valuation submitted by the applicant.

93 Ibid.

94 'Law as to Compensation for Immovable Properties Located within the Boundaries of the Turkish Republic of Northern Cyprus, which are within the Scope of Article 159, paragraph (4) of the Constitution (Law no. 49/2003).

95 *Xenides-Aresti v Turkey*, n80: "Most importantly, however, the terms of compensation do not allow for the possibility of restitution of the property withheld. Thus, although compensation is foreseen, this cannot in the opinion of the Court be considered as a complete system of redress regulating the basic aspect of the interferences complained of."

96 *Xenides-Arestis v Turkey*, n11, [37]–[40].

97 *Xenides-Arestis v Turkey*, n13, [55].

98 Ibid, [28]–[29].

99 The IPC proposed award included both loss of use and compensation for the value of the property whereas the Court's award was only for pecuniary damage in relation to the applicant's loss of use.

100 *Xenides-Arestis v Turkey*, n13, [59].

4.2 Eight test cases

The Court subsequently selected eight "test cases"[101] in order to examine the effectiveness of the new mechanism. In *Demopoulos and Others v Turkey*, the Court ruled the new remedy to be effective for purposes of Article 1 of Protocol No. 1 violations. It did not, however, make any ruling/finding as to its effectiveness regarding violations of Article 8. Conceding that "on its face" the remedy restricted claims only to property owners,[102] the Court noted that none of the applicants in *Demopoulos*, who were also owners of property, brought any Article 8 claims to the IPC[103] and there were no other precedents regarding the basis on which "the IPC or the TRNC courts could[104] or would provide redress". The Court was here referring to the fact that the evidence submitted by Turkey of cases having been successfully resolved under the new law were applications relating only to violations of the right to property. As the *Demopoulos* applicants who were claiming violations of their right under Article 8 as well as of their rights under Article 1 Protocol No. 1 had refused to apply to the IPC, despite the fact that they had been declared test cases by the Court, there was at the time no evidence before the Court regarding the provision and nature of redress for such Article 8 claims within the TRNC.

In *Demopoulos*, the Court rejected the applicants' (and the intervening Government's) arguments against the application of the rule to exhaust domestic remedies in their case; reiterating its position that remedies in the TRNC, and in particular the IPC procedure, should be regarded as domestic remedies under the Convention, it ruled that Article 35.1 was applicable to the test cases under consideration.[105] Further, in considering the effectiveness of the remedy, and having before it the evidence presented by the Respondent Government of applications to the IPC[106] that had been successfully resolved, by means of

101 *Demopoulos and Others v Turkey*, n10.

102 Ibid, [35]: "Under the provisions of the Law, the burden of proof rests upon the applicant who must prove beyond a reasonable doubt that, inter alia, the immovable property was registered in his name on 20 July 1974 (or that he is the legal heir to such a person), that he owned the movable property before 13 February 1975 and was forced to abandon it due to conditions beyond his own volition; and that according to the Land Registry records there are no other persons claiming rights to the claimed immovable property (section 6)."

103 Ibid, [133]: "Claimants who own property may make claims to the IPC in respect of non-pecuniary damages, which provision in Law 67/2005 is broad enough to encompass aspects of any loss of enjoyment of home."

104 The suggestion that the "TRNC courts" might provide redress for Article 8 violations was made by Sir Michael Wood on behalf of the Respondent Government at the Grand Chamber hearing of 18 November 2009; apparently the Court has accepted this proposition even though the remedy, the effectiveness of which was under consideration, was the Compensation law 67/2005 and the IPC as set up under its guidelines.

105 *Demopoulos and Others v Turkey*, n10, [87]–[103].

106 Ibid, [36]. The Court set out the powers and duties of the IPC as follows: "The IPC has the duties and powers to examine and reach decisions on applications, determine the amount and method of payment of compensation, collect written or oral testimony or hear witnesses, summon any person residing in the TRNC to give testimony or produce any document in his

compensation, restitution or exchange, it ruled that: "Law 67/2005 provides an accessible and effective framework of redress in respect of complaints about interference with the property owned by Greek Cypriots."[107] Consequently the *Demopoulos* applications were found to be inadmissible for non-exhaustion of domestic remedies.

4.3 Homes from the past[108]

Although, as mentioned above, in *Demopoulos*, the Court did not address the issue of the alleged violations of the right to respect of home, nonetheless it did state that the provision for non-pecuniary damages under the remedy (Law 67/2005 section 8(4)E)) was "broad enough to encompass aspects of loss of enjoyment of home". In addition, and in rejecting one of the applicants' complaint regarding an alleged violation of the right to respect of home as manifestly ill founded, the Court seized the opportunity to set out its current views regarding the protection afforded to Greek Cypriot IDPs under Article 8, several decades after they were evicted from their homes.[109] The Court reasoned that where there "has never been any, or hardly any, occupation by the applicant or where there has been no occupation for some considerable time, it may be that the links to that property are so attenuated as to cease to raise any, or any separate, issue under Article 8"; and in the absence of legal rights to occupation, such as ownership of the home, or some form of tenancy/occupancy protected by law, "such time has elapsed that there can be no realistic expectation of taking up, or resuming, occupation".

In two inadmissibility decisions, *Papayianni* and *Fieros*[110] shortly decided after *Demopoulos*, in which the Court joined a number of cases with Article 8 claims, the Court goes beyond *Demopoulos* in conceding that applicants without ownership "would be unable to take any claim based on Article 8 alone before the

possession, to compel a person to give evidence or produce a document in his possession, to award expenses to any persons summoned (section 13). The decisions of the IPC have binding effect and are of an executory nature similar to judgments of the judiciary and such decisions shall be implemented without delay upon service on the authorities concerned (section 14). It is an offence to refuse to produce any document or information required by the IPC or to fail to appear, or give evidence without legal excuse, a fine of TRY 2,000 being imposable on conviction (section 15) The Ministry responsible for financial affairs must make provision under a separate item of the Budget Law for each year for the payment of compensation awarded by the IPC and other expenses incurred by the application of the Law (section 18)."

107 Ibid, [127].

108 The phrase "homes from the past" appears for the first time in ibid, [136].

109 For a critical analysis of the Court's jurisprudence on this issue, see Paraskeva C., Meleagrou E. (2012–2013), "Homes from the Past: An Expiration Date for the Right to Respect for Home Under Article 8 of the European Convention on Human Rights", AIDH, Vol. VII, 845–877.

110 *Papayianni and Others v Turkey* (decision), Application nos. 479/07, 4607/10 and 10715/10, 6 July 2010. See also *Fieros and Others v Turkey* (decision), Application nos. 53432/99, 54086/00, 57899/00, 58378/00, 63518/00, 66141/01, 77752/01, 10192/02, 25057/02, 35846/02, 5 October 2010.

IPC". It goes further to reject outright the claims of all applicants to the protection of Article 8, except that of the present title holder. The remaining applicants, those with no title of ownership to the home, were either too young with "no concrete ties in existence at this moment in time"; or older applicants who, having lived for decades in the family home before 1974, but with no title of ownership, could not claim the protection of Article 8 under the Court's analysis, despite the enforced absence from their homes.[111]

Thus, after *Papayianni* and *Fieros*, ownership of a home is a prerequisite for a possible claim before the IPC, while the IPC remedy is only available for violations of the right to property. Moreover, the availability of non-pecuniary damages will depend on proving that the residence was a home. Establishing this, however, in light of the Court's analysis according to which the passage of time is the determinative factor, will be extremely difficult to do.

4.4 Effect of passage of time on the nature of the remedy for violations of the property rights of Cyprus IDPs

The Court in *Demopoulos*[112] pointed out that all the post-*Loizidou* applicants, who, under its well- settled jurisprudence, had retained title if not possession to their properties, claimed only pecuniary damages for the loss of use and not compensation for loss of their properties; the Court stated that the claims for loss of use could "in theory" continue indefinitely until a political settlement was achieved and that after so many decades, the claims of loss of use were "increasingly speculative and hypothetical". It was thus unrealistic to expect that the full benefits of the title could now be enjoyed.[113] The conclusion was "that the attenuation over time of the link between the holding of title and the possession and use of the property in question must have consequences on *the nature of the redress* that can be regarded as fulfilling the requirements of Article 35 § 1 of the Convention".[114]

111 These joined applications concern family members all claiming violations of the right to respect for home the position in which the vast majority of all Greek Cypriot IDPs remain in since 1974, i.e. they are members of displaced families who had been sharing the family home and only some of them were the actual title holders of the property where their home was. For the Court's previous approach, see *Zavou and Others v Turkey* (decision), Application no. 16654/90 ECHR, 26 September 2002: In that case, the Court did not seem to consider the absence of the applicants, who were not all property owners, from their home as a result of being forcibly displaced, to have deprived them of the protection of Article 8 of the Convention.

112 *Demopoulos and Others v Turkey*, n10, [109]–[118].

113 Ibid, [111]: "There has, it may be recalled, always been a strong legal and factual link between ownership and possession (see, for example, J.A. Pye (Oxford) Ltd and *J.A. Pye (Oxford) Land Ltd v the United Kingdom* [GC], Application no. 44302/02, ECHR 2007 X concerning extinction of title in adverse possession cases) and it must be recognised that with the passage of time the holding of a title may be emptied of any practical consequences."

114 Ibid, [113].

Consequently, the Court rejected the arguments of the applicants and the Cyprus Government that the remedy provided by the TRNC was overly restrictive regarding restitution of properties to the Greek Cypriot IDPs. It referred to its case law,[115] as described above, regarding ***restitutio in integrum*** and reiterated that: "If it is not possible to restore the position, the Court, as a matter of constant practice, has imposed the alternative requirement on the Contracting State to pay compensation for the value of the property." The Court went further to restate its jurisprudence regarding the discretion enjoyed by Contracting states to choose the remedy for breaches of the Convention they are held responsible for, even where the "illegality is on an international level". Despite the internationally recognised illegal occupation of Cyprus, nonetheless, and since the Court deals with individual applications as are those of the Cypriot IDPs, the Convention must apply in the same way.

The Court maintained its position that even in the occupied north of Cyprus, Turkey, as the Contracting state found in breach of the property rights of IDPs, is in the best position to choose and implement at a domestic level, an effective remedy such as it already had adopted pursuant to Law 67/2005. It was further satisfied, from the evidence submitted by Turkey, that the operation of the amended law, following its indications in *Xenides-Aresti*,[116] which now provided for restitution under certain circumstances, had already resulted in restitution of property in some cases.

4.5 The IPC[117] an effective remedy for violations of the rights of Greek Cypriot IDPs under Article 1 of Protocol No. 1 and Article 8: compensation rather than restitution

The Court in *Demopoulos* found that the TRNC compensation law and the IPC constitute an adequate and effective remedy for violations of Article 1 of Protocol No. 1. At the same time, it indicated and later confirmed in *Papayannis* and a number of post-*Demopoulos* cases that it could also provide such a remedy for Article 8 violations. The Court seems to consider it reasonable that the most likely remedy for these violations would be compensation and non-pecuniary damages and that restitution, although available, may be granted only in limited cases.

115 Ibid, [114].

116 *Xenides-Aresti v Turkey*, n80.

117 The IPC has been in operation since 2005. All data regarding the applications heard and settled or rejected are only available on its own website, where, clearly, compensation for expropriation of Greek Cypriot properties is by far the preferred remedy, restitution being granted only exceptionally. The extremely long delays in processing the applications are also obvious from the data, whereas the most commonly used phrase regarding "mention" meetings is their adjournment sine die. The volume of applications, never that high considering the numbers of Greek Cypriot IDPs, has dropped dramatically in the last few years as a result of the reported failures of the IPC to tackle such applications fairly and within a reasonable time.

While the Court maintained and repeated that under its jurisprudence where *restitutio in integrum* was not possible,[118] a Contracting Party had the alternative of paying compensation for the value of the property, at the same time in these cases of Greek Cypriot IDPs it introduced the additional factor of "the passage of time". Thus, it was justifiable to choose compensation over restitution as such passage of time affected the nature of the remedy; it made it also justifiable that only property owners could apply to the IPC for the violation of the right to home as again such passage of time demoted the vast majority of IDP homes into "homes from the past".

There is a remarkable analogy in the language adopted by the Court in its analysis regarding redress for violations of Article 1 of Protocol No. 1 and Article 8, in the *Demopoulos* decision. In both cases, the passage of time has weakened the link to property/home to such an extent that the right itself resembles an empty shell:[119] the title is "empty", the home is "from the past". And, whereas in the case of the Article 1 of Protocol No. 1 violation, this reasoning has a bearing on the redress that may become available, in the case of Article 8 violations, the Court's conclusion tantamounts to the exclusion from the scope of protection of respect for home of the vast majority of Greek Cypriot IDPs who do not hold title of ownership to their "erstwhile homes".

The implications of the *Demopoulos* inadmissibility decision for IDP rights to home and property under the ECHR, as interpreted by the Court, are considerable as illustrated by the admissibility decision in *Sargsyan v Azerbaijan*.[120] The Court discussed the effect that the passage of time has on the rights to property and home, referring both to *Demopoulos*[121] and *Varnava*.[122] The conclusion reached by the Court in *Sargsyan* is that, in the absence of a domestic remedy for the alleged violations, IDP applicants alleging continuous violations of the right to home and property will have to proceed at some point with an application to the Court; "remaining passive in the face of an unchanging situation would no longer

118 *Demopoulos and Others v Turkey*, n10, 116. The Court considered it arbitrary and unjust to oblige Turkey to restitute the properties to applicants who had left them behind 35 years previously. It rejected the argument of the applicants that there must be restitution in all cases except where there was material impossibility because such a proposition failed to take into account any legal and practical difficulties except "the permanent loss or destruction of the property". Turkey can take into account the position of third parties and it is contrary to the Court's jurisprudence to order the Respondent state to evict and rehouse large number of people in order to vindicate the human rights of victims of violations under the Convention.

119 Ibid, [137]: "The title is emptied, the links to that property are so attenuated as to cease to raise any, or any separate, issue under Article 8."

120 *Sargsyan v Azerbaijan* (decision) [GC], Application no. 40167/06, 16 June 2016. The Court considered claims of violation of Article 1 of Protocol No. 1 and Article 8, by an ethnic Armenian who was expelled from his home in Azerbaijan 20 years earlier, in the midst of the still unresolved conflict concerning Nagorno-Karabakh.

121 Ibid, [137], [139].

122 *Varnava and Others v Turkey* [GC], Application nos. 16064/90, 16065/90, 16066/90, 16068/90, 16069/90, 16070/90, 16071/90, 16072/90 and 16073/90, ECHR 2009-V.

be justified . . . excessive delay . . . may lead to the application being rejected as out of time."[123]

This conclusion puts the onus on IDPs to judge whether negotiations to reach a settlement in relation to the loss of homes and properties as a result of their displacement have any prospect of success or have stalled permanently and there is, therefore, no possibility of redress by means of a political settlement.

5 Concluding remarks

The inadmissibility decision in *Demopoulos* blocked the road to Strasbourg for Greek Cypriot IDPs, at least until the exhaustion of domestic remedies within the TRNC, i.e. application to the IPC and appeal to the High Administrative Court. The Court has so far shown unwillingness to consider the quality of Law 67/2005 and its application, the availability of restitution and/or the levels of compensation, the fairness of the process and the accessibility of the remedy to all Greek Cypriot IDPs who are currently property owners according to the records of the Land Registry of the Republic of Cyprus.[124]

It has been shown that the Court's decision to find the TRNC remedy both applicable and effective was largely a consequence of applying its jurisprudence on individual applicants' obligation to exhaust domestic remedies, on the one hand, and the obligation of Contracting states to remedy violations in ways that are in accordance with the Court's case law, on the other. Although the doctrine of the margin of appreciation allows the states a wide discretion as to the individual and general measures to be adopted, the Court retains the power to review these when it considers it appropriate to do so.

The passage of time has become a crucial factor affecting both the prospects of success in before the Court for IDPs and the nature of any domestic remedy when such is made available by the Respondent state, albeit with great delay. In the context of "frozen conflicts", IDPs stand to lose their separate right to respect of

123 *Sargsyan v Azerbaijan*, n120, [140].

124 In an inadmissibility decision, the only case that has so far been decided by the ECtHR, following exhaustion of domestic remedies, *Meleagrou and Others v Turkey* (decision), Application no. 1443/09, 02 April 2013, the Court rejected continued alleged violations of the rights to home and property of the applicants, insisting, while refusing to inquire into the availability of restitution, that restitution was only one of three remedies and holding that the non-recognition of legal titles to property as registered at present in the Land Registry of Cyprus was justified under TRNC legislation. More recently the Court has communicated two applications to Turkey with questions regarding the accessibility/effectiveness of the remedy for applicants in the same position as in the inadmissibility decision in Meleagrou and Others v Turkey, the fairness of calculating compensation for the value of the property , extreme delays/non-payment of compensation as well as the application of Articles 6 and 14 of ECHR, all of which go to the effectiveness of the remedy available within the TRNC. See *Loizou v Turkey*, Application no. 50646/2015, ECHR (communicated) 14 December 2015; *Joannou v Turkey*, Application no. 532440/2015, ECHR (communicated) 19 November 2015.

home and/or the full benefits of their title as the legal property owners, if a domestic remedy is finally introduced after a lengthy period of time (*Demopoulos, Papayianni, Fieros*). Alternatively, where the Respondent state fails to introduce a domestic remedy, in the context of lengthy and stalling political negotiations, the onus is on IDP applicants, displaced and dispossessed, to judge when to apply without "undue delay" to the Court. The Court has warned that undue delays will result in rejection of applications at the Court as out of time, thus leaving the IDP applicant without a remedy either in Strasbourg or at home.

In the case of the Greek Cypriot IDPs, the Court had failed to consider the hundreds of applications that had been lodged over the period of time when there was no remedy provided by Turkey.[125] Ironically, decades later, it dismissed them all once the pilot judgment procedure was concluded with the *Demopoulos* inadmissibility decision and the establishment of the IPC remedy that IDP applicants were now required to exhaust before resorting to the Court. Except that, at this late hour, IDP claims to homes had become null and void and the nature of the remedy that could realistically be available to them for violations of their right to property negated the expectation that the full benefits of title can now be enjoyed.

A state, responsible for forced expulsions, in violation of the rights to home and property of large numbers of IDPs, can now either wait for a long time before introducing a remedy to address expectations of redress, by now much reduced by the passage of time, or can routinely object that applications are out of time where there is no remedy and negotiations are stalling. Either way, the position of IDPs, as individual applicants in Strasbourg, in the context of long standing conflicts, is being seriously compromised. Hence the Court's realpolitik approach, in its recent case law, when addressing violations of the rights to home and property of individual IDPs (i.e. members of a larger population of similarly displaced persons): the states concerned must reach an agreement on a comprehensive political settlement of all such questions,[126] concerning return and/or compensation, pending which they should introduce property claims mechanisms to address the violation of property rights.[127]

125 In Xenides-Arestis, consideration of approximately 1400 post-Loizidou applications deriving from the same general cause was adjourned.

126 *Sargsyan v Azerbaijan*, n120, [216] : "While the issues raised fall within the Court's jurisdiction as defined in Article 32 of the Convention, it is the responsibility of the two States involved in the conflict to find a political settlement of the conflict. . . . Comprehensive solutions to such questions as the return of refugees to their former places of residence, re-possession of their property and/or payment of compensation can only be achieved through a peace agreement"; *Demopoulos*, n10, [85].

127 "[I]t would appear particularly important to establish a property claims mechanism, which should be easily accessible and provide procedures operating with flexible evidentiary standards, allowing the applicant and others in his situation to have their property rights restored and to obtain compensation for the loss of their enjoyment." *Sargsyan v Azerbaijan*, n120, [238]; *Chiragov v Armenia*, Application no. 13216/050, 16 May 2015, [199].

Bibliography

Books

Hitchens C. (1984), *Cyprus* (New York, Quartet Books). [Revised 3rd ed. as *Hostage to History: Cyprus from the Ottomans to Kissinger*, 1997 (London, Verso Books).]
Ker-Lindsay J. (2011), *The Cyprus Problem, What Everyone Meeds to Know* (Oxford, Oxford University Press).
Lambert-Abdelgawad E. (2008), *The Execution of Judgments of the ECtHR*, Human Rights, Files No. 19, 2nd ed. (Strasbourg: Council of Europe Publishing).

Book chapters

Costa J.P. (2002), "The Provision of Compensation Under Article 41 of the ECHR" in Fairgrieve D., Andenas M., Bell J. (eds.), *Tort Liability of Public Authorities in Comparative Perspective* (London, British Institute of International and Comparative Law).
Polakiewicz J. (2001), "The Execution of Judgments of the ECtHR" in Blackburn R., Polakiewicz J. *Fundamental Rights in Europe* (Oxford, Oxford University Press).

Journal articles

Coufoudakis V. (1982), "Cyprus and the European Convention on Human Rights: The Law and Politics of *Cyprus v Turkey*", *HRQ*, Vol. 4, 450–473.
Paraskeva C. (2009), "The Application of the 'Pilot Judgments Procedure' to the post-*Loizidou* Cases", *Annuaire International Des Droits De L' Homme*, Vol. IV, 573–588.
Paraskeva C., Meleagrou E. (2012–2013), "Homes from the Past: An Expiration Date for the Right to Respect for Home Under Article 8 of the European Convention on Human Rights", *Annuaire International des Droits de l'Homme*, Vol. VII, 845–877.
Wildhaber L. (2004), "The ECtHR in Action", *RitsLRev*, Vol. 21, 83.

Research papers

Anagnostou D. and Mungiu-Pippidi A. (2009), "Why Do States Implement Differently the European Court of Human Rights Judgments? The Case Law on Civil Liberties and the Rights of Minorities (work in progress)", JURISTRAS Project.

5 Inter-American and Colombian developments and contributions on the protection of persecuted internally displaced persons

Nicolás Carrillo-Santarelli

1 Introduction

The suffering and experiences of internally displaced persons (hereinafter, IDPs) are tragic and dramatic. Forcibly removed from their places of residence, fleeing due to threats, a founded fear of persecution or for other serious reasons,[1] their lifestyle is forced to undergo radical changes in ways that are seriously contrary to the fundamental rights and freedoms they are entitled to.

Such violations of the rights founded on the unconditional inherent worth or dignity[2] of human beings merit an adequate and appropriate legal response that provides effective protection, as demanded by two considerations: the necessity that law properly deals with the problems found in the society it regulates[3] and the importance of having solidarity with those who suffer, even when this implies progressively developing their full protection.[4] One could wonder why international law should deal with a "domestic" phenomenon as internal displacement and the answer lies in the acknowledgment that the violation of fundamental rights of human beings is an *erga omnes* problem that is beyond the mere "internal" affairs of States.[5] In spite of this, as mentioned by Ghráinne, there is a scarcity

1 Ghráinne B.N. (2015) "Internally Displaced Persons (IDPs)", *MPEncPIL*.

2 Sensen O. (2011) "Human Dignity in Historical Perspective: The Contemporary and Traditional Paradigms", *EJPT*, Vol. 10; Villán-Durán C. (2006), *Curso de Derecho Internacional de los Derechos Humanos* (Madrid, Trotta) 63, 92; Schachter O. (1983), "Human Dignity as a Normative Concept", *AJIL*, Vol. 77, 853; Andorno R., "Human Dignity and Human Rights as a Common Ground for a Global Bioethics", *JMP*, Vol. 34, 227–236; General Assembly resolution 41/120, *Setting international standards in the field of human rights* (4 December 1986), A/RES/41/120; Helsinki Final Act, 1 August 1975, Conference on Security and Co-Operation in Europe; Donnelly J. (1982), "Human Rights and Human Dignity: An Analytic Critique of Non-Western Conceptions of Human Rights", *APSR*, Vol. 76, 303–304, 310.

3 Remiro-Brotóns A. *et al.* (2010), *Derecho Internacional: Curso general* (Valencia, Tirant Lo Blanch), 37.

4 Clapham A. (2015), *Human Rights: A Very Short Introduction* (Oxford, Oxford University Press) xiii, 22, 24, 164–165.

5 Gómez Isa F., "International Protection of Human Rights' in Gómez Isa F. and de Feyter K. (eds.) (2006) *International Protection of Human Rights: Achievements and Challenges* (Bilbao,

of hard law provisions expressly dealing with the specific rights of IDPs, addressing their needs and tackling the challenges to their protection.[6] Yet this does not mean that the plight of IDPs is irrelevant or unregulated in international law, for three reasons. First, because some soft law provisions are founded on or reflect binding law, as happens with part of the Guiding Principles on Internal Displacement, which have addressed the issue and have been internalized in some countries, as Colombia;[7] second, because different norms, found across different international legal regimes, as argued in this chapter, provide human rights protection against internal displacement; and, third, because the case law of quasi-judicial and judicial international supervisory bodies has expressly dealt with the protection of IDPs and addressing their specific needs, as demonstrated below. This specificity of the legal responses that seek to properly address the concrete needs of the internally displaced answers to the demand of specialization, i.e. that the concrete needs of some victims and their specific situation are considered in ways that make law provide specialized protection to those in need.[8]

The need to protect the internally displaced is especially acute if one considers how appalling the phenomenon of mass-scale internal forced displacement is nowadays, with the Colombian case being especially poignant due to the fact that displacement has been used as a "war strategy"—as recognized by the United Nations—and the number of displaced.[9] In fact, the number of IDPs in Colombia is so high that it currently holds the unflattering title of ranking as the country with the highest number of internally displaced persons.[10] Given the seriousness of the phenomenon of internal displacement in Colombia, one could be tempted to think that a top-down normative approach would be best suited to make its authorities deal with the situation. Nevertheless, the contrary—a bottom-up

Universidad de Deusto) 20, 24–25, 31; McDougal M. and Lasswell H.D. (1959), "The Identification and Appraisal of Diverse Systems of Public Order", *AJIL*, Vol. 53, 4–5.

6 Ghráinne, n1.

7 Ibid; Office in Colombia of the High Commissioner for Human Rights, *Manual de Calificación de Conductas Violatorias*, Bogotá: Office of the United Nations High Commissioner for Human Rights, 2010, 235–236.

8 de Asís Roig R., "Hacia una nueva generalización de los derechos. Un intento de hacer coherente a la teoría de los derechos" in Campoy I. (ed.) (2006), *Una discusión sobre la universalidad de los Derechos Humanos y la inmigración* (Madrid, Dykinson) 37–38.

9 Ghráinne, n1; Edwards A., "Global Forced Displacement Hits Record High', 20 June 2016, UNHCR, http://www.unhcr.org/news/latest/2016/6/5763b65a4/global-forced-displacement-hits-record-high.html; Office in Colombia of the High Commissioner for Human Rights, *Recomendaciones de órganos internacionales de derechos humanos al Estado colombiano 1980–2000*, Bogotá: UNOHCR, 2000, 185.

10 Edwards, n9. In the UNHCR webpage, referred to therein, it is said that as of June 2016: "Colombia at 6.9 million, Syria at 6.6 million and Iraq at 4.4 million had the largest numbers of internally displaced people." This means that the number of IDPs has increased (Ní Ghráinne's estimation as of the time of publishing her piece was that there were 5.7 million IDPs in Colombia). Moreover, see: UNHCR The UN Refugee Agency, *Global Trends: Forced Displacement in 2015*, UNHCR, 2016, 30.

approach—can be relevant as well: given how they face the need to fulfil their duties to protect IDPs in such a mass scale, it may be worth looking at how the normative and practical experience of the Colombian authorities and the direct or immediate supervision of such fulfilment by the Inter-American system of human rights, which is the one most widely used by Colombian applicants, can both shed light on and prompt or suggest developments in the universal or general human rights system. After all, as mentioned by Antonio Remiro Brotóns, regional experiences may sometimes lead to changes in general international law.[11] For instance, pronouncements of the Inter-American Court of Human Rights on internal displacement and the rights of IDPs in cases against Colombia have been cited in cases against other countries in the region.

Accordingly, this chapter will explore how the Colombian experience and challenges regarding internal displacement have been addressed by the Inter-American and Colombian authorities, which has led them to demand and propose policies, doctrines and conclusions that may help to understand or develop standards universally or in other regions—after all, American doctrines have been adopted elsewhere, as happened with the *uti possidetis juris* one.[12] This study will be conducted in the following way. First, the chapter will explore how Colombian and Inter-American authorities have regarded the unlawfulness of internal displacement and the necessity of protecting those affected by it (Section 1). Then I will examine what they have said about the rights and guarantees of IDPs generally and in special circumstances and the legal status of internal displacement (Section 2). Finally, the chapter will explore the obligations of States before and after internal displacement takes place, including protection and humanitarian assistance duties and the question of reparations—including aspects of restitution, compensation and satisfaction—of the victims of internal displacement (Section 3). This section will also examine the obligations and—individual or simultaneous—responsibility of authorities and agents of persecution—both State and non-state, both during "ordinary" and "transitional" scenarios. I would like to make it clear that I have directly translated myself the citations of the Colombian Constitutional Court and legal materials found in this chapter, which are not officially available in English.

Before continuing, it is important to make a clarification: while, according to the Guiding Principles on Internal Displacement (hereinafter, the Guiding Principles), there can be IDPs who are not persecuted by State or non-state agents, such as those who "have been forced or obliged to flee or to leave their homes or places of habitual residence" as a result of natural disasters, the article will focus on those who flee from persecution, which is a particularly problematic situation in Colombia and other States in the Americas.

11 Remiro-Brotóns, n3, 62–63.

12 Ibid; Taylor Sumner B. (2004), "Territorial Disputes at the International Court of Justice", *DLJ*, Vol. 53, 2004, 1790; International Court of Justice, *Frontier Dispute, Judgment, I.C.J. Reports 1986, 554*, [20]–[26].

2 Recognition of the necessity of protecting internally displaced persons

Imagine the despair and suffering of someone who has been uprooted from their land, forced to have a completely different lifestyle, to lose the means of their income and perhaps be separated from their loved ones and friends. Maybe that person fled their home because of the persecution and threats directed at them or perhaps their relatives had been attacked and murdered. Sometimes, apart from all the drama of displacement, the displaced have an additional suffering due to the loss of connection to the land to which they feel attached for spiritual or cultural reasons, as happens to some indigenous peoples; or maybe displacement has an added toll due to the vulnerability of the victim, as happens with children. Sadly, this has been a reality in different countries, including Colombia, in which paramilitary groups—as described in the *Ituango Massacres v Colombia* case,[13] guerrillas and other actors—many belonging to what Kofi Annan calls the uncivil society,[14] such as drug cartels—have displaced people either to seize their lands and property or to intimidate and get rid of those who stand in the way of their objectives or are regarded as "the enemy".

Had those people fled to other countries, it would be clear that the law of refugees would protect them. As stipulated in Article 1 of the Convention relating to the Status of Refugees, those who have no State protection, have a well-founded fear of persecution and are "outside the country of [their] nationality" are considered refugees and thus enjoy the respective rights of the law of refugees, while those "who have not crossed an internationally recognized State border" are internally displaced persons, in accordance to the Guiding Principles on Internal Displacement. IDPs have remained in their States, perhaps due to difficulties of going abroad or because going to a different country altogether would be much more drastic and problematic. This being so, it can be asked if their situation is merely an internal or domestic one, especially if the State has not been the one persecuting them. Asserting this would be contrary to the developing humanization of international law, according to which the wellbeing and the respect of the dignity of human beings is not merely a local issue, which is the reason that explains why obligations are imposed on States of jurisdiction and other actors in order to protect victims. This demands asking whether international law international law responds to their needs concerning protection. If not, it should be modified *de lege ferenda*.

Given the mass scale of displacement in Colombia and the problems faced by the displaced, such questions have been presented to and examined by both Colombian authorities and international supervisory bodies, as the Inter-American ones, when the affected feel that they have found no effective remedies and

13 I/A Court H.R., *Case of the Ituango Massacres v Colombia,* Preliminary Objection, Merits, Reparations and Costs. Judgment of 1 July 2006. Series C No. 148, [177].

14 Annan K.A., "Foreword" in United Nations Office on Drugs and Crime, *United Nations Convention against Transnational Organized Crime and the Protocols Thereto*, United Nations, 2004, iii.

protection at the local level. What those authorities, both domestic and international, say, can thus contribute both to the progressive development *and* clarification of the protection of the internally displaced and the scope of their protection in *lex lata*, and so it is important to take a look at what they have said. Needless to say, insofar as what the Inter-American bodies determine in cases in which Colombia is not a party may pave the way for what those bodies, say, in future cases and must be taken into account by States in good faith. This is required by the notion of the "control of conformity with the Convention" developed by the Inter-American Court of Human Rights according to which the pronouncements and interpretations of that Court must be considered by State agents when their competences so permit.[15] Moreover, what those bodies conclude in cases in which Colombia is not a party can guide that State when handling its own displacement problematics, which explains why some relevant cases against other States will be explored in this chapter as well. As to the national level, special attention will be paid to the decisions of the Constitutional Court, insofar as it has explored issues about the fundamental rights of the displaced and have ordered other State agents to do things on their behalf when it has perceived that the proper protection of the displaced has failed or not taken place at all.

When facing the questions posed above, the Inter-American and Colombian authorities have agreed on the following: first, that internal displacement is a situation that is gravely contrary to the protection that human beings are entitled to by virtue of their dignity or inherent worth, including human rights—wherever they are found, including instruments not specifically or mainly devoted to their recognition and protection,[16] and, when applicable due to the presence of an armed conflict, international humanitarian law guarantees,[17] among other applicable norms on the protection of human dignity, which embody the much needed progressive and evolving humanization of international law.[18]

This is consistent with what the Guiding Principles say, since they are based on "international human rights law, humanitarian law, and refugee law by analogy".[19] It is noteworthy that in spite of such Principles being contained in a non-binding or soft law *instrument* (the content of which does reflect some binding standards),

15 I/A Court H.R., *Rights and guarantees of children in the context of migration and/or in need of international protection*, Advisory Opinion OC-21/14 of August 19, 2014, Series A No.21, [31]; Inter-American Court of Human Rights, *Control de Convencionalidad: Cuadernillo de Jurisprudencia de la Corte Interamericana de Derechos Humanos No. 7*, 2015.

16 I/A Court H.R., *"Other treaties" subject to the consultative jurisdiction of the Court (Art. 64 American Convention on Human Rights)*, Advisory Opinion OC-1/82 of 24 September 1982, Series A No. 1; I/A Court H.R., *The Right to Information on Consular Assistance in the Framework of the Guarantees of the due Process of Law*, Advisory Opinion OC-16/99 of October 1, 1999, Series A No.16.

17 Ghráinne, n1.

18 Meron T. (2006), *The Humanization of International Law* (Leiden, Martinus Nijhoff Publishers), xv.

19 Guiding Principles on Internal Displacement, E/CN.4/1998/53/Add.2, 11 February 1998, Introductory Note to the Guiding Principles, [7].

the Colombian Constitutional Court has considered that they *must* be observed by Colombian authorities.[20] In this sense, the Colombian Constitutional Court has argued that in spite of the Guiding Principles on Internal Displacement not having been adopted by means of an international treaty, the fact that they refer to the content of binding international norms and fill their gaps, along with their having a widespread acceptance, make it necessary for Colombian authorities to take them into account when interpreting law, protecting and serving displaced persons and when designing policies and norms.[21] This is an interesting and important example of the increased internalization and implementation of standards when it is believed that they are legitimate.[22] In addition to having an expressive[23] and cultural impact by drawing attention to the plight of the displaced and what their rights are, such internalized Principles can shed light on how to change both norms and practices that are contrary to the protection that IDPs are entitled to, something that both customary law and Article 2 of the American Convention on Human Rights demand.[24]

The identification of the entitlements and guarantees of internally displaced persons does not depend on formalities, insofar as internal displacement is regarded as contrary to human rights and other humanitarian obligations. Such guarantees apply not only if displacement is caused as a result of legal orders, but also when it is caused *de facto* in spite of domestic law prohibitions or when caused by non-state actors. In this sense, in the case of the *Moiwana Community v Suriname*, the Inter-American Court of Human Rights said the following:

> [T]he State asserts that [Moiwana survivors] may indeed move freely throughout the country. *Regardless of whether a legal disposition actually exists in Suriname that establishes such a right* [. . .] the Moiwana survivors' freedom of movement and residence is circumscribed by a very precise, *de facto restriction, originating from their well-founded fears* [. . .] which excludes them only from their ancestral territory.[25]

20 Ghráinne, n1, [25]–[26].

21 *Manual de Calificación de Conductas Violatorias*, n7, 235–236.

22 Koh H.H. (1997), "Why Do Nations Obey International Law?", *YLJ*, Vol. 106, 2601; Franck T.M. (2002), *Fairness in International Law and Institutions* (Oxford, Oxford University Press) 22.

23 On the expressive function that international norms and principles can have, see: Geisinger A. and Stein M.A. (2007), "A Theory of Expressive International Law", *VLR*, Vol. 60, 83, 86, 88–89, 94, 97, 130–131; McAdams R.H. (2015), *The Expressive Powers of Law: Theories and Limits* (Cambridge, Harvard University Press) 1–13.

24 I/A Court H.R., *Case of "The Last Temptation of Christ" (Olmedo-Bustos et al.) v Chile*, Merits, Reparations and Costs, Judgment of 5 February 2001, Series C No. 73, [87]; I/A Court H.R., *Case of Atala Riffo and daughters v Chile*, Merits, Reparations and Costs. Judgment of 24 February 2012, Series C No. 239, [80], [272], [279]; HRC, *The Nature of the General Legal Obligation Imposed on States Parties to the Covenant*, General Comment No. 31 [80], CCPR/C/21/Rev.1/Add. 13, Eightieth session, 26 May 2004, [13], [16]–[17].

25 I/A Court H.R., *Case of the Moiwana Community v Suriname*, Preliminary Objections, Merits, Reparations and Costs. Judgment of 15 June 2005, Series C No. 124, [119] (emphasis added).

Likewise, in the case of *Human Rights Defender et al. v Guatemala*, the same Court confirmed that:

> [T]he rights to freedom of movement and residence *may be violated either formally or by de facto restrictions*, if the State has not established the conditions or provided the means to exercise these rights. This occurs, for example, when a person is the victim of threats or harassment and the State does not provide the necessary guarantees to ensure that he can move around and live freely in the territory concerned, *even when the threats and harassment originate from non-state actors.*[26]

Apart from the idea that internal displacement is contrary to human rights even if it is caused by non-state threats and by *de facto* circumstances that are not approved by the State and its legal system, additional important conclusions can be inferred from the cited passages. This includes the idea that the rationale of providing protection to the internally displaced coincides with the one applicable to the protection of refugees as well as other forms of protection (such as the subsidiary protection status in the European Union or human rights prohibitions of return when there is a risk owing to personal features or a general situation of violence),[27] namely the necessity of protecting those who flee from persecution. Note how the Court refers, in the first quote, to *de facto* violations when people flee due to "well-founded" fears of persecution, an expression that is identical to the one found, for instance, in the Convention relating to the Status of Refugees (Article 1). Likewise, and despite the fact that some States—perhaps for political and unacceptable reasons such as the desire to not receive refugees—resist the idea, the United Nations High Commissioner for Refugees and other States accept that both States and non-state actors can be agents of persecution, and that those persecuted by *any* of them can be refugees.[28] This is an idea that the Inter-American Court also accepted in regards to IDPs, as in the *Human Rights*

26 I/A Court H.R., *Case of Human Rights Defender et al. v Guatemala*, Preliminary Objections, Merits, Reparations and Costs. Judgment of 28 August 2014. Series C No. 283, [166] (emphasis added).

27 European Court of Human Rights, Fourth Section, *Case of Sufi and Elmi v The United Kingdom*, Applications nos. 8319/07 and 11449/07, Judgment, 28 June 2011 (Final 28/11/2011), [30], [212]–[219]; European Court of Human Rights, Third Section, *Case of N. v Sweden*, Application no. 23505/09, Judgment, 20 July 2010 (Final 20/10/2010), [58–62].

28 UNHCR (The UN Refugee Agency), *Handbook and Guidelines on Procedures and Criteria for Determining Refugee Status under the 1951 Convention and the 1967 Protocol relating to the Status of Refugees*, UNHCR, Reissued 2011, 15, in which it is said that: "Persecution is normally related to action by the authorities of a country. it may also emanate from sections of the population that do not respect the standards established by the laws of the country concerned [. . .] Where serious discriminatory or other offensive acts are committed by the local populace, they can be considered as persecution if they are knowingly tolerated by the authorities, or if the authorities refuse, or prove unable, to offer effective protection."

Defender case. The Colombian Constitutional Court, likewise, in its decision *C-370/06*, "has acknowledged the presence of hundreds of thousands of persons in a situation of forced displacement, condemned to misery *by the action of armed illegal groups*".[29] This reality must have an adequate and effective legal response, lest victims are left unprotected.

It can be argued, then, that complementing the responsibility dimension, according to which those who displace persons without any international legal authorization have international criminal responsibility—as enshrined in Articles 7 and 8 of the Rome Statute—the entitlements or rights dimension determines that individuals who are displaced as a result of general violence or persecution, including those who have well-founded fears of persecution or being affected by such violence and flee from such situation, are entitled to legal protection under international law—to prevent gaps in some States. Such protection aims to safeguard the rights of the displaced, regardless of whether they cross national borders or not, as there is a close connection between persecution and the violation of rights. After all, as has been said in Colombia, the only difference between some refugees and IDPs is that the former flee their countries of origin and the latter remain in them, but both are "forced to abandon their homes".[30] Furthermore, as has been well pointed out by Bríd Ní Ghráinne, refugees and IDPs "may share the same experiences, needs, fears, and wants".[31] Regarding these ideas, in the case of *Chitay Nech et al. v Guatemala*, the Inter-American Court of Human Rights said that victims of displacement in that case suffered threats and persecutions,[32] which is something that refugees also sadly face. The idea of protecting all persecuted, wherever they are, and thus regardless of their having crossed borders or not, makes sense and is fair, since it would be unacceptable to deny protection to victims on the basis of their not going abroad, especially because borders are historically contingent, social creations and may change, while human beings have unconditional worth independently of formalities.

Granted, when addressing different situations, such as those of refugees and IDPs, nuanced different treatments may be acceptable to a certain extent, but the essentials and the fundamental guarantees owed to persons with the same needs should remain in all cases and law must ensure this, for instance, by providing the same protection via analogy when this is pertinent and necessary. This is something that has been recognized in practice. For instance, the Inter-American Court of Human Rights and the Committee on the Elimination of Racial Discrimination have clarified that *non-refoulèment* must also exist in relation to the internally-displaced. According to the latter, "States parties are obliged to ensure that the

29 Office in Colombia of the High Commissioner for Human Rights, *Compilación de jurisprudencia y doctrina nacional e internacional, Vol. VI*, Bogotá: UNOHCR, 2012, 874 (emphasis added).

30 *Manual de Calificación de Conductas Violatorias*, n7, 232.

31 Ghráinne, n1, [2].

32 I/A Court H.R., *Case of Chitay Nech et al. v Guatemala*, Preliminary Objections, Merits, Reparations, and Costs. Judgment of May 25, 2010, Series C No. 212, [163].

return of [. . .] refugees ***and displaced persons*** [to their homes of origin under conditions of safety] is voluntary and to observe the principle of non-refoulèment and non-expulsion of refugees."[33] For its part, the Inter-American Court has emphasized the need that IDPs return insofar as there are conditions of safety and they so desire;[34] while the Colombian Constitutional Court has said that the State has an obligation "to not coerce persons to return to their places of origin".[35] This echoes what the Guiding Principles on Internal Displacement mention in Principle 15, in which it is said that IDPs have "[t]he right to be protected against forcible return to or resettlement in any place where their life, safety, liberty and/or health would be at risk".

Apart from the requirement that not only refugees but also internally displaced persons are protected, as demanded by the same needs of protection and underlying rationales, there are other connections between the protection of refugees and that of the displaced, including the idea that IDPs have the right to seek refugee status by going abroad, which may happen when they feel that the State and its legal system can no longer protect them effectively or when they no longer trust them. This has been recognized in the Guiding Principles on Internal Displacement, which in Principle 2 mentions that those Principles "are without prejudice to the right to seek and enjoy asylum in other countries".

In the passage of the *Human Rights Defender* case quoted above, the Inter-American Court refers to freedom of movement and residence as being affected by internal displacement. This is logical because threats forcing people to leave their homes prevent them from enjoying their right to dwell and be wherever they choose. The question that ensues is whether this is the only right directly affected by internal displacement. Just as human rights law is not the only regime applicable in favor of IDPs, the answer, as confirmed by Colombian and Inter-American case law, is a negative one, because forced internal displacement is a situation that is contrary to several rights and freedoms, as explained in the next section.

3 The rights of the internally displaced

In regards to the question made at the end of the previous section about which rights are affected by internal displacement and which protection IDPs are entitled to, it is possible to begin by drawing attention to the fact that in addition to material damage there is a psychological anguish and harm caused to the internally displaced. Additionally, it is clear that in addition to the freedom of movement and residence, the following rights, among others, can be violated by internal

33 Committee on the Elimination of Racial Discrimination, *General recommendation XXII on article 5 of the Convention on refugees and displaced persons*, Forty-ninth session, 1996 (emphasis added).

34 Inter-American Court of Human Rights, *Desplazados: Cuadernillo de Jurisprudencia de la Corte Interamericana de Derechos Humanos No. 3*, 2015.

35 Office in Colombia of the High Commissioner for Human Rights, *Compilación de jurisprudencia y doctrina nacional e internacional, Vol. V*, Bogotá: UNOHCR, 2006, 727.

displacement: the right to personal integrity, because of the anguish and real fear felt by victims and the dramatic change of their living conditions; the right to privacy due to the violation by State or non-state actors, i.e. the agents of persecution, of their dwellings; the right to property (Principle 21 of the Guiding Principles) when others seize the goods owned by the displaced; the right to work when the displaced find no jobs in the places they move to, as may happen when those living in rural areas and who have worked in agriculture are forced to go to urban areas where they find no means of sustenance; the protection of family life and home; or the right to health when the conditions they live in in their new circumstances, for instance, in slums, affect such right and they receive no proper health services. Accordingly, all of the human rights that can be affected by internal displacement, including both civil and political right and economic, social and cultural rights of the internally displaced, among which the ones mentioned in this paragraph and others can be included, must be guaranteed. Those rights are enshrined in international human rights law, as revealed by Articles 7, 12 and 17 of the International Covenant on Civil and Political Rights; 7, 10 and 12 of the International Covenant on Economic, Social and Cultural Rights; and 5, 11, 17, 21, 22 and 26 of the American Convention on Human Rights.

This idea that multiple human rights are violated by forced displacement and that it causes several disruptions is recognized in the Introductory Note to the Guiding Principles on Internal Displacement, which mentions that it:

> [B]reaks up families, cuts social and cultural ties, terminates dependable employment relationships, disrupts educational opportunities, denies access to such vital necessities as food, shelter and medicine, and exposes innocent persons to such acts of violence as attacks on camps, disappearances and rape.

Specifically in relation to psychological suffering and other violations of human rights, the Guiding Principles on Internal Displacement recognize that they must be addressed by stressing that, when necessary, IDPs "shall have access to psychological and social services"; while in the case of the *Mapiripán Massacre v Colombia*, the Inter-American Court of Human Rights expounded the following:

> In most cases, the minimum conditions required by the displaced population to return to their homes, in terms of security and dignity for them, are lacking, and the significant negative effects of resettlement caused by forced internal displacement, in addition to its *grave psychological repercussions* for them, include: (i) *loss of the land and of their houses*, (ii) marginalization, (iii) loss of the household, (iv) *unemployment*, (v) deterioration of *living conditions*, (vi) *more illness and higher mortality*, (vii) loss of access to common property among the members of communities ["comuneros"], (viii) *food insecurity*, and (ix) social disintegration, as well as *impoverishment* and *accelerated deterioration of living conditions.*[36]

36 I/A Court H.R., *Case of the "Mapiripán Massacre" v Colombia*, Merits, Reparations and Costs, Judgment of 15 September 2005. Series C No. 134, [175] (emphasis added).

One example illustrates the preceding ideas. In the case of the *Ituango Massacres v Colombia*, the Inter-American Court of Human Rights opined that:

> [T]he destruction by the paramilitary group, with the collaboration of the Colombian Army, of the homes of the inhabitants of El Aro, and also of the possessions that were inside the homes, *in addition to being a violation of the right to the use and enjoyment of property, constitutes a grave, unjustified and abusive interference in their private life and home.* The alleged victims, who lost their homes, also lost the place where their private life took place.[37]

The confirmation that multiple rights are affected by internal displacement explains what the Inter-American Court of Human Rights said in the case of the *Afro-Descendant Communities Displaced from the Cacarica River Basin (Operation Genesis) v Colombia*:

> [O]wing to the complexity of the phenomenon of internal displacement and the *broad range of human rights it affects or jeopardizes*, and based on the circumstances of special vulnerability and defenselessness in which those displaced usually find themselves, *their situation can be understood as a de facto situation of lack of protection.* According to the American Convention, this situation obliges the States to adopt measures of a positive nature to reverse the effects of their said situation of weakness, vulnerability and defenselessness, *even in relation to the actions and practices of private third parties.*[38]

The Colombian Constitutional Court closely follows this idea about a *de facto* violation caused by displacement and has added an interesting additional consideration, which is that when internal displacement is widespread or massive and no effective protection is given to the victims, such *situation* is unconstitutional. This is a novel and important idea. Why so? Because the traditional constitutional control carried out by bodies as the Colombian Constitutional Court is oriented towards the identification and expulsion of legal norms without constitutional hierarchy when they contradict the Constitution i.e. when they are unconstitutional—due to its being the supreme norm of the State. Yet, the rationale of the Court concerning internal displacement is that it is a *situation* that is so dire and contrary to the fundamental values and standards of protection of the Constitution, due to its gravity, that it is unconstitutional and the Court can identify it as such and order the elimination of this situation in order to protect the victims. This is an argument that is not necessarily restricted to domestic or

37 I/A Court H.R., *Case of the Ituango Massacres v Colombia*. Preliminary Objection, Merits, Reparations and Costs. Judgment of 1 July 2006. Series C No. 148, [197] (emphasis added).

38 I/A Court H.R., *Case of the Afro-descendant communities displaced from the Cacarica River Basin (Operation Genesis) v Colombia*, Preliminary Objections, Merits, Reparations and Costs. Judgment of 20 November 2013, Series C No. 270, [315] (emphasis added).

Colombian law and is somehow echoed by the Inter-American Court's consideration that the situation of displacement in Colombia can be considered as *de facto* contrary to human rights law, as argued in the last quotation. The Constitutional Court's exact words, made in the case *T-025 of 2004*, which was drafted by magistrate Manuel José Cepeda, were that a "repeated and constant violation of fundamental rights that affects multiple persons, and whose solution demands the intervention of different entities" can be regarded as an "unconstitutional situation" when the respective authorities have failed for long to address the issue, due to the gravity and widespread nature of the violation, along with the omission of the State to protect. The legal consequence of this finding is that all persons affected by the same unconstitutional situation are entitled to the same measures of protection ordered by the Court in one case addressing it, even if they did not personally file an application. The Court concluded that the situation of internal displacement in Colombia had all of these features and hence it was regarded as unconstitutional.[39] Just as the Colombian Court adopted a flexible approach regarding the provision of protection measures in favor of all individuals in the same situation of displacement, even if they have not resorted to filing certain applications or have not been individually identified by authorities, the Inter-American Court of Human Rights has similarly adopted a favorable flexible approach. It did so by permitting to determine or identify who will benefit from reparations and decisions adopted by the Court at a stage later than the initial proceedings, by considering, as in the *Operation Genesis v Colombia* case, that:

> [B]earing in mind the scope and nature of the facts of the case, as well as the time that has passed, the Court finds it reasonable that it is difficult to identify and to individualize each of the presumed victims, especially in the case of displaced populations, in a vulnerable situation, that are difficult to locate. On this basis, the Court considers it reasonable that the initial list of presumed victims presented by the Commission could have varied during the processing of this case, and therefore, in application of Article 35(2) of the Rules of Procedure, the Court will take into account the list presented by the representatives in their motions and arguments brief.[40]

Returning to the idea that forced displacement affects multiple rights, and in accordance with what the Inter-American and Colombian Court have said, it can be concluded that measures seeking to protect and benefit all IDPs must be designed so as to address all of the rights affected or threatened by internal displacement, including those identified above, as the right to life, the right to

39 *Compilación de jurisprudencia y doctrina nacional e internacional,* n35, 695–744; Constitutional Court of Colombia, T-025 of 2004, Judgment, 22 January 2004.

40 I/A Court H.R., *Case of the Afro-descendant communities displaced from the Cacarica River Basin (Operation Genesis) v Colombia,* Preliminary Objections, Merits, Reparations and Costs. Judgment of 20 November 2013, Series C No. 270, [42].

personal integrity, including both its physical and psychological or spiritual dimensions; the right to protection of the family and family union; and others explored below, such as the right to a minimum sustenance, among others. This is because the situation of internal displacement, which constitutes a *de facto*—rather than a normative—contradiction of multiple human rights, requires that all of those rights are remedied and protected. Moreover, since *all* affected rights must be addressed, this includes not only civil and political rights but also economic, social and cultural rights, some of which were directly or indirectly referred to in the passage of the *Mapiripán Massacre v Colombia* case quoted above. This is demanded because, after all, internal displacement can affect all categories or classifications of human rights and all of them are important for human beings in their different dimensions. This is related to the interdependency and interrelation of all human rights, which according to the Vienna Declaration and Programme of Action imply that all "human rights are universal, indivisible and interdependent and interrelated" and that accordingly they must be treated "in a fair and equal manner, on the same footing, and with the same emphasis".[41] Furthermore, the Guiding Principles on Internal Displacement refer to economic, social and cultural rights of the internally displaced as their rights-holders, such as the right to health (Principle 19; Colombian Constitutional Court decision T-025/2004)[42] or the right to education (Principle 23; decision T-602 of 2003 of the aforementioned Constitutional Court),[43] confirming and supporting the findings of the Constitutional Court. The third section of this chapter will further explore protection measures in regards to economic, social and cultural rights.

In regards to the rights of the displaced, it could be asked if a certificate of some sort may be required by State authorities to identify those entitled to them. In that regard, concerning the fulfilment of the rights of IDPs and the identification of those entitled to measures of protection, there had been discussions in Colombia as to whether displaced persons had a right to be formally identified as such and if this identification, for instance, materialized in documents certifying their status, could be a condition that had to be satisfied in order to benefit from those measures and protection policies. This is an issue related to the human right "to recognition everywhere as a person before the law", found in, among others, Articles 3 of the American Convention on Human Rights (under the heading "Right to Juridical Personality") and 16 of the International Covenant on Civil and Political Rights and also in Principle 20 of the Guiding Principles on Internal Displacement, which says that from that right it follows that "authorities concerned shall issue to them all documents necessary for the enjoyment and exercise of their legal rights" and "shall facilitate the issuance of new documents or the replacement

41 Vienna Declaration and Programme of Action, Adopted by the World Conference on Human Rights in Vienna on 25 June 1993, [I.5].

42 Office in Colombia of the High Commissioner for Human Rights, *Compilación de jurisprudencia y doctrina nacional e internacional, Vol. V*, Bogotá: UNOHCR, 2006, 724.

43 Ibid, 679; Constitutional Court of Colombia, T-602 of 2003, Judgment, 23 July 2003.

of documents lost in the course of displacement, without imposing unreasonable conditions". Regarding these issues, the Constitutional Court of Colombia, in judgment *T-602 of 2003*, said that inclusion in the Colombian Single Registry of Displaced Population (*Registro Unico de Población Desplazada)* has the purpose of *facilitating* the provision of State or international cooperation assistance, but cannot be regarded as decisively or exclusively "conferring the status or condition of being a displaced person". As a result, the very fact of someone having been forced to flee her or his home alone suffices for them to be entitled to protection and assistance, even lacking a certificate.[44]

When addressing the rights of IDPs and the guarantees and protection that must be given to them, it is unavoidable to explore the demand that while all IDPs are vulnerable and thus all of them require special protection given the extreme adversity they face,[45] some individuals under certain circumstances or specially protected displaced persons must benefit from "special measures of protection". These are required by general international human rights norms in some cases, as it happens for instance with children;[46] and as is sometimes envisaged in treaties that either focus on the protection of certain individuals—such as women or persons with disabilities under some universal and Inter-American treaties[47] or on protection from certain abuses, such as torture and cruel, inhuman, or degrading punishment or treatment, which also exist in the Inter-American system.[48] Such demands respond to the phenomenon and necessity of the specialization[49] of international human rights law, given the need to address specific needs of protection and to tackle widespread dynamics of violence or abuses against some persons or by some actors. Logically, given how internal displacement may affect some persons more harshly,[50] it is only logical that the protection of IDPs follows this same logic of specialization. In that regard, the Inter-American Court of Human Rights said in the case of the "*Mapiripán Massacre" v Colombia* that:

44 Ibid; *Compilación de jurisprudencia y doctrina nacional e internacional*, n35, 675.

45 Ibid, 685–686; *Manual de Calificación de Conductas Violatorias*, n7, 240.

46 I/A Court H.R., *Juridical Condition and Human Rights of the Child*, Advisory Opinion OC-17/02 of 28 August 2002, Series A No. 17, [38]; article 19 of the ACHR.

47 Examples include the Inter-American Convention on the Prevention, Punishment and Eradication of Violence Against Women "Convention of Belém do Pará"; the Inter-American Convention on the Elimination of all Forms of Discrimination Against Persons with Disabilities (the previous two Inter-American treaties, for instance, are included in the Basic Documents Pertaining to Human Rights in the Inter-American System, edited by the Secretariat of the Inter-American Court of Human Rights, 2012); or the Convention on the Rights of the Child, the Convention on the Rights of Persons with Disabilities or the Convention on the Elimination of All Forms of Discrimination against Women at the Universal Level.

48 See, for instance: the Inter-American Convention to Prevent and Punish Torture and the Inter-American Convention on Forced Disappearance of Persons.

49 de Asís Roig, n8, 37–38.

50 American Court of Human Rights, *Desplazados: Cuadernillo de Jurisprudencia de la Corte Interamericana de Derechos Humanos No. 3*, 2015, 6–7, 11 onwards.

> The reasons for and expressions of the acute vulnerability of displaced persons have been characterized from various perspectives. Said vulnerability is reinforced by their rural origin and, in general, it especially affects women—who are heads of households and constitute more than half the displaced population—girls and boys, youths, and elderly persons.[51]

Likewise, in the case of the *Ituango Massacres v Colombia*, the same Inter-American Court held that certain displaced persons are more at risk or with greater vulnerability, as may happen with some women from rural areas, because, in its words, "[t]he accentuated vulnerability of the displaced is increased by the fact that they come from rural areas and that women are usually more affected, since they are the household heads and represent more than half the displaced population."[52] Similarly, in *Chitay Nech et al. v Guatemala*, the Court held that children may also be at greater risk due to the fragmentation of families caused by forced displacement, which has an impact on their rights and guarantees.[53]

The need of specially protecting some displaced—while recognizing that all IDPs are entitled to protection—has been recognized in Principle 9 of the General Principles on Internal Displacement, which mentions that: "States are under a particular obligation to protect against the displacement of indigenous peoples, minorities, peasants, pastoralists and other groups with a special dependency on and attachment to their lands." Principle 4, in turn, says that:

> Certain internally displaced persons, such as children, especially unaccompanied minors, expectant mothers, mothers with young children, female heads of household, persons with disabilities and elderly persons, shall be entitled to protection and assistance required by their condition and to treatment which takes into account their special needs.

Likewise, Principle 18.3 states that: "Special efforts should be made to ensure the full participation of women in the planning and distribution of [. . .] basic supplies." In fact, the need of special protection is so important that it has been mentioned that when the specific vulnerability of children, especially unaccompanied ones, pregnant women, women with small children, women who provide the income of their families, persons with disabilities or the elderly do not receive humanitarian assistance in a way that takes into account their vulnerability, they are victims of discrimination,[54] which is consistent with the notion of indirect discrimination.[55]

51 I/A Court H.R., *Case of the "Mapiripán Massacre" v Colombia*, Merits, Reparations and Costs, Judgment of 15 September 2005. Series C No. 134, [175].

52 I/A Court H.R., *Case of the Ituango Massacres v Colombia*. Preliminary Objection, Merits, Reparations and Costs. Judgment of 1 July 2006. Series C No. 148, [212].

53 I/A Court H.R., *Case of Chitay Nech et al. v Guatemala*, Preliminary Objections, Merits, Reparations and Costs. Judgment of 25 May 2010, Series C No. 212, [171].

54 *Manual de Calificación de Conductas Violatorias*, n7, 248–249.

55 I/A Court H.R., *Case of Atala Riffo and daughters v Chile*, Merits, Reparations and Costs. Judgment of 24 February 2012, Series C No. 239, [80]; I/A Court H.R., *Juridical Condition*

The Colombian Constitutional Court, in turn, said in judgment *T-602* of 2003 that the protection of the internally displaced must be based on "affirmative action" and approaches that are sensitive to "gender, age, ethnicity, disabilities and sexual orientation [. . .] while seeking to satisfy the needs of the most vulnerable groups, as children, the elderly of persons with disabilities".[56] Accordingly, the Constitutional Court said, for instance in judgment *T-025* of 2004, that children must benefit from health services that take into account their needs and from access to education, rights that must be ensured.[57]

Colombian and Inter-American decisions have satisfactorily responded to the demand of specialization. This is important insofar as it has led to ordering special protection and to raising awareness of the special needs of some internally displaced persons. In that regard, for instance, the Inter-American Court of Human Rights has referred to indigenous and members of certain communities by saying that due to their special attachment to their lands in religious or cultural terms among others displacement gravely affects them. Their uprooting disrupts such connection, has a negative impact on the maintenance of traditions or beliefs and may also cause suffering to those members due to their losses caused by displacement. Consequently, those persons are entitled to special measures of protection that address their specific needs. The Court has examined this in the cases of *Chitay Nech et al. v Guatemala* and *Rio Negro Massacres*, against the same State. In the former case, the Inter-American Court of Human Rights said the following:

> [F]orced disappearance affected the members of the Chitay Rodriguez family in a particularly grave manner due to their connection with the Mayan indigenous group [. . .] the energetic connection with the land has a fundamental importance in the Mayan vision, for which the abandonment of the community not only was made material for the families that had to flee, but also signified a greater cultural and spiritual loss [. . .] the displacement of the next of kin of Florencio Chitay Nech out of his community provoked a rupture with his cultural identity [. . .] the relationship of the indigenous groups with their territory has been recognized as crucial for their cultural structures and their ethnic and material survival [. . .] forced displacement of the indigenous peoples out of their community or from their members can

and Rights of the Undocumented Migrants, Advisory Opinion OC-18/03 of 17 September 2003, Series A No. 18, [103]; Committee on Economic, Social and Cultural Rights, *The equal right of men and women to the enjoyment of all economic, social and cultural rights (art. 3 of the International Covenant on Economic, Social and Cultural Rights)*, General Comment No. 16, E/C.12/2005/4, Thirty-fourth session, [13]; European Court of Human Rights, Grand Chamber, *Case of Oršuš and others v Croatia*, Application no. 15766/03, Judgment, 16 March 2010, [85], [153]; and [2], [14] of the Joint Partly Dissenting Opinion to that judgment.

56 *Compilación de jurisprudencia y doctrina nacional e internacional*, n35, 684; Constitutional Court of Colombia, T-602 of 2003, Judgment, 23 July 2003.

57 Ibid, 724–725; Constitutional Court of Colombia, T-025 of 2004, Judgment, 22 January 2004.

> place them in a special situation of vulnerability, that for its destructive consequences regarding their ethnic and cultural fabric, generates a clear risk of extinction and cultural or physical rootlessness of the indigenous groups, *for which it is indispensable that the States adopt specific measures of protection* considering the particularities of the indigenous peoples, as well as their customary law, values, uses, and customs, in order to prevent and revert the effects of said situation [. . .] the Chitay Rodriguez brothers were prohibited from enjoying from the coexistence of their family due to the well-founded fear of returning to their place of origin, when other next of kin had disappeared, as well as the need to feed and educate themselves [. . .] this situation of rupture of the family structure is evident today [. . .] the forced disappearance had as its purpose to punish not only the victim but also his community and his family [. . .] the forced disappearance of Florencio Chitay Nech aggravated the situation of displacement and the cultural uproot that the family suffered. In this way, the disintegration of their land affected the members of the Chitay Rodriguez family in a particularly grave manner due to their condition as Mayan indigenous persons.[58]

4 Protection, assistance and reparations in favor of internally forced displaced persons

While some displaced require measures that take into account their specific needs as concluded in the previous section, *all* displaced persons undergo tragic circumstances and hence are entitled to specific measures of protection as demanded by international legal standards. Displacement is a *de facto* serious situation. Accordingly, it is important to look at the common needs and problems that the displaced persons face. These are addressed via, among other things, specific standards and measures that deal with such specific needs, including, on the one hand, the right to restitution and voluntary return and, on the other both the entitlement to humanitarian assistance and protection from threats and the right to reparations. To this effect, all participants in abuses, while it is clear that States are under an obligation to repair when they breach their duties to respect (including the duty to abstain from causing displacement) or protect from displacement, I argue below that in addition to States, in those cases in which law does not already do so, norms must be enacted *de lege ferenda* since non-state actors should be legally obliged to abstain from causing, being complicit in or aggravating displacement and so should be under a duty to fully repair when they cause or aggravate the displacement and the suffering of IDPs (with the State being able and encouraged to freely give more than what it is required to). This is so in both ordinary and transitional scenarios, as explored in this final section.

58 I/A Court H.R., *Case of Chitay Nech et al. v Guatemala*, Preliminary Objections, Merits, Reparations, and Costs. Judgment of 25 May 2010. Series C No. 212, [145]–[147], [161]–[162] (emphasis added).

We will now turn to examine how these elements have been dealt with in the experience of the Inter-American and Colombian levels of governance.

The first aspect I will address is the one related to the protection of all the rights of IDPs. These include economic, social and cultural rights, rights under international humanitarian law—the violation of which may cause forced displacement as recognized in case law[59]—and all other internationally recognized rights founded on human dignity, as those examined in the previous section, which must all be respected. Inter-American and Colombian authorities have confirmed that all of those rights must be protected in a way that takes into account their particularities. In relation to the economic, social and cultural rights of the internally displaced, for instance, it is important to observe that the Colombian Constitutional Court refers to the need of ensuring a minimum level of satisfaction of some of those rights, which coincides with the opinion of the Committee on Economic, Social and Cultural Rights that States have "a minimum core obligation to ensure the satisfaction of, at the very least, minimum essential levels of each of the rights".[60] Regarding these minimum core obligations towards IDPs, the Inter-American Commission on Human Rights has highlighted the importance that society debates how State authorities must conduct social policies or adopt "social policy" to benefit the displaced population.[61] The Colombian Constitutional Court on its part has expressed that IDPs have a right to a minimum sustenance, which requires authorities to provide IDPs with food, water, basic housing, clothing and health services.[62] Likewise, Principle 18 of the Guiding Principles refers to "the right to an adequate standard of living" of IDPs, which includes, "at the minimum", the following: "(a) Essential food and potable water; (b) Basic shelter and housing; (c) Appropriate clothing; and (d) Essential medical services and sanitation." This is consistent with the idea put forward by the Inter-American Court of Human Rights in the *Street Children* case that "the fundamental right to life includes, not only the right of every human being not to be deprived of his life arbitrarily, but also the right that he will not be prevented from having access to the conditions that guarantee a dignified existence".[63]

The previous measures fall under the positive duties of States to bring about the enjoyment of economic, social and cultural rights, insofar as they seek to *fulfil* them by facilitating and providing such enjoyment; but apart from them, States are also required to abstain from violating the rights of the internally displaced

59 *Compilación de jurisprudencia y doctrina nacional e internacional*, n35, 674, 689, 691–692, 703, 721, 723.

60 Committee on Economic, Social and Cultural Rights, *The nature of States parties' obligations (art. 2, para. 1, of the Covenant)*, General comment No. 3, Fifth session, 1990, [10].

61 Inter-American Commission on Human Rights, *Access to Justice as a Guarantee of Economic, Social, and Cultural Rights: A Review of the Standards Adopted by the Inter-American System of Human Rights*, OEA/Ser.L/V/II.129, Doc. 4, 7 September 2007, [238].

62 Ibid, 722–723.

63 I/A Court H.R., *Case of the "Street Children" (Villagrán-Morales et al.) v Guatemala*, Merits, Judgment of 19 November 1999. Series C No. 63, [144].

(obligation to respect) and to *protect* them, for instance by ensuring that other entities and actors "do not deprive individuals of their access" to such enjoyment. This corresponds to the triad of the obligations "to respect, to protect and to fulfil" discussed by the Committee on Economic, Social and Cultural Rights, among others, in its Twelfth General Comment on the "right to adequate food".[64] This classification of duties sheds light on what States such as Colombia are required to do in response to internal displacement, which must always be adequately dealt with in all its dimensions in order to protect those affected by it. This is particularly so in the case of massive or systematic violations, as discussed by the Colombian Constitutional Court and explored in the previous section when analyzing the concept of a factual unconstitutional situation. The idea that those duties clarify the extent, scope and nature of the measures that authorities must implement is explained by the idea that states are under an obligation to respect and to provide protection and assistance, to which all internally displaced persons are entitled. This is reflected in Principles 3 and 5 of the Guiding Principles on Internal Displacement, which say that authorities "shall respect and ensure respect for their obligations under international law" and that:

> 1. National authorities have the primary *duty* and responsibility to provide *protection and humanitarian assistance* to internally displaced persons within their jurisdiction. 2. Internally displaced persons have the *right to request and to receive* protection and humanitarian assistance from these authorities. They shall not be persecuted or punished for making such a request. (emphasis added)

Naturally, all rights must be protected, which implies, for instance, that civil and political and other rights have to be protected and respected as well, for instance obliging States to protect IDPs from further persecution and threats. The previous conclusions about the nature of State obligations and the binary protection-humanitarian assistance that flows from them and responds to the needs of the displaced have been recognized in case law. In this regard, for instance, the Colombian Constitutional Court said in judgment *T-025 of 2004* that:

> [T]hrough the provision of humanitarian assistance authorities *fulfill the core duty related to the dignified subsistence of displaced persons.* Such humanitarian assistance refers both to emergency humanitarian help, which is provided once displacement occurs, and also to the component of minimum assistance during the stages of economic restitution and return [. . .] in relation to emergency humanitarian assistance, the Court clarifies that the *duration* of the minimum State obligation to provide urgent humanitarian help is, in principle, the one set forth in law: three months, that can be extended for

64 Committee on Economic, Social and Cultural Rights, *The right to adequate food (art. 11)*, General Comment 12, E/C.12/1999/5, Twentieth session, 12 May 1999, [15].

> three additional months in relation to certain subjects. The Chamber considers that this period determined by the legislator is not manifestly unreasonable [. . .] That being said, insofar as the period mentioned in the law mainly responds to the two aforementioned reasons, the Court clarifies that there are two categories of displaced persons that, because of their specific conditions, are entitled to a minimum right to receive emergency humanitarian help for a time period that is longer than the one set forth under the law: those a) individuals who are under extraordinary urgency circumstances; and b) persons who are not capable of sustaining themselves through a project of stabilization or socioeconomic restitution, such as children who have no one who looks after them or the elderly who, because of their advanced age or their health conditions, cannot gain an income; or women who look after their families and must spend all their time and efforts to take care of young children or the elderly under their tutelage. In these events, it is justified that the State keeps on providing the humanitarian assistance that is required for the dignified sustenance of the affected until the moment when the respective circumstance has been overcome—that is to say, until the moment in which the extraordinary urgency has ceased or the persons who could not sustain themselves and others acquire the conditions to do so.[65]

From the Colombian Court's assessment, it is possible to conclude that all IDPs are entitled to some humanitarian assistance measures, the purpose of which is permitting them to have a minimum sustenance and standard of living while they can regain or obtain the ability to generate income and satisfy their basic needs. This is required due to the fact that their displacement and the disruption of their lifestyles deprive them of their jobs and other rights and conditions and so, for a time, they need assistance. Yet, rather than formalities, what matters is that the situation is actually overcome and that the affected truly have the capacity to live in good and satisfactory conditions before assistance is withdrawn. This explains the reason why the State continues to have a duty to provide assistance to those who, due to their added vulnerabilities, do not have the ability to live without such support. Therefore, it is possible to conclude that humanitarian assistance, as understood by Colombian authorities, is not merely a gratuitous gesture but it actually entails an obligation of the State for as long as it is necessary given the disruption faced by victims. In this sense, in the *Operation Genesis v Colombia* case, the Inter-American Court of Human Rights stressed that the State has "obligations to ensure humanitarian assistance and a safe return".[66] Hence, that Court supported the argument of the Inter American Commission on Human Rights,

65 *Compilación de jurisprudencia y doctrina nacional e internacional*, n35, 723–724 (emphasis added).

66 I/A Court H.R., *Case of the Afro-descendant communities displaced from the Cacarica River Basin (Operation Genesis) v Colombia*, Preliminary Objections, Merits, Reparations and Costs, Judgment of 20 November 2013, Series C No. 270, [324].

which considered that humanitarian assistance, along with the facilitation of—voluntary and safe, it must be said return are *legal* obligations of States in favor of IDPs. Logically, the State is free and actually encouraged to go beyond what is legally and mandatorily required of it—as enshrined in the Principles on Reparation prepared by Theo van Boven[67] and may provide additional assistance to victims of forced internal displacement. It is therefore convenient to take a look at the arguments of the Commission, which were the following:

> The Commission indicated that the State's responsibility did not arise merely from the fact that it had played an "important role from the start," but that "it continued to be constituted owing to the failure to comply with its minimum obligations" towards the displaced population. It pointed out *two obligations of "special relevance": the obligation to provide and facilitate humanitarian assistance, and that of facilitating the return of those displaced.* On this point, it indicated with regard to the difference between humanitarian aid and reparation to the victims of forced displacement that *"humanitarian assistance is part of the State's general obligation towards any inhabitant with such needs, while reparation involves an obligation under international law to repair the consequences of a conduct that violated the Convention and thus reinstate, to the extent possible, the rights of the victims".*[68]

It can thus be said that apart from humanitarian assistance, there are duties to facilitate return and to repair. In regards to reparations, to my mind, it is important to identify who the parties responsible for the violation and lack of enjoyment of the rights of the displaced are, because they will have a responsibility to repair them—even an internationally legal responsibility for non-state actors who breach international legal duties of their own, in case they have them, as may happen when they have breached international criminal law or norms imposed on them by the sources of international law; and/or a social or domestic duty to repair when domestic law determines so, even if those actors lack international duties in a given case. For the sake of the full reparation of victims, both domestic and international laws should hold those actors responsible, lest victims, for instance, are not entitled to demand satisfaction from them. This requires exploring why, in addition to the obligations of States, it is important to interpret the dimension of "respect" of IDPs in light of current developments in international human rights law and related regimes, in which there are increasing demands of respect by non-state actors and

67 Principle 15 of the Basic Principles and Guidelines on the Right to a Remedy and Reparation for Victims of Gross Violations of International Human Rights Law and Serious Violations of International Humanitarian Law (Basic Principles); van Boven T. (2010), "The United Nations Basic Principles and Guidelines on the Right to a Remedy and Reparation for Victims of Gross Violations of International Human Rights Law and Serious Violations of International Humanitarian Law", *United Nations Audiovisual Library of International Law*, 3.

68 Ibid, [295] (emphasis added).

for holding them accountable. Such are the developments in international criminal law or, by analogy, in the field of business and human rights, which demonstrates that there can be a non-state—e.g. corporate—duty to respect that is binding in serious cases such as those related to breaches of *jus cogens* or international criminal law.[69] Accordingly, this evolutionary interpretation that considers the context or *corpus juris* in which the protection of human beings, which are forcibly displaced is embedded, also calls for holding non-state actors, as agents of persecution, accountable and binds them at the very least to respect the rights of IDPs, beginning with the obligation to not displace anyone. The Guiding Principles acknowledge this demand when they say, for instance, that they "shall be observed by all [. . .] groups and persons" (Principle 2); that they provide guidance to all of them (Introductory Note; Introduction: Scope and Purpose); or that internally displaced persons "shall be protected against discriminatory practices of recruitment into *any* armed forces *or groups*" (Principle 13; emphasis added).

Since non-state and State actors can be agents of persecution and cause or intensify the effects of displacement, then they will be under a duty to repair and face all the other consequences of responsibility, including offering guarantees or assurances that they will no longer cause displacement directly or with threats (non-repetition) and to cease any ongoing actions causing displacement (cessation).[70] Furthermore, States will be responsible if they fail to provide the aforementioned required humanitarian assistance, which is mandatory and related to the legitimacy of law, State power and sovereignty—partly grounded on the respect, promotion and protection of human rights[71]—or if they fail to facilitate a safe and voluntary return (see below). In such circumstances, States will be in breach of their duties which are both duties of result—concerning the core sustenance and satisfaction elements—and of means, for example, in relation to the requirement that States exercise due diligence to prevent attacks against those who return to the places from which they were displaced. As to reparations which include, as appropriate, restitution, compensation and satisfaction,[72] responsible States must repair. Yet, since often non-state actors cause persecution, *de lege ferenda* all agents of persecution should have a duty to repair in case it does not

69 Knox J.H. (2011), "The Human Rights Council Endorses 'Guiding Principles' for Corporations", *ASIL Insights*, Vol. 15; Ruggie J.G. (2012), "Kiobel and Corporate Social Responsibility", *Issues Brief*, Harvard Kennedy School, John F. Kennedy School of Government, 3–4; Portmann R. (2010), *Legal Personality in International Law*, (Cambridge, Cambridge University Press) 166–167, 280.

70 ILC, *Articles on Responsibility of States for Internationally Wrongful Acts*, Yearbook of ILC, 2001, Vol. II (Part Two), 2001, articles 30 and 31; Basic Principles, n67, Principles 15, 18 through 23.

71 I/A Court H.R., *Juridical Condition and Human Rights of the Child*, Advisory Opinion OC-17/02 of 28 August 2002, Series A No. 17, Concurring Opinion of Judge A.A. Cançado Trindade, [13], [15], [19]; Ratner S.R. (2015), *The Thin Justice of International Law: A Moral Reckoning of the Law of Nations* (Oxford, Oxford University Press) 73, 78–79, 83–84, 92–98.

72 Basic Principles, n67, Principle 18; n77, infra.

exist yet, including an obligation to apologize and provide assurances of non-repetition[73] and with *those* actors that have deprived victims of their goods, be they State persecutors or not, being under an obligation to return them to the displaced. Otherwise, reparations may not be full in some cases if non-state actors are under no duty to repair. This is why the acknowledgement in the Colombian peace agreement with the FARC—mentioned below—that all perpetrators must repair is so important. Furthermore, States must diligently try to ensure that goods are properly returned to their rightful owners. In situations in which States breach their duties of respect—including the duty of not being complicit in causing or aggravating displacement—protection or fulfilment, and non-state actors generate displacement or abuse the displaced, they must provide reparations to the victims whilst the effects of *all* violations need to be addressed. It must be borne in mind that the principle of individual responsibility demands that everyone is accountable for its own conduct, which explains why there can be simultaneous responsibilities of all those who in one way or another participate in or contribute to a violation when different actors breach legal obligations of their own.[74] Accordingly, there may be cases in which the State is held accountable for having failed to behave diligently in order to try to protect the displaced, with the non-state agents of persecution, as members of armed groups, being prosecuted for the perpetration of crimes against humanity or war crimes.

Concerning the ideas presented in this paragraph regarding restitution by all persecutors or actors who seize the goods of the displaced, it is useful to point out that the Declaration of Basic Principles of Justice for Victims of Crime and Abuse of Power mentions how:

> Offenders or third parties responsible for their behaviour should, where appropriate, make fair restitution to victims, their families or dependants. Such restitution should include the return of property or payment for the harm or loss suffered, reimbursement of expenses incurred as a result of the victimization, the provision of services and the restoration of rights.

I will now move to the analysis of the rights to restitution or restoration and to freely and safely return to the original residence of the displaced. One of the problems closely associated with forced displacement relates to land dispossession which is a serious problem in Colombia. In the *Operation Genesis* case, the Inter-American Court of Human Rights ordered land restitution measures after finding

73 Basic Principles, ibid, [15], [20]–[23].

74 I/A Court H.R., *International Responsibility for the Promulgation and Enforcement of Laws in Violation of the Convention (Arts. 1 and 2 of the American Convention on Human Rights)*, Advisory Opinion OC-14/94 of 9 December 1994, Series A No.14, [52], [54]–[57]; International Court of Justice, *Application of the Convention on the Prevention and Punishment of the Crime of Genocide (Bosnia and Herzegovina v Serbia and Montenegro), Judgment, I.C.J. Reports 2007*, 43, [419]–[420]; Cheng B. (2006), *General Principles of Law as Applied by International Courts and Tribunals* (Cambridge, Cambridge University Press) 208–210.

that the State failed to comply with its obligations towards those affected by internal displacement. In its words:

> [A]s a result of the State's failure to comply with its obligation to ensure the right to collective ownership [. . .] the communities of the Cacarica have suffered harm that goes beyond the mere detriment to their collective wealth. The body of evidence reveals that they have a special relationship with the lands they inhabit and that, consequently, they were profoundly affected not only by being *dispossessed* of these lands, but also by the fact that the illegal exploitation of the natural resources by third parties was permitted. Accordingly, in order to avoid a repetition of such acts, *the Court orders the State to restore the effective use, enjoyment and possession of the territories* recognized by law to the Afro-descendant communities assembled in the Cacarica Community Council.[75]

As mentioned above, along with humanitarian assistance and reparations, there is a State duty to conduct measures seeking to ensure the right of the displaced to return. Given its importance, special attention must be paid to such right to return to the places of origin and the corresponding State obligations to ensure it. This is due to the fact that return may *partly* revert and put an end to the situation of displacement—acknowledging that this is necessary when desired by the victims but also that some rights and harm cannot be repaired via restitution.[76] In this regard, Inter-American case law has identified the following main standards: a) return must be voluntary, which means that the displaced have the right to decide to settle elsewhere or to return to the places they were displaced from; b) constant consultation with the displaced must take place when planning and ensuring the return of IDPs; and c) return must be made in conditions of safety that the State is obliged to try to bring about (obligation of means), with the State being under a duty to keep supervising that those who have returned live in safety. All of these principles are interrelated (e.g. if someone decides to return, the State has the due diligence duty to protect them and to consult with them about the measures to be implemented to guarantee their return and will also be under an obligation of ensuring their continued safety). The following passages illustrate these points and how each standard is connected with the others.

75 I/A Court H. R., *Case of the Afro-descendant communities displaced from the Cacarica River Basin (Operation Genesis) v Colombia*, Preliminary Objections, Merits, Reparations and Costs, Judgment of 20 November 2013, Series C No. 270, [459] (emphasis added).

76 ILC, *Articles on Responsibility of States for Internationally Wrongful Acts*, Yearbook of ILC, 2001, vol. II (Part Two), 2001, articles 34 through 37; ILC, *Draft articles on Responsibility of States for Internationally Wrongful Acts, with commentaries*, 2001, [2] of the Commentary to Article 34 95; I/A Court H.R., *Case of Rodríguez Vera et al. (The Disappeared from the Palace of Justice) v Colombia*, Preliminary Objections, Merits, Reparations and Costs. Judgment of 14 November 2014. Series C No. 287, [543].

As to the first standard, the Inter-American Court of Human Rights said in the *Human Rights Defender et al. v Guatemala* case that: "the State must guarantee adequate conditions of safety so that [the displaced] can return to their places of residence, *if appropriate and if they so wish*".[77] Regarding consultations, the Court has said, for instance, that:

> When community members eventually are satisfied that the necessary conditions have been reached so as to permit their return, the State shall guarantee their safety. To that effect, upon the community members' return to Moiwana Village, the State shall send representatives every month to Moiwana Village during the first year, in order to consult with the Moiwana residents. If the community members express concern regarding their safety during those monthly meetings, the State must take appropriate measures to guarantee their security, which shall be designed in strict consultation with said community members.[78]

Something similar was expressed in the *Mapiripán* case, in which the Court argued that:

> When the former inhabitants decide to return to Mapiripán, the State must guarantee their security. For this, the State must send official representatives to Mapiripán every month during the first year, to verify order and *conduct consultations* with the residents in the town. If during these monthly meetings the townspeople express concern regarding their safety, the State must take such steps as may be necessary *to ensure it, and these actions will be designed in consultation with the beneficiaries of the measures.*[79]

Regarding the third identified standard about the *right* to return, which reflects the *due diligence* obligation to protect those who *decide* to return, with the subsidiary duty to ensure resettlement elsewhere in safe conditions if this is not really possible, the Court said, in the *Ituango Massacres v Colombia* case, that:

> [S]ome inhabitants of Ituango do not wish to return to La Granja and El Aro, because they fear they will continue to be threatened by the paramilitary groups. *It is possible that this situation will not change until an effective investigation has been completed and also judicial proceedings that result in the clarification of the facts and the punishment of those responsible.* When the

77 I/A Court H.R., *Case of Human Rights Defender et al. v Guatemala*, Preliminary Objections, Merits, Reparations and Costs. Judgment of 28 August 2014. Series C No. 283, [256] (emphasis added).

78 I/A Court H.R., *Case of the Moiwana Community v Suriname*, Preliminary Objections, Merits, Reparations and Costs, Judgment of 15 June 2005, Series C No. 124,[212].

79 I/A Court H.R., *Case of the "Mapiripán Massacre" v Colombia* Merits, Reparations and Costs, Judgment of 15 September 2005, Series C No. 134, [313] (emphasis added).

> former inhabitants, who have not already done so, *decide to return to Ituango, the State must guarantee their security, which should include monitoring the prevailing situation in a way and for the length of time that will guarantee this security. If it is not possible* to establish these conditions, the State must provide the necessary and sufficient resources to ensure that the victims of forced displacement may *resettle* in similar conditions to those they had before these events, in a place they freely and voluntarily choose.[80]

Similarly, in the case of the *Operation Genesis*, the Inter-American Court argued the following:

> The Court is also aware that the members of the Cacarica communities *feel insecure, particularly owing to the presence of armed agents. It is possible that this situation will not change until public order is re-established and until effective investigations and judicial proceedings are conducted that result in the clarification of the facts and the punishment of those responsible.* Therefore, the Court considers, as it has in other cases, that *the State must guarantee that the conditions of the territories that the State must restitute, as well as of the place where the members of the Cacarica communities live at present, are adequate for the safety and decent life of those who have returned and also of those who have not yet done so.* To this end, the State must send periodically—at least once a month—official representatives to the territories from which these persons were displaced and, in particular, to the Peace Communities ("Esperanza de Diós" and "Nueva Vida"), *for the five years that follow notification of this Judgment, in order to verify the situation of public order and, consequently, they must meet with the communities or the designated representatives of the latter.* If, during these monthly meetings, the inhabitants of the communities *express concern about their safety, the State must take the necessary measures to guarantee this, and these measures must be designed in collaboration with the beneficiaries of such measure.*[81]

The previous two citations highlight three important aspects: first, that it may happen that the State, in spite of its best efforts, is unable to permit a safe return of IDPs to their places of origin, event in which it will bear no legal accountability on that count but must ensure resettlement *in similar conditions* in a safe place they accept to go to. This condition of similarity is aimed, to my mind, at making the displaced live in similar conditions to the ones they had before and thus for their lifestyle to not be drastically altered, seeking to address and revert, to the extent

80 I/A Court H.R., *Case of the Ituango Massacres v Colombia*, Preliminary Objection, Merits, Reparations and Costs, Judgment of 1 July 2006, Series C No. 148, [404] (emphasis added).

81 I/A Court H.R., *Case of the Afro-descendant communities displaced from the Cacarica River Basin (Operation Genesis) v Colombia*, Preliminary Objections, Merits, Reparations and Costs. Judgment of 20 November 2013, Series C No. 270, [460] (emphasis added).

that it is possible, the fact that internal displacement causes victims "suffering [. . .] alterations in their living conditions, and [. . .] other consequences of a non-material or non-pecuniary nature".[82] The second aspect that the Court stresses is the necessity that States hold non-state abusers accountable to prevent them from repeating their misdeeds, which are encouraged or facilitated by impunity conditions. Finally, it is stressed that the guarantee of the safety and enjoyment of the rights of the formerly displaced must be a constant one, lest displacement takes place again; and must be conducted in consultation with the victims, confirming that the different standards (voluntariness, consultation, safety) are interrelated.

Furthermore, just as the standards on return are interrelated, so is the right to return itself connected with the other consequences and duties emerging from a situation of displacement, such as the reparation of victims, including restitution, *if possible*, or compensation otherwise (satisfaction is always required, I think, given how neither restitution nor compensation can fully eliminate the effects of the violations). This is echoed in General Recommendation XXII of the Committee on the Elimination of Racial Discrimination, which says that "displaced persons have the right *freely* to return to their homes of origin under conditions of *safety*", with States being obliged to ensure that their return "is voluntary" and that displaced persons have, "after their return to their homes of origin, the right to have *restored to them property* of which they were deprived [. . .] *and to be compensated appropriately for any such property that cannot be restored to them.* Any commitments or statements relating to such property made under duress are null and void."[83]

To conclude this section, given the current context in Colombia, in which many displaced lost their possessions, and some illegitimate possessors have attempted to keep the property rightfully belonging to the displaced by invoking agreements entered into by them with a consent that was neither full nor free, it is convenient to take a look at what has been said regarding the internally displaced in the peace negotiations between the Government and the FARC group. In that regard, the Agreement on the Victims of Conflict, the joint draft of which was published on 15 December 2015, expressly refers to the displaced, recognizing that "millions of Colombians are victims of forced displacement"; and setting forth that IDPs must receive special attention, given how "the consequences of [. . .] violations are more serious when perpetrated against [. . .] displaced persons and refugees"; specifying that conduct causing forced displacement cannot benefit from amnesties or pardons; and determining that displaced peasants must benefit from effective reparation provided by actors responsible for violations committed during the Colombian armed conflict. Moreover, the Agreement indicates that programs that seek to bring about and permit the return or resettlement of the displaced to their homes of origin must be carried out by the Government and that lands must be restituted. The same considerations were included in the Final Agreement on the

82 I/A Court H.R., *Case of the Plan de Sánchez Massacre v Guatemala*, Reparations, Judgment of 19 November 2004, Series C No. 116, [83].

83 Committee on the Elimination of Racial Discrimination, *General recommendation XXII on article 5 of the Convention on refugees and displaced persons*, op. cit., [2] (emphasis added).

Termination of Conflict and the Construction of a Stable and Lasting Peace between the government and the FARC, which includes recognitions of the wrongfulness of forced displacement and provisions against the impunity of forced displacement; on the protection of IDPs, their rights to return, restitution and other elements of reparations; and their participation in political life.[84] Given the need to protect victims in ways that reflect and take into account their specific needs, as the ones caused by a situation of armed conflict in which many civilians were persecuted, these express commitments are welcome and it is to be hoped that peace indeed flourishes in Colombia, because the persistence of conflict could perpetuate internal displacement, which would be tragic.

6 Conclusions

Colombia has undergone a terrible situation of armed confrontation for too many years, one of the features of which has been a large-scale situation of internal displacement that has affected an excessively large number of persons. Even one victim would be too many, but the massiveness of displacement in Colombia calls for special attention so that it does not take place in the future and victims have their rights fully repaired, including their right to *freely* decide, without any direct or indirect coercion, to return in conditions of safety.

While legal decisions may seem insufficient given the dire circumstances, it is to be applauded that, among other bodies, regional and local judicial authorities that have had to closely examine the situation of the displaced in Colombia have lived up to what is expected of them, both by declaring how internal displacement is seriously contrary to human rights and other standards, both domestic and regional, and by ordering the protection of victims in a way that takes into account their specific needs and all of their rights. The alteration of the living conditions of victims is serious in itself and often has sent those affected to other places in which their situation worsens, given the difficulty of finding jobs or health services, for example. It is to be hoped that the conflict in Colombia finally comes to an end and internal displacement never again takes place. Such displacement, however, must not be forgotten, so as to remember something that must be

84 Provisions on the reparations and protection of IDPs are found in the different versions of the agreement between the Colombian Government and the FARC, including not only the version that was defeated in the referendum of 2016 but also the version approved afterwards by Congress, which was finally approved domestically. See: *Acuerdo Final para la Terminación del Conflicto y la Construcción de una Paz Estable y Duradera* (Final Agreement on the Termination of Conflict and the Construction of a Stable and Lasting Peace), 24 November 2016, 3, 13, 15, 17, 51, 54, 126, 131, 133–135, 144, 151, 182–184, 295, 298, 304, 306, 308; *Acuerdo sobre las Víctimas del Conflicto: "Sistema Integral de Verdad, Justicia, Reparación y No Repetición", incluyendo la Jurisdicción Especial para la Paz; y Compromiso sobre Derechos Humanos*, 15 December 2015, 3, 9–10, 12–13, 22, 28, 47, 54–55; *Acuerdo Final para la Terminación del Conflicto y la Construcción de una Paz Estable y Duradera* (Final Agreement on the Termination of Conflict and the Construction of a Stable and Lasting Peace), 24 August 2016, 4, 14, 113, 115, 117, 123, 131.

avoided and prevented; and because the standards and initiatives developed and proposed by judicial authorities, negotiators, activists and others can inspire both the identification and codification of existing standards that benefit the displaced elsewhere and also inspire progressive development. That being said, it would be unfair and risky to deem that no standards applicable to internal displacement exist outside the Americas, because States have specific obligations and the internally displaced do have specific rights that answer to the demand of recognizing concrete rights that take their specific needs into account (i.e. demand of specialization), even if not always expressly identified as pertaining to the displaced. Authorities and interpreters must make an effort to identify and implement them rather than believe that they must be created anew; and Colombian and Inter-American contributions, made after witnessing the plight of so many, can shed light on their content. Logically, stronger guarantees and measures may and must be developed. No one deserves to be internally displaced and it is hard to imagine what those who have had to endure such situation have been through. They must be the center of our analysis and have our solidarity.

Altogether, the fact that millions of Colombians have been forcibly displaced from their homes of origin due to threats or violence is a situation that, in itself, in addition to being tragic is seriously contrary to international and domestic human rights standards, and affects a multiplicity of rights, as has been declared by the Colombian Constitutional Court and by the Inter-American Court of Human Rights. When exploring cases related to internal displacement, these judicial authorities have provided arguments, orders and conclusions that call for benefiting all those affected by internal displacement, without formalities standing in the way; for recognizing all of the rights of the displaced and ordering their full and appropriate reparation; and for ensuring that authorities comply with their duties to provide humanitarian assistance, protection and the satisfaction of the rights to return in free and safe conditions and to restitution among others to which the internally displaced are entitled. Such contributions, along with developments made in the transitional negotiations in Colombia and the identification of the importance and need of holding all agents of persecution accountable put forward in this chapter can both provide guidance to other regions and the universal system of human rights and clarify why the internally displaced already have strong guarantees of protection in the humanitarian *corpus juris*. A sad, tragic and unacceptable situation as the Colombian one, in which forced displacement is so prevalent, can thus provide lessons, factual, ethical and legal, that can be learned from in other places in which displacement occurs or may take place. Furthermore, as argued in the previous paragraph, the displaced must be at the center of the analysis of this situation that violates so many rights.

Bibliography

Books

Cheng B. (2006), *General Principles of Law as Applied by International Courts and Tribunals* (Cambridge, Cambridge University Press).

Clapham A. (2015), *Human Rights: A Very Short Introduction* (Oxford, Oxford University Press).
Durán C.V. (2006), *Curso de Derecho Internacional de los Derechos Humanos* (Madrid, Trotta).
Edwards A., "Global Forced Displacement Hits Record High", 20 June 2016, UNHCR.
Franck T.M. (2002), *Fairness in International Law and Institutions* (Oxford, Oxford University Press).
Geisinger A. and Stein M.A. (2007), "A Theory of Expressive International Law", *Vanderbilt Law Review*, Vol. 60, 77–131
McAdams R.A. (2015), *The Expressive Powers of Law: Theories and Limits* (Harvard University Press).
Meron T. (2006), *The Humanization of International Law* (Leiden, Martinus Nijhoff Publishers).
Portmann R. (2010), *Legal Personality in International Law* (Cambridge, Cambridge University Press).
Ratner S.R. (2015), *The Thin Justice of International Law: A Moral Reckoning of the Law of Nations* (Oxford, Oxford University Press).
Remiro-Brotóns A. *et al.* (2010), *Derecho Internacional: Curso general* (Valencia, Tirant Lo Blanch).

Book chapters

Annan K.A., "Foreword" in United Nations Office on Drugs and Crime, *United Nations Convention against Transnational Organized Crime and the Protocols Thereto*, United Nations, 2004, iii–iv.
de Asís Roig R., "Hacia una nueva generalización de los derechos. Un intento de hacer coherente a la teoría de los derechos" in Campoy I. (ed.) (2006), *Una discusión sobre la universalidad de los Derechos Humanos y la inmigración* (Madrid, Dykinson), 35–58.
Gómez Isa F. (2006), "International Protection of Human Rights" in Gómez Isa F. and de Feyter K. (eds.) (2006), *International Protection of Human Rights: Achievements and Challenges* (Bilbao, Universidad de Deusto).

Journal articles

Andorno R. (2009), "'Human Dignity and Human Rights as a Common Ground for a Global Bioethics', *Journal of Medicine and Philosophy*, Vol. 34, 223–240.
Donnelly J. (1982), "Human Rights and Human Dignity: An Analytic Critique of Non-Western Conceptions of Human Rights", *American Political Science Review*, Vol. 76, 303–316.
Ghráinne B.N. (2015), "Internally Displaced Persons (IDPs)", *Max Planck Encyclopedia of Public International Law*.
Knox J.H. (2011), "The Human Rights Council Endorses 'Guiding Principles' for Corporations", *ASIL Insights*, Vol. 15.
Koh H.H. (1997), "Why Do Nations Obey International Law?", *Yale Law Journal*, Vol. 106, 2599–2659.
McDougal M. and Lasswell H.D. (1959), "The Identification and Appraisal of Diverse Systems of Public Order", *American Journal of International Law*, Vol. 53, 1–29.

Ruggie J.G. (2012), "Kiobel and Corporate Social Responsibility", *Issues Brief*, Harvard Kennedy School, John F. Kennedy School of Government, 1–7.

Schachter O. (1983), "Human Dignity as a Normative Concept", *American Journal of International Law*, Vol. 77, 848–854.

Sensen O. (2011), "Human Dignity in Historical Perspective: The Contemporary and Traditional Paradigms", *European Journal of Political Theory*, Vol. 10, 71–91.

Taylor Sumner B. (2004), "Territorial Disputes at the International Court of Justice", *Duke Law Journal*, Vol. 53, 1779–1812.

van Boven T. (2010), "The United Nations Basic Principles and Guidelines on the Right to a Remedy and Reparation for Victims of Gross Violations of International Human Rights Law and Serious Violations of International Humanitarian Law", *United Nations Audiovisual Library of International Law*, 1–7.

6 Forced displacement, dispossession and property

Cambodia

Rhona Smith, Ratana Ly and Chantevy Khourn[1]

1 Introduction

Displacement of persons and land dispossession in Cambodia has been on a nationwide scale. The Khmer Rouge period of Democratic Kampuchea is probably the most widely known example. The Paris Peace Accords 1991 laid the foundation for the rebuilding of Cambodia, a country besieged by external and internal conflict for many years. Relative peace and stability has ensued, but the legacy of the events of the 1970s and 1980s remain all too present, compounded by historical legacies of colonisation, invasion and occupation.

The Cambodian context is inevitably shaped by Cambodia's complex history, its 'almost-continuous entrapment in the rivalries of outside forces',[2] which is discussed in this chapter primarily as it affects land rights.[3] As will be shown, individual land titles were introduced to Cambodia by the French colonial occupiers but abolished completely by the communist party by 1976. Although there is now a system of land titling and registration as well as systems for addressing contestations of land claims, land does remain one of the most prominent unresolved human rights issues in the country. Many people are still trying to resolve historical land claims and secure tenure.

A chronological approach is taken in this chapter to ensure an holistic understanding of the issues, although this chapter focuses on the events of the late twentieth century when dispossession ultimately became national policy. Case studies of Khmer people who had land before 1970 are used to examine the impact of historical events narrated herein. Names of the individuals, although

* The authors are each researching and writing in their individual academic capacities. As such, neither the UN nor Actionaid is involved and the final text does not necessarily reflect either of their views. The authors began working together in 2013 through Raoul Wallenberg Institute of Human Rights and Humanitarian Law academic programmes in Cambodia.

1 The authors are grateful to Dr Hap Phalthy for his advice on (post-1989) land laws and policies.

2 Church P. (ed.) (2009), *A Short History of Southeast Asia* (John Wiley) 5th ed, 12.

3 For more detailed reports and analyses of the history of Cambodia, see, inter alia, Chandler D. (2008), *A History of Cambodia*, (Westview Press) 4th ed., and the other texts below.

not the locations, have been changed.[4] Their experiences are representative of that of thousands of other Khmers. As will be demonstrated, there is still no coherent policy or approach to restoring property, land and housing to those displaced persons of Cambodia.

2 Historical background

Historically, all land in what is now known as Cambodia belonged to the king. Chandler notes that the notion of inalienable ownership of land, as distinct from land use, does not seem to have developed in pre-Angkorean Cambodia.[5] Land left fallow for three years reverted to state control[6] and use of land was controlled by the king. Land was primarily used for agriculture, i.e. rice farming. During the Angkorean period, the king oversaw considerable development of land, including extensive complex irrigation systems.[7] Indeed, skilful maximisation of natural resources, backed up by slavery and servitude, ensured the great success and political strength of successive kingdoms albeit dramatic expansion and growth ultimately contributed to their demise at the end of the thirteenth century.[8] By the early nineteenth century, Cambodia was, effectively, unmapped, unlike its neighbours. A period of invasion and occupation (by Vietnamese and Thai forces) characterised the first half of the nineteenth century – 'the darkest portion of Cambodia's recorded history prior to the Armageddon of the 1970s'.[9] Neither land titling nor rights was a feature of this period of civil unrest. The population remained rural and generally poor, rice farming being more subsistence orientated at this point and communities often isolated with little infrastructure.

1863 brought the establishment of the French protectorate.[10] Land titling was introduced and royal decrees permitted French ownership of land. By 1905 feudal landholdings were officially abolished.[11] 139,559 hectares were given to settlers in 8,532 land grants.[12] Road and rail infrastructure were (re)developed facilitating

4 Full details on file with authors. Name were changed for ethics' reasons but each individual kindly consented to his/her experiences being used.

5 Chandler, n3, 22.

6 Ibid, 22.

7 Evans D. et al. (2013), 'Uncovering archaeological landscapes at Angkor using lidar' *PNAS*, Vol.110, No. 31, 12595–12600.

8 Today the remains of some of these complexes are often listed as one of the wonders of the world, one of the largest religious complexes in the world and probably the largest pre-industrial complex supporting over half a million people –Evans D. et al. (2007), 'A comprehensive archaeological map of the world's largest preindustrial complex at Angkor, Cambodia', *PNAS*, Vol. 104, No. 36, 14277–14282.

9 Chandler, n3, 141.

10 Tully J. (2003), *France on the Mekong: A History of the Protectorate in Cambodia 1863–1953* (University Press of America).

11 Yuon H. (1982), 'The peasantry of Kampuchea: colonialism and modernization' in Kiernan B. and Boua C. (eds.), *Peasants and Politics in Kampuchea 1942–1981* (Zed Press) 36.

12 Ibid, 37.

movement throughout the Kingdom. However, on 9 March, 1945, Japanese forces usurped French forces throughout Indochina. A few days later, King Sihanouk of Cambodia declared Cambodia independent from France and proclaimed the country Kampuchea, albeit that Japanese forces were present. France regained *de facto* power by an agreement early in 1946.

King Sihanouk oversaw the departure of the French in 1953[13] and the re-establishment of Cambodian independence.[14] What is often regarded as a halcyon period of relative peace and prosperity followed. A land survey in 1950 records 437,888 landowners with 1,120,321 surveyed plots and 2,040,599 declared plots.[15] Land was 'very parcellized',[16] most plots being rice fields. Landowners often owned several plots, scattered rather than contiguous. This remains common in Cambodia with some people choosing to grow crops in disparate areas distant from their home, usually due to soil conditions. Hou Yuon recorded that, excluding Phnom Penh, in 1950, there were 7.22 recorded plots for each recorded landowner.[17] Nevertheless, many rural people were sharecroppers or tenant farmers: those with larger land holdings planted the best part of the land, renting out the rest. Debt bondage and semi-feudal systems resulted as the poorest rural people borrowed to rent land, plant and produce. Hu Nim noted a trend towards land ownership concentration – the number of plots less than five hectares drops from 92 to 85.6% between 1956 and 1962, while the number of medium (five to ten hectares) and large (more than ten hectares) plots increases.[18] Regional variations remained with a density of very small landholdings in central Cambodia (the central rice lands along the Mekong river).[19]

Changes in land concentrations impacted on population flow, census data records movement towards the larger urban developments of Phnom Penh, Battambang, Siem Reap, Pursat and Kratie[20] from the poorer provinces.[21] The seeds of discontent and disillusionment were sown. With American forces building in southern Viet Nam and the political and economic situation deteriorating in Cambodia, peasant revolts broke out sporadically, people disappeared and the King's power base was challenged by the strengthening Communist Party of Kampuchea.[22] The Communist Party maintained links with Viet Nam and senior

13 Withdrawal was finalised after the Geneva talks and peace agreement promulgated elections of 1955.

14 Cambodia joined the United Nations in 1953.

15 n11, 35.

16 Ibid, 35.

17 Ibid, 36.

18 Nim H. (1982), 'Land tenure and social structure in Kampuchea' in Kiernan and Boua, n11, 74.

19 Ibid, 75.

20 The most common transliteration of the Khmer names is used in this chapter. Note that other texts may spell place names differently.

21 Nim, n18, 75 quoting *Annuaire Statistique Retrospectif du Cambodge* 1958–1960.

22 Son Ngoc Minh was the first Cambodian communist leader. On the rise of the Communist Party of Kampuchea, see also Etcheson C. (1984), *The Rise and Demise of Democratic Kampuchea* (Westview Press).

members made visits to Hanoi.[23] Lon Nol became Prime Minister in 1966, having previously served in the military and as defence minister. His troops were used in the suppression of several uprisings, land dispossession and migration were often causal factors. In the Samlaut rebellion of 1967–1968, many peasants were reacting against what they saw as land grabbing by officials. [24] Peasants had lost 'their' land without adequate compensation when the government decided to build a sugar refinery at Kompong Kol in 1966. Unrest and insecurity continued and large numbers of people were forced (or 'chose') to move from their homes and villages. Forced displacement occurred and many peasants and villagers fled from the unrest. Anger was directed against the king and the government officials; Lon Nol resigned/retired as Prime Minster in 1967.

There appeared to be a lack of consistent registration of land and parts of most provinces were falling to the communists. The Khmer Rouge were active in many uprisings and rebellions, disturbances spread, subversion was brutally oppressed and many died. Land, when taken, was not returned and adequate compensation was not provided for those dispossessed. State structures and control were slowly fracturing.

During this period, Cambodia nevertheless ratified the Convention on the Prevention and Punishment of Genocide (in 1950), the Geneva Conventions (in 1958) and the Hague Convention and Protocol for the Protection of Cultural Property (in 1962). In the 1970s, all would be engaged as conflict engulfed the country.

3 The early 1970s: the Khmer Republic and civil war

Lon Nol was reinstated by King Sihanouk in 1968 but, in 1970, he effected a coup d'etat and the King went into exile. From China, the king called on the peasant masses to rebel, which they did en masse. The Khmer Republic was proclaimed in October 1970. Lon Nol led offensives against the north Vietnamese forces with the support of the USA. Cambodia was being increasingly drawn into the Indochina (Viet Nam) war and suffered from extensive 'covert' USA bombing raids.[25] It was USA policy to bomb Cambodia especially along the border where communists were allegedly supporting the north Vietnamese (including the

23 Commentators agreed that Saloth Sar/ Pol Pot visited Hanoi for meetings – see Chandler D. (1999), *Brother Number One, A Political Biography of Pol Pot* (Westview Press) rev. ed.; and Short P. (2004), *Pol Pot – The History of a Nightmare* (Hodder Headline).

24 Kiernan B., 'The Samlaut Rebellion 1967–68', in Kiernan Boua, n11.

25 See, Arne-Westad O. and Quinn-Judge S. (eds.) (2006), *The Third Indo-China War; Conflict between China, Vietnam and Cambodia 1972–79* (Routledge) 1st ed.; Nalty B. (2000), *Air War over South Vietnam 1968–1975: Comprehensive Coverage from the Tet Offensive to the Collapse of South Vietnam, Waging War in South Vietnam, Cambodia, and Laos* (Air Force History and Museums Program). Etcheson notes that the US dropped three times the quantity of explosives on Cambodia between 1970 and 1973 than it had dropped on Japan during World War II: Etcheson, n22, 99.

Vietcong). Huge swathes of land were destroyed and people were once again on the move. Food security continued to be a problem and the regime appeared dependant on USA for food and armaments.[26] Nationalism grew. At the same time, the Khmer Rouge were mounting a propaganda campaign. Conflict engulfed the country and the Khmer Republic became ever less effective in terms of governance and addressing the concerns and needs of the population.

Inevitably during this period, many people moved from their homes. In this chapter, we will follow several individuals. The three sets of testimonies are woven through the history enabling a deeper understanding of the reality including what motivated people's decisions vis-à-vis land and property. Ms Minea, Mrs Sophorn and Mrs Sopheap were neighbours in Trapaing Veng village, Sroyov commune, Steng Sen district, Kampong Thom province. They were farmers. Ms Minea was in her early 30s during Lon Nol's regime. She lived with her parents in Trapaing Veng village (the village is about 5km from Kampong Thom provincial town). Her parents had inherited numerous plots of land for rice farms. Mrs Sopheap and her older sister, Mrs Sophorn, were in their early 20s. Their parents were the ones who had the most land plots in the village. According to Ms Minea, her family and other villagers left their village to live in Tuol Pneat (located in the same commune but more remote) in late 1970 due to the fighting between government's military (Lon Nol's troops) and the rebellious military (Pol Pot's troops). The civil war had spread throughout the country and in conjunction with military action along the eastern border (Viet Nam) meant many people fled their home and left their lands.

In 1973 (based on their memory but they were not quite sure whether late 1972 or early 1973), they all left Tuol Pneat and moved to Domrey Chaon Klaa village, Kampong Thom provincial town because Pol Pot's troops had taken over their area. Their village was destroyed and they could no longer farm on their land. Ms Minea recalled that her family lived in a small cottage made from palm leaves that always flooded during rainy season[27] and that her father decided to do some rice farming on someone else's land nearby. These two families lived in Kampong Thom provincial town until the downfall of Lon Nol regime.

The communists continued to strengthen in numbers and organisation. Civil war brought outbreaks of violence across the country. Corruption and inefficiency in tandem with a failure to quell civil unrest ensured the Khmer Republic was never fully operational. Land issues were not addressed: security deteriorated; land was expropriated; and people were displaced.

4 1975–1979: Khmer Rouge period

By 1975, communist party troops were effectively blockading Phnom Penh, starving the capital of food and munitions. Chandler estimates around 2 million

26 Etcheson, ibid, 89–103.

27 Seasons in Cambodia are often binary – rainy (approximately June–November) and dry (approximately December–May).

refugees were in the city.[28] Lon Nol flew out in March 1975 and the communist troops marched in on 17 April 1975. Almost everyone was immediately told to leave Phnom Penh and go into the countryside, initially on the pretext of avoiding USA bombing.[29] Mr Sokha, our next case study, at that time had two private houses, one in Phnom Penh, and the other in Kampong Thom province. Forced to leave Phnom Penh when the Khmer Rouge forces took over, Mr Sokha went to Chamkar Leou district, Kompong Cham province (thinking that Chamkar Leou would have enough food due to its arable land) and was given a small plot of land to build a house by Angkar.[30] Our final case study is Ms Sreymom who was also living in Phnom Penh when the Khmer Rouge moved in. She and her family initially went to Chamkar Leou district, Kompong Cham to live with relatives. Angkar later ordered a move to a different village in Chamkar Leou to work. Angkar provided a big plot of land (the whereabouts of the original owner was unknown) on which many families, including Sreymom's family built small houses. While the land belonged to Angkar and Angkar could take the land back anytime, Angkar never did in the cases of Sokha and Sreymom.

The actions of the communist regime of Democratic Kampuchea which controlled the country until 7 January 1979 are well documented and analysed.[31] Forced displacement of people and land dispossession were national policies. As Tyner explains, for the Khmer Rouge to succeed in their goal of establishing a pure communist state, self-reliant and neither dominated nor exploited by any other state, 'the complete annihilation of all non-Communist social relations and material practices' was required with Cambodia being 'literally wiped clean, smashed, unmade' and 'killed' before Democratic Kampuchea could be built.[32] Article 12 in the 1976 Constitution of Democratic Kampuchea provided that all peasants are the masters of the rice paddies and fields, although this is obviously interpreted in a line with the agriculture collectivisation policies.[33] There was no place for individual land rights. Following the evacuation of Phnom Penh, mass population displacement occurred throughout the country as people were moved to collectives

28 Chandler, n3, 254.

29 See, inter alia, Short, n23, chapter 8; Martin M. (1994), *Cambodia – A Shattered Society* (trans. Mark McLeod) (University of California) 170 et seq; Vickery M. (1984), *Cambodia 1975–1982* (Allen & Unwin) 72 et seq on the evacuation of Phnom Penh and settlements in the countryside.

30 'Angkar' (sometimes transliterated from Khmer as Angka) meant 'organisation' and was the term applied to the general political organisation in the country – Angkar ruled the land, Angkar took people away for questioning and the Angkar promulgated its policies.

31 See, inter alia, Chandler, n23; Kiernan B. (2004), *How Pol Pot Came to Power: Colonialism, Nationalism and Communism in Cambodia 1930–1975* (Yale University Press); Short, n23; Becker E. (1998), *When the War was Over: Cambodia and the Khmer Rouge Revolution* (Perseus Books).

32 Tyner J. (2008), *The Killing of Cambodia: Geography, Genocide and the Unmaking of Space* (Ashgate) 119.

33 The literature supra n31 provides further information on the ideology, policies and practices of the Khmer Rouge re land and agriculture.

and the family unit abolished. Children were separated from their parents as forced labour and the agrarian socialist revolution plans were implemented.

As for Ms Minea, Mrs Sophorn and Mrs Sopheap, both families were forced to leave their houses in 1975. After the downfall of Lon Nol regime, it was not just those who lived in Phnom Penh who were forced to move: those who lived in provincial towns were also forced (by Angkar) to move to the countryside. Ms Minea's family were moved to Cheay Sbei village while the others moved to Panha Chi. Both villages are located in Sontuk district. The two families were treated as Pra-Chea-Chon Tmey (new (17 April) civilians).[34]

'You are forbidden to travel freely'[35] was one Angkar slogan. Social structure was dismantled, individualism being replaced by collectivism on a scale and at a speed hitherto unseen.[36] The slogans of Angkar were reinforced in the new constitution of Democratic Kampuchea (January 1976), which abolished private property: 'Away with individual private property; build collective property' and 'Once there is no individual property, then we can work for a perfect revolutionary society.'[37]

Mrs Sophorn said first the two families moved to live in Cheay Sbei village. All people who lived in Kampong Thom provincial town were forced to leave their houses to live in rural areas of the province.[38] Later, her mother-in-law's relative called her to live in Panha Chi village because one of her relatives was one of Pol Pot's officers (he held a role comparable to commune chief today). Hence, Mrs Sophorn's family (including Mrs Sopheap) moved to Panha Chi village, close to the provincial town. However, they and other Panha Chi villagers were later forced to move out to a more remote area as Pol Pot's officers reportedly held a grudge against them. Ultimately, Mrs Sophorn's family (not including her in-laws, just her husband, her parents and Mrs Sopheap) were listed to move to Chong Da village where they stayed until the end of the regime.

One in four people died during the Democratic Kampuchea period, whether through malnutrition, illness, overwork or being killed.[39] Those who could, fled. The people whose stories are related in this chapter stayed in Cambodia. None

34 Pra-chea-chon Tmey refers to those villagers or people who did not follow the Khmer Rouge rebellions before the downfall of Lon Nol's regime. They were mostly targeted for mass killing.

35 Locard H. (2005), *Pol Pot's Little Red Book: the Sayings of* Angkar (Silkwork Books) 295 (saying 414).

36 Chandler, n23 explores the ideological evolution shaping this period of history in Cambodia.

37 Locard, n35, respectively saying 367 on page 276 and saying 385 on page 284.

38 Any people who did not join Angkar before 1975 and lived in the town were called New Civilians. They were often killed by Angkar as they were seen as capitalists who exploited farmers/workers. Old Civilians joined Angkar even before Angkar took over the country and often lived in the villages (many of which were under the control of Angkar before 1975); they had more privileges and often were chosen to be the leaders.

39 See, for example, the ECCC statement that up to 3 million people perished – http://www.eccc.gov.kh/en/ about-eccc – or Rummel R.J. who suggests one in two died, 'Statistics of Democide'– http://www.hawaii.edu/ powerkills/SOD.CHAP4.HTM.

remained in their previous homes. The testimonies provide a brief insight into this time. Mrs Sophorn recalled:

> My place, Chong Da, was like one big commune, if today we can call [it] their main office . . . people [victims] were arrested and brought to Chong Da from everywhere . . . during the day time those people were guarded by Chlop[40] and the little children [the children of those victims] just played the dust in front of the house without knowing that they were soon killed . . . the adults all looked very sad as they all knew that they were soon killed . . . and at night those people were gone . . . they were all killed in Chong Da.

The three women shared similar stories on how hard they had to work day by day. They woke up early in morning, around 4am, and went to work in the field without having any meal until around 1pm when they had a half bowl of watery rice with green leaves. They were offered two meals per day. They all said they have seen many dead bodies or bloodied bodies of those just killed in the forest but they said nothing. All they did was to keep on working and make sure they were not arrested and killed. Mrs Sopheap narrated:

> One family from Trapaing Veng village, named Ram, her husband was Lon Nol's soldier . . . she also lived in Chong Da village and worked really hard . . . she had one baby daughter. Later she was found out about her husband's work . . . Pol Pot's Chlop told her that Pol Pot's Chlop will bring her including her baby to reunite with her husband . . . Many people were brought to kill in the forest of Chong Da village during that night.

According to Mrs Sopheap and Mrs Sophorn, many people were killed in Chong Da village especially those new civilians who were moved from Phnom Penh or anyone whose relatives were formerly Lon Nol's officers. They said that many women whose husbands worked as Lon Nol's soldiers were tricked into believing that Chlop would bring them to be reunited with their husbands; they were killed.

During this period, no one had individual land titles, most land title documentation was destroyed, almost everyone had been forcibly displaced and many entire families perished. Those who survived inevitably were affected by their experiences, as indeed have been their children.[41] Approaches to land use and property (as well as life) changed when it had been proved how easily titles (and lives) could be extinguished.

Tensions with Viet Nam continued, despite the January 1973 Paris Peace Accords officially ending the Vietnamese war, but Cambodians still fled there to

40 The Chlop were Pol Pot's security guards.

41 There are many studies on PTSD among survivors and on the state of mental health of Cambodians and Cambodian refugees.

escape the Khmer Rouge. There is no doubt that Viet Nam retained an interest in its neighbour and an invasion/liberation[42] began at the end of 1978.[43]

5 1979: People's Republic of Kampuchea and civil conflict

In January 1979, the Vietnamese reached Phnom Penh marking the end of Democratic Kampuchea. Between 1979 and 1980, Cambodia was a country on the move. Some people returned to their villages of origin and home provinces in the hope of finding somewhere familiar after losing family and witnessing atrocities; others were afraid to return to their home villages as they had fled when their properties were destroyed; and others were concerned about the potential for growing sufficient crops to feed their family or fearful of the violence and civil conflict that still characterised pockets of the Cambodian countryside. A 'continuous wave of Khmer refugees' reached the Thai border,[44] forced to forage, en route, for food and water. An unexpected consequence was the lack of attention paid to rice planting, which, in conjunction with weather conditions, led to famine.[45] In combination, reclaiming property, even just returning to pre-Khmer Rouge era homes, was neither a priority nor particularly practicable for many.

Right after the fall of Democratic Kampuchea, in January 1979, for example, Mr Sokha did not think of leaving Chamkar Leou district. He recalls his main concern being food. If he left Chamkar Leou, he did not know where to go to or whether there would be food and accommodation; besides, he had no means to travel. In addition, his village chief provided common land plots (collective ownership) as part of the solidarity groups (krom samaki) for agricultural purposes, so he decided to stay. When the food provided was not enough for his family, he thought of moving, trying to get information on whether there would be work in other places.

As for Ms Sreymom, in 1979, right after the Khmer Rouge regime fell, she and her family decided to return to Phnom Penh. En route, they learnt that Khmer Rouge forces were still present, so they returned to Chamkar Leou and simply

42 The choice of noun is dependent on political viewpoints – authors also vary in their categorisation of the Vietnamese action. Tensions over ethnic Vietnamese people in Cambodia remain potent and the situation is contentious in twenty-first century Cambodia –Ehrentraut S. (2011), 'Perpetually temporary: citizenship and ethnic Vietnamese in Cambodia', *Ethnic and Racial Studies*, Vo. 34, No. 5, 1–20; Nguyen L., Sperfeldt C. (2012), 'A Boat Without Anchors – a report on the legal status of ethnic Vietnamese minority populations in Cambodia under domestic and international laws governing nationality and statelessness' (Jesuit Refugee Service); Chhim K. et al. (2014), *Life Before Expulsion: Community History from Vietnamese Minorities in Kampong Chhnang* (Kdei Karuna); Keo D. and Ly R. (2015), 'Reflections on the river: Khmer perception of Ethnic Vietnamese in Bralai Meas before the Khmer Rouge regime' (Kdei Karuna).

43 See Morris S. (1999), *Why Vietnam Invaded Cambodia – Political Culture and the Causes of War* (Stanford University Press).

44 Martin, n29, 215.

45 Chandler n3 notes, on page 279, that the rice harvest doubled in size in 1980.

took an empty house, close to their relatives, to live in. The original owner had moved somewhere else during the Khmer Rouge regime as part of the forced transfer and no one in the village objected to them occupying it.

There were many unoccupied properties and reports of people returning to find their houses locked up and secure, especially in the cities and towns, seemingly untouched from 1975.[46] However, the situation was fluid. New government officials were given property in Phnom Penh; and property in the countryside was occupied by Vietnamese soldiers. Other property in the city was taken over and, in effect, squatted in, by former villagers who moved to the city, in search of food, work or safety.[47]

Mr Sokha and Ms Sreymom were affected by poverty, forcing their next moves. Mr Sokha headed to Phnom Penh (in late 1979), having received information that there were jobs available and given he had a relative working for the government. His priority was to get a job with his relative rather than to reclaim his house in Phnom Penh. Ms Sreymom's husband went to Phnom Penh in 1980, although this was to sell bread. He discovered that their home was occupied by someone else and, rather than challenging it, he simply returned to Chamkar Leou.

The government gave 'certain' houses in Phnom Penh to people working for the government; they could then bring their families to live with them. Different ministries were in charge of different blocks of the city. For example, the Food Department of the Ministry of Commerce was in charge of Psar Thmey area, so employees of this Department would be given houses there. That was the case for Mr Sokha, although he recalls that he could request to change to his original house, but thought that inconvenient. At that time, people were not permitted to select and occupy empty houses in Phnom Penh if they did not work for the government. This, however, did not stop some people moving to the city and occupying houses or building on empty land. Virtually noone was evicted at this time as long as the empty houses they took were not within a certain area that the government reserved for its departments. Buying and selling houses was not possible as houses still belonged to the state and, in theory, could be reclaimed. However, in reality, the state generally did not reclaim property in the city because there were so many empty houses.[48]

Democratic Kampuchea was replaced by the People's Republic of Kampuchea (PRK)[49] with the Vietnamese progressively extending control throughout the country, although resistance remained, in places strengthened by external support. The Democratic Kampuchea regime (then in exile) retained Cambodia's seat at

46 E.g. Vickery n29, 227 and 234 for examples.

47 Ibid, 239.

48 As noted above, virtually everyone had left Phnom Penh in 1975 and it had become, in effect, a ghost city.

49 The People's Republic of Kampuchea was not formally recognised in the UN. A coalition including the Khmer Rouge continued to occupy Cambodia's seat at the UN until 1993. The Peoples Republic of Kampuchea was recognised *de facto* by many states, albeit not necessarily *de jure*.

the UN. In 1980, Cambodia signed the International Covenants on Economic, Social and Cultural Rights and Civil and Political Rights and the Convention on Elimination of all forms of Discrimination Against Women, although these were only acceded to twelve years later.

Around this time, Ms Sreymom's husband returned to sell bread in Phnom Penh and ended up securing a government job. The government then gave her husband a house shared with another family (not the original owner). The family moved back in 1981. Ms Sreymom informally (meaning without legal entitlement or recognition) sold 'their' house in Chamkar Leou (the empty house which she had taken in 1979). There was no legal title or document; village chiefs were often happy to let people buy and sell houses informally, the chief receiving some 'commission' money for such uncontested transactions. Ms Sreymom mentioned that in late 1980s, the owner of the house in Phnom Penh, given by the government to her families in 1981, returned, but did not say anything to indicate that he wanted the house back. Ms Sreymom remains living in this same house.

In the countryside, ensuring a good rice harvest was a priority. The collectivisation of cultivation introduced by the People's Republic of Kampuchea continued until the late 1980s; 'private ownership was not recognized'.[50] Ms Minea moved back to Trapaing Veng village before Mrs Sopheap and Mrs Sophorn. She had lost her father to malnutrition during the Khmer Rouge period so she moved to Trapaing Veng village with her mother and built a house on her old (1970) land (her house had been destroyed). Mrs Sopheap and Mrs Sophorn first left Chong Da village and moved to Poh Khav village for a few months. They did not dare return to Trapaing Veng and were unaware others had returned to live in the village. Ms Minea visited them and encouraged them back. However, Mr Som,[51] a former neighbour, and his family had already built a house on their old land. As their land was already occupied, Mrs Sopheap decided to build a house on Mr Som's land. When asked why Mr Som had built a house on her former land instead of his, Mrs Sopheap indicated her land was more like a small hill and did not flood during rainy season. The two families did not argue about this issue but later Mr Som's house went on fire, so the families decided to switch their land back. Mrs Sopheap built a house on her old land while Mr Som moved back to his original land. This demonstrates how many land 'transactions' were conducted without title or rights.

Many factors influenced the property decisions of people. Emotional factors were often determinative – Mr Sokha said that he did not want to go back to his original house because it reminded him of his family members who died during the Khmer Rouge regime; furthermore, his original house had been used by Angkar to store iron in, so in order to live in that house, he would have to move all the iron elsewhere. Social and security factors were also relevant. In 1982/3, where the situation had improved, the government was more relaxed with respect to land occupation. This was particular so in Phnom Penh where the government

50 Chandler n3, 279.
51 Name changed although this person died around 2006.

continued to build strength and stability. Although the land, in theory, belonged to the state, people bought and sold land informally. Mr Sokha bought another house close to his relatives so that they could protect one another in case of emergency. Although the buying and selling was informal, Mr Sokha remains in that house today. He also said that at the time, people did not know whether there would be more wars, so instead of going back to their original houses, they stayed where they thought they were safer and prepared to flee if war broke out again.

It was not until 1989 that a sub-decree provided that people could buy from the state for their individual ownership. Furthermore, if people built a house by themselves on empty land, they did not have to pay to the state to secure ownership over that house.[52]

There were many factors influencing the housing decisions of people:

1. Location. People often needed to grow food or keep animals. People would disregard their previous home if the land was unsuitable and, in effect, 'trade up' to an available property with better land for the required crops and husbandry. Mr Sokha said that he was only able to get 18kg of rice a month working for the government, so his family needed to grow food and raise animals, his original flat was not suitable to ensure a supply of food.[53]
2. National security. Khmer Rouge forces were still strong. In 1983 or 1984, some resistance movements against People's Republic of Kampuchea announced that if they won over the *de facto* Phnom Penh government, they would give the original land to its owners. The thought and fear of fleeing was constant.
3. Ethnic issues. The unwritten policies of the *de facto* Phnom Penh government towards certain race/ethnicities also affected people's right to return home. During the Khmer Rouge regime and later, the relationship between Viet Nam and China soured. During the period of Viet Nam's control over Phnom Penh, Vietnamese Cambodians and ethnic Khmers were better treated than Chinese Cambodians in terms of getting a job in the government or advancing their position. In the early years, many Vietnamese were accommodated in Phnom Penh and the provinces working with the emergent Cambodian authorities. Vickery notes verified reports of Vietnamese settlements in urban areas, although found them not excessive.[54] At least in the initial years (1979 to early 1981), Chinese Cambodians found it more difficult to get jobs in the government, meaning also that they could not get houses from the government in Phnom Penh. (Indeed, as the situation

52 Sub-decree on Granting House Ownership to the Cambodian Citizens, No.25ANK, 22 April 1989, Art 1(2), Art 5.

53 In the country, Vickery n29 notes, on page 298, that policies of the PRK were favourable to those of Sihanouk or Pol Pot as far as most peasants were concerned. This is most likely due to the increase in food supplies and potential for people to grow their own rice once more.

54 Vickery, ibid, Postscript 1983, 296.

improved, more Chinese Cambodians came to Phnom Penh, while ethnic Khmer Cambodians moved to the provinces.)

Mr Sokha stated that if he had known that his original house would be so expensive today, he would have asked for it when he first came back to Phnom Penh. Many Cambodians are in a similar situation but at that juncture, properties had no quantifiable monetary value and there was no policy supporting property ownership.

Although the 1981 Constitution provides that confiscation of private property of citizens was prohibited,[55] unclear ownership of houses in the city made it easy for those who were working for the government to arbitrarily take houses. In 1985, Mr Sokha recalled Sangkat (village chief) in Psar Tmey claiming houses from some owners 'to reorganize Psar Tmey area'. Many people left the area with little or no compensation, scared of challenging the communist government; others insisted on remaining; and some are still living there.

The new government strengthened with support from Viet Nam and Hun Sen became Prime Minister, a post he still holds today.[56] A series of reforms were implemented by the new government, including new laws allowing for the buying, selling and inheriting of land. In 1985, the Sub-Decree on the Management of the Use of Agricultural Law was adopted[57] – the first land law passed after the years of state land ownership.

6 1989–1991: the state of Cambodia/PRK

In 1989, the People's Republic of Kampuchea became the State of Cambodia. The Constitution formulated in 1981 (with the Vietnamese authorities) was revised. Article 14 defined state property and Article 15 gave Cambodian citizens the right to own, use and inherit land but not to buy and sell it.[58] It should be noted that agricultural and forested land also received some degree of protection with approval needed for changes.

1989 also brought a legal milestone on ownership of housing in Phnom Penh.[59] Prior ownership of housing was not explicitly addressed, rather the new provisions related to all land, hitherto state land, allocated to individuals by the state. Some government employees thereby gained recognition of *de facto* ownership of the houses in which they were living. While ownership before 1979 was not recognized

55 Constitution of the People's Republic of Kampuchea, 25 June 1981, Art 18.

56 Differing views of the government and rise to prominence of several Khmer politicians still prominent today, see Mehta H., Mehta J. (1999), *Hun Sen, Strongman of Cambodia* (Graham Brash); Strangio S. (2014), *Hun Sen's Cambodia*, (Yale University Press).

57 No.06ANK, 6 May 1985.

58 Constitution of the People's Republic of Kampuchea, 25 June 1981, Arts 15–17.

59 See Sub-decree on Granting House Ownership to the Cambodian Citizens No 25 ANK, 22 April 1989; and then Circular on the implementation of sub-decree on granting house ownership to Cambodian citizens living in Phnom Penh, circular no. 05SRC, June 5, 1989.

by law,[60] some village chiefs allowed people to reclaim their pre-1979 land and homes, sometimes leaving newcomers, who were farming that land, landless.[61] This was simply *ad hoc* practice of village chiefs, with claims to former lands based on memory and validated by oral corroboration. Occasionally former land title documents were used, albeit informally (meaning without legal effect – the state prohibited land ownership before 1979 so officially authorities did not accept evidence of historic land ownership).

Although Cambodians now had the right to occupy, use and sell their newly allocated land, the habit of occupying empty houses continued.[62] Sporadic land registration was made available for agricultural land. Village and commune authorities had to approve of registration applications as a first stage. The system was woefully under-resourced and many disputes arose over conflicting land claims. In many instances, commune-level possession was recognised but another person (a third party) could go through the whole title registration process for the same, or part of the same, land and the commune-recognised occupier could be forced to move. This became more of an issue as land concessions grew with development. It is not uncommon for hundreds of small holding occupiers to find themselves effectively homeless when a titular landowner seeks to exercise his or her rights over land currently occupied by subsistence farmers without land title documentation.

The Vietnamese forces formally withdrew in September 1989, although challenges remained for the State of Cambodia, not least in exercising control over the entire country. These challenges were exacerbated by international politics on foreign support for both the government and the government in exile. Armed conflict continued and many people remained displaced. Others left when faced with the ongoing uncertainty of governance and sporadic violence.

In Paris in October 1991, agreements were reached with the Cambodian government, the four principal factions in Cambodia (including the State of Cambodia and the Khmer Rouge) and a wide range of third states including Cambodia's neighbours in Southeast Asia and all five permanent members of the Security Council.[63] The parties engaged in the conflict and supporting various

60 Sub-decree on Granting House Ownership to the Cambodian Citizens, No.25ANK, 22 April 1989, Art 1(2).

61 Phalthy H., *The Implementation of Cambodia's Laws on Land Tenure*, PhD Thesis, 2010 (on file with the authors), 65.

62 For many years later, people would occupy properties oblivious to the changes in the law on property rights.

63 The participating states were Australia, Brunei Darussalam, Cambodia, Canada, the People's Republic of China, the French Republic, the Republic of India, the Republic of Indonesia, Japan, the Lao People's Democratic Republic, Malaysia, the Republic of the Philippines, the Republic of Singapore, the Kingdom of Thailand, the Union of Soviet Socialist Republics, the United Kingdom of Great Britain and Northern Ireland, the United States of America and the Socialist Republic of Viet Nam. Yugoslavia and Zimbabwe also participated in the conference.

factions were therefore involved in the process to secure a lasting peace. However, Roberts questions the longterm aim of the settlement and its benefit for the Cambodian people, concluding 'the peace process was aimed at foreign powers, not at Cambodians'.[64] Land, for example, was not addressed, despite the emerging problems of the practicalities of mass resettlement in a country essentially without a land registration and titling system.

7 1991–1993: the UN transitional authority period in Cambodia

At the conclusion of the Paris Peace Conference in 1991, an agreement on a comprehensive political settlement of the Cambodian conflict and a declaration on the rehabilitation and reconstruction of Cambodia were adopted.[65]

The UN Transitional Authority in Cambodia (UNTAC) was then established by the UN Security Council.[66] The UN would oversee the transition of Cambodia to full independent self-government, and therefore a functioning UN member state. Repatriation was a major component of the agreement – 360,000 refugees on the Thai–Cambodian border were to return to Cambodia (no specifics as to whether to pre-1970 or 1975 homes or to a place of choice – the need for security, work and food were key considerations for many refugees); basic infrastructure, public utilities and essential services were to be rolled out in a rehabilitation component; human rights and respect for the rule of law was to be secured; and a military component was tasked with ensuring withdrawal of foreign forces, destruction of weapons, maintenance of ceasefire and mine clearance.[67] Berdal and Leifer note that this was the most ambitious and expensive undertaking to date in the peacekeeping experience of the UN.[68]

UNTAC was charged with providing assistance where necessary in repatriating Cambodian refugees and displaced persons,[69] something that was dealt with in more detail by Annex 4 of the Agreement on a comprehensive political settlement of the Cambodian conflict.[70] The choice of domicile and right to property were recognised therein.[71] Annex 5 articulated the principles for a new constitution of

64 Roberts D. (2001), *Political Transition in Cambodia 1991–99: Power, Elitism and Democracy* (Curzon) 30.

65 See letter dated 30 October 1991 from the Permanent Representatives of France and Indonesia to the United Nations addressed to the Secretary-General, UN Doc A/46/608; S/23177 30 October 1991.

66 UNSC Resolution 745 (1992) of 28 February 1992.

67 See Heder S. and Leagerwood J. (eds.) (1996), *Propaganda, Politics and Violence in Cambodia – Democratic Transition under United Nations Peace-keeping* (M.E. Sharpe); Roberts, n64.

68 USD 1.7 billion. Berdal M. and Leifer M. (1996), 'Cambodia' in Mayall J. (ed.), *The New Interventionism 1991–1994: United Nations Experience in Cambodia, Former Yugoslavia and Somalia* (Cambridge University Press) 25.

69 Paris Peace Accords, n63 Annex 2, Article XII.

70 Paris Peace Accords n63.

71 Ibid, Annex 4, [4].

Cambodia, the supreme law, which was to include a declaration on protection from arbitrary deprivation of property or deprivation of private property without just compensation.[72]

A land law was passed in 1992,[73] although Diepart notes some regarded it as a mechanism for further enrichment of the wealthy rather than for securing fair land titling for all.[74] In the new Constitution, land rights are recognised and protected for all Khmer,[75] although the constitution per se is not necessarily directly justiciable. This marked the beginning of modern Cambodian law, a period in which greater engagement with the international system was signified by ratification of several human rights treaties.[76] Civil conflicts continued for a few years (the Khmer Rouge did not abide by the Paris Agreement in spite of being a signatory) but UNTAC successfully oversaw elections in 1993.

8 1993–2016: post-transition Kingdom of Cambodia

The United Nations Transitional Authority left Cambodia in 1993, although many UN agencies retain large presences and offices in the country. Cambodia received (and continues to receive) considerable aid and technical assistance investment and support from a wide range of actors. There is a large density of non-governmental and civil society organisations, both national and international, in the country. Some of this support has focussed on land titling. A major land administration, management and distribution programme sought to programmatise the government's response to the lack of land titles in the country, supported by a range of donors and partners.

The land concession system[77] is the biggest factor in displacement and land ownership in contemporary Cambodia. With the withdrawal of sanctions and embargoes, Cambodia developed a burgeoning free market economy. Property

72 Ibid, Annex 5, [2]

73 Land Law no 100K, 13 October 1992.

74 Diepart J.C., 'The fragmentation of land tenure systems in Cambodia: peasants and the formalization of land rights' French Technical Committee on 'Land Tenure and Development', GRET, 2015, 13.

75 Article 44 provides that all persons, individually or collectively, shall have the right to ownership; only Khmer legal entities and citizens of Khmer nationality shall have the right to own land; and legal private ownership shall be protected by the law.

76 Cambodia has, as of January 2017, accepted eight out of nine core international human rights treaties, one of the strongest ratification records in the region. It has only signed the International Convention on the Protection of the Rights of all Migrant Workers and Members of their Families.

77 Areas of land are leased by the government commonly to commercial enterprises (economic land concessions) as well as to the poor and landless to live on and grow crops (social land concessions) – see, inter alia, Land Law 2001. For a visual representation of the extent of land concessions, see 'The Great Cambodian Giveaway: Visualizing Land Concessions over Time, 1993–2013', A Licadho Media Project, http://www.licadho-cambodia.org/concession_timelapse/.

prices in the capital and other key areas have boomed and urban renewal brings high rise developments aimed at wealthy Cambodians and foreign investors as well as the ever growing number of expatriates.

Land Law 2001 recognises the possession rights of those Cambodian people who had enjoyed peaceful uncontested possession of their land before the act came into force yet who are not formally recognised as landowners.[78] It does not per se recognise pre-1970 title claims. It also prevents people from taking state land although the state may provide land to citizens in social concessions.[79] In the situation in which the authorities seize people's contested land, the affected people can bring the claim against the state within three years. Otherwise, that land will be considered as state land.[80] The government has continued to adopt various policies to solve land issues including issuing a sub-decree to create the Cadastral Commission in 2002.[81] This Cadastral Commission addresses many local land disputes.[82] However, disputes are often also brought to members of parliament (National Assembly and Senate), direct to the governors of provinces and direct to the Prime Minister. These may be deflected back to local authorities, 'mediation' may ensue and the issue may or may not be resolved to the satisfaction of the person/s raising the issue. There remains no single system for categorically and legally resolving land title disputes and conflicting title claims are not uncommon, with some claiming registered title and others claiming possession. Old, pre-1970 titles are also occasionally produced but hold little legal weight.

Numerous sub-decrees, circulars, and proclamations have since been adopted to govern and to solve land issues. However, land remains a critical issue and there have been continuous protests concerning the land issues, leading to many land rights activists being arrested. Many NGOs are heavily involved in supporting dispossessed people despite the tensions caused with provincial and national government.[83]

9 Property rights of those displaced

As this chapter traces, displacement of people in Cambodia was not a solitary event. Rather, there were serial displacements – French colonialisation and early industrialisation; localised revolts and spreading unrest in the 1960s; US bombing

78 Chapter 4, Land Law 2001, see, in particular, Article 30.

79 Cambodian Law Land, NS/RKM/0801/14, 30 August, 2001, Art 17.

80 Cambodian Law Land, ibid, Art 33.

81 See Sub-decree on the Organization and Functioning of the Cadastral Commission," No.47ANK/BK, 31 May 2002.

82 For an early review, see GTZ, 'Towards institutional justice? A review of the work of Cambodia's Cadastral Commission in relation to land dispute resolution, 2006, http://documents.worldbank.org/ curated/en/309161468222269820/pdf/408230Towards01nal0Justice01PUBLIC1.pdf.

83 The 2015 Law on Non-Governmental Organisations is widely cited as restricting the work of NGOs in this, and other, areas.

campaigns and civil conflict in the late 1960s and early 1970s; mass displacement and deurbanisation in the 1970s; Vietnamese occupation and uncertainty in 1979; state ownership in the 1980s – each causing some or all people to leave their homes and lands. The evolution of property rights, land titling and returning people in the 1990s brought further displacement and dispossession when returnees found their property occupied. The Cambodian situation arguably differs from other conflicts, when people flee to safety, in that many people were forced not just to leave their homes in the 1970s, but then were told where to live and work. Angkar could move people around from province to province. During Angkar's rule, Angkar gave people houses or land belonging to people who had left their houses or land (either fleeing or being moved by the Angkar). In other words, during Khmer Rouge regime, people were already living in other people's houses or land, they were used to the idea that other people took their houses and they took other empty houses since during Khmer Rouge regime there was no ownership. During the years of civil unrest that followed, people settled in whichever property they found themselves living. It was normal for people to live in property that was not hitherto theirs.

The situation is complex and remains a challenge for the government. Many of those displaced in the 1970s, who are still alive, have not yet returned to their previous land or been compensated for its loss but then, there is also a question of where 'home' is for those who were forcibly displaced then moved by the Angkar, then settled in some unoccupied house during the years of civil unrest. The idea of reclaiming a former property often did not arise. The UN Principles on Housing and Property Restitution for Refugees and Displaced Persons are rarely, if ever, mentioned or claimed. Those who did return to previous property have frequently faced new challenges from land concessions encroaching on, or near, their property as Cambodia continues its rapid development.[84] There remain many people without full land title for the land on which they live and grow rice, despite the increased efforts of the government to facilitate titling. Frequently such people are relatively poor subsistence farmers lacking education and awareness of the land titling system, or indeed the wherewithal to access commune, village and cadastral authorities to pursue land titling. In terms of the Land Law, general possession must be unambiguous, non-violent, continuous and in good faith.[85] This can open to challenge the claims of those engaged in more public protests over land concessions and encroachment activities. Their claim can be prejudiced due to the violence or perceived lack of good faith.

In the city, as well as many towns and villages, original houses have been demolished and new buildings have replaced them. There are some people who lost their houses during the Khmer Rouge regime who feel that they have been

84 See OHCHR, 'A human rights analysis of economic and other land concessions in Cambodia, Report of the Special Rapporteur on the situation of human rights in Cambodia, Surya Subedi', A/HRC/21/63/Add.1/Rev.1 and addendum.

85 Article 38, Land Law 2001.

treated unfairly. However, in many instances, documents to prove ownership were destroyed or lost. One solution to address the loss of housing during Pol Pot regime would be to improve the economic standard of living of all Cambodians. Everyone could then afford homes and land. This would also help the country move towards the future, rather than dwelling in the past.

Land grabbing, deforestation, encroachment, economic, social, tourist and other land concessions have caused problems in recent years.[86] The former Special Rapporteur on adequate housing summed up the position thus:

> Years of civil war and conflict, followed by land grabbing on a massive scale, have exacerbated land disputes and skewed land ownership patterns to the disadvantage of the rural and urban poor. Land management systems have been unable to address a combined result of the absence of land records which were destroyed during the Khmer Rouge period, an undeveloped and non-transparent land registration system, the absence of cadastral index maps, inadequate land laws and procedures, unclear delineation of State land and the weakness of the justice system.[87]

The government is now developing a more holistic approach to land management. Although the lack of comprehensive and uncontested titling is a legacy of the historic displacements, many of those dispossessed of their land during the 1970s and 1980s are unlikely to ever be able to reclaim it or secure compensation.

In Cambodia, the tragedy of displacement and dispossession is that so many of the poorest rural populations and indigenous people have fragile, tenuously documented legal connections to the land on which they live, fish and farm. The dichotomy of land use, progress and development has disproportionately affected many of the poorest in the countryside and led to the forced relocation of many of those who had moved to the cities to seek a better future. Meanwhile, a small but influential sector of Cambodian society continues to get wealthier and the poverty gulf widens. What is notable is that in the twenty-first century, Cambodia is characterised by a strong civil society and a greater awareness of rights and freedoms than was hitherto the case. Ever more land rights disputes are raised at various levels as the language of human rights and understanding of the constitutional property rights and land laws strengthens. That Cambodian people are incredibly resilient is beyond question given the history outlined above; as is the case that they deserve fair land settlements and the stability and security which comes with recognition of land tenure.

86 See, inter alia, OHCHR, n84; Cambodian Human Rights and Development Association, 'A growing divide: disputes without resolutions. The land rights situation in Cambodia in 2015' April 2015, Adhoc.

87 Report of the Special Rapporteur on adequate housing as a component of the right to an adequate standard of living, Miloon Kothari, Mission to Cambodia, UN Doc E/CN.4/2006/41/Add.3 (2006), [26].

The history of Cambodia outlined in this chapter evidences challenges posed when an entire country's population is forcibly deprived of all land title and possession. The process of registering historic land titles is complex, compounded by the period of time many people had been dispossessed, the number of properties which a family may have occupied (by forced displacement and then subsequent displacement or voluntary relocation), the lack of comprehensive records and the tenuous historic title claims of many former peasants and subsistence farmers. There is no tribunal in accordance with the Pinheiro Principles, and no likelihood of all displaced persons ever having restored to them housing, property and land of which they were arbitrarily deprived during the tumultuous years of last century.[88] For many Cambodians, that is all in the past:[89] development and progress, freedom and prosperity are the priorities.

Bibliography

Books

Arne-Westad O. and Quinn-Judge S. (eds.) (2006), *The Third Indo-China War; Conflict between China, Vietnam and Cambodia 1972–79* (Routledge) 1st ed.

Becker E. (1998), *When the War was Over: Cambodia and the Khmer Rouge Revolution* (Perseus Books).

Chandler D. (2008), *A History of Cambodia*, (Westview Press) 4th ed.

Chandler D. (1999), *Brother Number One, A Political Biography of Pol Pot* (Westview Press) rev. ed.

Chhim K. et al. (2014), *Life Before Expulsion: Community History from Vietnamese Minorities in Kampong Chhnang* (Kdei Karuna).

Church P. (ed.) (2009), *A Short History of Southeast Asia* (John Wiley) 5th ed.

Heder S. and Leagerwood J. (eds.) (1996), *Propaganda, Politics and Violence in Cambodia – Democratic Transition under United Nations Peace-keeping* (M.E. Sharpe).

Keo D. and Ly R. (2015), 'Reflections on the river: Khmer perception of ethnic Vietnamese in Bralai Meas before the Khmer Rouge regime' (Kdei Karuna).

Kiernan B. (2004), *How Pol Pot Came to Power: Colonialism, Nationalism and Communism in Cambodia 1930–1975* (Yale University Press).

Kiernan B. and Boua C. (eds.), *Peasants and Politics in Kampuchea 1942–1981* (Zed Press).

Locard H. (2005), *Pol Pot's Little Red Book: the Sayings of* Angkar (Silkwork Books).

Morris S. (1999), *Why Vietnam Invaded Cambodia – Political Culture and the Causes of War* (Stanford University Press).

88 Principle 2, United Nations Principles on Housing and Property Restitution for Refugees and Displaced Persons.

89 Demographically, most Cambodians were born after the end of the Khmer Rouge period. The most recent full census is 2008 http://www.nis.gov.kh/nis/census2008/PressReleaseEng.pdf – when the median age of the population was 21.9 with a projection for 2017 of a median of 25.4, see table available on http://www.stat.go.jp/info/meetings/cambodia/pdf/rp12_ch10.pdf (Japan supported the census). UNFPA note that one in three Cambodians was aged 15–29, http://cambodia.unfpa.org/en/node/15237.

Nalty B. (2000), *Air War over South Vietnam 1968–1975: Comprehensive Coverage from the Tet Offensive to the Collapse of South Vietnam, Waging War in South Vietnam, Cambodia, and Laos* (Air Force History and Museums Program).
Roberts D. (2001), *Political Transition in Cambodia 1991–99: Power, Elitism and Democracy* (Curzon).
Short P. (2004), *Pol Pot – The History of a Nightmare* (Hodder Headline).
Tully J. (2003), *France on the Mekong: A History of the Protectorate in Cambodia 1863–1953* (University Press of America).
Tyner J. (2008), *The Killing of Cambodia: Geography, Genocide and the Unmaking of Space* (Ashgate).
Vickery M. (1984), *Cambodia 1975–1982* (Allen & Unwin).

Book chapters

Berdal M. and Leifer M. (1996), 'Cambodia' in Mayall J. (ed.), *The New Interventionism 1991–1994: United Nations experience in Cambodia, former Yugoslavia and Somalia* (Cambridge University Press).
Nim H. (1982), 'Land tenure and social structure in Kampuchea' in Kiernan B. and Boua C. (eds.), *Peasants and Politics in Kampuchea 1942–1981* (Zed Press).

Journal articles

Ehrentraut S. (2011), 'Perpetually temporary: citizenship and ethnic Vietnamese in Cambodia' *Ethnic and Racial Studies*, Vol. 34, No. 5, 1–20.
Evans D. et al.(2013), 'Uncovering archaeological landscapes at Angkor using lidar' *Proceedings of the National Academy of Sciences,* Vol.110, No. 31, 12595–12600.
Evans D. et al. (2007), 'A comprehensive archaeological map of the world's largest preindustrial complex at Angkor, Cambodia', *Proceedings of the National Academy of Sciences*, Vol. 104, No. 36, 14277–14282.

Research papers

Cambodian Human Rights and Development Association, 'A growing divide: disputes without resolutions. The land rights situation in Cambodia in 2015' April 2015, Adhoc.
Diepart J.C., 'The fragmentation of land tenure systems in Cambodia: peasants and the formalization of land rights' French Technical Committee on 'Land Tenure and Development', GRET, 2015.
GTZ, 'Towards institutional justice? A review of the work of Cambodia's Cadastral Commission in relation to land dispute resolution', 2006, http://documents.worldbank.org/curated/en/309161468222269820/pdf/408230Towards01nal0Justice01PUBLIC1.pdf (13 September 2017).
Nguyen L. and Sperfeldt C. (2012), 'A Boat Without Anchors – a report on the legal status of ethnic Vietnamese minority populations in Cambodia under Domestic and International laws governing Nationality and Statelessness' (Jesuit Refugee Service).
Phalthy H., *The Implementation of Cambodia's Laws on Land Tenure*, PhD Thesis, 2010 (on file with the authors).

7 Forcible displacement as a weapon of war in the Syrian conflict

Lessons and developments

Yasmine Nahlawi

1 Introduction

The Syrian conflict was born out of peaceful anti-government protests in 2011 to which the government, under the rule of President Assad, responded with brutal force. It is estimated that over the course of this conflict, over ten per cent of the Syrian population has been either killed or injured[1] and over one half of the population has been displaced – the United Nations (UN) estimates that as of May 2017, there are 5.4 million Syrian refugees as well as 6.1 million internally displaced persons (IDPs).[2] As this chapter highlights, the process by which such displacement has occurred gives rise to significant international legal questions regarding the obligations of various actors – including the host State, the UN and non-State actors (NSAs) – to prevent the displacement of civilian populations but also to guarantee, in the event that displacement does occur, minimum rights for the displaced.

This chapter analyses relevant developments in Syria pertaining to forcible displacement with reference to existing international legal norms (for example, under international humanitarian law – IHL – or international human rights law – IHRL) as well as international case law and evaluates relevant State practice and *opinio juris* arising from the Syrian conflict to assess the emergence or reinforcement,

* Special thank you to two interviewees from Syria, whose identities will remain anonymous for security purposes, who provided witness accounts on the evacuation processes in each of Daraya and East Aleppo. One interviewee was a member of the Local Council of Daraya City and another was a member of a civilian team in East Aleppo that advised and supported the military representatives involved in negotiating the terms of the evacuation of the city. I am extremely grateful to them both for their time and for the critical and insightful information that I obtained from them.

1 Black I., 'Report on Syrian conflict finds 11.5% of population killed or injured' (*The Guardian*, 11 February 2016) https://www.theguardian.com/world/2016/feb/11/report-on-syria-conflict-finds-115-of-population-killed-or-injured.

2 'Syria Regional Refugee Response' (*Office of the UN High Commissioner for Refugees*, December 2017) http://data.unhcr.org/syrianrefugees/regional.php; 'Syria Emergency' (*Office of the UN High Commissioner for Refugees*, May 2017) http://www.unhcr.org/uk/syria-emergency.html.

if any, of customary norms pertaining to forcible displacement and the rights of the forcibly displaced. The discussions of these legal issues, as further explained below, reflect the categorisation of the Syrian conflict as a non-international armed conflict (NIAC) in which the forcible displacement undertaken was primarily internal (i.e. within State boundaries).[3] However, given the ongoing nature of the conflict as well as the lack of international judicial mechanisms to establish international criminal responsibility of perpetrators,[4] it should be cautioned that the consequences of the developments described in this chapter may not yet have fully manifested.

Given the complexity of the Syrian conflict as well as the wide-ranging violations pertaining to forcible displacement that have occurred throughout the country, this chapter focuses on two specific cases,[5] namely the forced evacuations of Daraya and East Aleppo in August and December 2016, respectively. These two cases were chosen because of the gravity of their scale and because each brings to light unique issues pertaining to the international legal framework governing the prohibition against forcible displacement. However, it should be stressed that these two cases provide only a glimpse into a much wider pattern of forcible displacement that has been perpetrated across Syria since the conflict began.

2 Displacement from Daraya

Daraya was a city of 80,000 inhabitants approximately eight kilometres from the Syrian capital of Damascus and was one of the first cities to join the revolution against the Assad regime in 2011.[6] It came under the control of armed opposition groups in 2012, after which it was subjected to siege and military bombardment by Assad forces. Following roughly four years of war and siege, opposition representatives from Daraya succumbed to negotiations with the regime to

3 On Syria's characterisation as a NIAC, *see* Human Rights Council, Report of the Independent International Commission of Inquiry on the Syrian Arab Republic (16 August 2012) UN Doc A/HRC/21/50, [12].

4 Syria is not a party to the International Criminal Court (ICC) and any attempt to refer the situation to the ICC through the United Nations Security Council (UNSC) risks veto by Russia and China, as was the case in May 2014 when France submitted a draft resolution in this regard. There is also no regional court system to which victims of atrocities in Syria can turn. *See* UNSC Draft Resolution (22 May 2014) UN Doc S/2014/348.

5 Forcible displacement may have been perpetrated by multiple sides to the Syrian conflict, including by ISIS, opposition forces and Kurdish forces. However, this chapter restricts its focus to forcible displacement committed by the Assad regime given the disproportionate responsibility that it bears in this regard, most particularly taking into account the enormous scale under which it has pursued this strategy in cities across Syria (as described in this chapter).

6 Dearden L., 'Syria war: UN warns "the world is watching" as regime forces evacuate civilians and rebels from Daraya' (*The Independent*, 26 August 2016) http://www.independent.co.uk/news/world/middle-east/syria-war-news-latest-daraya-civilians-and-rebels-evacuate-besieged-damascus-suburb-after-four-years-a7211276.html; 'Syria civil war: aid convoy reaches besieged Daraya' (*Aljazeera*, 2 June 2016) http://www.aljazeera.com/news/2016/06/syria-civil-war-aid-daraya-160601124835991.html.

determine the fate of the estimated remaining 4,000 residents (both combatants and civilians).[7] According to an interviewee from the Local Council of Daraya City (Daraya Local Council – a local and elected body established in October 2012 to implement local rule in opposition-held Daraya),[8] three civilian negotiators represented the residents of Daraya, all of whom were either current or previous members of the city's Local Council. The regime was represented by Kinana Hwaijeh, a news broadcaster for the official State news channel and daughter of General Ibrahim Hwaijeh of the Syrian air force.[9]

The final agreement, reached between Daraya city and the Assad regime on 24 August 2016, was not produced in written form.[10] Daraya Local Council, however, released a statement outlining the general terms of the agreement.[11] First, opposition fighters and their families would be evacuated with light arms to opposition-controlled Idlib governorate. Second, civilians would have the option of being evacuated to either Idlib or to regime-controlled Kiswah, where they would be processed within a matter of hours and without any harm done to them (civilians were not given an option to stay in their homes). Third, Daraya residents who had fled to nearby Muadamiya over the past four years could also be evacuated to either Idlib or Kisweh. It was stipulated that the above evacuations must be completed within 72 hours.[12] Finally, the regime would release any women and children detainees in its prisons who were from the city of Daraya who could then, presumably, rejoin their families in either Idlib or Kisweh. Evacuations from Daraya were conducted on 26–27 August 2016.

The evacuation of Daraya as well as the events leading up to it pose a number of international legal questions surrounding the legal framework pertaining to forcible displacement of an internal nature (i.e. within State boundaries) as well

7 Report of the Secretary-General, 'Implementation of Security Council resolutions 2139 (2014), 2165 (2014), 2191 (2014) and 2258 (2015)' (16 September 2016) UN Doc S/2016/796, [7]; Report of the Secretary-General, 'Implementation of Security Council resolutions 2139 (2014), 2165 (2014), 2191 (2014) and 2258 (2015)' (20 July 2016) UN Doc S/2016/631, [47].

8 'About Us' (*Local Council of Daraya City*, 2014) http://darayacouncil.org/index.php/%D8%A7%D9%84%D9%85%D8%AC%D9%84%D8%B3-%D8%A7%D9%84% D9%85%D8%AD%D9%84%D9%8A/%D9%85%D9%86-%D9%86%D8%AD%D9%86.html (Author's translation).

9 Jabbour S., 'Daraya: Agreement for forcible displacement amidst international silence' (*Aljazeera*, 1 September 2016) http://www.aljazeera.net/news/reportsandinterviews/2016/9/1/%D8%AF%D8%A7%D8% B1%D9%8A%D8%A7-%D8%A7%D8%AA%D9%81%D8%A7%D9%82-%D8%AA%D9%87%D8%AC% D9%8A%D8%B1-%D9%82%D8%B3%D8%B1%D9%8A-%D9%88%D8%B3%D8%B7-%D8%B5%D9% 85%D8%AA-%D8%A7%D9%84%D8%B9%D8%A7%D9%84%D9%85 (Author's translation).

10 The implications of this are discussed below.

11 'Statement' (*Local Council of Daraya City*, 12 October 2016) https://www.facebook.com/daraya.council/posts/558647077663198:0.

12 Abdulrahim R., 'Syrian rebels reach deal to evacuate besieged Damascus suburb' (*Wall Street Journal*, 25 August 2016) https://www.wsj.com/articles/syrian-rebels-reach-deal-to-evacuate-besieged-damascus-suburb-1472154630 [hereinafter Abdulrahim Syrian Rebels Reach Deal].

as that pertaining to the rights of the forcibly displaced. This section focuses on two major issues. The first is whether the evacuation of the city satisfied any of the exceptions to the prohibition against forcible displacement under both IHL and IHRL given that this prohibition is not considered to be absolute under international law. The second is whether the evacuation was 'forced' given that it was implemented pursuant to a formal agreement with civilian representatives from the city. These questions are addressed in turn.

2.1 Was the evacuation justified?

The international prohibition against forcible displacement can be found in multiple international legal and soft law instruments, including in Principle 6(2) of the Guiding Principles on Internal Displacement (Guiding Principles);[13] Article 7(1)(d) Statute of the International Criminal Court (ICC Statute) (as a crime against humanity);[14] and in texts pertaining to NIACs (which Syria embodies[15]) including Article 17(1) Additional Protocol II to the Geneva Conventions (APII),[16] Article 8(2)(e)(viii) ICC Statute[17] and Rule 129 of the ICRC's rules on customary international humanitarian law.[18] Syria is party to neither APII nor the ICC Statute and is thus not bound by their provisions. As for the Guiding Principles, they do not constitute an international treaty, although they have been described as 'minimum standards' pertaining to forcible displacement that are premised on existing laws of IHL, IHRL and custom and that enjoy widespread support among States.[19] Their provisions, therefore, while not intrinsically

13 'Guiding Principles on Internal Displacement' (*UN Office for the Coordination of Humanitarian Affairs*, 1998) Principle 6(2) http://www.unhcr.org/uk/protection/idps/43ce1cff2/guiding-principles-internal-displacement.html.

14 Article 7(1)(d) prohibits both deportations (displacement outside the boundaries of a State) and forcible transfer (displacement within the boundaries of a State). Rome Statute of the International Criminal Court (adopted 17 July 1998, entered into force 1 July 2002) 2187 UNTS 3 Art 7(1)(d) [hereinafter ICC Statute]. *See also Prosecutor v Krstić* (Judgement) IT-98-33-T (2 August 2001), [521] [hereinafter *Krstić* case] (differentiating between deportation and forcible transfer).

15 UN Doc A/HRC/21/50, n3, [12].

16 Protocol Additional to the Geneva Conventions of 12 August 1949 and Relating to the Protection of Victims of Non-International Armed Conflicts (adopted 8 June 1977, entered into force 7 December 1978) 1125 UNTS 609 Art 17 [hereinafter APII].

17 ICC Statute, n14, Art 8(2)(e)(viii).

18 'Rule 129. The Act of Displacement' (*ICRC*, 2017) https://ihl-databases.icrc.org/customary-ihl/eng/docs/v1_rul_rule129.

19 'Guiding Principles on Internal Displacement', n13, Introductory note by Francis M. Deng; Lavoyer J.P. (1998), 'Guiding Principles on Internal Displacement: a few comments on the contribution of international humanitarian law', *IRRC*, Vol. 38, 324, 468; Kälin W. (2005), 'The Guiding Principles on Internal Displacement as international minimum standard and protection tool', *RSQ*, Vol. 24, 27, 29–31 [hereinafter Kälin Guiding Principles]; Abebe A.M. (2011), 'Special rapporteurs as law makers: the developments and evolution of the normative framework for protecting and assisting internally displaced persons', *IJHR*, Vol. 15, 286, 286–87.

binding, may contain normative weight through their reflection of existing norms. In this respect, it is important to note that the prohibition against forcible displacement has become prominently recognised as a customary norm of international law in both international armed conflicts (IACs) and NIACs, a conclusion affirmed by the International Criminal Tribunal for the Former Yugoslavia (ICTY) in the cases *Prosecutor v Krnojelac* (*Krnojelac* case) and *Prosecutor v Blagojević and Jokić* (*Blagojević* case), as well as by international legal scholars including Jacques and Kälin.[20]

The prohibition against forcible displacement in NIACs, however, is not considered to be non-derogable. All of the above-mentioned texts, with the exception of Article 7(1)(d) ICC Statute, which lists forcible displacement as a crime against humanity, suggest that exceptions to this rule can be made if 'the security of the civilians involved or imperative military reasons so demand'.[21] While these exceptions are not explicitly listed for forcible displacement as a crime against humanity, they can be implicitly accepted as defining this prohibition, for example as stipulated within Article 7(1)(d) ICC Statute. Article 7(2)(d) ICC Statute, for example, defines '[d]eportation or forcible transfer' as 'forced displacement . . . without grounds permitted under international law', which presumably refers to the two exceptions stipulated within the other legal texts.[22] In the case *Prosecutor v Simić, Tadić, and Zarić* (*Simić* case), the ICTY similarly discussed the legal framework pertaining to the crime against humanity of forcible displacement with reference to the two exceptions (of security of civilians and imperative military necessity) stipulated within IHL texts.[23]

The ICTY's *Blagojević* case clarifies the interpretation of the two exceptions to the prohibition against forcible displacement. As for the first exception, namely the security of civilians, it stated that an evacuation can be authorised 'when the area in which the population is located is in danger as a result of "military operations" or "intense bombing"'.[24] In such a case, the ICTY stressed that 'a military commander may, and is in fact duty bound to, evacuate the population',[25] a notion that is affirmed by Jacques to constitute a customary

20 *Prosecutor v Krnojelac* (Judgement) IT-97-25-A (17 September 2003), [222] [hereinafter *Krnojelac* Appeal]; *Prosecutor v Blagojević and Jokić* (Judgement) IT-02-60-T (17 January 2005), [629] [hereinafter *Blagojević* case]; Jacques M. (2012), *Armed Conflict and Displacement: The Protection of Refugees and Displaced Persons under International Humanitarian Law* (Cambridge University Press) 70–71, 152–53; Kälin W. (2008), 'Guiding Principles on Internal Displacement: annotations', *ASILBrookInst*, Vol. 38, 27–29 https://www.brookings.edu/wp-content/uploads/2016/06/spring_guiding_principles.pdf [hereinafter Kälin Annotations].

21 *See supra* n13, n16–18.

22 ICC Statute, n14, Art 7(2)(d). *See also* Schabas W. (2010), *The International Criminal Court: A Commentary on the Rome Statute* (Oxford University Press) 164–165.

23 *Prosecutor v Simić, Tadić, and Zarić* (Judgement) IT-95-9-T (17 October 2003), [127] [hereinafter *Simić* case].

24 *Blagojević* case, n20, [598].

25 Ibid.

norm in both IACs and NIACs.[26] In terms of the second exception of 'imperative military reasons', the *Blagojević* case clarifies that evacuations can be authorised when 'the presence of the population hampers military operations'.[27] Importantly, however, it stressed, a notion further emphasised in the case *Prosecutor v Karadžić* (*Karadžić* case), that 'it is unlawful to use evacuation measures [based on imperative military reasons] as a pretext to remove the [civilian] population and [effectuate] control over a desired territory.'[28] This notion receives support from the ICRC commentary to Article 17 APII as well as Kälin's annotations to the Guiding Principles on Internal Displacement, both of which affirm that 'imperative military reasons cannot be justified by political motives.'[29]

Applying this framework to the Daraya case, it is unlikely that the Daraya evacuation satisfied either exception to the prohibition against forcible displacement. Importantly, the evacuation of combatants in addition to civilians meant that there were no security or military needs to evacuate civilians. Had the evacuation been pursued purely for civilian safety or for military necessity, then logically, only civilians should have been evacuated to safer areas. The evacuation of both civilians and combatants from Daraya is a strong indicator that the primary driver of displacement was, in fact, the political motive of establishing regime control over the city and, therefore, in violation of the terms stipulated by the *Blagojević* and *Karadžić* cases that it is unlawful to use an evacuation in order to '[effectuate] control over a desired territory'.[30]

The unlawful nature of the Daraya evacuation can also be extracted – albeit indirectly – from *opinio juris* manifested by the Syrian regime itself. The regime refrained from characterising the evacuation as a displacement or even evacuation of the population, but rather consistently framed it as an anti-terrorism operation in line with its wider characterisation of the Syrian conflict as one between the State and terrorist groups. Additionally, the negotiated Daraya deal, although formally achieved between representatives of the Assad regime and Daraya city, was not produced in writing. An interviewee from Daraya Local Council commented:

> The regime did not want anything written on paper which would attribute responsibility to it, this was its policy. It did not produce written agreements in the previous ceasefire agreements of Moadamiya, Barzeh, or Qadam.

The above likely reflect a conscious decision on behalf of the Assad regime to depict the Daraya evacuation as an anti-terrorism operation rather than as a displacement of the population given its understanding that its involvement in

26 Ibid; Jacques, n20, 52–53.
27 *Blagojević* case, n20, [598].
28 Ibid, [597]; *Prosecutor v Karadžić* (Judgement-Volume I of IV) IT-95-5/18-T (24 March 2016), [492] [hereinafter *Karadžić* case].
29 Zimmermann B. *et al.* (1987), *Commentary on the Additional Protocols of 8 June 1977 to the Geneva Conventions of 12 August 1949* (Brill/Nijhoff) 1473; Kälin Annotations, n20, 32.
30 *Blagojević* case, n20, [597]; *Karadžić* case, n28, [492].

forcibly displacing civilians from Daraya would entail its international legal responsibility.

The UN's stance towards the Daraya evacuation constitutes an additional indicator regarding its unlawful nature. The same interviewee revealed:

> When we asked the office of UN Special Envoy to Syria Staffan de Mistura if it could oversee any evacuation process to ensure that violations did not take place, it failed to respond to our request, but told us only indirectly that this would not be possible as this would make it involved in the process of forcible displacement.

Sure enough, a September 2016 report of then-UN Secretary-General, Ban Ki-moon, carefully articulated that '[t]he United Nations was not a part of the agreement, nor did it support the evacuation.'[31] In a statement shortly following the Daraya evacuation, UN Under-Secretary-General for Humanitarian Affairs and Emergency Relief Coordinator, Stephen O'Brien, affirmed:

> [A]greements resulting in a mass evacuation of civilians after a prolonged period of besiegement do not comply with international humanitarian law and human rights law. Let us be clear, all sieges, a medieval tactic, must be lifted. This should not be through any type of agreement which results in the forced displacement of the civilian population. What happened in Daraya should not be precedent setting for other besieged areas in Syria. It is imperative that all those displaced are allowed to return voluntarily, in safety and in dignity, to their homes as soon as the situation allows it.[32]

The UN's condemnation of the Daraya evacuation and its refusal to play any official part in it reinforces the view that the evacuation constituted an unlawful forcible displacement. It also, however, gives rise to another compelling question pertaining to the responsibility that the UN should assume towards such illegal situations. On the one hand, the UN was unable to prevent the grave, systematic and sustained IHL violations inflicted on the civilian population in Daraya in the months and years prior to the negotiations to evacuate the city, conditions, which themselves – as detailed in the next section – led directly to the situation of forcible displacement. On the other hand, the UN had the opportunity to at least mitigate abuses that were likely to occur throughout the evacuation process. The role of the UN and wider international community in such instances has not been adequately addressed in international law and receives further consideration in Section 3.2 below. The next section, however, discusses in greater depth the legal

31 UN Doc S/2016/796, n7, [7].

32 'Statement on Darayya and the situation in other besieged areas in Syria' (*UN Office for the Coordination of Humanitarian Affairs*, 30 August 2016) https://docs.unocha.org/sites/dms/Documents/ERC_USG%20 Stephen_OBrien_Statement_on_Darayya.pdf.

nature of the Daraya evacuation agreement, more specifically whether the conclusion of such an agreement, which received the endorsement of civilian representatives, could legitimise an otherwise unlawful process.

2.2 Was the evacuation 'forced'?

Given that Daraya's evacuation arguably did not meet either of the exceptions to the prohibition against forcible displacement articulated under IHL, IHRL, the Guiding Principles on Internal Displacement and customary international law, it is important to determine whether it was actually 'forced', given that it was undertaken following the conclusion of a formal agreement between the State and Daraya city. As mentioned previously, all three negotiators who represented the city were civilians and, therefore, the question becomes whether their formal consent to the evacuations on behalf of the city's residents means that the evacuation was not forced.

It is well established in the context of IACs that agreements on behalf of civilians have no bearing on the legality of forcible displacement. Article 7 of the Fourth Geneva Convention (GCIV), for example, states that '[n]o special agreement shall . . . restrict the rights' conferred by the Convention on protected persons,[33] which include as per Articles 49 and 147 protection against forcible transfers (forcible displacement within the boundaries of a State) and deportations (forcible displacement outside the boundaries of a State).[34] ICTY case law provides support to this provision as discussed in *Prosecutor v Naletilić and Martinović* (*Naletilić* case):

> [A]n agreement between two military commanders or other representatives of the parties in a conflict does not have any implications on the circumstances under which a transfer is lawful. Military commanders cannot consent on behalf of the individual.[35]

In this case, therefore, the ICTY affirmed in the context of IACs that the conclusion of an agreement by military or other representatives for the evacuation of a civilian population (in the absence of compelling security or military imperatives) cannot bestow legality on such a process. The ICTY did not, however, extend this conclusion to forcible displacements conducted in NIACs, which more accurately reflects the nature of the Syrian conflict.[36]

In this sense, it is worth examining the ICTY's *Simić* case, which evaluated forcible displacement as a crime against humanity and thus prohibited in both times

33 Geneva Convention Relative to the Protection of Civilian Persons in Time of War (adopted 12 August 1949, entered into force 21 October 1950) 75 UNTS 287 Art 7 [hereinafter GCIV].

34 Ibid Arts 49, 147. *See also* n14.

35 *Prosecutor v Naletilić and Martinović* (Judgement) IT-98-34-T (31 March 2003), [523] [hereinafter *Naletilić* case].

36 *See* n3.

of peace and war, including in both IACs and NIACs as affirmed in the ICTY's *Krnojelac* case.[37] In the *Simić* case, the ICTY stated, similarly to its conclusions in the *Naletilić* case, that 'agreements concluded by military commanders or other representatives of parties in a conflict cannot make displacement lawful.'[38] Importantly, it relied on the *Naletilić* case as a basis for this finding even though the *Naletilić* case dealt with forcible displacement as a war crime while the *Simić* case dealt with it as a crime against humanity.[39] This offers a strong argument that the conclusion of an agreement on behalf of a civilian population fails to bestow legality on an otherwise unlawful forcible displacement, whether in the context of crimes against humanity, IACs or NIACs. This seems to be agreed to by Jacques, who notes only in general terms that agreements on behalf of a civilian population cannot substitute for individual consent in the context of forcible displacements.[40]

The UN's stance towards the Daraya evacuation further supports the argument that agreements on behalf of a civilian population in the context of a NIAC cannot make an otherwise unlawful forcible displacement lawful. As mentioned above, UN Under-Secretary-General for Humanitarian Affairs and Emergency Relief Coordinator, Stephen O'Brien, emphasised in a statement following the evacuation that 'agreements resulting in a mass evacuation of civilians after a prolonged period of besiegement do not comply with international humanitarian law and human rights law.'[41] Similarly, in response to the evacuation of Al-Waer neighbourhood in the city of Homs in March 2017, UN Secretary-General António Guterres published in a report that '[t]he United Nations has not been involved in the negotiations or evacuations around such agreements, which do not appear to meet international legal standards or adhere to humanitarian principles.'[42]

It is important in this context to consider the effect that individual consent might have had on the process of displacement, for example if the residents of Daraya requested such an evacuation or otherwise consented to it. The *Naletilić* case, for example, stressed that '[t]ransfers motivated by an individual's genuine wish to leave, are lawful',[43] a conclusion that was reiterated in the *Simić* case.[44] Individual consent to displacement would, in fact, be reflective of a broader right to freedom of movement embodied within Article 12 of the International Covenant on Civil and Political Rights (ICCPR) to which Syria is a signatory.[45]

37 *Krnojelac* Appeal, n20, [221].
38 *Simić* case, n23, [127].
39 Ibid.
40 Jacques, n20, 135.
41 'Statement on Darayya and the situation in other besieged areas in Syria', n32.
42 Report of the Secretary-General, 'Implementation of Security Council resolutions 2139 (2014), 2165 (2014), 2191 (2014), 2258 (2015) and 2332 (2016)' (19 April 2017) UN Doc S/2017/339, [52].
43 *Naletilić* case, n35, [519].
44 *Simić* case, n23, [125].
45 International Covenant on Civil and Political Rights (adopted 16 December 1966, entered into force 23 March 1976) 999 UNTS 171 Art 12 [hereinafter ICCPR].

To evaluate this question, it is important to assess the nature of any consent given to an evacuation process, namely whether it is given freely or under duress. The ICTY in the *Krnojelac* case stressed that the 'essential element is that the displacement be involuntary in nature, where the relevant persons had no real choice'.[46] The term 'real choice' is key, as it distinguishes between consent based on fear and consent based on genuine choice. The *Simić* case adds that 'an apparent consent induced by force or threat of force should not be considered to be real consent',[47] meaning that displacement that occurs pursuant to civilians' consent in the literal sense will still be considered forced if they had no genuine choice in reaching this conclusion.[48]

Evaluating the ICTY's findings with respect to the Daraya evacuation requires a brief overview of the humanitarian situation within the city prior to the commencement of negotiations. In the words of UN Under-Secretary-General for Humanitarian Affairs and Emergency Relief Coordinator, Stephen O'Brien:

> This evacuation followed four years of unrelenting siege during which children starved, people resorted to eating grass and the town was subjected to an onslaught of fighting, including aerial bombardment, and severe restrictions on freedom of movement for civilians, as well as on commercial and humanitarian goods.[49]

Indeed, Daraya was under siege by the Assad regime from November 2012 to August 2016.[50] Only two humanitarian aid convoys were allowed into the city throughout these four years, both in June 2016. The first convoy contained items such as anti-lice shampoo, mosquito nets, vaccines and baby formula, although no food as was desperately required by the population.[51] The second convoy contained food for 2,400 people (Daraya's estimated population at that point was 4,000) but was immediately followed by an escalated military campaign by the Assad regime which entailed the use of over three hundred barrel bombs over the next ten days,[52] themselves indiscriminate and highly destructive weapons prohibited under UN Security Council (UNSC) Resolution 2139 on Syria as well as under customary international humanitarian law due to their inherently indiscriminate nature.[53]

46 *Prosecutor v Krnojelac* (Judgment) IT-97-25-T (15 March 2002) [475] [hereinafter *Krnojelac* case].

47 *Simić* case, n23, [125].

48 Jacques, n20, 59–60, 135, 138; Schabas, n22, 165.

49 'Statement on Darayya and the situation in other besieged areas in Syria', n32.

50 Human Rights Council, 'Report of the Independent International Commission of Inquiry on the Syrian Arab Republic' (11 August 2016) UN Doc A/HRC/33/55, [34].

51 Ibid, [35].

52 Ibid; Abdulrahim R., 'Bombs follow aid into besieged Syrian towns' (*Wall Street Journal*, 20 June 2016) http://www.wsj.com/articles/bombs-follow-aid-into-besieged-syrian-towns-1466467006 [hereinafter Abdulrahim Bombs Follow Aid]; UN Doc S/2016/631, n7, [47].

53 UNSC Res 2139 (22 February 2014) UN Doc S/RES/2139, [3]; 'Rule 1. The Principle of Distinction between Civilians and Combatants' (*ICRC*, 2017) https://ihl-databases.icrc.

This dismal humanitarian situation occurred against the backdrop of an even wider military campaign against Daraya. Between January 2014 and February 2016, for example, an estimated 6,800 barrel bombs were dropped on the city.[54] Residents and local officials reported that incendiary weapons were also dropped on residential areas.[55] All of the city's hospitals were targeted and destroyed throughout the years under siege; Daraya's last remaining hospital was hit with incendiary weapons on 19 August 2016, only a few days before the evacuation agreement was concluded.[56] Such conditions largely reflect those described in the *Simić* case, in which the ICTY elaborated that:

> A lack of genuine choice may be inferred from, inter alia, threatening and intimidating acts that are calculated to deprive the civilian population of exercising its free will, such as the shelling of civilian objects, the burning of civilian property, and the commission of – or the threat to commit – other crimes 'calculated to terrify the population and make them flee the area with no hope of return'.[57]

The conditions inflicted on the city of Daraya therefore not only give rise to concern regarding the commission of various war crimes (including those pertaining to the use of indiscriminate and proscribed weapons,[58] the targeting of civilian and other protected objects such as hospitals[59] and the use of starvation as

org/customary-ihl/eng/docs/v1_rul_rule1; 'Rule 11. Indiscriminate Attacks' (*ICRC*, 2017) https://ihl-databases.icrc.org/customary-ihl/eng/docs/v1_rul_rule11; 'Rule 71. Weapons that Are by Nature Indiscriminate' (*ICRC*, 2017) https://ihl-databases.icrc.org/customary-ihl/eng/docs/v1_rul_rule71.

54 'Syria: terrifying eyewitness video of life under siege and barrel bombs must spur humanitarian lifeline' (*Amnesty International*, 19 April 2016) https://www.amnesty.org/en/press-releases/2016/04/syria-terrifying-eyewitness-video-of-life-under-siege-and-barrel-bombs/.

55 'No going back: forced displacement in the Syrian conflict' (*Syrian American Council*, February 2017), 8 – https://d3n8a8pro7vhmx.cloudfront.net/sacouncil/pages/167/attachments/original/1486567664/ Displacement_Paper_Version_by_Julie_F.pdf?1486567664; Abdulrahim Syrian Rebels Reach Deal, n12.

56 'Syria's civil war: 'Last hospital in Daraya bombed'' (*Aljazeera*, 19 August 2016) http://www.aljazeera.com/ news/2016/08/syria-civil-war-daraya-hospital-bombed-160819101838839.html.

57 *Simić* case, n23, [126].

58 UN Doc S/RES/2139, n53, [3]; 'Rule 71. Weapons that Are by Nature Indiscriminate', n53; 'Rule 84. The Protection of Civilians and Civilian Objects from the Effects of Incendiary Weapons' (*ICRC*, 2017) https://ihl-databases.icrc.org/customary-ihl/eng/docs/v1_rul_rule84; 'Rule 85. The Use of Incendiary Weapons against Combatants' (*ICRC*, 2017) https://ihl-databases.icrc.org/customary-ihl/eng/docs/v1_rul_rule85.

59 APII, n16, Art's 11, 13; ICC Statute, n14, Art 8(2)(e)(i-ii); 'Rule 1. The Principle of Distinction between Civilians and Combatants', n53; 'Rule 7. The Principle of Distinction between Civilian Objects and Military Objectives' (*ICRC*, 2017) https://ihl-databases.icrc.org/customary-ihl/eng/docs/v1_rul_rule7; 'Rule 11. Indiscriminate Attacks', n53; 'Rule 28. Medical Units' (*ICRC*, 2017) https://ihl-databases.icrc.org/customary-ihl/eng/docs/v1_rul_rule28.

a weapon of war),[60] but they also reinforce the conclusion that even had civilians provided individual consent to the evacuation, this would not have been based on any genuine choice. As an interviewee stated: 'We knew that the alternative was genocide. We knew that Daraya's fall was only a matter of time.' A representative of Assad's office also reportedly told negotiators that anything short of the complete evacuation of civilians would lead the army to 'kill them all, the civilians'.[61] As similarly described by the ICTY in the case *Prosecutor v Gotovina, Ćermak, and Markač* (*Gotovina* case), there was clearly an 'environment in which those present had no choice but to leave' in order to ensure their survival, meaning that the displacement was forcible even if civilians had in theory chosen or consented to it.[62]

Importantly, the starve-or-surrender tactic employed by the Assad regime against Daraya was not an isolated incident. Rather, it was also pursued in other areas across the country, including in Homs,[63] Moadamiyah,[64] Wadi Barada[65] and more.[66] In Homs, for example, the regime used a combination of '[m]assacre, rape, detention, siege, starvation, denial of medical care, targeted bombing of civilians and civilian infrastructure, sectarian militias, [and] psychological warfare' in order to take control of the city over several stages and to forcibly displace residents of opposition-held areas, including through negotiated deals.[67] East Aleppo, discussed in the next section, represents yet another compelling case study that gives rise to important international legal questions regarding the framework of forcible displacement.

60 APII, n16, Art 14; ICC Statute, n14, Art's 7(1)(b) and 7(2)(b); 'Rule 53. Starvation as a Method of Warfare' (*ICRC*, 2016) https://ihl-databases.icrc.org/customary-ihl/eng/docs/v1_rul_rule53.

61 Barnard A., Saad H., 'Besieged town of Daraya agrees to surrender to Syrian government' (*New York Times*, 25 August 2016) https://www.nytimes.com/2016/08/26/world/middleeast/daraya-syria-assad-surrender.html?_r=0; Jabbour, n9.

62 *Prosecutor v Gotovina, Ćermak, and Markač* (Judgement) IT-06-90-T (15 April 2011), [1745] [hereinafter *Gotovina* case].

63 *See* 67.

64 'Syrians in rebel Damascus suburb start to evacuate in deal' (*Reuters*, 2 September 2016) http://uk.reuters.com/article/uk-mideast-crisis-syria-idUKKCN11812I.

65 Esnor J., 'Syrian rebels evacuated out of besieged Wadi Barada after government forces capture strategic water springs' (*Telegraph*, 30 January 2017) http://www.telegraph.co.uk/news/2017/01/30/syrian-rebels-evacuated-besieged-wadi-barada-government-forces/.

66 *See* 'Timeline: Syria's 13 'people evacuation' deals' (*Aljazeera*, 16 May 2017) http://www.aljazeera.com/ indepth/features/2017/04/timeline-syria-people-evacuation-deals-170413084313089.html.

67 'No return to Homs: a case study on the demographic engineering in Syria' (*PAX*, 21 February 2017), 13, 27–28 - https://www.paxforpeace.nl/publications/all-publications/no-return-to-homs. *See also* 'Syria rebels agree to leave Homs' besieged al-Waer' (*Aljazeera*, 13 March 2017) http://www.aljazeera.com/news/2017/03/syria-rebels-agree-leave-homs-beseiged-al-waer-170313134154656.html.

3 Displacement from East Aleppo

Aleppo, once Syria's most populated city and its economic capital,[68] was split in 2012 into an opposition-controlled East and a State-controlled West.[69] After it came under opposition control, East Aleppo became the target of regular attacks by the Assad regime and came under complete siege in July 2016.[70] Thereon after, the humanitarian situation quickly deteriorated and induced the city to strike a deal with the regime in December 2016 similar to that of Daraya, which called for the evacuation of East Aleppo in return for the safety of its residents.[71] This agreement, too, bears important lessons regarding the international legal prohibition against forcible displacement.

The negotiated agreement to evacuate East Aleppo was brokered by Russia and Turkey and involved representatives from both the Assad regime and the opposition of East Aleppo. The individual responsible for conducting negotiations on behalf of East Aleppo was Al-Farouk Ahrar (pseudonym), a military commander of the Ahrar al-Sham opposition group.[72] According to an interviewee who was a political opposition leader in East Aleppo, Al-Farouk's efforts were supported by a team of five civilians (including the interviewee himself) whose role was to act as intermediaries between Al-Farouk (and armed opposition groups more generally) and the civilians within the city. This team of intermediaries consisted of one representative from the Local Council of Aleppo City (a local and elected body established in March 2013 that established local rule in opposition-held East Aleppo), one representative from the Free Syrian Lawyers (a professional organisation of pro-opposition Syrian lawyers), two political opposition leaders and one medical doctor.

In contrast to the Daraya agreement, the East Aleppo deal was put in writing. Signed on 13 December 2016, the agreement bears the signatures of Zayd Saleh, head of the Security and Military Committee in Aleppo and representative of the Assad regime; Vladimir Savchenko, Russian Lieutenant General and representative of the Russian government; negotiation representative for the regime Omar

68 Human Rights Council, 'Report of the Independent International Commission of Inquiry on the Syrian Arab Republic' (2 February 2017) UN Doc A/HRC/34/64, [21].

69 Francis E., Barrington L., 'Aleppo endgame nears as evacuation resumes' (*Reuters*, 21 December 2016) http://www.reuters.com/article/us-mideast-crisis-syria-idUSKBN14A1CL.

70 Report of the Secretary-General 'Implementation of Security Council resolutions 2139 (2014), 2165 (2014), 2191 (2014) and 2258 (2015)' (18 October 2016) UN Doc S/2016/873, [4].

71 Report of the Secretary-General, 'Implementation of Security Council resolutions 2139 (2014), 2165 (2014), 2191 (2014), 2258 (2015) and 2332 (2016)' (20 January 2017) UN Doc S/2017/58, [4].

72 'Syrian regime's representative in Aleppo agreement negotiations is brother of Fateh Al-Sham Leader' (*Enab Baladi*, 14 December 2016) http://english.enabbaladi.net/archives/2016/12/syrian-regimes-representative-aleppo-agreement-negotiations-brother-fateh-al-sham-leader/.

Rahmoun; and opposition representative Al-Farouk Ahrar.[73] The four provisions of this agreement were the following: 1) Evacuation of armed fighters with light weapons only; 2) Evacuation of armed fighters, in addition to civilians who wish to leave, towards Western Aleppo; 3) Guarantee by Syrian and Russian forces for the safety of evacuees until the exchange point of Uqdat Al-Raqqah in Western Aleppo suburbs, at which point regime busses providing transportation to the evacuees would return to regime-controlled territory; and 4) Commitment to a ceasefire from both sides throughout the evacuation process.[74]

As a result of this agreement, an estimated 36,000 people were evacuated from East Aleppo, primarily to opposition-held territory, between 15 and 22 December 2016.[75] Approximately 500 civilians chose to remain in the city.[76] While there are many similarities between the Daraya and East Aleppo evacuation deals, the East Aleppo case gives rise to its own set of legal questions pertaining to the prohibition against forcible displacement. This section discusses some of these issues, namely whether the evacuation from East Aleppo can be described as forcible displacement given that the negotiated agreement offered civilians a choice to remain within the city and what role the international community should have assumed in this situation. These issues are examined in turn.

3.1 Was the evacuation 'forced'?

The first manner by which the Daraya and East Aleppo deals differed from each other is that the former stipulated that all inhabitants within the city must be evacuated (both civilians and combatants), while the East Aleppo deal only specifically called for the evacuation of combatants. As for civilians, the East Aleppo deal determined that only 'civilians who wished to leave' would be evacuated,[77] meaning that, in writing at least, the East Aleppo deal did not compel civilians to leave their homes. However, as with the analysis conducted with respect to the Daraya case, it is important to stress that security of civilians or imperative military necessity notwithstanding, civilians' choice to undergo displacement rather than to remain in their homes can still be regarded as forced if the choice is not genuine. As the ICTY determined in the *Krnojelac* and *Simić* cases,[78] the conclusion of a deal, the specific terms of such a deal or even the provision of individual consent do not necessarily confer legality on a

73 Ibid.

74 Ibid.

75 UN Doc S/2017/58, n71, 1.

76 'The displacement agreement from Aleppo: how it happened? And how it has [*sic*] been done?' (*Jusoor*, December 2016), 6 - http://jusoor.co/content_images/users/1/contents/312.pdf.

77 'Syrian regime's representative in Aleppo agreement negotiations is brother of Fateh Al-Sham Leader', n72.

78 *See* n47–49. *See also Gotovina* case, n62, [1739]; *Naletilić* case, n35, [523].

process of displacement. What ultimately matters, as stressed in *Gotovina* case, is that 'people are moved against their will or without a genuine choice'.[79]

As with Daraya, the conditions inflicted on East Aleppo were clearly calculated to achieve the full displacement of the population. Even if this end goal was not expressly stated (for example, within the text of the evacuation deal), it was inevitable given the scale of the military campaign that was launched against the city prior to the conclusion of this agreement. In July 2016, for example, the regime cut off the Castillo road, which was the last remaining supply route into East Aleppo, and effectively placed an estimated 250,000–275,000 civilians under siege.[80] Indiscriminate attacks against the city between July and December 2016 employed proscribed weapons including barrel bombs, incendiary weapons and chemical weapons,[81] and targeted food, power and water sources within the city.[82] This led to the displacement of tens of thousands of civilians even before the official evacuation agreement was achieved.[83]

This overwhelming military offensive also targeted the city's hospitals, important not only because hospitals themselves are protected objects under IHL,[84] but also because of their vital role in providing emergency services for medical needs that become compounded in situations of war. According to the Syrian American Medical Society, an organisation providing medical and humanitarian relief in response to the Syrian crisis, there were seventy-three attacks on medical facilities and personnel in East Aleppo between June and December 2016.[85] A report by then-UN Secretary-General further revealed that each hospital in East Aleppo was hit at least twice as of October 2016, 'indicating the deliberate nature of some of those attacks'.[86] The Independent International Commission of Inquiry on Syria (Commission of Inquiry on Syria) – established

79 *Gotovina* case, n62, [1739].
80 UN Doc S/2016/631, n7, [10]; Report of the Secretary-General, 'Implementation of Security Council resolutions 2139 (2014), 2165 (2014), 2191 (2014) and 2258 (2015)' (16 August 2016) UN Doc S/2016/714, [4]; UN Doc S/2016/796, n7, 2. A temporary ceasefire in October 2016 allowed for the limited distribution of humanitarian aid in East Aleppo. Report of the Secretary-General, 'Implementation of Security Council resolutions 2139 (2014), 2165 (2014), 2191 (2014) and 2258 (2015)' (15 November 2016) UN Doc S/2016/962, [4].
81 UN Doc A/HRC/34/64, n68, [51]–[60]; 'Breaking Aleppo' (*Atlantic Council*, February 2017), 32–35, 44–45 http://www.publications.atlanticcouncil.org/breakingaleppo/wp-content/uploads/2017/02/BreakingAleppo.pdf.
82 UN Doc S/2016/714, n80, [6]; UN Doc S/2016/873, n70, [19]; UN Doc A/HRC/34/64, n68, [41]–[47].
83 Report of the Secretary-General, 'Implementation of Security Council resolutions 2139 (2014), 2165 (2014), 2191 (2014) and 2258 (2015)' (14 December 2016) UN Doc S/2016/1057, [5].
84 APII, n16, Art 11; ICC Statute, n14, Art's 8(2)(e)(ii); 'Rule 28. Medical Units', n59.
85 'The failure of UN Security Council Resolution 2286 in preventing attacks on healthcare in Syria' (*Syrian American Medical Society*, January 2017) https://foundation.sams-usa.net/wp-content/uploads/ 2017/01/SAMS-2286-Report.pdf.
86 UN Doc S/2016/873, n70, [34].

pursuant to UN Human Rights Committee Resolution S-17/1 to investigate violations of IHRL, to ascertain the facts surrounding such violations and to identify those responsible for them[87] – concluded that '[b]y the time pro-Government forces recaptured the city in late December, no hospitals were left functioning' and that the patterns 'strongly suggest the deliberate and systematic targeting of medical infrastructure as part of a strategy to compel surrender'.[88]

Assad and Russian forces, both of which were involved in carrying out the military attacks against East Aleppo, each consistently denied the targeting of civilian areas and protected objects such as hospitals as well as the use of indiscriminate weapons, which at least reinforces *opinio juris* regarding the unlawfulness of such attacks.[89] Nevertheless, their well-documented military campaign against East Aleppo was clearly aimed at achieving forcible displacement as a means of establishing regime control over the city. This was emphasised by Under-Secretary-General for Humanitarian Affairs and Emergency Relief Coordinator, Stephen O'Brien, in October 2016:

> Let me be clear — eastern Aleppo is besieged by the Syrian Government. No United Nations assistance has entered in nearly four months. Food is so scarce that many people survive on one meal of rice a day, and what is available in local markets is sold at vastly inflated prices. At the same time, civilians are being bombed by Syrian and Russian forces, and if they survive that they will starve tomorrow. The tactics are as obvious as they are intolerable — make life intolerable; make death likely; push people from starvation to despair to surrender; push people to leave on green buses.[90]

Therefore, despite the apparent element of choice for civilians to leave or remain within East Aleppo as per the written evacuation agreement, the conditions inflicted on the city left civilians with no genuine choice but to evacuate in fear for their safety, thus constituting forcible displacement.

It should be mentioned that armed opposition groups in East Aleppo were also implicated in launching indiscriminate mortar and rocket attacks against

87 Human Rights Council Res S-17/1 (23 August 2011) UN Doc A/HRC/RES/S-17/1 Art 12.

88 UN Doc A/HRC/34/64, n68, [30]–[32].

89 'Breaking Aleppo', n81, 29; 'Russia rejects Syria war crimes claim over hospital attacks' (*BBC News*, 16 February 2016) http://www.bbc.co.uk/news/world-middle-east-35586886; 'President al-Assad to Denmark's TV 2: Moderate opposition is a myth . . . We won't accept that terrorists will take control of any part of Syria-VIDEO' (*Syrian Arab News Agency*, 6 October 2016) http://sana.sy/en/?p=89763; 'President Al-Assad to BBC News: we are defending civilians, and making dialogue' (*Syrian Arab News Agency*, 10 February 2015) http://sana.sy/en/?p=28047; 'Full transcript of AP interview with Syrian President Assad' (*Fox News*, 22 September 2016) http://www.foxnews.com/world/2016/09/22/full-transcript-ap-interview-with-syrian-president-assad.html.

90 UNSC 7795th Meeting (26 October 2016) UN Doc S/PV.7795, 3.

regime-held West Aleppo. Such attacks, documented in major opposition offensives including in July and October 2016, killed civilians in West Aleppo and forced others to flee from their homes.[91] This gives rise to the responsibility of these NSAs for violations of IHL, which is binding on all parties to an armed conflict (both State and non-State).[92] However, the atrocities committed by the Assad regime were not only of a far greater scale than those committed by armed opposition groups, but were also directly responsible for the organised forcible displacement described thus far.

3.2 Role of the international community

Another major difference between the Daraya and East Aleppo evacuations pertains to the seemingly contradictory stance of the UN towards each of them, specifically with regards to whether or not it supported these evacuations. As detailed in the previous analysis on the Daraya evacuation, the UN refused to play any official part in the process given concerns that this would involve it in an unlawful practice and was careful to stress that it 'was not a part of the [Daraya] agreement, nor did it support the evacuation.'[93] Also worth mentioning is the UN's response to the evacuations conducted in Al-Waer neighbourhood in the city of Homs in March 2017. UN Secretary-General António Guterres published in a report that:

> The United Nations has not been involved in the negotiations or evacuations around such agreements, which do not appear to meet international legal standards or adhere to humanitarian principles. The United Nations has repeatedly expressed its concern at any local agreement that is preceded by the decimation of an area and results in the forced displacement of some parts of the civilian population. I would like to remind parties involved in such agreements that, under international humanitarian law, the forced displacement of civilians for reasons relating to the conflict is permissible solely in order to guarantee their security or for imperative military necessity. Forced displacement for any other reason relating to the conflict is prohibited and may constitute a war crime. Any evacuation of civilians must be safe, voluntary and to a place of their choosing.[94]

91 UN Doc S/2016/631, n7, [9]; UN Doc S/2016/714, n80, [5]; UN Doc S/2016/962, n80, [5].

92 Berkes A. (2016), '*De Facto* Regimes and the Responsibility to Protect' in Barnes R. and Tzevelekos V.P. (eds.), *Beyond Responsibility to Protect: Generating Change in International Law* (Intersentia) 162; Rondeau S. (2016), 'The responsibility to protect doctrine, and the duty of the international community to reinforce international humanitarian law and its protective value for civilian populations' in Barnes R. and Tzevelekos V.P. (eds.), *Beyond Responsibility to Protect: Generating Change in International Law* (Intersentia) 256.

93 *See* n31.

94 UN Doc S/2017/339, n42, [52].

With respect to East Aleppo, however, the stance of the UN seemed to have reversed. Then-UN Secretary-General Ban Ki-moon, for example, offered express support for the conclusion of an evacuation agreement in East Aleppo:

> We understand that there are ongoing negotiations between the parties for an evacuation deal, facilitated by Russia and Turkey. We support those efforts and stand ready to help implement and oversee such an agreement, which we understand may now be imminent. We remind all parties of their obligations under international humanitarian law to prioritize the safe passage of civilians out of eastern Aleppo and to ensure that those who have surrendered or have been captured are treated humanely and in line with international law.[95]

Subsequent to this statement, the UNSC adopted Resolution 2328, which accepted direct UN involvement in the East Aleppo evacuation process, even if only through the observation and monitoring of the situation. Specifically, this Resolution:

> [Requested] the United Nations and other relevant institutions to carry out adequate, neutral monitoring and direct observation on evacuations from the eastern districts of Aleppo and other districts of the city, and to report as appropriate thereon.[96]

The UN's seemingly contradictory stance in the East Aleppo evacuation as compared to those of Daraya and Al-Waer requires further discernment of what its role (and that of other international actors) should be when forcible displacement is pursued in the context of wider mass atrocity situations.

On close analysis, it becomes apparent that although the UN assumed opposing courses of action for the Daraya and Al-Waer evacuations as opposed to the East Aleppo evacuation, its legal position was, in fact, unchanged. Importantly, when the UN accepted involvement in the East Aleppo evacuation in the form of monitoring and direct observation, it did so based on the expectation (although deeply flawed, as discussed below) that this evacuation satisfied (or would satisfy) the conditions for a lawful evacuation as opposed to an unlawful forcible displacement. This is apparent through the wording of Paragraph 2 of UNSC Resolution 2328, which stressed that 'these evacuations must be conducted in accordance with international humanitarian law and principles and . . . must be voluntary and to final destinations of [civilians'] choice.'[97]

This passage within UNSC Resolution 2328 highlights two ways in which the UN maintained – or attempted to maintain – that the East Aleppo evacuation satisfied or would satisfy the requirements for a lawful evacuation. First, it

95 UNSC 7834th Meeting (13 December 2016) UN Doc S/PV.7834, 2.
96 UNSC Res 2328 (19 December 2016) UN Doc S/RES/2328, [3].
97 Ibid, [2].

emphasised that the evacuation 'must be conducted in accordance with international humanitarian law and principles'.[98] This provision can be interpreted as not only calling for the lawful treatment of evacuees during and after the process of displacement in accordance with IHL (discussed further in the next section), but also as demanding that the evacuation itself be justified under IHL, for example by satisfying one or both of the exceptions to the prohibition against forcible displacement, namely the security of civilians or military necessity.[99]

Second, UNSC Resolution 2328 stressed that the East Aleppo evacuation must be 'voluntary and to final destinations of [civilians'] choice'.[100] As described earlier in this chapter, consent to an evacuation can overcome its otherwise unlawful nature and would, in fact, be representative of the right to freedom of movement as per Article 12 ICCPR.[101] However, it has also been stressed that such consent must be given freely as opposed to under duress.[102]

Despite the UN's attempt to justify its involvement in the East Aleppo evacuation process by referring to it as compliant with IHL and/or as premised on the voluntary consent of the evacuees, the reality was that the evacuation did not meet these international legal standards and, in fact, constituted an instance of unlawful forcible displacement. This represented the official conclusion published by the Commission of Inquiry on Syria in its February 2017 report:

> As warring parties agreed to the evacuation of eastern Aleppo for strategic reasons – and not for the security of civilians or imperative military necessity, which permit the displacement of thousands – *the Aleppo evacuation agreement amounts to the war crime of forced displacement.*[103]

As stated by the Commission of Inquiry, it is clear that the East Aleppo evacuation was not undertaken for reasons of military necessity or security of civilians, the two exceptions to the prohibition against forcible displacement as per IHL.[104] Similar to the analysis conducted with respect to the Daraya case,[105] the evacuation of combatants from East Aleppo meant that there was no remaining military imperative to evacuate civilians, neither was there any remaining fear for their security. Similarly, any consent provided in the context of the East Aleppo evacuation can be deemed invalid given the coercive environment surrounding the displacement process, which effectively meant that civilians who 'elected' to leave the city were not, in fact, exercising a genuine choice. This seems to be acknowledged within

98 Ibid.
99 *See* n21–29 and accompanying text.
100 UN Doc S/RES/2328, n96, [2].
101 *See* nn43–45 and accompanying text.
102 *See* nn46–48.
103 UN Doc A/HRC/34/64, n68, [93] (emphasis added).
104 *See* nn21–29 and accompanying text.
105 *See* n30 and accompanying paragraph.

Resolution 2328 itself, as it calls in Paragraph 2 for the protection of civilians 'who choose *or who have been forced* to be evacuated' from East Aleppo.[106] This phrase offers a clear recognition that there was an element of coercion underlying the East Aleppo evacuation despite calls within the Resolution that the evacuation must be voluntary.

For humanitarian or other reasons, the UN became involved – although indirectly – in a clearly unlawful forcible displacement of civilians from East Aleppo. It was careful, however, not to portray its involvement as such, but rather attempted to frame the process as an evacuation that would both conform to IHL and be premised on the voluntary consent of the evacuees. This means that legally speaking, the UN was consistent with its positions in both the Daraya and Al-Waer evacuations in which it stressed that it could not and would not become involved in unlawful forcible displacement.

Questions regarding the potential international legal responsibility of the UN or other international actors for their involvement in a process of forcible displacement have never been brought forward before an international judicial body. Clearly, however, the UN's position with respect to all of the Daraya, Al-Waer and East Aleppo evacuations points to its belief that it should not be involved in such unlawful processes. Examining this issue from a wider perspective, it is argued that the role of the UN and other international actors should arise far before they are forced to make the difficult choice of, on the one hand, participating in an unlawful forcible displacement that may mitigate abuses against evacuees, or, on the other hand, standing back and doing nothing in the name of non-involvement in an unlawful process. Principle 5 of the Guiding Principles on Internal Displacement offers some support on this point:

> All authorities and international actors shall respect and ensure respect for their obligations under international law, including human rights and humanitarian law, in all circumstances, so as to prevent and avoid conditions that might lead to displacement of persons.[107]

This Principle emphasises that respecting and ensuring respect for IHL and IHRL obligations can help to avoid situations in which civilians become subject to forcible displacement, a notion that is met with the support of international legal scholars.[108]

A preventative role of international actors in minimising the risk of forcible displacement furthermore reflects the essence of the emerging 'responsibility to

106 UN Doc S/RES/2328, n96, [3] (emphasis added). *See also* UN Doc A/HRC/34/64, n68, [104].

107 Guiding Principles on Internal Displacement, n13 Principle 5.

108 Jacques, n20, 20; Kälin Annotations, n20, 25; Lavoyer, n19, 468; Bugnion F. (2004–2005), 'Refugees, internally displaced persons, and international humanitarian law', *Fordham International Law Journal*, Vol. 28, 1397, 1407.

protect' (R2P) doctrine. This doctrine, although not a binding treaty, was endorsed unanimously through UN General Assembly (UNGA) Resolution 60/1 in 2005 and is thus representative of State consensus.[109] R2P imparts a primary responsibility on a host State to protect its population from mass atrocity crimes – namely genocide, war crimes, crimes against humanity and ethnic cleansing – and attributes a secondary responsibility to the international community to take positive measures to assist the State in its prevention obligations.[110] In the case that such prevention efforts fail, R2P calls on States to react to the commission of these crimes, including through the authorised use of armed force if necessary and as a last resort.[111] Although a great deal of controversy persists with respect to the enforcement of R2P – most particularly with respect to the role that the use of force can or should assume under this doctrine – one of the underlying assumptions within the doctrine, namely that the international community as a whole bears a degree of responsibility for preventing and reacting to mass atrocity crimes, holds fundamental agreement as demonstrated through the consensus in adopting UNGA Resolution 60/1.

Therefore, with respect to both East Aleppo and Daraya, the focus of the UN, and indeed of the wider international community, should have been to take positive measures to prevent or address the underlying causes that contributed directly to the outcome of forcible displacement, namely the sustained IHL and IHRL violations described in previous sections.[112] Unfortunately, however, not only did the UN support and become directly involved in the East Aleppo displacement process through monitoring and observation and not only was it unable to protect the civilians of East Aleppo from the sustained IHL and IHRL violations that contributed directly to the forcible displacement, but it was also unable to ensure the protection of the evacuees during and after their transportation to non-State controlled areas within Syria. Legal issues pertaining to the protection of IDPs from both East Aleppo and Daraya are discussed in the next section.

4 IDP protection rights

In addition to calling for an evacuation of East Aleppo that was voluntary and conformed to IHL, UNSC Resolution 2328 further stressed that 'protection must be provided to all civilians who choose or who have been forced to be evacuated

109 UNGA Res 60/1 (24 October 2005) UN Doc A/RES/60/1.

110 International Commission on Intervention and State Sovereignty, 'The Responsibility to Protect: The Report of the International Commission on Intervention and State Sovereignty' (*International Development Research Centre*, 2001), [2.30]–[2.31] http://www.un.org/ga/search/view_doc.asp?symbol=A/59/565; UNGA, '2005 World Summit Outcome' UNGA 60th Session UN Doc A/60/L.1 (2005), [138]–[39]; Evans G. (2008), *The Responsibility to Protect: Ending Mass Atrocity Crimes Once and for All* (Brookings Institution Press) 42.

111 Ibid.

112 *See* nn49–62 and 80–88 and accompanying text.

and those who opt to remain in their homes.'[113] This provision presents another dimension to the rights of the displaced, namely their protection throughout and after the process of displacement. Importantly, Jacques states that the 'conditions under which displacement is actually carried out constitute an essential element for the determination of the lawfulness of the displacement',[114] meaning that even displacements undertaken for the justified reasons of military necessity or the security of civilians can nevertheless incur the international legal responsibility of the parties involved for a failure to protect the rights of the displaced during or subsequent to the process of displacement. Such rights include, as per the Guiding Principles on Internal Displacement (supported by existing international legal norms, as discussed below), the rights to life, accommodation and 'conditions of safety, nutrition, health and hygiene'.[115] Kälin stresses that these obligations 'apply, in principle, whether or not displacement is permissible',[116] which means that obligations to uphold the rights of the displaced apply irrespective of the legality of the displacement itself (similar to how the obligation to observe IHL exists regardless of whether the actual use of force is lawful).

The general protections that must be accorded to the internally displaced, applicable to those who were displaced from both East Aleppo as well as Daraya, are laid out in Principle 7(2) of the Guiding Principles on Internal Displacement:

> The authorities undertaking such displacement shall ensure, to the greatest practicable extent, that proper accommodation is provided to the displaced persons, that such displacements are effected in satisfactory conditions of safety, nutrition, health and hygiene, and that members of the same family are not separated.[117]

This Principle, therefore, endeavours to guarantee basic rights of accommodation, safety, nutrition, health and hygiene for the internally displaced and is premised on existing provisions under both IHL and IHRL. Under IHL, for example, both Article 17(1) APII as well as the ICRC's Rule 131 on customary humanitarian law affirm the above-mentioned rights for the displaced in NIACs (as in Syria).[118] Under IHRL, a number of provisions from the ICCPR as well as from the International Covenant on Economic, Social and Cultural Rights (ICESCR) – both of which Syria is a party to – further reinforce protection rights for the

113 UNSC Res 2328, n96, [2].

114 Jacques, n20, 57.

115 'Guiding Principles on Internal Displacement', n13, Principles 7(2), 8, 10–12, 18, 21; APII, n16, Art 17(1); 'Rule 131. Treatment of Displaced Persons' (*ICRC*, 2017) https://ihl-databases.icrc.org/customary-ihl/eng/docs/v1_rul_rule131; 'Rule 133. Property Rights of Displaced Persons' (*ICRC*, 2017) https://ihl-databases.icrc.org/customary-ihl/eng/docs/v1_rul_rule133.

116 Kälin Annotations, n20, 37.

117 'Guiding Principles on Internal Displacement', n13, Principle 7(2).

118 APII, n16, Art 17(1); 'Rule 131. Treatment of Displaced Persons', n115.

displaced. Such rights are enshrined, for example, in Article 6 ICCPR right to life;[119]Article 12 ICCPR right to freedom of movement;[120] and Article 11(1) ICESCR right to an 'adequate standard of living', which includes 'adequate food, clothing and housing'.[121]

It is unclear, however, who bears the primary responsibility for ensuring the above-mentioned rights of IDPs, and the Guiding Principles themselves, as illustrated below, fail to provide a satisfactory answer to this question. On the one hand, the Syrian authorities not only represent the State, but they furthermore hold primary culpability for the forcible displacements in both Daraya and East Aleppo as has already been detailed. On the other hand, however, a large proportion of civilians from both cities were displaced to areas under opposition control, meaning that they came under the direct care of opposition forces rather than of the State itself.

Examining this issue from an IHL perspective, it is recalled that obligations to respect the laws of war are binding on all parties to an armed conflict.[122] In NIACs, for example, Common Article 3 to the Geneva Conventions states that 'each *Party* to the conflict shall be bound to apply, as a minimum, the following provisions.'[123] The reference to 'parties' and not 'States' has been interpreted as encompassing NSAs in the scope of application.[124] APII in turn 'develops and supplements [Common Article 3] without modifying its existing conditions of application',[125] meaning that its provisions also apply to both State and non-State actors involved in NIACs.[126] The Guiding Principles on Internal Displacement support this approach, as Principle 2(1) stresses that the document 'shall be observed by all authorities, groups and persons irrespective of their legal status and applied without any adverse distinction'.[127] With respect to the Syrian cases of Daraya and East Aleppo, these provisions imply that both the State and non-State actors are obligated to uphold the rights of the displaced in terms of securing their accommodation, safety, nutrition, health and hygiene as per Article 17(1) APII as well as the ICRC's Rule 131 on customary humanitarian law.[128] They do not,

119 ICCPR, n45, Art 6.

120 Ibid, Art 12.

121 International Covenant on Economic, Social and Cultural Rights (adopted 16 December 1966, entered into force 3 January 1976) 993 UNTS 3 Art 11(1) [hereinafter ICESCR].

122 Berkes, n92, 162; Rondeau, n92, 256.

123 GCIV, n33, Art 3 (emphasis added).

124 Ryngaert C., van de Meulebroucke A. (2012), 'Enhancing and enforcing compliance with international humanitarian law by non-state armed groups: an inquiry into some mechanisms', *JCSL*, Vol. 16, 443, 464; Murray D. (2014), 'How international humanitarian law treaties bind non-state armed groups', *JCSL*, Vol. 20, 101, 125; Berkes, n92, 162.

125 APII, n16, Art 1. *See also* Murray, n124, 125; Cassese A. (2008), 'The status of rebels under the 1977 Geneva Protocol on Non-International Armed Conflicts', *ICLQ*, Vol. 30, 416, 424.

126 Berkes, n92, 162; Rondeau, n92, 256.

127 'Guiding Principles on Internal Displacement', n13, Principle 2(1).

128 *See* n118.

however, indicate which party holds primary responsibility for the fulfilment of these rights.

Further guidance in this respect can be extracted from the ICTY's *Blagojević* case, which stressed that 'the evacuating party' assumes the primary responsibility in upholding the rights of the displaced in both international and non-international armed conflicts.[129] It premised this conclusion on Article 49 GCIV, which imparted such protection obligations on '[t]he Occupying Power undertaking such transfers or evacuations'.[130] The Trial Chamber noted that although no similar provision exists within APII with respect to NIACs, it 'does not find any reason why this general principle should not be applicable also to non-international armed conflicts'.[131] Principle 7(2) of the Guiding Principles reinforces this conclusion and states that '[t]he authorities undertaking such displacement' shall ensure the aforementioned rights of the displaced to accommodation, safety, nutrition, health and hygiene.[132] In both Daraya and East Aleppo, the forcible displacements were pursued primarily by the Assad regime, thus imparting primary responsibility on it in upholding the rights of the displaced as per the above provisions deriving from IHL.

An examination of the same issue from an IHRL perspective, however, proceeds differently. While there is a compelling argument that IHRL norms are binding on both State and non-State actors (although this notion is in itself controversial),[133] it is commonly recognised that the State holds the primary responsibility to ensure the fulfillment of human rights for individuals under its jurisdiction. Under the concept of due diligence, for example, a State assumes a minimum 'standard of care' to ensure that applicable human rights norms are upheld by all parties within its jurisdiction, including by NSAs.[134] In this manner, a State can be held responsible for human rights breaches, even those committed by NSAs, if it fails to exercise due diligence to prevent or address them.[135] Additionally, in the *Case of Ilaşcu and Others v Moldova and Russia* (*Ilaşcu* case), the European Court of Human Rights found that a State's human rights obligations continue to exist even if it does not exercise effective control over parts of its territory, as may be the case in situations

129 *Blagojević* case, n20, [599].
130 GCIV, n33, Art 49.
131 *Blagojević* case, n20, [599].
132 'Guiding Principles on Internal Displacement', n13, Principle 7(2).
133 *See* Rodenhäuser T. (2012), 'Human rights obligations of non-state armed groups in other situations of violence: the Syria example', *IHLS*, Vol. 3, 263, 269; A/HRC/21/50 (n3), [134]. *See*, however, Hessbruegge J.A. (2005), 'Human rights violations arising from conduct of non-state actors', *BHRLR*, Vol. 11, 21, 31; McCorquodale R. (2002), 'Overlegalizing silences: human rights and nonstate actors', *ASILP*, Vol. 96, 384, 385.
134 Heieck J. (2016), 'The responsibility not to veto revisited: how the duty to prevent genocide as a jus cogens norm imposes a legal duty not to veto on the five permanent Members of the Security Council' in Barnes R. and Tzevelekos V.P. (eds.), *Beyond Responsibility to Protect: Generating Change in International Law* (Intersentia) 112.
135 Ryngaert C. (2015), 'State responsibility and non-state actors' in Noortmann M. *et al.* (eds.), *Non-State Actors in International Law* (Hart Publishing) 164; Rodenhäuser, n133, 269.

of armed conflict. The Court conceded that 'such a factual situation reduces the scope of [a State's] jurisdiction', although it nevertheless determined that the State would still possess a duty to 'endeavour, with all the legal and diplomatic means available to it *vis-à-vis* foreign States and international organisations, to continue to guarantee the enjoyment of the rights and freedoms defined in the Convention'.[136]

With respect to forcible displacement, therefore, the IHRL framework imparts a primary obligation on the State, rather than the party undertaking displacement as per IHL, to uphold the rights of the displaced. This obligation would continue to exist, under the concept of due diligence and the findings of the *Ilaşcu* case, even if the State fails to exercise authority over a certain part of its territory. This is reflected in Principle 3(1) of the Guiding Principles, which stresses that '[n]ational authorities have the primary duty and responsibility to provide protection and humanitarian assistance to internally displaced persons within their jurisdiction.'[137] In the case of Syria, this attributes primary responsibility to the Assad regime for the protection of the displaced from Daraya and East Aleppo. This means that even if the evacuees were resettled to opposition-held territory in which the regime did not hold *de facto* control, the Syrian State retained a degree of responsibility to ensure and uphold their rights.

In the Syrian case, therefore, all of IHL, IHRL and the Guiding Principles on Internal Displacement reinforce the primary responsibility of the Syrian authorities to ensure the rights of the internally displaced from Daraya and East Aleppo, both as the party which undertook the forcible displacements but also as the party representing the State. An important question emerges, however, regarding who the primary bearers of this responsibility would be had the forcible displacement been undertaken primarily by NSAs. In such a case, Principle 7(2) of the Guiding Principles, deriving from IHL and placing such responsibility on the 'authorities undertaking such displacement', would point to NSAs, whereas Principle 3(1), deriving from IHRL and imparting responsibility on '[n]ational authorities', would point to the host State.

There is no clear explanation within the Guiding Principles or within academic commentary (most particularly, within Kälin's detailed annotations on the Guiding Principles) regarding the distinction between Principles 7(2) and 3(1) (most particularly, in the context of NIACs), neither is the apparent contradiction between their provisions addressed or explained. Guidance from the UN similarly fails to offer any conclusive determination regarding the primary bearers of responsibility towards IDPs, as it places '[p]rimary responsibility for protecting internally displaced persons . . . with the national authorities of the country', but simultaneously acknowledges that '[i]n situations of armed conflict, all parties to the conflict, both State and non-State actors, have a responsibility to . . . [provide]

136 *Case of Ilaşcu and Others v Moldova and Russia* (App no 48787/99) ECHR 8 July 2004, [333] [hereinafter *Ilaşcu* case].

137 'Guiding Principles on Internal Displacement', n13, Principle 3(1).

protection and assistance to the civilian population.'[138] Importantly, even in the latter situation of armed conflict, the UN fails to offer guidance regarding the attribution of primary responsibility for the protection of IDPs (for example, whether this should be made on the basis of the party that undertakes the displacement or the party that holds effective control over the territory to which IDPs are displaced). Such ambiguities must be addressed in order to allow for the clear identification of bearers of responsibility towards IDPS in situations of forcible displacement, particularly within NIACs.

Despite the clear legal responsibility of the Assad regime under all of IHL, IHRL and the Guiding Principles to guarantee the rights of the internally displaced from both Daraya and East Aleppo, interviewees from both cities affirm that it assumed no such responsibilities towards the vast majority who were resettled to opposition-controlled territory. Any humanitarian efforts that did materialise to assist these IDPs were conducted by the UN or by other aid agencies out of a humanitarian motive rather than pursuant to efforts or facilitations by the regime to fulfil its obligations in this regard.[139] Additionally, despite such humanitarian efforts, conditions facing these displaced persons were lacking in the minimum standards and protections. Idlib, for example, to where many of the Daraya and East Aleppo evacuees were displaced, was already home to 700,000 IDPs, more than 130,000 of whom were staying in makeshift camps.[140] This meant that basic services – including the provision of aid, medical care and housing – were extremely strained.[141] Furthermore, clashes and infighting existed between various armed opposition factions,[142] which, although seemingly not directed against civilians or IDPs, inevitably contribute to a deteriorated security situation. Such conditions ran counter to the provisions of Principles 7(2), 18 and 19 of the Guiding Principles detailing the rights of IDPs to accommodation, safety, nutrition, health and hygiene.[143]

Not only did the Syrian authorities fail to assume their obligations towards IDPs from Daraya and East Aleppo, but they furthermore, along with Russian forces, deliberately and indiscriminately targeted areas to which they had resettled (most particularly, Idlib).[144] This included, for example, a particularly egregious

138 'Handbook for the Protection of Internally Displaced Persons' (*UN Office of the High Commissioner for Rights*, 2009) 9–10 – http://www.unhcr.org/4c2355229.pdf.

139 UN Doc S/2017/58, n71, [7]–[8] ; 'Clarifications on the Daraya evacuation process' (*Local Council of Daraya City*, 28 August 2016) https://www.facebook.com/daraya.council/posts/539308612930378.

140 'What next for Syrians who fled Aleppo?' (*International Rescue Committee*, 20 January 2017) https://www.rescue.org/article/what-next-syrians-who-fled-aleppo.

141 'Aleppo battle: what next for the evacuees?' (*BBC News*, 21 December 2016) http://www.bbc.co.uk/ news/world-middle-east-38340165; 'Can Aleppo's displaced survive in Idlib?' (*Al-Monitor*, 5 January 20187) http://www.al-monitor.com/pulse/originals/2017/01/syria-aleppo-displaced-idlib-lack-opportunities.html# ixzz4XNjldrWb.

142 UN Doc S/2017/339, n42, [12].

143 'Guiding Principles on Internal Displacement', n13, Principles 7(2), 18–19.

144 *See* UN Doc S/2017/339, n42, [20]–[21]; Report of the Secretary-General,

chemical attack on the city of Khan Sheikhoun in Idlib province on 4 April 2017 which led to the deaths of 29 IDPs.[145] UN Special Envoy to Syria Staffan de Mistura forewarned of such consequences when he stated in December 2016 that '[i]f there is no political agreement and a ceasefire, Idlib will become the next Aleppo.'[146] President Assad himself signalled intent to make Idlib the target of 'cleaning' in an October 2016 interview:

> You cannot cut, because Idlib is adjacent to Turkey, it's right on the Syrian-Turkish borders. So you cannot cut; you have to clean. You have to keep cleaning this area and to push the terrorists to Turkey to go back to where they come from, or to kill them. There's no other option.[147]

The indiscriminate attacks against Idlib, including against areas known to host IDPs, violate Principle 10(2) of the Guiding Principles on Internal Displacement, which prohibits '[a]ttacks or other acts of violence against internally displaced persons who do not or no longer participate in hostilities' and which specifically mentions attacks on IDP 'camps or settlements' as part of this prohibition.[148] Additionally, Lavoyer points out that IDPs, as long as they do not take up arms, are accorded civilian protection rights under IHL.[149] As such, the fundamental IHL rules of distinction as well as the prohibition against indiscriminate attacks continue to apply to IDPs.[150]

Overall, therefore, the Assad regime not only fell short of taking measures to uphold the rights of the displaced from Daraya and East Aleppo (as per its obligations under IHL and IHRL as the evacuating party and as the party representing the State, respectively), but it furthermore subjected areas to which they were known to have resettled to indiscriminate bombardment. This had detrimental effects on the safety and well-being of IDPs in violation of their rights stipulated within the Guiding Principles on Internal Displacement and supported

'Implementation of Security Council resolutions 2139 (2014), 2165 (2014), 2191 (2014), 2258 (2015) and 2332 (2016)' (16 February 2017) UN Doc S/2017/144 Table 1; Report of the Secretary-General, 'Implementation of Security Council resolutions 2139 (2014), 2165 (2014), 2191 (2014), 2258 (2015) and 2332 (2016)' (22 March 2017) UN Doc S/2017/244 Table 1; 'Russian Warplanes Target IDPs in Idlib City' (*Syrian Network for Human Rights*, 11 April 2017) 2 http://sn4hr.org/wp-content/pdf/english/Russian_aircraft_targets_displaced_people_in_Idlib_en.pdf.

145 Priyanka Gupta, 'Khan Sheikhoun attack survivors recall horror' (*Aljazeera*, 5 May 2017) http://www.aljazeera.com/indepth/features/2017/05/khan-sheikhoun-attack-survivors-recall-horror-170503130351120.html.

146 'Aleppo battle: What next for the evacuees?', n141.

147 'President al-Assad's interview given to Russia's Komsomolskaya Pravda newspaper-VIDEO' (*Syrian Arab News Agency*, 14 October 2016) http://sana.sy/en/?p=90442.

148 'Guiding Principles on Internal Displacement', n13, Principle 10(2).

149 Lavoyer, n19, 470.

150 'Rule 1. The Principle of Distinction between Civilians and Combatants', n53; 'Rule 11. Indiscriminate Attacks', n53.

by existing IHL and IHRL. Additionally, there remain a host of other issues pertaining to the rights of IDPs from Daraya, East Aleppo and elsewhere that have not been adequately addressed at the national or international levels, including on their rights to return to their homes and to property restitution or compensation.[151] While these issues will perhaps be addressed through the conclusion of a political agreement to end the conflict, it is currently unclear whether or how IDPs will be guaranteed these rights in a post-conflict Syria.

5 Conclusion

This chapter established that neither the Daraya nor the East Aleppo evacuations in Syria satisfied the recognised exceptions (under both IHL and IHRL) to the international legal prohibition against forcible displacement, namely the security of civilians or military necessity. Analysis of both cases further revealed that the evacuations were not conducted pursuant to the consent of civilians despite the conclusion of formal agreements involving civilian representatives of the respective cities. As such, it is more befitting that the Daraya and East Aleppo cases – in international political and legal discourse – are referred to as displacements rather than evacuations.[152]

As discussed in this chapter, the UN assumed significantly contrasting roles in the Daraya and East Aleppo displacements despite maintaining a consistent legal position regarding its non-involvement in such unlawful processes. In Daraya, the UN was opposed to the evacuation of civilians and refused to assume any role within the process. In East Aleppo, however, it formally endorsed the evacuation although it stressed that it must conform to IHL and IHRL norms and must be conducted on a voluntary basis (neither of which it did). This discrepancy highlights a need for further discussion regarding the role that the international community can or should assume in situations in which forcible displacement is inevitable in the context of wider mass atrocity situations. It was suggested that a greater emphasis on prevention efforts by the international community – as

151 *See*, for example, Unruh J.D. (2016), 'Weaponization of the land and property rights system in the Syrian civil war: facilitating restitution?', *JISB*, Vol. 10, 453, 458–463; 'Housing land and property (HLP) in the Syrian Arab Republic' (*Norwegian Refugee Council*, May 2016) https://www.nrc.no/globalassets/pdf/ reports/housing-land-and-property-hlp-in-the-syrian-arab-republic.pdf; Chulov M., 'Iran repopulates Syria with Shia Muslims to help tighten regime's control' (*The Guardian*,14 January 2017) https://www.theguardian.com/world/2017/jan/13/irans-syria-project-pushing-population-shifts-to-increase-influence?CMP=share_btn_fb; 'Silent sectarian cleansing: Iranian role in mass demolitions and population transfers in Syria' (*Naame Shaam*, May 2015) http://online.wsj.com/public/resources/documents/NaameShaamReport 05182015.pdf; Khatib L. *et al.*, 'Western policy towards Syria: applying lessons learned' (*Chatham House*, March 2017) 10 – https://www.chathamhouse.org/sites/files/chathamhouse/publications/research/2017-03-15-western-policy-towards-syria-lessons-learned.pdf.

152 The term 'evacuation' implies that the displacement is justified under international law. *Blagojević* case, n20, [597].

advocated by the emerging R2P doctrine – can help to mitigate the risk of forcible displacement in the first instance.

Another issue that was noted within this chapter to require further clarification and development of the law pertains to the specific bearers of responsibility for the protection of IDPs. It was highlighted that IHL imparts such protection responsibilities primarily on the party that undertakes the displacement (whether State or non-State), while IHRL attributes them primarily to the State. In Syria, both IHL and IHRL frameworks point to the primary responsibility of the Assad regime for ensuring the protection of IDPs, although it was noted that the two frameworks may not always act in convergence (for example, in situations in which forcible displacement is undertaken by NSAs rather than State forces). Additionally, the Guiding Principles on Internal Displacement fail to address this discrepancy, but rather contain contrasting provisions (Principles 3(1) and 7(2)) that invoke IHRL and IHL frameworks, respectively, without distinguishing between their spheres of application. Given that questions pertaining to IDP rights in Syria will become increasingly prominent over the coming months and years, especially as IDPs seek to return to their homes and seek property restitution and/or compensation, this legal issue must receive increased attention from the international community.

Bibliography

Books

Evans G. (2008), *The Responsibility to Protect: Ending Mass Atrocity Crimes Once and for All* (Brookings Institution Press).

Jacques M. (2012), *Armed Conflict and Displacement: The Protection of Refugees and Displaced Persons under International Humanitarian Law* (Cambridge University Press).

Schabas W. (2010), *The International Criminal Court: A Commentary on the Rome Statute* (Oxford University Press).

Zimmermann B. *et al.* (1987), *Commentary on the Additional Protocols of 8 June 1977 to the Geneva Conventions of 12 August 1949* (Brill/Nijhoff).

Book chapters

Berkes A. (2016), '*De Facto* Regimes and the Responsibility to Protect' in Barnes R. and Tzevelekos V.P. (eds.), *Beyond Responsibility to Protect: Generating Change in International Law* (Intersentia).

Heieck J. (2016), 'The Responsibility Not to Veto Revisited: How the Duty to Prevent Genocide as a Jus Cogens Norm Imposes a Legal Duty Not to Veto on the Five Permanent Members of the Security Council' in Barnes R. and Tzevelekos V.P. (eds.), *Beyond Responsibility to Protect: Generating Change in International Law* (Intersentia).

Rondeau S. (2016), 'The Responsibility to Protect Doctrine, and the Duty of the International Community to Reinforce International Humanitarian Law and its Protective Value for Civilian Populations' in Barnes R. and Tzevelekos V.P.

(eds.), *Beyond Responsibility to Protect: Generating Change in International Law* (Intersentia).

Ryngaert C. (2015), 'State Responsibility and Non-State Actors' in Noortmann M. *et al.* (eds.), *Non-State Actors in International Law* (Hart Publishing).

Journal articles

Abebe A.M. (2011), 'Special rapporteurs as law makers: the developments and evolution of the normative framework for protecting and assisting internally displaced persons', *International Journal of Human Rights*, vol. 15, 286.

Bugnion F. (2004–2005), 'Refugees, internally displaced persons, and international humanitarian law', *Fordham International Law Journal,* Vol. 28, 1397.

Cassese A. (2008), 'The status of rebels under the 1977 Geneva Protocol on Non-International Armed Conflicts', *ICLQ,* Vol. 30, 416.

Hessbruegge J.A. (2005), 'Human rights violations arising from conduct of non-state actors', *Buffalo Human Rights Law Review*, Vol. 11, 21.

Kälin W. (2005), 'The Guiding Principles on Internal Displacement as international minimum standard and protection tool', *Refugee Survey Quarterly*, Vol. 24, 27.

Kälin W. (2008), 'Guiding Principles on Internal Displacement: annotations', *American Society of International Law and the Brookings Institution*, Vol. 38, https://www.brookings.edu/wp-content/uploads/2016/06/spring_ guiding_ principles.pdf.

Lavoyer J.P. (1998), 'Guiding Principles on Internal Displacement: a few comments on the contribution of international humanitarian law', *International Review of the Red Cross,* Vol. 38, 324.

McCorquodale R. (2002), 'Overlegalizing silences: human rights and nonstate actors', *ASIL Proceedings*, Vol. 96, 384.

Murray D. (2014), 'How international humanitarian law treaties bind non-state armed groups', *Journal of Conflict & Security Law*, Vol. 20, 101.

Rodenhäuser T. (2012), 'Human rights obligations of non-state armed groups in other rituations of violence: the Syria example', *International Humanitarian Legal Studies,* Vol. 3, 263.

Ryngaert C. and van de Meulebroucke A. (2012), 'Enhancing and enforcing compliance with international humanitarian law by non-state armed groups: an inquiry into some mechanisms', *Journal of Conflict & Security Law*, Vol. 16, 443.

Unruh J.D. (2016), 'Weaponization of the land and property rights system in the Syrian civil war: facilitating restitution?', *Journal of Intervention and State Building,* Vol. 10, 453.

8 Collective dislocation

Crimes of displacement, property deprivation and discrimination under international criminal law

Matthew Gillett[1]

1 Introduction

Displacement, discrimination and property crimes collectively fuel a self-reinforcing cycle of criminality that can result in the mass expulsion of peoples from their homelands. Many cases prosecuted at the International Criminal Tribunal for the former Yugoslavia ("ICTY") have borne out this paradigm.[2] Several cases scheduled for the International Criminal Court ("ICC") allege discriminatory expulsions and will raise questions of the nature and proof of forcible displacement.[3] As such, it is important to examine the nature of crimes related to and causative of the mass displacement of people, and to assess the means by which such criminal allegations can be substantiated in international courts.

The conventional view of ethnic cleansing[4] sees killings, rapes, torture and beatings being perpetrated on an ethnic basis with the intent of driving the remaining victims out of a territory. Many cases prosecuted under international criminal law bear out this conception. However, ethnic cleansing is not only carried out through brutal physical violence against human victims. It can also be achieved through administrative, financial and other measures that target peoples' livelihoods and means of survival. As invidious as these methods of administrative expulsion are, they are equally under-researched. In the absence of informed analysis of ethnic

1 Matthew Gillett is a Trial Attorney and Appeals Counsel at the ICTY. Any views expressed in these materials are those of the author alone and do not necessarily reflect the views of the ICTY or the United Nations in general.

2 Acquiviva G. (2011), "Forced Displacement and International Crimes", UNHCR, *Legal and Protection Policy Research Series*, 13.

3 For example, forcible transfer and displacement carried out on a large scale and along ethnic lines in the Democratic Republic of Congo feature centrally in the confirmed charges against *Ntaganda* at the ICC; see *Decision Pursuant to Article 61(7)(a) and (b) of the Rome Statute on the Charges of the Prosecutor Against Bosco Ntaganda*, 9 June 2014, [123] and [148].

4 The Commission of Experts on the former Yugoslavia defined ethnic cleansing as follows: "The expression 'ethnic cleansing' is relatively new. Considered in the context of the conflicts in the former Yugoslavia, 'ethnic cleansing' means rendering an area ethnically homogenous by using force or intimidation to remove persons of given groups from the area." Commission of Experts, First Interim Report (S/25274), [55].

cleansing as a holistic phenomenon, the understanding of how expulsion occurs will remain fragmented and undeveloped. The analysis in this chapter seeks to shine light on the various means ranging from direct physical violence to regulatory measures used to force people to leave their homes and communities.

This study explores the legal landscape applicable to the triple threat of displacement crimes, property crimes and persecution. After setting out the legal elements of the crimes, the analysis then examines the type of evidence that can demonstrate these crimes. Using case studies, it explores the interconnectedness of these various forms of violent and non-violent expulsion.

2 The nature of displacement crimes

In light of the crimes dealt with at international criminal courts, which include murder, rape and genocide, there is sometimes an under-appreciation of the gravity of displacement crimes. However, in many conflicts, displacement crimes are the most severe in terms of sheer numbers of victims. For example, after concluding a visit to the former Yugoslavia during the conflict in the 1990s, Mr Tadeusz Mazowiecki, Special Rapporteur of the Commission on Human Rights, noted that:

> Over 2.1 million people have been displaced from their homes since the war in Bosnia and Herzegovina began – nearly 50 per cent of the population recorded in the census of 1991. Some 800,000 of them are estimated to have sought refuge outside Bosnia and Herzegovina; the rest are seeking refuge inside the country.[5]

The Special Rapporteur observed that large-scale population movements were used "in order to achieve 'ethnic cleansing'".[6] He noted the use of various methods, ranging from murder, to rape, to administrative measures, such as dismissal from work of non-Serbs who refused to take up dangerous work in the Bosnian Serb Army and evictions from homes, utilized to remove the population.[7]

Perhaps because of its widespread practice, forcible displacement is a crime of multiple labels. In their volume on forcible displacement, Grant Dawson and Sonia Farber note that "forcible displacement wears many linguistic guises: expulsion, transfer, deportation, migration, dislocation-illegal, involuntary, forced, coerced, and unlawful. Despite these various monikers, the objective, and too often the result, is still the same: the removal of a group of people, which often leads to their destruction."[8] Capturing the range of descriptives applied to forced displacement of peoples is necessary and enlightening. It highlights the importance of

5 Fifth periodic report on the situation of human rights in the territory of the former Yugoslavia submitted by Mr Tadeusz Mazowiecki, Special Rapporteur of the Commission on Human Rights, pursuant to paragraph 32 of Commission resolution 1993/7 of 23 February 1993; E/CN.4/1994/47, 17/11/1993 (Mazowiecki Report), [13].

6 Mazowiecki Report, ibid, [14].

7 Mazowiecki Report, ibid, [87]–[91].

8 Dawson G., Farber S. (2012), *Forcible Displacement Through the Ages* (Martinus Nijhoff) 1.

distinguishing between legitimate and illegitimate conduct, which results in the movement of peoples out of their homes. Not all transfers or deportations are legal, just as not all dislocations or expulsions are illegal. For example, civilian populations may be expelled from their homes where necessary for their own safety or where required by imperative military necessity, as discussed below. It is the function of international criminal law to elucidate the border between justified movements of persons and unlawful expulsions that amount to international crimes.

Disentangling illegal forced displacement from legitimate conduct resulting in population movements requires a holistic view of the phenomenon of displacement.

Historically, the record of forcible displacement is as long as the record of the interaction of human societies. Examples abound of mass expulsions over the centuries, some in conjunction with warfare and some conducted in highly organized strategic ways. In the 1500s CE, Incas used a system called *mitima*, or resettlement, to entrench their conquest of communities in Latin America. The occupants of newly conquered territories would be transported to other parts of the Inca Empire. In order to prevent excessive disorder, the resettlees were sent to areas resembling their original territory. Transferring peoples in this way immersed them in communities of compliant subjects, thereby facilitating their own acceptance of the Inca system, and at the same time moved productive subjects of the Inca Empire into the newly acquired territory. Equally important was the indirect effect of dislocating peoples to areas where the common culture became that of the Inca Empire.[9] Other expulsions throughout the ages have incorporated a mix of violent and regulatory measures to achieve their aims. For example, the Ottoman Government systematically expelled towards the Syrian deserts (and killed) over a million members of the Armenian minority in 1915. In 1944, the Tatars in Crimea were expelled en masse to other areas in the Soviet Union as a form of collective punishment for their collaboration with the Nazis during the Second World War. Other mass expulsions have continued to be perpetrated throughout the decades after the Second World War, including in the former Yugoslavia as described in more detail below.[10] In this light, it can be seen that the use of combined violence and regulatory coercion to move populations has a long pedigree.

To understand illegal forms of displacement, it is also apposite to look first to the underlying interests that are at stake. In *Stakic*, a trial chamber of the ICTY explained the rationale for criminalizing deportation (and forcible transfer)[11] as follows:

9 Dawson and Farber, ibid, 26–28.

10 For the details of these and other incidents, see Dawson, Farber, ibid, 3–42.

11 Deportation and forcible transfer are typically distinguished according to the final destination of the victims; when victims are forced across a State border, it is considered as deportation, whereas forcible transfer typically refers to displacements within a State; Hall C.K. (2008), “Article 7 Crimes against Humanity, B.I.2 (d) ‘Deportation or Forcible Transfer of Population’, and B.II.(d) ‘Prohibited Movements of Population’” in Triffterer O. (ed.), *Commentary on the Rome Statute of the International Criminal Court – Observers’ Notes,*

> The protected interests behind the prohibition of deportation are the right and expectation of individuals to be able to remain in their homes and communities without interference by an aggressor, whether from the same or another State. The Trial Chamber is therefore of the view that it is the *actus reus* of forcibly removing, essentially uprooting, individuals from the territory and the environment in which they have been lawfully present, in many cases for decades and generations, which is the rationale for imposing criminal responsibility and not the destination resulting from such a removal.[12]

Along with the right of individuals to stay in their communities, the Appeals Chamber of the ICTY also referred to the motivating "right not to be deprived of his or her property by being forcibly displaced to another location".[13] The Appeals Chamber's framed the underlying rights in terms that are close to, but not identical with, rights contained in the International Covenant on Civil and Political Rights, particularly Article 12(1), which provides that "Everyone lawfully within the territory of a State shall, within that territory, have the right to liberty of movement and freedom to choose his residence" and Article 17(1), which provides that: "No one shall be subjected to arbitrary or unlawful interference with his privacy, family, home or correspondence, nor to unlawful attacks on his honour and reputation."[14]

The risk of dispossession increases precipitously when an individual or family is removed from their home, because they have to pass ownership of their property to the local authorities and/or because no one is left to care for the property in their absence.[15] Thus displacement concerns not just the unsettling effects of being removed from one's home but also the potentially deadly possibility of being segregated from one's basic means of survival.

When examining the nature of displacement crimes, it is axiomatic that they can be perpetrated not only by direct physical force by also by more subtle means. The Appeals Chamber of the ICTY has noted that "the term 'forced', when used in reference to the crime of deportation, is not to be limited to physical force but includes the threat of force or coercion, such as that caused by fear of violence, duress, detention, psychological oppression or abuse of power against such person or persons or another person, or by taking advantage of a coercive environment."[16]

Article by Article (München/Oxford/Baden-Baden, C.H. Beck/Hart/Nomos) 2nd ed., 194–200, 247–251.

12 *Prosecutor v Stakic*, IT-97-24-T, ICTY, TC, Judgement, 31 July 2003, [677].

13 *Prosecutor v Stakic*, No. IT-97-24-A, ICTY, AC, Judgement, 22 March 2006, [277]. *Prosecutor v Krnojelac*, IT-97-25-A, Judgement, 17 September 2003, [218].

14 International Covenant on Civil and Political Rights, of 16 December 1966, 999 UNTS 171 ("ICCPR").

15 As noted by the Trial Chamber in *Krstic*, the harm caused by deportation includes "abandoning one's home, losing property and being displaced under duress to another location" *Prosecutor v Krstic*, Judgment, IT-98-33-T, 2 August 2001, [523].

16 Stakic, n13, [281]; *Prosecutor v Krnojelac*, IT-97-25-T, TC, Judgement, 15 March 2002, [475], citing *Krstic*, n15, [529].

Certainly, there are many cases of overt acts being charged as deportation and/or forcible transfer. For example, in the Kenya situation the Pre-Trial Chamber of the ICC considered violent physical acts such as killing, looting and destruction of property as the coercive acts through which the displacement occurred.[17] However, more nefarious methods are often employed in conjunction with overt violence to force peoples to depart their homes.

These less overtly violent means of expelling individuals and groups are often overshadowed by the sheer brutality of direct expulsions through physical violence and intimidation. Nonetheless, administrative expulsions can gravely impact large sectors of society and can have a profound effect on the well-being and even the survival of whole communities. Accordingly, this analysis addresses also administrative forms of expulsion, in order to explore their nature and the contentious issues that arise when investigating and prosecuting such conduct.

The use of a range of measures to perpetrate large-scale displacement is also a common feature that emerges from the record of displacements. Regulatory measures that can impede peoples' rights and coerce them to leave their homes are often imposed cumulatively with outright violence against members of the targeted community. In *Stakic*, a witness explained the pressure on non-Serbs to leave Prijedor, stating:

> [W]e no longer had any rights there. We no longer had the right to live, let alone own anything. Any day, somebody could come, confiscate your car, take away your house, shoot you, without ever being held responsible for it.[18]

It is notable that the witness's account references several rights violations that are recognised under international law: the right to life, the right to the free enjoyment of the home, the right to security and the right of victims to an adequate investigation and remedy into violations of their rights.[19] It is also notable that the witness recounts these violations in a successive, interconnected manner, which is typical of the underlying triggers of displacement.[20] As noted by the Commission of Experts in its report on the former Yugoslavia, acts that caused and were associated with ethnic cleansing included "mass murder, torture, rape and other forms of sexual assault; severe physical injury to civilians; mistreatment of civilian prisoners and prisoners of war; use of civilians as human shields; destruction of personal, public and cultural property; looting, theft and robbery of personal

17 *Prosecutor v Ruto and Sang*, Ch. II, ICC-01/09-01/11-373, 23 January 2012, [251], [255], [260]–[261], [265]–[266], [277].

18 *Stakic*, n12, [691] citing *Witness B*, T. 2263.

19 For the right to life, see ICCPR, Article 6, Universal Declaration of Human Rights (UDHR), Article 3; for the right to the free enjoyment of the home, see ICCPR, Article 17, UDHR, Article 12; for the right to security, see ICCPR Article 9, UDHR, Article 3, and the right of victims to an adequate investigation and remedy for violations of their rights, see ICCPR, Article 2(3), UDHR, Article 8.

20 See Acquiviva, n2, 15.

property; forced expropriation of real property; forceful displacement of civilian population; and attacks on hospitals, medical personnel and locations marked with the Red Cross/Red Crescent emblem".[21]

With this survey of the nature of forced displacement and related crimes along with the underlying interests that are protected in mind, the analysis now addresses the specific legal elements of these offences.

3 The legal elements of displacement crimes

Ethnic cleansing covers a gamut of crimes, ranging from murders to rape to misappropriations of property. The most specific crimes that are addressed in this chapter are deportation and forcible transfer, as well as persecution through these means. Displacement, whether through deportation or forcible transfer, is a crime in and of itself and does not require the commission of any other acts in order to be criminally punished. Deportation was recognized as a crime against humanity in the Nuremberg Charter.[22] Forcible transfer of population was included in the Rome Statute to make clear that transfers within a State's borders can also constitute a crime against humanity.[23] At the ICTY and the ICTR, the jurisprudence has recognized that forcible transfer can constitute the crime against humanity of "other inhumane acts" or an underlying act of persecution, as the statutes only explicitly list deportation as a crime against humanity.[24]

Having explored the nature of, and underlying interests protected by, these criminal prohibitions, it is important to examine the legal elements of these offences and highlight the legal questions that remain unresolved or subject to debate, particularly in relation to regulatory forms of expulsion.

There is a long pedigree of prohibitions against forcible displacement crimes. For example in the Lieber Code of 1863,[25] Article 23 mandated that "private citizens are no longer murdered, enslaved, or carried off to distant parts, and the inoffensive individual is as little disturbed in his private relations as the commander of the hostile troops can afford to grant in the overruling demands of a vigorous war." Subsequently, the prohibition against the forcible removal of peoples was enshrined in the Nuremberg Charter, adopted 8 August 1945.[26] Article 6(b)

21 Final Report of The Commission of Experts Established Pursuant to Security Council Resolution 780 (1992), S/1994/674, [134].

22 Hall, n11, 194–195.

23 Robinson D. (2001), "Article 7 (1)(d)—Crime Against Humanity of Deportation Or Forcible Transfer of Population" in Lee R.S. (ed.), *The International Criminal Court: Elements of Crimes and Rules of Procedure and Evidence* (Ardsley, Transnational Publishers) 86–88, 86.

24 Stakic, n13, [317].

25 The "Lieber Instructions" were a set of principles for the conduct of armed hostilities prepared by Francis Lieber and promulgated by President Lincoln which were in operation during the American Civil War; The Lieber Code (Washington, D.C., 24 April 1863).

26 Agreement by the Government of the United States of America, the Provisional Government of the French Republic, the Government of the United Kingdom and Northern Ireland and

included deportation as a war crime and Article 6(c) included deportation as a crime against humanity. The International Military Tribunal at Nuremberg interpreted deportation to cover expulsions both within and without a State's borders.[27] Deportation was also considered a crime in the Judgement of the post-Second World War International Military Tribunal,[28] the Charter of the International Military Tribunal for the Far East,[29] (Allied) Control Council Law No. 10,[30] the International Law Commission's Principles of International Law Recognised in the Charter of the Nuremberg Tribunal (IMT)[31] and the 1954 Draft Code of Offences against the Peace and Security of Mankind.[32] Forcible displacement was prohibited in Geneva Convention IV of 1949, and this prohibition was extended to forcible displacement in non-international armed conflicts in Additional Protocol II of 1977 to the Geneva Conventions.[33]

The following analysis looks, first, to the requirements under the Rome Statute of the ICC as well as the corresponding legal requirements that apply at the *ad hoc* Tribunals. It primarily focuses on jurisprudence emerging from the ICTY that has dealt with forcible displacement crimes in many of its judgments. The detailed examination is necessary as it provides the legal underpinnings and parameters for the prohibited conduct that constitutes expulsion. It sets out the consequences for those responsible for intentionally violating the rights of victims to freely choose their place of residence within their national State and not to have their family life and home interfered with.

3.1 Forcible displacement as a crime against humanity

Displacement crimes are typically charged in international proceedings as crimes against humanity, particularly as forcible transfer and deportation. Crimes against

the Government of the Union of Soviet Socialist Republics for the Prosecution and Punishment of the Major War Criminals of the European Axis, Protocol, 8 August 1945, Art. 6(a), 59 Stat. 1544, 82 *UNTS*, 279.

27 Stakic, n12, [684].

28 Stakic, n13, [276] referring to IMT Judgment, Vol I (1947), 227.

29 Stakic, ibid, referring to Article 5(c).

30 Stakic, ibid, referring to Article II(1)(c).

31 Stakic, ibid, referring to Principle VI(c).

32 Stakic ibid.

33 See, e.g., IV Geneva Convention Relative to the Protection of Civilian Persons in Time of War of 12 August 1949, Article 49 ("Individual or mass forcible transfers, as well as deportations of protected persons from occupied territory to the territory of the Occupying Power or to that of any other country, occupied or not, are prohibited, regardless of their motive"); Protocol Additional to the Geneva Conventions of 12 August 1949 and relating to the protection of victims of non-international armed conflicts (Protocol II), Geneva, 8 June 1977, 1125 *UNTS* (1979) 609, Article 17 ("The displacement of the civilian population shall not be ordered for reasons related to the conflict unless the security of the civilians involved or imperative military reasons so demand. Should such displacements have to be carried out, all possible measures shall be taken in order that the civilian population may be received under satisfactory conditions of shelter, hygiene, health, safety and nutrition").

humanity are serious attacks on human dignity or a grave humiliation/degradation of human beings.[34] They are considered so grave that they concern not just the victim or only the State involved but impact on humanity as a whole, justifying the direct application of international law.[35] Crimes against humanity are prohibited and punishable in war and in times of peace. They are not isolated or sporadic events but instead must be part of the large-scale (*widespread* practice) or organized commission of such crimes (*systematic* practice).[36] Although crimes against humanity overlap with domestic crimes such as murder, torture or cruel treatment, they can be distinguished because additional elements must be proved to show that a crime against humanity has been committed, namely, the link between the underlying crime and the existence of a widespread or systematic attack against a civilian population.[37]

In general, the following contextual elements must be shown for crimes against humanity: the existence of a widespread or systematic attack directed against a civilian population; the accused's acts were part of the widespread or systematic attack directed against the civilian population; and the accused was aware of the attack on the civilian population and that the acts for which he is criminally responsible comprised part of that attack.[38] Importantly, at the ICC there is an additional requirement that the widespread or systematic attack be "pursuant to or in furtherance of a State or organizational policy to commit such attack."[39] It is also noteworthy that, whereas at the ICTY, the Prosecution must also show the existence of an armed conflict (this is a jurisdictional requirement at the ICTY), at the ICC, the Rome Statute does not require the existence of an armed conflict to prove a crime against humanity.

Looking to the definitions of the underlying crimes, the "deportation or forcible transfer of population" under Article 7(1)(d) of the Rome Statute concerns forced displacements of persons from where they are lawfully present without grounds permitted under international law. The Elements of Crimes of the Rome Statute clarify that the term "forcibly" is not restricted to physical force, but may include threat of force or coercion, such as that caused by fear of violence, duress, detention, psychological oppression or abuse of power against such person or persons or another person or by taking advantage of a coercive environment.[40]

34 Cassese A., Gaeta P. (2008), *International Criminal Law*, 2nd ed. (Oxford University Press) 98.

35 Cassese and Gaeta, ibid, 981–01.

36 Rome Statute of the International Criminal Court, Rome, 17 July 1998, 2187 *UNTS*, Article 7(1).

37 In the context of the International Criminal Court, it is also necessary to show that the crimes were committed pursuant to a State or organizational policy; Rome Statute, ibid, Article 7(2).

38 *Prosecutor v Kunarac, Kovac and Vukovic*, IT-96-23& IT-96-23/1-A, AC, 12 June 2002, [85].

39 Rome Statute, n36, Article 7(2)(a).

40 Elements of Crimes, International Criminal Court, fn 12, https://www.icc-cpi.int/NR/rdonlyres/336923D8-A6AD-40EC-AD7B-45BF9DE73D56/0/ElementsOfCrimesEng.pdf?

In terms of the distinction between the two crimes, deportation is commonly seen as forcible displacement across a State border, whereas forcible transfer typically refers to displacements within a State.[41] At the ICTY, it has been clarified that whereas the ultimate location of the displaced person does not form part of the elements of forcible transfer; deportation has an additional element requiring that the person crosses a *de jure* or *de facto* international border.[42]

At the ICTY, forcible displacement is usually charged in three ways: first, under Article 5(d) as deportation. Second, under Article 5(i) as other inhumane acts through forcible transfer. Third, under Article 5(h) as persecution, which is the denial of fundamental rights to persons because of the identity of the group or collectivity to which they belong.[43] The forced character of the displacement is determined by the victim's absence of genuine choice in their displacement. The forced character of the transfer may be shown not only by the use of physical force but may also include threat of force or coercion, such as that caused by fear of violence, duress, detention, psychological oppression or abuse of power or by taking advantage of a coercive environment. As regards the level of causative influence that the perpetrator's acts must rise to, the Trial Chamber in *Gotovina* appeared to use a standard of the "primary and direct" cause of the displacement.[44] In Popovic *et al*, the Trial Chamber held for deportation that:

> [W]hatever the form of forced displacement as discussed below, be it by physical force, coercion or creation of coercive conditions, it must be as a result of the force—the act of the accused—that the persons are displaced across a border. In other words, for the crime of deportation it is not sufficient to prove force on the part of the accused and the ultimate location of the victims across a border. The Prosecution must also establish the link between the two elements. To do otherwise is to leave a constituent element of the crime related not to the acts of the accused but to chance or, in many cases, to a choice made by a victim. This cannot be consistent with the concept of actus reus of a crime.[45]

In relation to the requirement[46] that the victims be "lawfully present" in the location from which they are expelled, the Trial Chamber in *Popovic et al.* held

41 Goy B. (2017), "Article 7(1)(d)" in Klamberg M. (ed.), *Commentary on the Law of the International Criminal Court* (Brussels, Torkel Opsahl Academic EPublisher); *Ruto and Sang*, n17, [268].

42 *Prosecutor v Đorđević*, AC, IT-05-87/1-A, 27 January 2014, fn 2159, emphasis in original, referring to Stakic, n13, [317]; *Prosecutor v Popovic*, Judgment, IT-05-88-T, 10 June 2010, [892], [904].

43 While the same conduct cannot be the basis for convictions for both deportation and forcible transfer, it can be the basis for convictions for both persecution and either of deportation or forcible transfer; *Prosecutor v Stanisic and Zupljanin*, IT-08-91-A, 30 June 2016, [1092].

44 *Prosecutor v Gotovina and Markac*, IT-06-90-T, TC, Judgement, Vol.2, [743]–[1744].

45 *Popovic*, n42, [893].

46 Popovic, ibid, [891].

that this term should be given its common meaning and should not be equated to the legal concept of lawful residence.[47] At the ICC, the question of whether lawful presence should be determined under national or international law was ultimately left for the Court to decide.[48]

The concepts of absence of genuine choice and lawful presence will likely be the focus of litigation and further jurisprudential development in future cases at the ICTY and at other international tribunals. In particular, it is unclear whether courts will make reference to domestic law to determine lawful presence and, if not, what standard they will apply to determine lawful presence.

The displacement of the civilian population may be lawful where it is necessary "for the security of the persons involved or for imperative military reasons".[49] Evacuation is therefore an exceptional measure that is permitted when, for example, an area is in danger as a result of military operations or is liable to be subjected to intense bombing or when the presence of persons in an area hampers military operations. However, it is unlawful to use evacuation measures based on imperative military reasons as a pretext to remove the population and effectuate control over a desired territory.[50] In this respect, a case-by-case analysis will be necessary and appropriate. At the ICC, the *Ntaganda* Pre-Trial considered that the displacement of civilians was "not justified by the security of the civilians involved or by military necessity, as there [was] no indication of any precautionary measures having been taken before these acts of displacement were carried out or any reasons linked to the conduct of military operations".[51]

To determine whether deportation has occurred, it is necessary to assess whether the victims have been expelled across a border. In *Stakic*, the Prosecution noted that "it may be difficult to exactly determine the location of the borders of a country . . . particularly in situations of armed conflict" and that "internal displacement is frequently a prelude to the further transfer of individuals outside of the country."[52] The Trial Chamber adhered to this view, holding that "as many, if not most, conflicts are in some way connected with claims to territory it is often difficult, particularly several years after the conflict ends, to establish the exact or even an approximate location of a particular border at the relevant time."[53] On this basis, the Trial Chamber held that forcibly displacing persons across *de facto* borders, including constantly shifting front-lines could suffice to establish deportation. However, the Appeals Chamber overturned this aspect of the Trial

47 Popovic, ibid, [900].

48 Robinson D. (2001), "Article 7(1)(d)—Crime Against Humanity of Deportation Or Forcible Transfer of Population" in Lee R.S., Friman H. (eds.), *The International Criminal Court: Elements of Crimes and Rules of Procedure and Evidence* (Ardsley, Transnational Publishers), 86–88.

49 *Popovic*, n42, [901].

50 *Popovic*, ibid, [901]–[903].

51 *Ntaganda*, n3, [68].

52 *Stakic*, n12, [664].

53 *Stakic*, ibid, [676].

Chamber's findings. It held that while *de facto* borders could in some circumstances be sufficient to constitute frontiers for deportation, constantly shifting front-lines were not sufficient.[54]

3.2 Forcible displacement as a war crime

When displacement crimes are charged as war crimes, the Prosecution must always establish the contextual (also known as "chapeau") elements. War crimes cover conduct committed during armed conflict wthat is criminalized under international humanitarian law. War crimes prohibitions are largely based on the Hague Regulations on the Means and Methods of War (1899 and 1907) as well as the Geneva Conventions of 1949 and Additional Protocols of 1977.[55] Although war crimes overlap with domestic crimes such as murder or rape, they can be distinguished because additional elements must be proved to show that a war crime has been committed.

Under the Rome Statute of the ICC, it must always be shown that the conduct took place in the context of and was associated with an armed conflict (either international or non-international) and that the perpetrator was aware that the crimes were linked to the armed conflict. The Rome Statute appears to also require that the crimes were committed as part of a plan or policy or as part of a large-scale commission of such crimes.[56]

At the ICTY, the contextual elements are largely identical to those at the ICC. The Prosecution must show that the crime was committed during an armed conflict, that the crime was closely related to an armed conflict (nexus requirement); that the accused was aware of the nexus and that the victims were taking no active part in the hostilities (or, in the case of objects, were not military targets) and the perpetrator was aware or should have known this.[57] Additionally, at the ICTY it must be shown that the crime is criminalized under international law and sufficiently serious, that is to say that it must constitute a breach of a rule protecting important values and the breach must involve grave consequences for the victim.[58]

The primary provisions in the Rome Statute of the ICC by which forcible transfer and deportation can be charged as war crimes are: unlawful deportation or transfer (Article 8(2)(a)(vii)); the transfer, directly or indirectly, by the Occupying Power of parts of its own civilian population into the territory it occupies, or the deportation or transfer of all or parts of the population of the occupied territory within or outside this territory (Article 8(2)(b)(viii));

54 *Stakic*, ibid.
55 Cassese and Gaeta, n34, 81–82.
56 Rome Statute, n36, Article 8(1).
57 This requirement applies where a crime punishable under Article 3 is based on Common Article 3 IV GC, n33.
58 *Prosecutor v Tadić*, IT-94-1-AR72, Decision on the Defence Motion for Interlocutory Appeal on Jurisdiction, 2 October 1995.

ordering the displacement of the civilian population for reasons related to the conflict, unless the security of the civilians involved or imperative military reasons so demand (Article 8(2)(e)(viii)).[59]

Jurisprudence detailed above from crimes against humanity cases will generally apply when assessing the legality of a population movement.[60] For example, questions over the nature of the border that must be crossed for deportation and the circumstances in which population displacements may be justified and legitimate will be determined in the same manner for war crimes as for crimes against humanity. The major difference between forcible displacement as a war crime and as a crime against humanity, aside from the fact that crimes against humanity cover conduct committed outside of armed conflict, is that the former can only be committed against victims qualifying as protected persons under the Geneva Conventions and Additional Protocols.[61] While there is no formal requirement that victims of crimes against humanity be protected persons under international humanitarian law, the extent to which that requirement would apply de facto for crimes against humanity is unsettled and has not been subject to definitive treatment in the jurisprudence of the international courts.

3.3 Forcible displacement as genocide

The Appeals Chamber of the ICTY has held that forcible transfer "does not constitute in and of itself a genocidal act".[62] Similarly, the International Court of Justice has held that ethnic cleansing, in the sense of operations to render an area ethnically homogenous, cannot in and of themselves "be designated as genocide: the intent that characterizes genocide is to 'destroy, in whole or in part' a particular group, and deportation or displacement of the members of a group, even if effected by force, is not necessarily equivalent to destruction of that group".[63]

Nonetheless, in certain contexts forcible displacement can also form a part of the underlying conduct constituting genocide. The definition of genocide explicitly refers to forcibly transferring children from a group to another group as an underlying act of genocide.[64] The most well-known example of transferring children in modern times is that of the stolen generation of Aboriginal children in Australia who were transferred to European ethnicity families from 1910 to 1970. History contains other examples of removing the younger members of a group. For example, in 1609 the Spanish military under Phillip II expelled

59 Rome Statute, n36, Article 8.

60 *Prosecutor v Prlic*, IT-04-74-T, 29 May 2013, Vol.1, [132].

61 See *Prosecutor v Katanga*, ICC-01/04-01/07, 7 March 2014, Judgment pursuant to Article 74 of the Statute, [788]–[790].

62 *Prosecutor v Krstic*, IT-98-33-A, 19 April 2004, AC, Judgement, [33].

63 *Case concerning Application of the Convention on the Prevention and Punishment of the Crime of Genocide (Bosnia and Herzegovina v Serbia and Montenegro)*, Judgment, I.C.J. Reports 2007, 43, [190].

64 Rome Statute, n36, Article 6(e).

Muslims who had converted to Catholicism, known as Moriscos, due to ongoing suspicion as to their loyalties. In doing so, the Catholics separated the Morisco children and allowed them to stay in Spain on the basis that they could still be converted to Catholicism.[65]

On a separate note, at the ICTY, it has been held that the treatment of the Srebrenica survivors, which included their forcible displacement from Srebrenica and their suffering with the uncertainty as to the fate of their male relatives, was sufficient to constitute the underlying genocidal act of causing serious mental harm.[66]

To prove genocide, it is always necessary to demonstrate the specific intent to destroy the national, religious, racial or ethnic group, in whole or in part. Because of this requirement, genocide will typically only be charged in the most extreme circumstances of targeted attacks against one of these protected groups and it would be extremely rare that it would be charged for population movements *simpliciter* without any associated murders or other crimes of serious physical violence.

3.4 Related crimes

3.4.1 Property crimes

There are several property crimes that are relevant to the analysis of expulsion. As with crimes of forcible displacement, property crimes under international criminal law have a history extending back at least as far as the Lieber Code of 1863. This early codification of the law applicable during armed conflict indicated a basic division whereby public goods went to the victorious entity but private goods remained the property of individual citizens and penalties applied to the appropriation of that property without lawful justification.

At the ICC, property crimes include pillage under Article 8(2)(b)(xvi) (international armed conflicts) and 8(2)(e)(v) (non-international armed conflicts). It is notable that the elements of crimes require that the Prosecution show that the perpetrator "intended to deprive the owner of the property and to appropriate it for private or personal use".[67] If the property is deprived for some other use, such as a public purpose, the elements of the crime will not be demonstrated.

Other crimes that are potentially relevant to regulatory expulsions are Destruction and Appropriation of Property, under Article 8(2)(a)(iv) (equivalent to Article 2(d) of the ICTY Statute) (international armed conflicts); and the war crime of Destroying or Seizing the Enemy's Property, under Article 8(2)(b)(xiii) (international armed conflicts), 8(2)(e)(xii) (non-international armed conflicts). Also of potential relevance are the crimes against religious and cultural buildings: intentionally directing attacks against buildings dedicated to religion, education,

65 Dawson, Farber, n8, 27–28.
66 *Prosecutor v Tolimir*, IT-05-88/2-A, 8 April 2015.
67 ICC Elements of Crimes, n40, 26.

art, science or charitable purposes, historic monuments, hospitals and places where the sick and wounded are collected, provided they are not military objectives, under Article 8(2)(b)(ix) (international armed conflicts) and Article 8(2)(e)(iv) (non-international armed conflicts).

At the ICTY, there are several provisions prohibiting the interference with property, including Article 3(b), which covers "wanton destruction" or "devastation" of cities, town and villages; Article (3)(d), which includes as a war crime, "seizure of, destruction or wilful damage done to institutions dedicated to religion, charity and education, the arts and sciences, historic monuments and works of art and science"; and Article (3)(e), which prohibits the crime of plunder. The crime of plunder has been defined as: "all forms of unlawful appropriation of property in armed conflict for which individual criminal responsibility attaches under international criminal law, including those acts traditionally described as '"pillage"'.[68]

For Article (3)(d) of the ICTY Statute, which includes as a war crime, "seizure of, destruction or wilful damage done to institutions dedicated to religion, charity and education, the arts and sciences, historic monuments and works of art and science", the Prosecution must establish that: (i) an act has caused damage to, or destruction of, an institution dedicated to religion, charity and education, the arts and sciences, historic monuments and works of art and science; (ii) the damaged or destroyed institution was not used for military purposes at the time of the act; and (iii) the act was carried out with intent to destroy or damage or in reckless disregard of the likelihood of the destruction or damage to the institution in question.

3.4.2 Discriminatory crimes (persecution)

The process of criminal expulsion on a large scale will almost inevitably involve persecution against the targeted group. In some ways, persecution forms an umbrella crime, as it encompasses other crimes when they are committed with the specific intent to discriminate on prohibited grounds.

At the ICC, persecution requires a showing that the perpetrator severely deprived, contrary to international law, one or more persons of fundamental rights, such as the right to life or the security of the person, that the perpetrator targeted such person or persons by reason of the identity of a group or collectivity or targeted the group or collectivity as such. The included groups listed in the Rome Statute are political, racial, national, ethnic, cultural, religious, gender as defined in Article 7, paragraph 3, of the Statute, or other grounds that are universally recognized as impermissible under international law and that that conduct was committed in connection with any other crime listed under the Rome Statute.

The ICTY jurisprudence defines the elements of persecution under Article 5(h) of the ICTY Statute as follows: the *actus reus* is an act or omission that (a) discriminates in fact and (b) denies or infringes on a fundamental right laid down

68 *Prosecutor v Kordić and Čerkez*, IT-95-14/2-A, Judgement, 17 December 2004, [79].

in customary international law or treaty law; and it must also be shown that (c) where the underlying act is not specified as a crime under Article 5 of the ICTY Statute, that the cumulative effect of all the underlying acts of the crime of persecution must reach a level of gravity equivalent to that for other crimes against humanity. For example, in *Brdjanin*, the Trial Chamber found that in light of the cumulative effect of the denial of the rights to employment, freedom of movement, proper judicial process and proper medical care in the context of the conflict, fundamental rights had been infringed and persecution committed.[69] The *mens rea* is dual: (a) the underlying act or omission must have been carried out deliberately/intentionally and (b) with the intention to discriminate on political, racial, religious or ethnic grounds.

While litigation and jurisprudence on the crime of persecution largely focuses on the specific intent, or *dolus specialis*, of the accused, it is notable that the elements of persecution also require a demonstrated impact on the victim. By requiring a showing of severe deprivation or denial of a fundamental right, the formulations of the crime of persecution at international courts seek to ensure that only the most grave instances of persecution are brought before them.

In relation to forcible displacement type crimes, the approach taken at the ICC subtly differs from that taken at the *ad hoc* tribunals. Whereas the ICC requires the underlying act of persecution to be committed "in connection with" an existing crime listed under the Statute, the *ad hoc* Tribunal definition has no such enumerated-crime requirement. Viewed holistically, persecution at the ICC can be seen as an empty vessel crime – as it will not be established without adding the content of an additional enumerated crime.[70] Conversely, at the ICTY, persecution can, theoretically, be established independently of any other enumerated crime occurring.[71] The benefit of the broad ICTY formulation is flexibility to adapt to new forms of discriminatory conduct; the drawback is a potentially over-expansive reach that, from some perspectives, does not satisfy the fundamental requirements of predictability and comprehensibility.[72]

The preceding survey sets out the elements of discrete crimes. However, these legal exigencies should not overshadow the interrelationship of the actual perpetration of these crimes particularly in the context of forcible displacement. Evidence gathered in investigations for widespread and organized ethnic cleansing shows that expelling people *en masse* is typically conducted through a combination of misappropriation of property, violent abuses and deprivation or restriction of

69 *Prosecutor v Brdjanin*, IT-99-36, [1049].

70 See Cryer R. *et al.* (2010), *An Introduction to International Criminal Law and Procedure*, 2nd ed. (Cambridge University Press) 260.

71 See, e.g., *Prosecutor v Brdjanin*, n69, [1049] referring to the denial of the rights to employment, freedom of movement, proper judicial process, and proper medical care.

72 See Cryer, n70, 260 ("This requirement was included because of the concern of several States about the possible elasticity of the concept of persecution. The fear was that any practices of discrimination, more suitably addressed by human rights bodies, would be labelled as 'persecution', giving rise to international prosecutions").

rights.[73] As the following section of the analysis shifts from legal elements to factual application, the correlative nature of these crimes emerges from the evidentiary materials examined.

4 Proving displacement crimes: principles and practice

At first, it may seem a simple task to prove forcible displacement crimes. Ask the victims whether they were forced to leave their homes and who forced them. But the reality of large-scale forced population movements is often more complex, multi-factorial, and disputed than, for example, the classic example of European Jews being deported from their homes in crowded trains during the Holocaust.

International courts rightfully and properly insist on proof beyond reasonable doubt of each element of charged forcible displacement crimes. Other fundamental fair trial rights, such as the right to adequate time and facilities to prepare a defence, the right to trial without undue delay and the right to confront Prosecution witnesses, govern all international trials.[74] When addressing allegations of forced displacement on a massive scale, international courts have a daunting task. This task is all the more exacting due to the unsettled legal parameters of some key elements of forcible displacement crimes, such as the nature of the borders that must be crossed for forcible transfer to convert to deportation, the level of *mens rea* required on the part of the perpetrators and the level of causation required to establish criminal liability.

At the international criminal tribunals, the standards and burdens of proof adhere to the principles set out in international human rights instruments such as the International Covenant on Civil and Political Rights and the European Convention on Human Rights.[75] Under Article 66 of the Rome Statute of the ICC, all accused are presumed innocent and the burden falls on the Prosecution to prove the guilt of the accused beyond reasonable doubt. Other international courts have analogous provisions. At the ICTY, Article 21(3) of the Statute of the ICTY provides that all accused before the Tribunal are entitled to the presumption of innocence until proved guilty beyond reasonable doubt.[76] The cases at the international tribunals frequently involve allegations based on circumstantial evidence. In these situations, the guiding rule is that where more than one inference is reasonably open from the facts established by the evidence and one or more of those inferences is inconsistent with the guilt of the accused, an acquittal must be entered for the relevant count.[77]

73 See examples herein.

74 See, e.g., Rome Statute, ICTY Statute, ICTR Statute.

75 See Cryer, n70, 430–431.

76 Rule 87(A) of the Rules of the ICTY provides in so far as relevant: "A finding of guilt may be reached only when a majority of the Trial Chamber is satisfied that guilt has been proved beyond reasonable doubt."

77 *Prosecutor v Thomas Lubanga Dyilo*, Judgment pursuant to Article 74 of the Statute, 14 March 2012, ICC-01/04-01/06, [111]; *Prosecutor v Omar Hassan Ahmad Al Bashir*,

With those general standards in mind, it is apposite to examine how displacement crimes are actually proved. In order to prove the elements of the crimes to the requisite standard, it is usually necessary to gather evidence from a variety of sources. These sources can include witness testimony, documents, photographs, videos and physical objects, such as shell casings and ligatures.

Commencing with the underlying offence, testimony from the ground-level witnesses will establish the immediate circumstances in which the victims left their homes – the violence or fear created by the surrounding events and the impact of being uprooted suddenly from one's community and expelled to another land. For example, in the *Milutinovic et al.* case, which concerned the expulsion of Kosovo Albanians by the police and army of Serbia and the Former Republic of Yugoslavia, the Trial Chamber recounted the evidence of three victim witnesses – Mehmet Mazrekaj, K58 and K20 from the village of Beleg. The witnesses described a typical paradigm – the FRY and Serb armed forces entered Beleg; villagers were forced out of their homes and rounded up into central locations; some men were killed (either before or after they were captured); women, children and old men were searched for weapons and valuables; the armed forces verbally abused the Kosovo Albanians, beat some of the men, and raped some of the women at night and then the victims were forced to leave in a convoy to Albania.[78] The conditions were confusing, with the soldiers wearing a mix of uniforms, the vehicles including tanks and mounted heavy weapons and villagers being herded from house to house in terrifying circumstances.[79] These witnesses testified and/or provided statements for the Prosecution to tender at trial.

While victim witnesses may be sufficient to describe the crime, frequently it will be necessary to call witnesses from the perpetrator forces to prove the manner in which the crimes were ordered. In *Milutinovic et al.*, the Prosecution sought to prove that the displacement of several hundred thousand Kosovo Albanians was carried out intentionally and on a discriminatory basis by the Serb military and police forces acting in accordance with a joint criminal enterprise headed by Slobodan Milosevic from March to May 1999. Proving this broader allegation was assisted by the evidence of insider witnesses, including one who was a member of the armed forces who carried out the crimes. He described his involvement in expelling Kosovo Albanian civilians and the deliberate burning of houses in villages in Đakovica/Gjakova municipality during April 1999. He stated:

> [A]ll of us who took part in that operation, found it, if I can say, unpleasant to expel women, children, elderly persons and invalids. I know the KLA

Judgment on the appeal of the Prosecutor against the "Decision on the Prosecution's Application for a Warrant of Arrest against Omar Hassan Ahmad Al Bashir", 3 February 2010, ICC-02/05-01/09-73, 33; *Prosecutor v Delalić, Mucić, Delić, and Landžo*, IT-96-21-A, Judgement, 20 February 2001 (*Čelebići* Appeal Judgement), [458].

78 *Prosecutor v Milan Milutinovic et al.*, IT-05-87-T, TC, Judgement, 26 February 2009, Vol.2, [52]–[69].

79 *Milutinovic*, ibid, [52]–[69].

> pretty well and I've not seen a single woman of 70 years old or a child or anybody in the KLA, people like that cannot be fighters and terrorists. Or people in wheelchairs. But we expelled them all from the baby in the cradle to the elderly people in wheelchairs and that's the problem that I have today.[80]

Establishing the organized and concerted nature of the crimes is also assisted by showing the magnitude of the expulsions. In the *Milutinovic et al.* case, the Chamber referred to reports of various international organisations, including the report of the United Nations High Commissioner for Refugees, to obtain approximate numbers of displaced people. One UNHCR report that the Trial Chamber relied on recorded over 700,000 Kosovo Albanians who fled to outside countries, in the period March to July 1999.[81] On the basis of this and other evidence, the Trial Chamber concluded that:

> The manner in which the VJ and MUP dealt with the KLA was often heavy-handed and involved indiscriminate violence and damage to civilian persons and property, further exacerbating rather than ameliorating the situation in Kosovo. The consistent eye-witness accounts of the systematic terrorisation of Kosovo Albanian civilians by the forces of the FRY and Serbia, their removal from their homes, and the looting and deliberate destruction of their property, satisfies the Chamber that there was a campaign of violence directed against the Kosovo Albanian civilian population, during which there were incidents of killing, sexual assault, and the intentional destruction of mosques. It was the deliberate actions of these forces during this campaign that caused the departure of at least 700,000 Kosovo Albanians from Kosovo in the short period of time between the end of March and beginning of June 1999. Efforts by the MUP to conceal the killing of Kosovo Albanians, by transporting the bodies to other areas of Serbia, as discussed in greater detail below, also suggest that such incidents were criminal in nature.[82]

The Trial Chamber's summation of the crimes committed during this campaign refers to not only forcible displacement but also property destruction and persecution. It demonstrates that the evidence used to prove the core crimes of displacement was also relevant to, and indicative of, these other crimes.

Thus far the analysis has addressed the broad category of expulsion crimes, primarily consisting of violent expulsions through physical force and direct threats delivered personally to the victims. However, expulsions can be perpetrated through multiple means, including non-violent administrative instruments and means. Instances in history rebound, including, for example, the clearance of the

80 *Milutinovic*, ibid, [1172].
81 *Milutinovic*, ibid, [1150].
82 *Milutinovic*, ibid, [1178].

Scottish Highlands by land owners seeking to maximize profits from sheep farming.[83] This type of expulsion is particularly contentious as it sits close to the blurred line between unlawful forced displacement and regulatory conduct with regrettable but lawful consequences.[84]

To prove crimes relating to administrative expulsion, certain types of evidence are particularly apposite. For example, this form of displacement is often rationalized and legitimized by laws and regulations intended to encourage the targeted groups to leave their homes or to discourage them from returning.[85] In such cases, the laws or regulations themselves will provide an important starting point for the assessment of the alleged criminality. Experts[86] or international[87] witnesses can be used to explain regulations and the manner in which they were implemented across the society. This can assist to demonstrate that regulations that are ethnically neutral on their face can nonetheless have a discriminatory impact, overly burdening one ethnic or sectarian group in order to speed up its expulsion from a territory.

In his fifth report on the human rights situation in Bosnia during the Yugoslav conflict, the Special Rapporteur on Human Rights, Mr Tadeusz Mazowiecki, noted that: "[O]n 15 April 1993 the Mostar city authorities adopted Statute No.266/93, which severely restricted the provision of humanitarian relief to displaced people . . . those living in abandoned flats were given a deadline by HVO forces to leave by 9 May 1993. In some cases the deadline was enforced with arson and threats of death."[88] An estimated 10,000 Muslims were affected by this decree, demonstrating the large numbers of people that can be subjected

83 Dawson, Farber, n8, 30–32.

84 Similarly, see the discussions of the legality of the forced displacement of 1.4 million people due to the construction of the Three Gorges dam in China; Dawson, Farber, ibid, 39–41.

85 Documentary evidence is a prevalent feature in international trials, particularly at the ICTY, and there is no general prohibition on the use of hearsay evidence. The jurisprudence of the international tribunals allows for the introduction of documentary evidence through various means, including through motions from the bar table. Examples of documents that are particularly relevant for proving displacement, property deprivation and discriminatory crimes include public records, laws and regulations; reports of governmental and non-governmental organizations; and demographic reports. The registration records of displaced persons are often taken by UNHCR representatives stationed at major border crossings or collection points during armed conflicts and other disasters resulting in large-scale population flows.

86 An expert is a person who, by virtue of some specialised knowledge, skill or training can assist the Chamber in understanding or determining an issue of a technical nature that is in dispute; *Prosecutor v Bosco Ntaganda*, Decision on Defence preliminary challenges to Prosecution's expert witnesses, 9 February 2016, ICC-01/04-02/06, [9].

87 During the conflict in the former Yugoslavia, as in most conflicts, there were many international workers and representatives present in various capacities. The parties will often call these internationals as witnesses to provide evidence from the viewpoint of a non-party to the conflict. They can be journalists, ambassadors, members of peace-keeping forces and NGO representatives.

88 Mazowiecki Report, n5, [52].

to forcible displacement. Mazowiecki recounted how the forced evictions of Muslims from Mostar continued over several months during 1993.[89]

A hotly contested example of the use of regulatory instruments to forcibly displace people on an ethnic basis is provided by the *Gotovina et al.* proceedings. That case concerned the expulsion of many thousands of ethnic Serbs who were living in the Krajina region during Croatia's campaign to re-take that area in 1995. Prior to that date, the Krajina region of Croatia was held by ethnic Serbs who had attempted to establish their own ethnic entity called the Republika Srpska Krajina. To prove that the Croatian leadership intended to expel the Krajina Serb civilians, the Prosecution pointed to legislation that it alleged was designed to discourage non-Croats from returning to the Krajina region after they had left. One example was the Law on the Temporary Takeover of Property and Administration of Property ("Law on Temporary Takeover").[90] The law handed over possession of abandoned property to the Croatian authorities and allowed them to re-assign the property to people, such as those displaced by the conflict, present in the Croatian territory. As noted by the Trial Chamber when assessing this evidence, this law was apparently ethnically neutral on its face.[91] However, the Prosecution argued that by requiring the legitimate owner to return to Croatia in order to reclaim their property within an initial 30-day deadline (this was later changed to 90 days), the law effectively prevented Serbs who were unable to re-enter Croatia from repossessing their property while pretending to provide a mechanism for so doing.

The Prosecution called the international witness Elisabeth Rehn, who was the Special Rapporteur of the UN Commission on Human Rights on the situation of human rights in the territory of the former Yugoslavia between 27 September 1995 and early 1998. Rehn reported that various obstacles continued to prevent Croatian Serbs from regaining possession of their properties and that, by March 1997, not a single case brought before a local property claims commission had resulted in a Serb owner regaining possession of a property. She also reported on 14 January 1998 that less than ten per cent of the 200,000 Serbs who fled after Croatia's military operations in 1995 had returned to the Krajina. Defence witnesses were called to argue that the short time limit to return and demand to re-take possession (90 days) was intended to encourage home owners to return to the area. However, the Trial Chamber rejected the Defence witnesses on this issue, finding that the "motives underlying and the overall effect of the legal instruments was to provide the property left behind by Krajina Serbs in the liberated areas to Croats and thereby deprive the former of their housing and property".[92]

At the appeal stage of proceedings, the Appeals Chamber found that the convictions against two of the accused (Ante Gotovina and Mladen Markac) were

89 Mazowiecki Report, ibid, [53].

90 *Prosecutor v Ante Gotovina et al.*, IT-06-90-T, TC, Judgement, 15 April 2011, [2092].

91 *Gotovina*, ibid, [2092] ("At the outset, the Trial Chamber notes that the text of the legal instruments does not refer to ethnicities and does not make any distinctions based on ethnicity").

92 *Gotovina*, ibid, [2098].

insufficiently founded. This was due to reasons other than the discriminatory legislation. However, the Appeals Chamber acknowledged that there was such discriminatory legislation in place but held that it was insufficient in and of itself to convince the Appeals Chamber that the exodus of the Krajina Serbs was forced.[93] Because of the particular circumstances surrounding the Appeals Chamber's findings in the *Gotovina* case,[94] the Appeals Chamber's dismissal of the discriminatory legislation as a basis for criminal liability should not be seen as precluding the use of such evidential material to prove the intent to forcibly displace populations on an ethnic basis, thus constituting persecution.

The difficulty with expulsions carried out through less violent means, such as through administrative procedures, is separating legitimate from illegitimate conduct. In this respect, some examples of evidence from international trials help to demonstrate the fact-specific analyses that Chambers conduct.

In the *Stakic* case, the Trial Chamber noted that, in the context of the large-scale exodus of non-Serbs from Prijedor, a local official, on 9 April 1993 given by the then former Chief of the SJB, Simo Drljača, stated:

> As to the extensive work performed by the administrative-legislative bodies, it is enough to say that more than 20,000 cases of emigration by Muslim and Croat citizens were registered. When the German TV came to prove that we were forcefully expelling Muslims and Croats, we showed them more than 20,000 visas, guarantees and requests for voluntary emigration for economic reasons.[95]

Addressing this, and other similar evidence that ostensibly seemed to indicate a voluntariness to the departures, the Trial Chamber found that "the atmosphere in the municipality of Prijedor during the time relevant to the Indictment was of such a coercive nature that the persons leaving the municipality cannot be considered as having voluntarily decided to give up their homes."[96] Proving that the perpetrator forces created circumstances that deprived the victims of the ability to freely choose whether to leave or stay is an arduous but often critical requirement in situations of administrative expulsion.

A related manner that can be used to prove the involuntary nature of the expulsion is the demonstration of discriminatory employment practices, forcing people of one ethnicity to leave. The case of *Stanisic and Zupljanin* concerned high-level officials from the Bosnian Serb police forces. Having surveyed the evidence, the Trial Chamber concluded that there was a common criminal plan that sought to expel non-Serbs from several municipalities in Bosnia. One of the indicia of the criminal plan and one of the forms of discrimination was the dismissal of non-Serbs from

93 *Prosecutor v Gotovina et al.*, IT-06-90-A, Appeal Judgement, 16 November 2012, [95].
94 In this respect, see the strongly worded dissenting opinions attached to the Appeals Judgement.
95 Stakic, n12, [705] citing Exh. D99.
96 Stakic, ibid, [707].

their posts. The Trial Chamber noted that: "Muslims and Croats were dismissed from key positions in the army, the police, the judiciary, local enterprises, the media, hospitals, and other public institutions and enterprises."[97] It referred to a decision of the Crisis Staff of the Autonomous Region of the Krajina, of 11 May 1992, which held that "management posts in Krajina enterprises must be filled by persons who are absolutely loyal to the Serbian Republic of Bosnia and Herzegovina."[98] It noted evidence showing that "non-Serbs who managed to retain their positions due to a war time assignment were assessed by the Commission for the Standardisation of Staff, which in turn determined whether there were Serb citizens who could adequately replace non-Serbs still holding positions."[99] Depriving and granting jobs on the basis of ethnicity has a direct impact on people's ability to support themselves and their families and can constitute a means of removing many persons of the targeted ethnicity without even firing a weapon.

Inasmuch as forcible displacement is frequently conducted through multiple reinforcing methods of discrimination, proving the criminal nature of these acts also typically requires multiple sources of evidence. Victim witnesses constitute the primary and most direct means of showing that the departures were forced and not voluntary. At the same time, they will not usually be able to provide accurate accounts of the specific numbers of victims of these typically large-scale crimes. Demonstrating the scale of the crimes requires verifiable records of population movements, such as UNHCR registration documents, along with testimony from expert witnesses or international workers, who can contextualise and explain the figures or raw data contained in the registration documents or corresponding regulations. Even with the forced nature of the expulsions established, it is still necessary to show the existence and source of the intent behind the expulsions. To do so, insider witnesses are often necessary. And in order to check that the movements were not carried out for the safety of the population or imperative military reasons, the internal documents of the responsible forces (typically military or police forces) will provide an essential resource, including *ex post facto* laws on non-return that can be used to assist in assessing the intent behind the removal of the population. In light of the invidious but large-scale impact of administrative expulsion, it will be important for investigations to go behind the terms of facially neutral regulatory instruments to assess their true impact and determine whether they were intended to impose a discriminatory and disproportionate burden on one sector of society.

5 Conclusion

The preceding analysis demonstrates forcible displacement is often conducted through a variety of mutually reinforcing means, including direct displacement,

97 *Prosecutor v Stanisic and Zupljanin*, IT-08-91-T, 27 March 2013, Vol.2, [279].
98 *Stanisic and Zupljanin*, ibid, [280].
99 *Stanisic and Zupljanin*, ibid, fn 820.

property crimes and persecution. The law concerning forcible displacement, property deprivation, and discriminatory crimes has developed through the jurisprudence of the international tribunals, particularly at the ICTY, but questions as to the nature of the border crossing necessary for deportation and the level of causation of the perpetrator's acts remain unsettled.

The practice of investigating, litigating and adjudicating these crimes has shown the value of gathering multiple sources of evidence, from witness testimony, to documents of international organizations, to the orders and regulations of the perpetrating forces and authorities. Nonetheless, proving charges for these crimes within the context of a criminal trial upholding high standards of fairness and due process is a demanding undertaking. In the context of administrative expulsions, linking the discriminatory instruments to practices on the ground will assist in showing that facially neutral regulations may in fact have strong persecutory implications intended to expel a particular group of society.

Mass movements of peoples can alter the situation on the ground, sometimes for several generations, but questions of accountability will persist and often hamper true reconciliation if they are not adequately addressed. The experience of the ICTY has shown that forcible displacement, related property crimes and persecutory crimes are highly prevalent during societal conflicts and deeply interlinked in their perpetration. Exploring and analysing the law and practice relevant to these offences is a necessary endeavour in order to ensure the constant development and streamlining of the litigation of allegations of large-scale ethnic cleansing.

Bibliography

Books

Cassese A. and Gaeta P. (2008), *International Criminal Law*, 2nd ed. (Oxford University Press).

Cryer R. *et al.* (2010), *An Introduction to International Criminal Law and Procedure*, 2nd ed. (Cambridge University Press).

Dawson G. and Farber S. (2012), *Forcible Displacement Through the Ages* (Martinus Nijhoff).

Book chapters

Goy B. (2017), "Article 7(1)(d)" in Klamberg M. (ed.), *Commentary on the Law of the International Criminal Court* (Brussels, Torkel Opsahl Academic EPublisher).

Hall C.K. (2008), "Article 7 Crimes against Humanity, B.I.2 (d) 'Deportation or Forcible Transfer of Population', and B.II.(d) 'Prohibited Movements of Population'" in Triffterer O. (ed.), *Commentary on the Rome Statute of the International Criminal Court – Observers' Notes, Article by Article* (München/Oxford/Baden-Baden, C.H. Beck/Hart/Nomos) 2nd ed., 194–200.

Robinson D. (2001), "Article 7 (1)(d)—Crime Against Humanity of Deportation Or Forcible Transfer of Population" in Lee R.S. (ed.), *The International Criminal*

Court: Elements of Crimes and Rules of Procedure and Evidence (Ardsley, Transnational Publishers) 86–88.

Research papers

Acquiviva G. (2011), “Forced Displacement and International Crimes”, UN High Commissioner for Refugees, *Legal and Protection Policy Research Series.*

Appendix

UN and other documentation

International Documents

Treaties

Convention (II) with Respect to the Laws and Customs of War on Land and its annex: Regulations concerning the Laws and Customs of War on Land. The Hague, 29 July 1899.

Convention (IV) respecting the Laws and Customs of War on Land and its annex: Regulations concerning the Laws and Customs of War on Land. The Hague, 18 October 1907 reprinted in 2 *AJIL* (1908) 90 (Supp) 1.

Peace Treaty of Constantinople, 15 November 1913, Annex.

Convention Between Greece and Bulgaria Respecting Reciprocal Emigration, 14 *AJIL* (Oct, 1920) No 4, Supplement, 356-60.

Treaty of Peace with Turkey signed at Lausanne, 24 July 1923.

Convention Concerning the Exchange of Greek and Turkish Populations, signed at Lausanne, January 30, 1923 to be found in 18 *AJIL* (Apr 1924) No 2, Supplement, 84-90.

The Berlin (Potsdam) Conference, July 17-August 2, 1945, Protocol of the Proceedings, August 1, 1945, <http://avalon.law.yale.edu/20th_century/decade17.asp>

Agreement by the Government of the United States of America, the Provisional Government of the French Republic, the Government of the United Kingdom and Northern Ireland and the Government of the Union of Soviet Socialist Republics for the Prosecution and Punishment of the Major War Criminals of the European Axis, Protocol, 8 August 1945, 59 Stat. 1544, 82 *UNTS* 279.

Geneva Convention for the amelioration of the condition of the wounded and sick in armed forces in the field (I GC), 75 *UNTS* No 970.

Geneva Convention for the amelioration of the condition of the wounded, sick and shipwrecked members of the armed forces at sea (II GC), 75 *UNTS* No 971.

Geneva Convention relative to the treatment of prisoners of war (III GC), 75 *UNTS* No 972.

Geneva Convention Relative to the Protection of Civilian Persons in Time of War of 12 August 1949 (IV), 75 *UNTS* No 973.

Convention for the Protection of Human Rights and Fundamental Freedoms, better known as the European Convention on Human Rights ("ECHR"), *ETS* No 5.

Convention relating to the Status of Refugees, Geneva, 28 July 1951, 189 *UNTS* 137.

Convention on the Settlement of Matters Arising out of the War and the Occupation between the United Kingdom of Great Britain and Northern Ireland, France, the United States of America and the Federal Republic of Germany, Bonn, May 26, 1952, <http://treaties.fco.gov.uk/docs/fullnames/pdf/1959/TS0013%20(1959)%20CMND-656%201952%2026%20MAY,BONN%3BCONVENTION%20ON%20SETTLEMENT%20OF%20MATTERS%20ARISING%20OUT%20OF%20WAR&THE%20OCCUPATION%20BETWEEN%20NI,FRANCE,USA&FEDERAL%20REPUBLIC%20OF%20GERMANY_1.pdf?>

The Korean War Armistice Agreement, Panmunjom, Korea, July 27, 1953 <http://www.usfk.mil/Portals/105/Documents/SOFA/G_Armistice_Agreement.pdf>

International Covenant on Civil and Political Rights (adopted 16 December 1966, entered into force 23 March 1976) 999 UNTS 171.

International Covenant on Economic, Social and Cultural Rights (adopted 16 December 1966, entered into force 3 January 1976) 993 UNTS 3.

Convention on the Elimination of Discrimination of All Forms of Racial Discrimination, adopted and opened for signature and ratification by General Assembly resolution 2106 (XX) of 21 December 1965, 660 *UNTS* 195.

Convention on the Non-Applicability of Statutory Limitations to War Crimes and Crimes against Humanity, Adopted and opened for signature, ratification and accession by General Assembly resolution 2391 (XXIII) of 26 November 1968.

OAU Convention Governing the Specific Aspects of Refugee Problems in Africa, 10 September 1969, *UNTS* No. 14691.

American Convention on Human Rights, "Pact of San Jose", Costa Rica, 22 November 1969, Organization of American States, B-32.

International Convention on the Suppression and Punishment of the Crime of Apartheid, Adopted by the General Assembly of the United Nations on 30 November 1973, 1015 *UNTS* No I 14861.

Protocol Additional to the Geneva Conventions of 12 August 1949 and Relating to the Protection of Victims of International Armed Conflicts (Protocol I), 8 June 1977, 1125 *UNTS* 3.

Protocol Additional to the Geneva Conventions of 12 August 1949 and relating to the protection of victims of non-international armed conflicts (Protocol II), Geneva, 8 June 1977, 1125 UNTS (1979) 609.

Convention on the Elimination of All Forms of Discrimination against Women, New York, 18 December 1979, 1249 *UNTS* 13.

Inter-American Convention to Prevent and Punish Torture, Cartagena de Indias, 9 December 1985, Organization of American States.

Indigenous and Tribal Peoples Convention, 1989 (No. 169).

Convention on the Rights of the Child. New York, 20 November 1989, 1577 *UNTS* I-27531.

Bosnia and Herzegovina, Agreement No 1, 22 May 1992.

Cotonou Agreement (Liberia), 25 July 1993, <http://www.unhcr.org/refworld/docid/3ae6b5796.html>

Inter-American Convention on Forced Disappearance of Persons, Belém do Pará, 9 June 1994, Organization of American States.

Inter-American Convention on the Prevention, Punishment and Eradication of Violence Against Women "Convention of Belém do Pará", Belém do Pará, 9 June 1994, Organization of American States.

Dayton Peace Agreement, Annex 7, (1995).

Interim Agreement for Peace and Self-government in Kosovo, S/1999/648, 7 June 1999, <http://peacemaker.un.org/sites/peacemaker.un.org/files/990123_RambouilletAccord.pdf>

Inter-American Convention on the Elimination of all Forms of Discrimination Against Persons with Disabilities, Guatemala City, 7 June 1999, Organization of American States.

Agreement on Cessation of Hostilities between the Government of the Federal Democratic Republic of Ethiopia and the Government of the State of Eritrea, 18 June 2000, Volume 2138, I-37273.

Pact on Security, Stability and Development in the Great Lakes Region, 14 and 15 December 2006, <http://peacemaker.un.org/sites/peacemaker.un.org/files/061215_PactonSecurityStabilityDevelopmentGreatLakes.pdf>

Protocol on the Protection and Assistance to Internally Displaced Persons adopted by the International Conference on the Great Lakes Region, adopted on 29 November 2006, <https://www.icglr.org/index.php/en/the-pact> and <http://www.refworld.org/pdfid/52384fe44.pdf>

Protocol on the Property Rights of Returning Persons, 30 November 2006, <https://www.icglr.org/images/Pact%20ICGLR%20Amended%2020122.pdf >

Convention on the Rights of Persons with Disabilities. New York, 13 December 2006, 2515 *UNTS* I-44910.

African Union Convention for the Protection and Assistance of Internally Displaced Persons in Africa, adopted in Kampala, Uganda, 23 October 2009.

Peace Agreement of the Democratic Republic of the Congo and Le Congres National pour la Defense du Peuple, 23 March 2009, <http://peacemaker.un.org/sites/peacemaker.un.org/files/CD_090323_Peace%20Agreement%20between%20the%20Government%20and%20the%20CNDP.pdf>

African Union Convention for the Protection and Assistance of Internally Displaced Persons in Africa, 23 October 2009.

Agreement between the Government of the Republic of Sudan and the Sudan People's Liberation Movement on Temporary Arrangements for the Administration and Security of the Abyei Area, 20 June 2011, <http://peacemaker.un.org/sites/peacemaker.un.org/files/SD_110620_AgreementTemporaryArrangementsAbyeiArea.pdf>

Agreement on the Establishment of the Extraordinary African Chambers within the Senegalese Judicial System, Senegal-African Union, Aug. 22, 2012, 52 I.L.M. 1024 (2013).

Agreement on the Statute of the Chambers, Senegal-African Union, Jan. 30, 2013, 52 I.L.M. 1028.

Ceasefire Agreement between the Government of Sudan and the Justice and Equality Movement-Sudan, 10 February 2013, <http://peacemaker.un.org/sites/peacemaker.un.org/files/SD_130210_CeasefireGoSJEMSudan.pdf>

Agreement on the Resolution of the Conflict in the Republic of South Sudan, Addis Ababa, 17 August 2015.

Colombian Government-Farc Agreement: Acuerdo Final para la Terminación del Conflicto y la Construcción de una Paz Estable y Duradera (Final Agreement on the Termination of Conflict and the Construction of a Stable and Lasting Peace), 24 November 2016 and 24 August 2016 versions.

Colombian Government-Farc Agreement: Acuerdo sobre las Víctimas del Conflicto: "Sistema Integral de Verdad, Justicia, Reparación y No Repetición", incluyendo la

Jurisdicción Especial para la Paz; y Compromiso sobre Derechos Humanos (Agreement on the Victims of Conflict: "Integral System of Truth, Justice, Reparations and Non-Repetition", including the Special Peace Jurisdiction), 15 December 2015.

Comprehensive Agreement on Respect for Human Rights and International Humanitarian Law between the Government of the Republic of the Philippines and the National Democratic Front of the Philippines, <http://peacemaker.un.org/sites/peacemaker.un.org/files/PH_980316_Comprehensive%20Agreement%20on%20Respect%20for%20Human%20Rights.pdf>

Statutes/Codes/Charters

The Lieber Code (Washington D.C., 24 April 1863).

United Nations, *Charter of the International Military Tribunal – Annex to the Agreement for the prosecution and punishment of the major war criminals of the European Axis ("London Agreement")*, 8 August 1945, <http://www.unhcr.org/refworld/docid/3ae6b39614.html>

Allied Control Council No. 10: Punishment of Persons Guilty of War Crimes, Crimes against Peace and against Humanity, Berlin, 20 December 1945.

Charter of the International Military Tribunal for the Far East, Tokyo, 19 January 1946, amended on 26 April 1946.

Statute of the International Criminal Tribunal for the former Yugoslavia, < http://www.icty.org/x/file/Legal%20Library/Statute/statute_sept09_en.pdf>

Rome Statute of the International Criminal Court, Rome, 17 July 1998, 2187 *UNTS*, Treaty no. 38544.

Elements of Crimes, International Criminal Court, <https://www.icc-cpi.int/NR/rdonlyres/336923D8-A6AD-40EC-AD7B-45BF9DE73D56/0/ElementsOfCrimesEng.pdf?>

Principles/Declarations/Draft Articles

Affirmation of the Principles of International Law Recognized by the Charter of the Nuremberg Tribunal, G.A. Res. 95(1)., UN. Doc A/64/Add.l, (1946) 188.

Bangkok Principles on the Status and Treatment of Refugees, 31 December 1966 (adopted by the Asia-African Legal Consultative Committee).

'Basic Principles on the Protection of Civilian Populations in Armed Conflicts', UN General Assembly resolution, A/RS/2675, 9 December 1970.

Principles of international co-operation in the detection, arrest, extradition and punishment of persons guilty of war crimes and crimes against humanity, UN General Assembly resolution 3074 (1973).

United Nations, Economic and Social Council, Commission on Human Rights, E/CN.4/1998/53/Add.2, 11 February 1998 *Guiding Principles on Internal Displacement* (1998), <http://www.ohchr.org/EN/Issues/IDPersons/Pages/Standards.aspx>

UN Principles on Housing and Property Restitution for Refugees and Displaced Persons (Pinheiro Principles) (2005), <http://globalinitiative-escr.org/wp-content/uploads/2013/05/Pinheiro-Principles-Publication.pdf>

Basic Principles and Guidelines on the Right to a Remedy and Reparation for Victims of Gross Violations of International Human Rights Law and Serious Violations of International Humanitarian Law, UN Doc. /RES/60/147, (Dec. 16, 2005).

Basic principles for a peaceful settlement of the Nagorno-Karabakh conflict, Madrid, 29 November 2007, <http://www.deutscharmenischegesellschaft.de/wp-content/uploads/2016/04/Madrid-Principles-%E2%80%93-Full-Text-20071129.pdf >

Declaration Relating to Moslem Properties in Greece, to be found in 18 *AJIL* (Apr 1924) No 2, Supplement.

Universal Declaration on Human Rights, < http://www.ohchr.org/EN/UDHR/Documents/UDHR_Translations/eng.pdf>

Declaration on the Right to Leave and the Right to Return, Adopted by the Uppsala Colloquium, Uppsala, Sweden 21 June 1972.

Declaration on the Protection of Women and Children in Emergency and Armed Conflict, General Assembly resolution 3318 (XXIX) of 14 December 1974.

Helsinki Final Act, 1 August 1975, Conference on Security and Co-Operation in Europe.

General Assembly resolution 40/34, *Declaration of Basic Principles of Justice for Victims of Crime and Abuse of Power* (29 November 1985), A/RES/40/34.

Strasbourg Declaration on the Right to Leave and Return, Adopted on 26 November 1986.

Draft Declaration on freedom and non-discrimination in respect of the right of everyone to leave any country, including his own, and to return to his country, by Mubanga-Chipoya, E/CN.4/Sub.2/1987/10.

Declaration and Concerted Plan of Action in Favour of Central American Refugees, Returnees and Displaced Persons, CIREFCA 89/13/Rev.1, 30 May 1989.

Declaration on Humanitarian Assistance and Gradual Repatriation of Temporary Refugees and Displaced Persons from the War in Bosnia and Herzegovina and in Croatia, Ljubljana, 2 July 1992.

Draft Code of Crimes against the Peace and Security of Mankind, Report of the International Law Commission on the work of its forty-eighth session, Yearbook of the International Law Commission, 1996, Vol. II (Part Two), 17.

Draft Declaration on Population Transfer and the Implantation of Settlers, E/CN.4/Sub.2/1997/23, 27 June 1997.

Cairo Declaration, Africa-Europe Summit under the Aegis of the OAU and the EU, Conseil/00/901, 3–4 April 2000.

World Conference on Human Rights, *Vienna Declaration and Programme of Action*, Vienna, 25 June 1993.

Declaration on the Rights of Indigenous People, adopted by Human Rights Council, Resolution 2006/2.

Nairobi Declaration on the Effective Implementation and Operationalization of the Protocol on Property Rights of Returning Persons in the Great Lakes Region, 23 April 2015, <http://icglr.org/images/Declaration-Ministers%20in%20charge%20of%20lands%20issues%20April%202015.pdf>

High Level Conference on the future of the European Court of Human Rights, Brighton Declaration (20 April 2012) <http://www.echr.coe.int/Documents/2012_Brighton_FinalDeclaration_ENG.pdf>

International Law Commission (2001) *Draft Articles on Responsibility of States for Internationally Wrongful Acts, with commentaries* (ARSIWA) Supplement No. 10 (A/56/10) chp.IV.E.1, Yearbook of the International Law Commission, Vol. II, Part Two, < http://legal.un.org/ilc/texts/instruments/english/commentaries/9_6_2001.pdf>

International Law Commission (2001) *Draft Articles on Responsibility of States for Internationally Wrongful Acts, with commentaries* (ARSIWA), Commentaries, Yearbook of the International Law Commission, Vol. II, Part Two, <http://legal.un.org/ilc/texts/instruments/english/commentaries/9_6_2001.pdf>

Reports

Report by the Commission on the Responsibilities of the Authors of War and on Enforcement of Penalties, 14 *AJIL* (Jan – Apr, 1920) No 1 / 2, 95.

Progress Report of the United Nations Mediator on Palestine, U.N. GAOR, Supplement No. 11, A/648 (1948), 14.

Introduction to the Annual Report of the Secretary-General on the Work of the Organization, U.N. GAOR, Supplement No. 1A, A/6701/Add.1 (1967) 7.

Report of the International Law Commission on the Work of its Second Session, U.N. GAOR, 5th Sess., Supp. No. 12, Principle 6(c), U.N. Doc. A/1316 (1950), reprinted in *Yearbook of the International Law Commission*, Vol. 2, 374 (1950).

Report of the Committee on the Exercise of the Inalienable Rights of the Palestinian People U.N. SCOR, U.N. Doc. S/12090 (1976) 8.

Report of the UN High Commissioner for Refugees to the Economic and Social Council, UN Doc.E/1985/62 (1985).

Report by EU observers on statements about violations of the second protocol to the Geneva Conventions concerning Ilok, 1 November 1991.

Final Report of the Commission of Experts Established Pursuant to Security Council Resolution 780 (1992), S/1994/674.

Fifth periodic report on the situation of human rights in the territory of the former Yugoslavia submitted by Mr Tadeusz Mazowiecki, Special Rapporteur of the Commission on Human Rights, pursuant to paragraph 32 of Commission resolution 1993/7 of 23 February 1993; E/CN.4/1994/47, 17/11/1993.

'The Human Rights Dimensions of Population Transfers including the Implantation of Settlers', Preliminary Report prepared by AS Al-Khasawneh and R Hatano, E/CN.4/Sub.2/1993/17 6 July 1993.

Preliminary Report of the Sub-Commission on Prevention of Discrimination and Protection of Minorities relating to Population Transfers, 1993.

Interim report of the Commission of Experts established pursuant to Security Council resolution 780 (1992), annexed to Letter dated 9 February 1993 from the Secretary-General addressed to the Security Council (S/25274, 10 February 1993).

UN Sub-Commission on Human Rights, Special Rapporteur on the Human Rights Dimensions of Population Transfer, including the Implantation of Settlers and Settlements, Final Report, UN Doc. E/CN. 4/Sub.2/1997/23, 27 June 1997.

Report of the Representative of the Secretary-General, Mr. Francis M. Deng, submitted pursuant to Commission resolution 1997/39. Addendum: Guiding Principles on Internal Displacement, 11 February 1998, E/CN.4/1998/53.

'Fragmentation of International Law: Difficulties Arising from the Diversification and Expansion of International Law', Report of the Study Group of the International Law Commission, U.N. Doc. A/CN.4/L.682, (Apr. 13, 2006), as corrected by U.N. Doc. A/CN.4/L.682/Corr.1 (Aug. 11, 2006) (finalized by Martti Koskenniemi).

Report of the International Law Commission, 58th session (1 May-9 June and 3 July-11 August 2006), UN Doc. A/61/10.

OHCHR, Report of the Special Rapporteur on adequate housing as a component of the right to an adequate standard of living, Miloon Kothari, Mission to Cambodia, UN Doc E/CN.4/2006/41/Add.3 (2006)

OHCHR, 'A human rights analysis of economic and other land concessions in Cambodia, Report of the Special Rapporteur on the situation of human rights in Cambodia, Surya Subedi', A/HRC/21/63/Add.1/Rev.1 and addendum, 24 September 2012.

Report of the independent international factfinding mission to investigate the implications of the Israeli settlements on the civil, political, economic, social and cultural rights of the Palestinian people throughout the Occupied Palestinian Territory, including East Jerusalem, A/HRC/22/63, 7 February 2013.

First report on crimes against humanity, Special Rapporteur Mr Sean D. Murphy, A/CN.4/680, 17 February 2015.

Report of the Special Rapporteur on the Human Rights of Internally Displaced Persons, A/HRC/32/35, 29 April 2016, 7.

Report of the Secretary-General, 'Implementation of Security Council resolutions 2139 (2014), 2165 (2014), 2191 (2014) and 2258 (2015)' (20 July 2016) UN Doc S/2016/631.

Report of the Secretary-General, 'Implementation of Security Council resolutions 2139 (2014), 2165 (2014), 2191 (2014) and 2258 (2015)' (16 August 2016) UN Doc S/2016/714.

Report of the Secretary-General, 'Implementation of Security Council resolutions 2139 (2014), 2165 (2014), 2191 (2014) and 2258 (2015)' (16 September 2016) UN Doc S/2016/796.

Report of the Secretary-General 'Implementation of Security Council resolutions 2139 (2014), 2165 (2014), 2191 (2014) and 2258 (2015)' (18 October 2016) UN Doc S/2016/873.

Report of the Secretary-General, 'Implementation of Security Council resolutions 2139 (2014), 2165 (2014), 2191 (2014) and 2258 (2015)' (15 November 2016) UN Doc S/2016/962.

Report of the Secretary-General, 'Implementation of Security Council resolutions 2139 (2014), 2165 (2014), 2191 (2014) and 2258 (2015)' (14 December 2016) UN Doc S/2016/1057.

Report of the Secretary-General, 'Implementation of Security Council resolutions 2139 (2014), 2165 (2014), 2191 (2014), 2258 (2015) and 2332 (2016)' (20 January 2017) UN Doc S/2017/58.

Report of the Secretary-General, 'Implementation of Security Council resolutions 2139 (2014), 2165 (2014), 2191 (2014), 2258 (2015) and 2332 (2016)' (16 February 2017) UN Doc S/2017/144.

Report of the Secretary-General, 'Implementation of Security Council resolutions 2139 (2014), 2165 (2014), 2191 (2014), 2258 (2015) and 2332 (2016)' (22 March 2017) UN Doc S/2017/244.

Report of the Secretary-General, 'Implementation of Security Council resolutions 2139 (2014), 2165 (2014), 2191 (2014), 2258 (2015) and 2332 (2016)' (19 April 2017) UN Doc S/2017/339.

Human Rights Committee (International Covenant on Civil and Political Rights)

General Comment No 15: The Positions of Aliens under the Covenant, 11 April 1986.
General Comment No. 27, Article 12 (Freedom of Movement), CCPR/C/21/Rev.1/Add.9, 2 November 1999.
General Comment No. 29, Article 4: Derogations during a State of Emergency, CCPR/C/21/Rev.1/Add.11., 31 August 2001.
General Comment No. 31, The Nature of the General Legal Obligation imposed on States Parties to the Covenant, CCPR/C/21/Rev.1/Add. 13, 26 May 2004.
Report of Human Rights Committee, Cyprus, CCPR A/32/44 (1977).
Report of the Human Rights Committee, Supplement No. 40, A/34/40 (1979).
Consideration of reports submitted by states parties under article 40 of the Covenant, Concluding observations of the Human Rights Committee, Israel, CCPR/C/79/Add. 93, 18 August 1998.
Consideration of reports submitted by states parties under article 40 of the Covenant, Concluding observations of the Human Rights Committee, Israel, CCPR/CO/78/ISR, 21 August 2003.
Consideration of reports submitted by States Parties under Article 40 of the Covenant, Concluding observations of the Human Rights Committee, Bosnia and Herzegovina, 22 November 2006, CCPR/C/BIH/CO/1.
Consideration of reports submitted by states parties under article 40 of the Covenant, Concluding observations of the Human Rights Committee, Colombia, CCPR/C/COL/CO/6, 4 August 2010.
Consideration of reports submitted by states parties under article 40 of the Covenant, Concluding observations of the Human Rights Committee, Israel, CCPR/C/ISR/CO/3, 3 September 2010.
Consideration of reports submitted by States Parties under Article 40 of the Covenant, Seventh periodic reports of States parties due in 2014, Colombia, CCPR/C/COL/7, 7 April 2015.
Concluding observations on the second periodic report of Bosnia and Herzegovina, adopted by the Committee at its 106th session (15 October – 2 November) 2012, CCPR/C/BIH/CO/2.
Concluding observations on the fourth periodic report of Cyprus, CCPR/C/CYP/CO/4, 30 April 2015.

Committee on Economic, Social and Cultural Rights

The nature of States parties' obligations (art. 2, para. 1, of the Covenant), General comment No. 3, Fifth session, 1990.
The right to adequate food (art. 11), General Comment 12, E/C.12/1999/5, Twentieth session, 12 May 1999.
The equal right of men and women to the enjoyment of all economic, social and cultural rights (art. 3 of the International Covenant on Economic, Social and Cultural Rights), General Comment No. 16, E/C.12/2005/4, Thirty-fourth session.

Human Rights Council

Resolution S-17/1 (23 August 2011) UN Doc A/HRC/RES/S-17/1.

Report of the Independent International Commission of Inquiry on the Syrian Arab Republic (16 August 2012) UN Doc A/HRC/21/50.

Report of the Independent International Commission of Inquiry on the Syrian Arab Republic (11 August 2016) UN Doc A/HRC/33/55.

Report of the Independent International Commission of Inquiry on the Syrian Arab Republic (2 February 2017) UN Doc A/HRC/34/64.

Council of Europe

Parliamentary Assembly, 'Crisis in former Yugoslavia', Recommendation 1198 (1992), 5 November 1992.

Parliamentary Assembly, 'Massive and flagrant violations of human rights in the territory of former Yugoslavia', Resolution 994 (1993), 3 February 1993.

Parliamentary Assembly, 'Execution of judgments of the European Court of Human Rights', Resolution 1226 (2000), <http://assembly.coe.int/nw/xml/XRef/Xref-DocDetails-EN.asp?FileID=16834&lang=EN>

Parliamentary Assembly, 'Humanitarian situation of the displaced Kurdish population in Turkey', Recommendation 1563 (2002), 29 May 2002.

Parliamentary Assembly, 'Refugees and displaced persons in Armenia, Azerbaijan and Georgia', Resolution 1497 (2006).

Parliamentary Assembly, 'Solving property issues of refugees and displaced persons', Resolution 1708 (2010).

Committee of Ministers (2003) *Resolution ResDH(2003)190 concerning the judgment of the European Court of Human Rights of 28 July 1998 in the Loizidou case against Turkey*, Resolution ResDH(2003)190 (2 December 2003), <http://hudoc.echr.coe.int/eng?i=001-71910>

Committee of Ministers (2003) *Resolution ResDH(2003)191 concerning the judgment of the European Court of Human Rights of 18 December 1996 in the Loizidou case against Turkey*, Resolution ResDH(2003)191 (2 December 2003), <http://hudoc.echr.coe.int/eng?i=001-71908>

Committee of Ministers, Resolution Res (2004) 3, On judgments revealing an underlying systemic problem, 12 May 2004.

Committee of Ministers, Recommendation to member states on internally displaced persons, Rec (2006) 6 100.

Committee of Ministers, Recommendation CM/Rec(2008) 2, on efficient domestic capacity for rapid execution of judgments of the European Court of Human Rights (Adopted by the Committee of Ministers on 6 February 2008 at the 1017th meeting of the Ministers' Deputies).

Committee of Ministers (2010) Memorandum prepared by the Secretariat of the Department for the Execution of Judgments of the ECHR (Directorate General of Human Rights and Legal Affairs), *Cases examined by the Committee of Ministers concerning the property rights and homes of displaced Greek Cypriots. Consequences of the inadmissibility decision adopted by the European Court on 5 March 2010 in the case of* Demopoulos v Turkey and 7 other cases, CM/Inf/DH(2010)21, parts II and III, <https://search.coe.int/cm/Pages/result_details.aspx?ObjectId=09000016805af4da>

Committee on the Elimination of Racial Discrimination

General recommendation XXII on article 5 of the Convention on refugees and displaced persons, Forty-ninth session, 1996.

Report of the Committee on the Elimination of Racial Discrimination, U.N. GAOR, 50th Sess., Supp. No. 18, 219, U.N. Doc. A/50/18 (1995) 26.

Other documents

Final Record of the Diplomatic Conference of Geneva of 1949, Vol. II (A), 821.

Diplomatic Conference on the Reaffirmation and Development of International Humanitarian Law Applicable in Armed Conflicts, *Official Records,* Vol. VI, CDDH/SR. 44, 30 May 1977, 291.

Commentary of 1958, IV Geneva Convention Relative to the Protection of Civilian Persons in Time of War of 12 August 1949.

International Committee of the Red Cross, Study on Customary International Humanitarian Law, 'Rules', <https://ihl-databases.icrc.org/customary-ihl/eng/docs/v1>

25th International Conference of the Red Cross, Geneva, 23–31 October 1986, Res. I.

GCC, Supreme Council, 10th session, Muscat, 18–21 December 1989, Final Communique, annexed to Letter dated 29 December 1989 from Oman to the UN Secretary-General, UN Doc. A/45/73-S/21065, 2 January 1990.

UK, Statement before the UN General Assembly, UN Doc. A/46/PV.89, 24 August 1992, 36.

US, Former Yugoslavia: Grave Breaches of the Fourth Geneva Convention (Second Submission) annexed to Letter dated 22 September 1992 to the UN Secretary-General, UN Doc. S/24583, 23 September 1992, Annex.

Executive Committee of the High Commissioner's Programme, Note on International Protection, 31 August 1993, A/AC.96/815.

ICRC, Working paper on war crimes submitted to the Preparatory Committee for the Establishment of an International Criminal Court, 14 February 1997.

Office in Colombia of the High Commissioner for Human Rights, *Recomendaciones de órganos internacionales de derechos humanos al Estado colombiano 1980–2000*, Bogotá: Office of the United Nations High Commissioner for Human Rights, 2000.

International Commission on Intervention and State Sovereignty, 'The Responsibility to Protect: The Report of the International Commission on Intervention and State Sovereignty' (*International Development Research Centre,* 2001) <http://www.un.org/ga/search/view_doc.asp?symbol=A/59/565>

Written Statement submitted to the ICJ, *Legal Consequences of the Construction of a Wall in the Occupied Palestinian Territory,* 30 January 2004.

Office in Colombia of the High Commissioner for Human Rights, *Compilación de jurisprudencia y doctrina nacional e internacional, Vol. V*, Bogotá: Office of the United Nations High Commissioner for Human Rights, 2006.

Office in Colombia of the High Commissioner for Human Rights, *Manual de Calificación de Conductas Violatorias*, Bogotá: Office of the United Nations High Commissioner for Human Rights, 2010.

UNHCR (The UN Refugee Agency), *Handbook and Guidelines on Procedures and Criteria for Determining Refugee Status under the 1951 Convention and the 1967 Protocol relating to the Status of Refugees*, UNHCR, Reissued 2011.
Office in Colombia of the High Commissioner for Human Rights, *Compilación de jurisprudencia y doctrina nacional e internacional, Vol. VI*, Bogotá: Office of the United Nations High Commissioner for Human Rights, 2012.
International Law Association (2014) *Study Group on Due Diligence in International Law, First Report by Duncan French (Chair) and Tim Stephens (Rapporteur)*, Report of the Seventy-Sixth Conference. Washington: International Law Association, <https://olympereseauinternational.files.wordpress.com/2015/07/due_diligence_-_first_report_2014.pdf>
International Law Commission, Crimes Against Humanity, 67th Session, A/CN.4/L.853, 2 June 2015.
'Land and Human Rights: Standards and Applications', United Nations Office of the High Commissioner for Refugees, 2015, HR/PUB/15/5/Add.1, 88.
Mandate of the Special Rapporteur on the human rights of internally displaced persons, 32/11, A/71/53, adopted 1 July 2016.
UNHCR The UN Refugee Agency, *Global Trends: Forced Displacement in 2015*, UNHCR, 2016.
'Translating the Kampala Convention into Practice: A Stocktaking Exercise', ICRC, February 2017.
'State Setting of the Present-day Bosnia-Herzegovina', Information Bulletin, Center for Constitutional Studies and Democratic Development.

United Nations Resolutions/Meetings

Security Council

Security Council resolution S/RES/365 (1974).
S/Res/385 (1976).
SC Resolution 687 (1991) 8 April 1991.
Security Council resolution 752, 15 May 1992.
S/Res/779 (1992).
Security Council, S/Res/819 (1993) 16 April 1993.
S/Res/859 (1993).
S/Res/874 (1993).
S/Res/906 (1994).
S/Res/896 (1994).
S/Res 993 (1995).
S/Res/999 (1995).
Security Council resolution 1009, 10 August 1995.
Security Council resolution 1019, 9 November 1995.
S/Res/1036 (1996).
S/Res/1078 (1996).
UNSC Draft Resolution (22 May 2014) UN Doc S/2014/348.
UNSC Res 2139 (22 February 2014) UN Doc S/RES/2139.
UNSC Res 2328 (19 December 2016) UN Doc S/RES/2328.
UNSC 7795th Meeting (26 October 2016) UN Doc S/PV.7795.
UNSC 7834th Meeting (13 December 2016) UN Doc S/PV.7834.

General Assembly

General Assembly Resolution 181 (II) (1947), 137.
General Assembly Resolution 194, A/810 (1948).
General Assembly Resolution A/Res/3236(XXIX) (1974).
General Assembly Resolution 37/253, A/37/51 (1983) 48.
General Assembly Resolution 55/116, A/Res/55/116 (Sudan).
General Assembly resolution 36/147 C, 16 December 1981.
General Assembly resolution 37/88 C, 9 December 1982.
General Assembly resolution 38/79 D, 15 December 1983.
General Assembly resolution 39/95 D, 14 December 1984.
Resolution 41/120 of the United Nations General Assembly, Setting international standards in the field of human rights, A/RE/41/120, 4 December 1986.
General Assembly Resolution 55/116, A/Res/55/116.
UNGA, '2005 World Summit Outcome' UNGA 60th Session UN Doc A/60/L.1 (2005).
UNGA Res 60/1 (24 October 2005) UN Doc A/RES/60/1.
General Assembly, A/Res/71/292, 22 June 2017.

Other Bodies

Commission on Human Rights, Res. 1995/77.
Commission on Human Rights, Res. 1996/73.
Sub- Commission resolution 1998/9, 20 August 1998.
Commission on Human Rights, Report on the 43rd session, Resolution 1987/4, E/1987/18 (1987).
UN Subcommission on Prevention of Discrimination and Protection of Minorities, Res. 1995/13, U.N. ESCOR, 50th Sess., at 20, U.N. Doc. EICN.4Sub.2119951L. 11Add.3 (1995).
United Nations, Commission on Human Rights, Sub-Commission on the Promotion and Protection of Human Rights (2005) *Housing and property restitution in the context of the return of refugees and internally displaced persons. Principles on housing and property restitution for refugees and displaced persons*, 28 June 2005, E/CN.4/Sub.2/2005/17, <https://documents-dds-ny.un.org/doc/UNDOC/GEN/G05/146/95/PDF/G0514695.pdf?OpenElement>

Websites (All weblinks in this book were checked on 22 September 2017)

Mid-Year Trends 2015', United Nations High Commissioner for Refugees, 3, <http://www.unhcr.org/56701b969.html#_ga=1.238359107.297000490.1455875838>
Zapater J., 'Prevention of Forced Displacement: The Inconsistencies of a Concept' (UNHCR: Policy Development and Evaluation Service) Research Paper No 186, April 2010, 3, < http://www.unhcr.org/uk/research/working/4bbb2a199/prevention-forced-displacement-inconsistencies-concept-josep-zapater.html?query=forced displacement>
Wolff S., 'Can Forced Population Transfers Resolve Self-determination Conflicts? A European Perspective', <http://www.stefanwolff.com/files/ethniccleansing.pdf>

'Exchange of Populations', <http://www.globalsecurity.org/military/world/war/exchange-of-population.htm>

Greer J.L., 'Critique of the ICRC's Customary Rules Concerning Displaced Persons: General Accuracy, Conflation, and a Missed Opportunity', 1, < https://www.nottingham.ac.uk/hrlc/documents/publications/hrlcommentary2007/acritiqueoficrcscustomaryrulesondisplacedpersons.pdf>

ICRC Database on Customary international humanitarian law, <https://www.icrc.org/customary-ihl/eng/docs/home>

The Act of Displacement, https://ihl-databases.icrc.org/customary-ihl/eng/docs/v2_rul_rule129

'Iraq: Forcible Expulsion of Ethnic Minorities', March 2003, Vol. 15, No. 3,<https://www.hrw.org/reports/2003/iraq0303/index.htm#TopOfPage>

Droege C., 'Developments in Legal Protection of Internally Displaced Persons: 10 Years of Experience since the Guiding Principles', 4, <https://www.icrc.org/eng/assets/files/other/09-2008-icrc-c-droege-guiding-principles.pdf>

Introductory Note by the Representative of the Secretary-General on Internally Displaced Persons Mr. Francis M. Deng, <http://www.ifrc.org/Docs/idrl/I266EN.pdf>

International Conference on the Great Lakes Region, 30 November 2006, <http://www.refworld.org/pdfid/52384fe44.pdf>

Stanley V., Senior Rural Development Specialist, World Bank Group, <http://www.worldbank.org/en/news/feature/2015/12/02/the-power-of-sharing-knowledge-helps-countries-tackle-forced-displacement>

Mdontswa T., Deputy Chief Land Claims Commissioner, South Africa Commission on Restitution of Land Rights, <http://www.worldbank.org/en/news/feature/2015/12/02/the-power-of-sharing-knowledge-helps-countries-tackle-forced-displacement>

Hill-Cawthorne L. (2014), 'The Grand Chamber Judgment in *Hassan v UK*', EJIL: Talk! < <https://www.ejiltalk.org/the-grand-chamber-judgment-in-hassan-v-uk/>

Information acquired from the Office of the High Commissioner for Human Rights, <http://indicators.ohchr.org/>

European Commission, 'Forced Displacement – Refugees and Internally Displaced People', ECHO Fact Sheet, June 2016, <http://ec.europa.eu/echo/files/aid/countries/factsheets/thematic/refugees_en.pdf>

'The Roadmap for Return of IDPs and Implementation of Abyei Protocol', 8 June 2008, <http://peacemaker.un.org/sites/peacemaker.un.org/files/SD_080608_Roadmap%20for%20Return%20of%20IDPs%20and%20Implementation%20of%20Abyei%20Protocol.pdf>

'Mutarule's Displaced Start Returning Home', 20 August 2015, <https://monusco.unmissions.org/en/mutarule%E2%80%99s-displaced-starts-returning-home>

Cohen R., 'Listening to the Voices of the Displaced: Lessons Learned', Brookings-Bern Project on Internal Displacement, September 2008, 9, <https://www.brookings.edu/wp-content/uploads/2016/06/09_internal_displacement_cohen.pdf>

Council of Europe (2017) *Pilot Judgments,* <http://www.echr.coe.int/Documents/FS_Pilot_judgments_ENG.pdf>

Cyprus 'spurns historic chance' (2004), < http://news.bbc.co.uk/1/hi/world/europe/3656753.stm>

Dream Homes Property Consultants (2013), <http://www.dreamhomesproperty consultants.com

Edwards A. (2016) *'Global forced displacement hits record high'*, <http://www.unhcr.org/uk/news/latest/2016/6/5763b65a4/global-forced-displacement-hits-record-high.html>

Handal A. (2007-ongoing) *Ciné-dérive cinema and new media production house*, <http://www.cine-derive.com/projects/DHPC>

This is Kiruna: How to Move a City (2016), < https://www.youtube.com/watch?v=WKvqJ05AsPY&t=547s>

Council of Europe, *The supervision process*, http://www.coe.int/en/web/execution/the-supervision-process>

Internal Displacement Monitoring Centre, <http://www.internal-displacement.org/countries/cyprus>

'Handbook for the Protection of Internally Displaced Persons' (*UN Office of the High Commissioner for Rights*, 2009) <http://www.unhcr.org/4c2355229.pdf>

'About Us' (*Local Council of Daraya City*, 2014) <http://darayacouncil.org/index.php/%D8%A7%D9%84%D9%85%D8%AC%D9%84%D8%B3-%D8%A7%D9%84%D9%85%D8%AD%D9%84%D9%8A/%D9%85%D9%86-%D9%86%D8%AD%D9%86.html>

'Aleppo battle: What next for the evacuees?' (*BBC News*, 21 December 2016) <http://www.bbc.co.uk/news/world-middle-east-38340165>

Barnard A. and Saad H., 'Besieged Town of Daraya Agrees to Surrender to Syrian Government' (*The New York Times*, 25 August 2016) <https://www.nytimes.com/2016/08/26/world/middleeast/daraya-syria-assad-surrender.html?_r=0>

'Breaking Aleppo' (*Atlantic Council*, February 2017) <http://www.publications.atlanticcouncil.org/breakingaleppo/wp-content/uploads/2017/02/Breaking Aleppo.pdf>

'Can Aleppo's displaced survive in Idlib?' (*Al-Monitor*, 5 January 20187) <http://www.al-monitor.com/pulse/originals/2017/01/syria-aleppo-displaced-idlib-lack-opportunities.html#ixzz4XNjldrWb>

'Clarifications on the Daraya Evacuation Process' (*Local Council of Daraya City*, 28 August 2016) <https://www.facebook.com/daraya.council/posts/539308612930378>

Francis E. and Barrington L., 'Aleppo endgame nears as evacuation resumes' (*Reuters*, 21 December 2016) <http://www.reuters.com/article/us-mideast-crisis-syria-id USKBN14A1CL>

'Full transcript of AP interview with Syrian President Assad' (*Fox News*, 22 September 2016) <http://www.foxnews.com/world/2016/09/22/full-transcript-ap-interview-with-syrian-president-assad.html>

'Housing Land and Property (HLP) in the Syrian Arab Republic' (*Norwegian Refugee Council*, May 2016) <https://www.nrc.no/globalassets/pdf/reports/housing-land-and-property-hlp-in-the-syrian-arab-republic.pdf>

Black I., 'Report on Syrian Conflict finds 11.5% of population killed or injured' (*The Guardian*, 11 February 2016) <https://www.theguardian.com/world/2016/feb/11/report-on-syria-conflict-finds-115-of-population-killed-or-injured>

Esnor J., 'Syrian rebels evacuated out of besieged Wadi Barada after government forces capture strategic water springs' (*The Telegraph*, 30 January 2017) <http://www.telegraph.co.uk/news/2017/01/30/syrian-rebels-evacuated-besieged-wadi-barada-government-forces/>

Khatib L. et al, 'Western Policy Towards Syria: Applying Lessons Learned' (*Chatham House*, March 2017) <https://www.chathamhouse.org/sites/files/chathamhouse/publications/research/2017-03-15-western-policy-towards-syria-lessons-learned.pdf>

Dearden L., 'Syria war: UN warns 'the world is watching' as regime forces evacuate civilians and rebels from Daraya' (*The Independent*, 26 August 2016) <http://www.independent.co.uk/news/world/middle-east/syria-war-news-latest-daraya-civilians-and-rebels-evacuate-besieged-damascus-suburb-after-four-years-a7211276.html>

Chulov M., 'Iran repopulates Syria with Shia Muslims to help tighten regime's control' (*The Guardian*,14 January 2017) <https://www.theguardian.com/world/2017/jan/13/irans-syria-project-pushing-population-shifts-to-increase-influence?CMP=share_btn_fb>

'No Going Back: Forced Displacement in the Syrian Conflict' (*Syrian American Council*, February 2017) <https://d3n8a8pro7vhmx.cloudfront.net/sacouncil/pages/167/attachments/original/1486567664/Displacement_Paper_Version_by_Julie_F.pdf?1486567664>

'No Return to Homs: A case study on the demographic engineering in Syria' (*PAX*, 21 February 2017) <https://www.paxforpeace.nl/publications/all-publications/no-return-to-homs>

'President Al-Assad to BBC News: We are defending civilians, and making dialogue' (*Syrian Arab News Agency*, 10 February 2015) <http://sana.sy/en/?p=28047>

'President al-Assad to Denmark's TV 2: Moderate opposition is a myth . . . We won't accept that terrorists will take control of any part of Syria-VIDEO' (*Syrian Arab News Agency*, 6 October 2016) <http://sana.sy/en/?p=89763> 'President al-Assad's interview given to Russia's Komsomolskaya Pravda newspaper-VIDEO' (*Syrian Arab News Agency*, 14 October 2016) <http://sana.sy/en/?p=90442>

Gupta P., 'Khan Sheikhoun attack survivors recall horror' (*Aljazeera*, 5 May 2017) <http://www.aljazeera.com/indepth/features/2017/05/khan-sheikhoun-attack-survivors-recall-horror-170503130351120.html>

Abdulrahim R., 'Bombs Follow Aid Into Besieged Syrian Towns' (*The Wall Street Journal*, 20 June 2016) <http://www.wsj.com/articles/bombs-follow-aid-into-besieged-syrian-towns-1466467006>

Abdulrahim R., 'Syrian Rebels Reach Deal to Evacuate Besieged Damascus Suburb' (*The Wall Street Journal*, 25 August 2016) <https://www.wsj.com/articles/syrian-rebels-reach-deal-to-evacuate-besieged-damascus-suburb-1472154630>

'Russia rejects Syria war crimes claim over hospital attacks' (*BBC News*, 16 February 2016) <http://www.bbc.co.uk/news/world-middle-east-35586886>

'Russian Warplanes Target IDPs in Idlib City' (*Syrian Network for Human Rights*, 11 April 2017) <http://sn4hr.org/wp-content/pdf/english/Russian_aircraft_targets_displaced_people_in_Idlib_en.pdf>

'Silent Sectarian Cleansing: Iranian Role in Mass Demolitions and Population Transfers in Syria' (*Naame Shaam*, May 2015) <http://online.wsj.com/public/resources/documents/NaameShaamReport05182015.pdf>

'Statement' (*Local Council of Daraya City*, 12 October 2016) <https://www.facebook.com/daraya.council/posts/558647077663198:0>

'Statement on Darayya and the situation in other besieged areas in Syria' (*UN Office for the Coordination of Humanitarian Affairs*, 30 August 2016) <https://docs.

unocha.org/sites/dms/Documents/ERC_USG%20Stephen_OBrien_Statement_on_Darayya.pdf>

Jabbour S., 'Daraya: Agreement for forcible displacement amidst international silence' (*Aljazeera*, 1 September 2016) <http://www.aljazeera.net/news/reportsandinterviews/2016/9/1/%D8%AF%D8%A7%D8%B1%D9%8A%D8%A7-%D8%A7%D8%AA%D9%81%D8%A7%D9%82-%D8%AA%D9%87%D8%AC%D9%8A%D8%B1-%D9%82%D8%B3%D8%B1%D9%8A-%D9%88%D8%B3%D8%B7-%D8%B5%D9%85%D8%AA-%D8%A7%D9%84%D8%B9%D8%A7%D9%84%D9%85>

'Syria civil war: Aid convoy reaches besieged Daraya' (*Aljazeera*, 2 June 2016) <http://www.aljazeera.com/news/2016/06/syria-civil-war-aid-daraya-160601124835991.html>

'Syria rebels agree to leave Homs' besieged al-Waer' (*Aljazeera*, 13 March 2017) <http://www.aljazeera.com/news/2017/03/syria-rebels-agree-leave-homs-beseiged-al-waer-170313134154656.html>

'Syria: Terrifying Eyewitness Video of Life under Siege and Barrel Bombs must Spur Humanitarian Lifeline' (*Amnesty International*, 19 April 2016) <https://www.amnesty.org/en/press-releases/2016/04/syria-terrifying-eyewitness-video-of-life-under-siege-and-barrel-bombs/>

'Syria's civil war: 'Last hospital in Daraya bombed'' (*Aljazeera*, 19 August 2016) <http://www.aljazeera.com/news/2016/08/syria-civil-war-daraya-hospital-bombed-160819101838839.html>

'Syrian Arab Republic' (*UN Office for the Coordination of Humanitarian Affairs*, January 2017) <http://www.unocha.org/syria>

'Syrian Regime's Representative in Aleppo Agreement Negotiations is Brother of Fateh Al-Sham Leader' (*Enab Baladi*, 14 December 2016) <http://english.enabbaladi.net/archives/2016/12/syrian-regimes-representative-aleppo-agreement-negotiations-brother-fateh-al-sham-leader/> accessed 2 March 201

'Syrians in rebel Damascus suburb start to evacuate in deal' (*Reuters*, 2 September 2016) <http://uk.reuters.com/article/uk-mideast-crisis-syria-idUKKCN11812I>

'The displacement agreement from Aleppo: How it happened? And how it has [*sic*] been done?' (*Jusoor*, December 2016) <http://jusoor.co/content_images/users/1/contents/312.pdf>

'The Failure of UN Security Council Resolution 2286 in Preventing Attacks on Healthcare in Syria' (*Syrian American Medical Society*, January 2017) <https://foundation.sams-usa.net/wp-content/uploads/2017/01/SAMS 2286 Report.pdf>

'Timeline: Syria's 13 'people evacuation' deals' (*Aljazeera,* 16 May 2017) <http://www.aljazeera.com/indepth/features/2017/04/timeline-syria-people-evacuation-deals-170413084313089.html>

'What next for Syrians who fled Aleppo?' (*International Rescue Committee*, 20 January 2017) <https://www.rescue.org/article/what-next-syrians-who-fled-aleppo>

National Instruments/Documents

'Turkish Republic of Northern Cyprus', 'Law as to Compensation for Immovable Properties Located within the Boundaries of the Turkish Republic of Northern Cyprus, which are within the Scope of Article 159, paragraph (4) of the Constitution' (Law no. 49/2003).

'Turkish Republic of Northern Cyprus', 'Law for the Compensation, Exchange and Restitution of Immovable Properties' (22 December 2005).

'Turkish Republic of Northern Cyprus', 'By-Law made under Sections 8 (2) (A) and 22 of the Law for the Compensation, Exchange and Restitution of Immovable Properties which are within the scope of sub-paragraph (b) of paragraph 1 of Article 159 of the Constitution', (20 March 2006).

UK Parliament. House of Commons (2005) *Cyprus, Session 2004–05* (HC 2004–05 113-I). Foreign Affairs Committee Publications, < https://www.publications.parliament.uk/pa/cm200405/cmselect/cmfaff/113/11305.htm>

Republic of Cyprus Official Gazette, 26 July 2002.

Constitution of the People's Republic of Kampuchea, 25 June 1981.

Cambodia, Sub-Decree on the Management of the Use of Agricultural Law, No.06ANK, 6 May 1985.

Sub-decree on Granting House Ownership to the Cambodian Citizens No 25 ANK, 22 April 1989.

Circular on the implementation of sub-decree on granting house ownership to Cambodian citizens living in Phnom Penh, circular no. 05SRC, June 5, 1989.

Sub-decree on Granting House Ownership to the Cambodian Citizens, No.25ANK, 22 April 1989.

Cambodia, Land Law no 100K, October 13, 1992.

Cambodian Law Land, NS/RKM/0801/14, 30 August, 2001, Art 17.

Cambodia Sub-decree on the Organization and Functioning of the Cadastral Commission," No.47ANK/BK, May 31, 2002.

Index

For Product Safety Concerns and Information please contact our EU
representative GPSR@taylorandfrancis.com
Taylor & Francis Verlag GmbH, Kaufingerstraße 24, 80331 München, Germany

www.ingramcontent.com/pod-product-compliance
Ingram Content Group UK Ltd.
Pitfield, Milton Keynes, MK11 3LW, UK
UKHW022015180926
475701UK00003B/371
* 9 7 8 0 3 6 7 5 9 2 3 3 2 *